COACHING
WITH THE
BRAIN IN MIND

Foundations for Practice

DAVID ROCK
LINDA J. PAGE, Ph.D.

WILEY

John Wiley & Sons, Inc.

This publication is designed to provide accurate and authoritative information in regard to the subject matter covered. It is sold with the understanding that the publisher is not engaged in rendering professional services. If legal, accounting, medical, psychological or any other expert assistance is required, the services of a competent professional person should be sought.

For general information on our other products and services please contact our Customer Care Department within the U.S. at (800) 762-2974, outside the United States at (317) 572-3993 or fax (317) 572-4002.

Wiley also publishes its books in a variety of electronic formats. Some content that appears in print may not be available in electronic books. For more information about Wiley products, visit our website at www.wiley.com.

Library of Congress Cataloging-in-Publication Data:

Rock, David.
    Coaching with the brain in mind : foundations for practice / by David Rock, Linda J. Page.
        p.   cm.
    Includes bibliographical references and index.
    ISBN 978-0-470-40568-0 (cloth)
        1. Employees—Coaching of. 2. Neurosciences. 3. Teaching—
    Psychological aspects. I. Page, Linda J. II. Title.
    HF5549.5.C53R63   2009
    658.3'124—dc22
                                                                    2009009765

Printed in the United States of America

10 9 8 7 6 5 4

David: to Lisa, Trinity, and India Rock
Linda: to Susan, Malika, and Chantal

Contents

PART II: HOW CAN WE BE HEALTHY?

Contents

PART IV: HOW CAN WE FEEL BETTER?

PART V: HOW CAN WE GET ALONG?

Contents

Preface: Who Should Read This Book?

Ishi is the name given to the last surviving member of the Yahi tribe when he was "captured" outside Oroville in north-central California in the year 1911. Workers caught sight of him when they were preparing to go home after a day at the slaughterhouse just outside of town. The "wild Indian," as he was described then, was wearing tattered remnants of clothes and seemed near starvation. Most of his fellow Yahi had been systematically exterminated over the previous five decades as a massive influx of prospectors and settlers arrived in Northern California searching for gold. Ishi was about 50 years old at the time of his capture, so he had been born around 1860. He had been living in the foothills north and east of the rich marshlands that have become Sacramento, the state capital of California. After most of his tribe had been decimated, he went into hiding with his uncle, mother, and a woman who was his wife or sister. They lived as much as possible as they had when their tribe numbered in the thousands, hunting deer and rabbits, gathering and cooking acorns, grains, and roots, and fishing in the tributaries of the Sacramento River. They also took cans of bean and flour from cabins. But they had to keep away from the invaders who had proven to be dangerous.

After the other members of Ishi's party died, he allowed himself to be captured on a late summer's evening. No one else in the world spoke his language. According to his people's customs, a person did not use his own name—that was for his family to reveal. He no longer had a family. The fugitive was turned over to anthropologist Alfred Kroeber, who arranged for him to live in the University of California's Anthropology Museum in San Francisco. After attempts to record and learn his language, linguists such as Edward Sapir discovered that his tribe's word for "man" or "person" was anglicized as "Ishi." So that became his name. Ishi was the object of great curiosity until his death from tuberculosis in 1916. His story was made popular again in 1961 when Theodora Kroeber, anthropologist Alfred's second wife, published *Ishi in Two Worlds: A Biography of the Last Wild Indian in North America*.

Ishi's brain was removed from his body after his death in clear violation of his wishes and his people's customs. In 2004 Orin Starn took up Ishi's story again, tracking his brain to the Smithsonian in Washington, DC. But it is not just *Ishi's* brain that captures our interest—it is the minds and brains of the people around him: the settlers who exterminated (their words) thousands of native people; the reporters who treated him as a curious, uncivilized "thing"; the anthropologists who, though in a very kindly way, saw him as in need of protection; and the scientists who thought they could learn something important about him from examining his disembodied brain.

Compared with people who thought of themselves as more civilized, Ishi proved to have advanced social and adaptive skills. After some time he made friends, laughed and explored, lent a helping hand around the museum and hospital, was respectful of others and adapted to his environment. He enjoyed teaching children and others the skills he knew, maintained a sense of dignity and held firm to his values. The point we are making is not to hold Ishi up as some icon, as nature's perfect Noble Savage. Rather, he proved simply to be a human being. On the surface, he was very different from the men and women of San Francisco a century ago. Ishi's experience shows us that the human brain, even that of a mature person who might be labeled primitive, is capable of supporting enormous changes in thinking and behavior, given the right context and relationships.

Coaching is a context that supports change across very large gaps between where a person is and where he or she wants to be. Professional coaching burst out of its start in the late 20th century ("No, not football, basketball, or athletic coaching!") to become a valuable tool in the corporate and personal change arsenal. According to Career Partners International (2008), 40% of 400 U.S. and Canadian business leaders interviewed chose coaching as their preferred method for leadership development. Research is accumulating that shows a return-on-investment (ROI) of five to eight times the cost of coaching, or 500% to 800%. But ROI results prove only that something has changed. For coaching to become an established profession (see Grant, 2003), it is even more important to know what is working and how.

WHAT WE ARE ASKING

Does Coaching Have Solid Theoretical and Conceptual Roots?

Our first goal in writing this book is to establish the deep theoretical foundations of coaching, its bedrock and the pillars that raise it above that bedrock, and to suggest that neuroscience provides a solid platform for the ongoing development of coaching.

Although research on the brain has been around much longer than professional coaching, (there is evidence of prehistoric brain surgery), new technologies have enabled phenomenal advances over the past two decades. Some unquestioned assumptions have been overturned. Neuroscience is beginning to reveal even more about the "what" and "how" of coaching and related practices such as leadership development.

How Can We Use Our Minds and Brains to Initiate and Maintain the Changes We Want to Make?

Our second goal is to demonstrate how setting goals, making connections, becoming more aware, seeking breakthroughs, and taking action—the "stuff" of coaching—parallel what neuroscientists tell us about how the brain operates. In fact, anyone who wants to harness the power of the mind to help others learn can benefit from what we are presenting here. Whether you are already a coach or not, we will show you how to become more effective in your own life, and more effective in how you help others, by understanding how the brain works. We will present examples and stories and techniques that draw on all the foundations for coaching practice.

Where are We Going?

We also wrote this book to acknowledge a revelation: We are all participating in the creation of a new brain.

Yes, this book covers decidedly contemporary fields such as coaching, the brain, and the mind, but we started it with the story about a "wild Indian" from a century ago and the questions his treatment raises about minds and brains then and now. If we pay attention to where people direct their attention, we can surmise the questions they are asking. And the questions people ask reveal their assumptions about reality. Saxton Pope, chief surgeon at the University of California hospital where Ishi died, removed Ishi's brain despite knowing that Ishi did not wish to be dissected after death. Starn suggests that Pope went against Ishi's wishes, despite the friendship the two men enjoyed, because he believed that Ishi's brain was of scientific importance. In other words, Pope paid attention to the brain because he believed it would reveal more about this primitive man than their five years of personal interaction and friendship had done. In particular, he may have believed, as scientists have up until recently, that the individual, disembodied brain equals mind. In its most primitive form, this belief assumes that if you can weigh or measure or ascertain the shape of a brain, you can know something important about how that brain operates or operated—you can know the mind and the personality and its thoughts. Although this simplistic assumption was disappearing even as Ishi was chipping arrowheads from blue Milk of Magnesia bottles, it still exists in a more elaborate form today: If you can describe the working parts of the brain in enough detail, you can see thoughts.

Compare this assumption to the contemporary claim by neuropsychiatrist Daniel Siegel (2007a) that "mind is using the brain to create itself" (p. 32). The "brain equals mind" assumption fits an older way of looking at the world that we have labeled "mechanistic." The "mind uses the brain" assumption fits a new approach that we label in these pages "systemic." This is more than just words, for in the century between the removal of Ishi's brain and its return to the descendants of a tribe that is likely related to him, science has discovered that the rules for understanding the brain are very different from the rules for understanding how things work in everyday life. If the brain and the mind are in any way related, then we need to know the new rules if we want to change our minds.

One of these new "systemic" rules is that attention changes the brain. If, as many physicists assert, the brain is a quantum environment, then asking a question and looking for an answer, or observing, has an effect on outcome. When scientists asked what Ishi's brain would reveal about his humanity, they were *not* paying attention to the fact that he had become deeply connected to the modern community around him and even contributed to this new society. What else do we require as proof of humanity?

Today we can see and talk with each other without physical wires and cables to connect us. We have pictures of the whole Earth that fuel our sense of being on a giant spaceship together. Yet we still question whether some people deserve being considered human. We still react to one another and to the world based on self-fulfilling assumptions. We continue looking for answers that result in suffering and inhumanity. As we compare the questions we ask now to the questions asked by scientists a century ago, we recognize the true challenge lying before coaching:

How do we use our minds to create fully functioning, healthy human brains?

If that question interests you, please come along with us by reading this book.

About the Authors

David Rock has done over 7,000 hours of executive and business coaching and has trained over 10,000 people as coaches. He launched Results Coaching Systems in 1998 and cofounded the coaching certificate programs at New York University in 2005. As well as being chief executive officer of Results Coaching Systems, David is now on the faculty at CIMBA, an international business school based in Europe, and a guest lecturer at Oxford University's business school. He is on the board of The Blue School, building a new approach to K-12 education. At the time of writing this book, he is completing a professional doctorate in the Neuroscience of Leadership. His approach to coaching is at the heart of wide-scale coaching programs at global organizations including EDS, Ericsson, and many others. In 2006 David coined the term "NeuroLeadership" and founded the NeuroLeadership Institute that brought together neuroscientists and global business leaders for the first NeuroLeadership Summit in May 2007, followed by further summits and a journal. His expertise lies in the science underpinning coaching and how to build coaching cultures in large organizations. He divides his time between Sydney, Australia, and New York City.

Linda Page, Ph.D., began her first career at Princeton University, where she studied sociology, anthropology, and linguistics. She later became a psychotherapist. She administered a master's program in counseling psychology, taught social and cognitive psychology in a doctoral program in the United States, and founded a coaching school—Adler

International Learning—in 1998 in Toronto, Canada. The school now has a presence in the United States and Europe. The multidisciplinary demands of coaching practice and neuroscience research and theory bring together many strands of her career and intellectual interests. Linda has been a member of the Society for Psychotherapy Research for many years. She helped organize research symposia for the International Coach Federation and now serves on the Research Advisory Board of The Foundation of Coaching. As a board member for the International Consortium for Coaching in Organizations, she helped develop a series of symposia that bring together small groups of business leaders, coaches, and trainers to develop mutual understanding of the challenges facing organizations internationally. She has also served on the boards of the Association of Coach Training Organizations and the Graduate School Alliance for Executive Coaching, which is developing a graduate-level curriculum for coach education. She is a regular contributor to *The Journal of Individual Psychology* and serves on the editorial board of *The International Journal for Coaching in Organizations.*

IN THE AUTHORS' WORDS

The two of us come from very different backgrounds and, indeed, different parts of the world. We see this as an advantage because coaches come from many different backgrounds, each with its own "bedrock" that, taken together, constitute the foundation of coaching. We intend in this book to remind us all of the foundational concepts that we are familiar with and to acquaint ourselves with other, less familiar bedrock. At the very least, we hope to participate in a dialogue that develops a common language and helps us understand one another. And we intend to help create a *discipline* of coaching by making sure that we acknowledge the contributions of those on whose shoulders we stand. For that reason, we have included many more references than is typical for books of this type. Further, we hope to build on the existing foundation of coaching by adding neuroscience as an evidence base for the discipline and profession of coaching.

Neither of us is a neuroscientist. Neither are we primarily scholarly theory producers, weaving together research data for academic texts and journals, although we both contribute in this way. We are both most interested in *applying* neuroscience discoveries to coaching and to leadership skills in general. That is, we are interpreters who hope to encourage people to make practical use of what is known about the brain. Ultimately, we have written this book because of the positive impact that understanding the brain has had on our own coaching practices as well as on our ability to train better coaches.

About This Book

This book is organized into parts and chapters. In the Introduction, we provide an overview so you may select specific parts for particular attention or chapters in a different order without missing the context of the whole. We introduce the questions whose answers reveal the emergence of coaching, neuroscience, and the potential for a new brain.

We have included a number of examples that are drawn from our experience. No names of actual persons are used, and the circumstances have been altered extensively. The types of situations are real and in some cases have been repeated many times.

Knowledge and Action, Action and Knowledge

Knowledge which is unable to support action is not genuine —and how unsure is activity without understanding!

–Rudolf Virchow

Rudolf Virchow was a 19th-century physician, anthropologist, social activist, and scientist who argued against the separation of science, or knowledge for its own sake, from practice based on that knowledge. As his quote states, "Knowledge which is unable to support action is not genuine." We want you to be able to make use of the theories in this book as practical tools, whether you yourself are a coach, a manager or executive, another helping professional, a business owner, a parent or spouse, or anyone who wants to have a more fulfilling and productive life. Applying that knowledge is what will make it *genuine* knowledge.

Coaching has been criticized as a set of techniques looking for a theory. The second part of Virchow's quote is " —and how unsure is activity without understanding!" Or, as Kurt Lewin, put it, "There is nothing so practical as a good theory." It is our hope that the full impact of this book will be to help coaching, coaches, clients, leaders, and all they touch transform theory into practice and vice versa.

Acknowledgments

We both wish to thank our teachers, mentors, students, and clients who have helped us understand coaching, leadership, and their potential. This has been a four-year project, and a team effort. Many thanks to coaching students from New York University coaching programs who helped research specific topics at the start of the project, including Cindy Cornell, Sue Dorward, Don Duffy, Gwyn Osnos, and Paulette Rao. And a big thanks to Judy Crater, too.

These colleagues have read and commented on all or portions of earlier manuscripts: Laura Atwood, William Bergquist, Vikki Brock, Kevin Cashman, Jean Davies, Lorne Ellingson, Suzan Guest, Mike Jay, Richard Kopp, Jeanie Nishimura, Ruth Orenstein, Robert Potvin, Pamela Ramadei, Pam Richarde, Jeannine Sandstrom, Melinda Sinclair, Lee Smith, Irene Stein, Lew Stern, Adria Trowhill, and others. We are grateful for their generous help. At the same time, they are not responsible for any lapses in these pages.

Thank you to our supportive and patient Wiley editor, Marquita Flemming. We continue to depend on the thoughtful work and generous spirit of neuroscientists to bring brain research to our minds and society, including Amy Arnsten, Leslie Brothers, Robert Coghill, Naomi Eisenberger, Matt Lieberman, Kevin Ochsner, Jeffrey Schwartz, Dan Siegel, Henry Stapp, Yi-Yuan Tang, and many others who also deserve our respect and gratitude.

David wishes to thank all the people who dedicate their lives to painstaking research to further our understanding of human nature.

Linda could not possibly have completed this book without the support of her colleagues at Adler International Learning, her daughters and grandchildren, and, more than anything else, the practical and loving input of her spouse, Susan.

DAVID ROCK
LINDA J. PAGE

What Are the Questions?

Ishi had grown up in the wilderness, but when his companions at the anthropology museum asked him to take them back to his old haunts in 1914, he was reluctant. Perhaps he did not want to be reminded of sad memories of his family and tribe, now all dead. But just as likely, he was a different person now. He had been living in San Francisco for three years, dressing and eating as others did, walking along the streets with his new friends, working in and welcoming visitors to the museum and volunteering in the hospital next door. He had seen things, trains and cars and electricity, that he could hardly have imagined as a younger man. Ishi may have had the sense, familiar to most of us, of not being able to go back. Some experiences have profound effects that go beyond incremental improvement of fingering an instrument or wielding a wrench or a kitchen knife. Some experiences seem to create a whole new mind—or, rather, to use the more dynamic verb form, a whole new way of minding, of using our brains to experience the world. Ishi, like all migrants, may have missed his past life terribly, but Ishi the San Francisco resident was no longer that person who showed up at the Oroville slaughterhouse on an August evening in 1911. How could he not have experienced what today we would call a transformation, a personal paradigm shift?

Shifts in how we perceive the world occur because what we experience changes the questions we ask. Seeking answers to questions we have never asked before changes our brains so we can *practice differently* and thereby craft new experiences. This is a process that has

1

undoubtedly gone on for many thousands of centuries, for as long as human beings have been conscious of themselves and their world. Because we now know that the brain is sensitive to experience, we can guess that Ishi's brain changed while he was in San Francisco, although no gross mea-surement of it could possibly reveal what those changes were. His presence certainly also changed those around him, as reading about him today has the potential for changing us.

Coaching is a practice that specializes in changing awareness, action, and the world around us. In systems language, this is called "co-evolution." People change their environment, and their different experiences in this changed environment change their brains so they can make new changes. Coaching enables us to see this process at a new level and therefore to practice it more consciously than ever before. But coaching is a relatively new practice. Where did it come from and where is it going?

This book was written to answer three basic questions:

- What is the conceptual and theoretical foundation for the practice of coaching?
- What are the more current pillars that lifted coaching above its foundational "bedrock"?
- To what extent might neuroscience provide a platform for the further development of coaching?

In this introduction, we reveal the underlying story we discovered as we sought to answer those questions: *Both coaching and neuroscience are examples of a widespread shift in how people think about themselves and the world.*

We tell this story and give an overview of the book under these headings:

- Coaching bedrock
  - Paradigms
  - Paradigm shift
- Coaching pillars
  - Systemic paradigm
  - What is coaching?
- Neuroscience platform
  - Why neuroscience and coaching?

- Organization of *Coaching with the Brain in Mind*
- What do we need to know about neuroscience?
  - Brain-shifting discoveries
  - Energy and information
  - What is a brain?
  - The brain in our hand
  - What is a mind?
  - What do relationships have to do with it?
  - Health and well-being
- What are we doing here?
- A note about the science of neuroscience

COACHING BEDROCK

HISTORICAL INTERLUDE

Coach and philosopher Julio Olalla (2008) has asked "Why coaching? Why now?" He noted that authorities in the Middle Ages, primarily church and feudal lords, enforced a knowledge chain of command. People with questions were discouraged from taking their own experience into account in order to arrive at answers. They were expected to consult a priest who consulted a book—usually the Bible or some other religious text. Galileo (1564–1642) provoked the Inquisition's wrath not only because he asserted that Earth orbited the Sun (and not the other way around) but primarily because he bypassed the "authorities" and sought knowledge based on experiment and observation of the natural world.

The period of European "Enlightenment" followed Sir Isaac Newton's (1643–1727) discovery of the principles of motion and gravity. His empirical approach had roots in ancient Greece, a society that social psychologist Richard Nisbett (2003) suggests was unique in its celebration of personal freedom, individuality, objective thought, rhetoric, and logic. Nisbett suggested that this heritage was related to the economic individualism of herding and fishing that was characteristic of early Greek society. Yet it must be noted that ancient Greece city-states were slave-based societies and that the individual freedom of the slave owners rested on the social labor of the slaves. However, the tradition of individual

(Continued)

3

truth-seeking and argument influenced scientific development in Europe more than 15 centuries later.

Newton's discoveries revolutionized physics. Explanations in classical mechanics, as his system has been called, assume singular causes leading in one direction to later effects. This mechanistic worldview permeated scholarly and popular thought and influenced subsequent natural and social sciences as well as philosophy. Logical positivism—the perspective that ideas are true, false, or meaningless—strongly influenced 20th-century science. And the belief, inherited from Greek traditions of argument, that a conflict of ideas gives rise to higher truths was consistent with an increasingly market-dominated economy.

The view that derives from Newton's approach is that "the truth is out there" waiting to be discerned by rational, value-free observers. Disagreements over what is true arise either because observers are biased by their subjectivity or because their measurements are inaccurate. In this paradigm, rational debate among differing observers roots out bias, and technological innovation provides more and more accurate measurement.

The replacement of medieval reliance on religious authority by Enlightenment reliance on scientific inquiry has proven tremendously successful. This is illustrated every day as we travel, work, and communicate in ways unimaginable a century ago. Over the past nearly four centuries since the Enlightenment, the adoption of the mechanistic worldview has resulted in an exponential increase in technological advances. However, by the mid-20th century, social and scientific trends began to reveal the limits of classical mechanics.

The practice of coaching can trace its foundation to several fields that developed during the centuries following the Enlightenment. Philosophy certainly existed well before the Enlightenment, but after empirical science loosened the church's hold on truth, contributions to ontology, or the study of the nature of human nature, were sought beyond Western philosophical traditions including from new disciplines of anthropology and sociology. Advances in medicine and health practices provided part of the foundation for coaching, as did the flowering of early-20th-century psychology, especially behaviorism. Many coaching techniques can be traced to psychotherapy, an application of health practices, philosophy, and psychology. Management theory also had a significant impact on coaching. As the 20th century began, well before coaching became widely practiced, each of these fields was heavily influenced by a set of ideas that characterize the mechanistic paradigm. These ideas emphasize:

- The individual over community or context
- Dualism rather than holism
- Objectivity as more privileged than subjectivity
- Determinism and not constructivism
- Hierarchy as more effective than collaboration

Paradigms

Application of the term "paradigm" to modern scientific thought is credited to Thomas Kuhn and his book *The Structure of Scientific Revolutions* (1962). According to Kuhn, a paradigm is a mental model or a set of beliefs through which we view the world. The paradigm we have referred to as "mechanistic" was employed in Western European and later in North American thinking from the time of Isaac Newton in the 17th to the mid-20th century. This paradigm is referred to in many other ways: classical or Newtonian mechanics, modern, rational, logical positivist, industrial, capitalist. In general, mechanism assumes that objective truth is the goal of inquiry, that understanding results from studying the bits and pieces that constitute phenomena, and that causes lead in only one direction to determine effects. Mechanism also assumes a universe that is rather like a clock. The existence and behavior of all its elements can be perfectly understood if only we can identify the causes that happened just before the moment we are trying to understand. And we can understand those prior causes by identifying what determined them. And on and on back to the beginning of time. Two big problems arise from this deterministic paradigm:

1. What do we do with our persistent human experience that the choices we make have some relevance to what happens in the world?

Is our conscious experience of facing and making choices just some irrelevant cosmic joke?

2. Early in the 20th century, physicists discovered that observations of behavior of very small particles did not fit the predictions of classical mechanics. It took several decades for this new "quantum mechanics" to shake the Newtonian assumptions of physics. Thus, the stage was set for a "paradigm shift."

Paradigm Shift

Kuhn (1962) also introduced the concept of the paradigm shift, a discontinuous and sometimes radical change in paradigm. Before his book appeared, scientific progress was commonly thought to consist of small discoveries accumulating to form larger, more significant explanatory theories. Kuhn disagreed that this was the only way progress happened in science. He argued that some discoveries are revolutionary and cause giant leaps forward. For example, Galileo's claim that the Earth was round shook the very foundation of how questions are formulated and answered. This was a major paradigm shift in human history.

Most of us have experienced a personal paradigm shift. Someone—a teacher, a relative, a friend, a therapist, a mentor, a coach—has made a remark or an observation that has profoundly changed how we think, feel, and behave. Richard Bandler and John Grinder, founders of NeuroLinguistic Programming (1975, 1976), draw on Gregory Bateson's influence in calling this "a difference that makes a difference." It is often described by metaphors, such as "a curtain lifted" or "the light went on" or "I'm seeing with new eyes." The biblical story of Saul on the road to Damascus is an example from religion. We suspect that Ishi's experience with the modern world may have created a personal paradigm shift for him.

Coaches are privileged to see paradigm shifts regularly in our work. A seemingly innocuous question can elicit a new way of thinking.

Looking more broadly at society as a whole, Alvin Toffler (1984) suggested that a paradigm shift could occur if one or more basic elements are significantly altered. For a system to undergo a dramatic shift, it must be pushed beyond the state that holds it in equilibrium. Coaches apply this principle to individuals or organizations, hoping to evoke an insight that will cause the client to "see with new eyes." When whole

Example: "I Couldn't have Done it without Her"

Russell had run successful campaigns for several elected officials. He credited his coach for helping him build his reputation among his party colleagues, but when they suggested that he run for office himself, he hesitated. "How," he wondered, "can I hide the fact that I have a coach? Won't people dismiss me for having to rely on someone else?" He conveyed his concern to his coach, who replied, "What are you in this for?" In pondering this simple question, Russell discovered a new way of looking at himself and his situation, one that relies less on how he looks to others and more on what he feels is true for him. He shifted his stance from trying to hide his use of coaching to presenting himself as a new kind of politician—one who openly applies coaching principles to his work with colleagues and constituents. The night Russell was nominated to run for office, he proudly introduced his coach to the assembled crowd, saying, "I couldn't have done it without her—and without every one of you."

societies begin to see with new eyes, existing assumptions come into question, the old equilibrium breaks down, and the resulting chaos provides fertile ground for new fields and practices. This is the story of how coaching came into being.

COACHING PILLARS

The mechanistic paradigm came into question during the later 20th century as scientific and technological advances, more global integration, and social and political conflict pushed Western societies beyond the equilibrium, however illusory, promised by scientific progress. Systems theory applied advanced mathematical concepts to help us see the order and promise in chaos and complexity. Experiments in physics accumulated to show that mechanism was a special case of quantum mechanics. Understanding the mental aspects of elite athletic performance and recognizing the elements of the change process expanded our capacity to optimize performance in many realms. Psychology and learning theory were released from their behaviorist straitjacket by the cognitive revolution that approached the mind as an active ingredient. Positive psychology and concepts related to emotional intelligence moved us beyond seeing health as merely absence of disease. And management theory embraced collaboration and leadership in order to move beyond hierarchical dead-ends. All these "pillars" reinforced community and context, holism, the importance of subjectivity, constructivism, and collaborative participation.

Systemic Paradigm

Coaching emerged as a practice in response to a rapidly changing world and a paradigm shift in a number of disciplines. Postmodernism rejects logical positivism, especially the idea that there is an objective truth that can be determined by a neutral observer. Postmodernism was influenced by social movements of the 1960s that identified dominant definitions of "reality" as themselves constituents of the social power structure. In this view, there is no such thing as a neutral observer. Postmodern inquiry uncovers (deconstructs) the assumptions in language and action that ignore subjective experience (Bergquist & Mura, 2005).

Globalization has spurred openness to diverse perspectives and the recognition that the same event may be interpreted differently by different participants.

Quantum physics proposed, and over the past century has proven, that the activity of an observer affects what we can discover about the behavior of subatomic particles. Since the brain's neurons consist of atoms and their subatomic constituents, is it not possible that the observational attention of the mind can affect the outcome of neuronal activity? This proposition is still being hotly contested, but early applications show promising results, ones that are explaining how self-directed change happens and what each of us can do mentally to change our brains. This research is made possible by the development of machines that provide a snapshot of the inside of a brain, measure electrical activity of a brain in action, and take a moving picture of the changes in brains. Thus, the concept of volition, or the ability of the mind to affect the brain by the exertion of "willpower," is being brought into the spotlight after spending a century in the shadow of behavioral and psychodynamic deterministic assumptions.

Although mechanistic approaches still have influence, coaches are trained to think systemically, to attend to values, to take a holistic perspective, to use a collaborative rather than a directive approach, and to focus on strengths rather than on weaknesses. Coaching applications that follow the subjective agendas of clients, that encourage their capacity to generate options and make choices, that aim for ever higher potential and treat them as whole human beings are further expressions of a new paradigm. The pillars we describe in this book provide support for coaching to promote these shifts:

- from observer to participant
- from passive to active
- from negative to positive
- from teaching to experiencing
- from telling to listening

The previous worldview took its name from discoveries in physics. We draw on the study of systems for the new name: the "systemic paradigm."

Let us be clear: As we see it, the mechanistic paradigm is not *entirely replaced* by the systemic approach. Newton's classical mechanics is not false—it is rather a special case of quantum principles. And systemic approaches in general are not new. Rather, much like classic figure-ground illustrations such as the vase and faces shown in introductory psychology classes, we can "see" the same phenomenon from different perspectives. Coaching is informed by both mechanistic and systemic paradigms. Many common coaching techniques, such as breaking large tasks into small steps, are rooted in thoroughly mechanistic radical behaviorism.

Yet if mechanistic modes of inquiry and practice had been adequate at the end of the 20th century, there would have been no need for coaching. Medical and psychological change agents tended to approach human problems separate from their social context. Individuals were divided into physical and mental, work and personal, spiritual and material, each with different professional attendants. In contrast, coaching seeks to help whole human beings balance the many different aspects of their lives and to improve their ability to function with one another, with their work, with the world, and with themselves. This is not instead of but in addition to already-existing professions.

This book contends that coaching is the most fitting application of the systemic paradigm among helping professions, arising at the turn of the 21st century because previous practices are weighed down by their Newtonian heritage.

Where a classical approach is useful, it continues to be used. Where new assumptions or techniques meet personal or organizational goals, they rightfully are pursued. This expands our global repertoire. For example, Westerners are learning Asian spiritual and health practices and Asians are learning Western industrial practices (Nisbett, 2003). The point is that we can choose which paradigm best suits our purposes. Awareness of choice is a principle that unites coaching theory and practice. Coaching arose at the end of the 20th century on pillars that showed there are more options for fulfilling human potential than mechanistic thought led us to believe. Coaching emerged as an embodiment of a new systemic paradigm.

What is Coaching?

It has been easier to say what coaching is *not* than to say precisely what it is—not athletic coaching (although it draws on the wisdom of the best sports coaching), not consulting, not mentoring, not psychotherapy, not counseling, not advising. . . .

Coach Mike Jay (1999) differentiates coaching from other professions such as teaching, managing, facilitating, counseling, consulting, mediating, or mentoring by how its context differs from these other activities: "The coach has no responsibility, accountability and authority [for the behavior of the client], and does not own the outcome" (p. 47).

Coaches are change agents who serve the interests of their clients. The definition of coaching by the International Coach Federation (2008) recognizes this focus on the client's interests, or "agenda":

> Coaches are trained to listen, to observe and to customize their approach to individual client needs. They seek to elicit solutions and strategies from the client; they believe the client is naturally creative and resourceful. The coach's job is to provide support to enhance the skills, resources, and creativity that the client already has.

Many similar definitions exist among coaching and coach training organizations.

Looking beyond coaching itself, David Orlinsky brought his experience as a professor in the multidisciplinary Department of Human Development at the University of Chicago to bear on the question of where coaching fits among others that use psychological or social means to induce change. Orlinsky combined the various definitions of coaching with his knowledge of other helping professions. In Figure I.1, we present the preliminary conclusions that Orlinsky (2007) drew.

	Constructive/Facilitative Change Agent(s)	Commercial/Expert Change Agent(s)	Coercive/Manipulative Change Agent(s)
Governing Norm	C/F change agent(s) are committed to serving the positive interests and wellbeing of their clients (defined jointly by the client, the profession, society-at-large, and the change agent(s) own informed expert judgment).	C/E change agent(s) serve their own interests through serving clients' interests, jointly adjusted through open market processes.	C/M change agent(s) are committed to serving the needs and interests of the change agent(s) with respect to the client, and/or those of the change agent(s) sponsoring agency.
Limiting Condition	C/F change agent(s) must subordinate own interests to those of clients, but must also protect their own legitimate interests as members of a professional community and as individuals.	C/F change agent(s) must operate within the general limits of legality applicable to their service industry.	C/M change agent(s) need to operate within the normative limits of the organization and community that legitimize their activities (or risk criminal charges if discovered).
Specific Examples	• Professional therapists, counselors, and coaches (of varied professional background) • Social workers (in addition to those in clinical or counseling settings) • Clergy (in their ministerial function and pastoral capacity) • Social/political reformers	• Business consultants • Fiduciary agents and advisers (legal, financial, and so on) • Salespersons and merchants	• Advertising agents and agencies • Business and political negotiators • Partisan political consultants and strategists • Ideological propagandists • Police, security, and military interrogators • Prosecutors and defense attorneys
Counterfeit-forms	• Quacks • Confidence artists	• Providers of expert services in grey areas	• Ideologically/religiously-based extremists (revolutionary or terrorist)

Figure I.1 *Provisional Typology of Generic Psychosocial Change Agents*
©2007 by David E. Orlinsky. Used with permission.

Clients come to coaches because they want help in effecting changes. These are not physical changes, such as we might go to a hairdresser or cosmetic surgeon for. So coaches fit into the general category of "psychosocial change agents." Other nonphysical change agents, such as salespeople, want us to change our buying behavior, and lawyers or accountants advise us how to do things differently, but coaches are not in the "commercial/expert" category like these change agents. And there are change agents such as negotiators, propagandists, and police or military interrogators who use "coercive/manipulative" means to induce change, also unlike coaches. Coaches, suggests Orlinsky, are "constructive/facilitative" change agents like therapists, counselors, social workers, clergy, and political reformers. Orlinsky further describes each of these three broad categories in terms of its governing norm, limiting condition, and counterfeit forms.

Like other constructive/facilitative change agents, for example, coaches operate under the norm of a commitment "to serving the positive interests and well-being of their clients (defined jointly by the client, the profession, society-at-large, & the change-agent's own informed expert judgment)" (Orlinsky, 2007, p. 3). Counterfeit agents in this category are individuals whom peer and government certification and ethical codes are designed to protect clients against: quacks and confidence artists.

If indeed coaches can be considered psychosocial change agents in the same constructive/facilitative category as therapists and counselors, how do these change agents differ? Orlinsky answered that question by comparing the practices of these three professional activities, as summarized in Figure I.2.

Forms of Constructive/Facilitative Psychosocial Practice		
Psychotherapy	Counseling	Coaching
Healing of distressing disorders through relief of suffering and correction of maladaptive habits, conflicts, attitudes from painful, symptomatic (abnormal) dysfunction to asymptomatic or adequate functionality	Solution of troubling problems through resolution of dilemmas and improvement of strategic coping from frustrating, impaired (inadequate) adaptation to competent or normal adaptation	Optimization of unrealized potential through development of talent and refinement of effective skills from unsatisfying, limited (average) performance to enhanced or outstanding effectiveness

Figure I.2 Differentiation of Psychosocial Practices in Psychotherapy, Counseling, and Coaching

©2007 by David E. Orlinsky. Used with permission.

Thus, according to Orlinsky's survey of coaching literature as compared with his knowledge of psychotherapy and counseling, coaching is a psychosocial change intervention that optimizes "unrealized potential through development of talent & refinement of effective skills from unsatisfying, limited ('average') performance to enhanced or 'outstanding' effectiveness" (Orlinsky, 2007, p. 5). This is a definition that not only tells us what coaches do, it also differentiates coaching from two related practices.

NEUROSCIENCE PLATFORM

At the same time as coaching has emerged, and consistent with the new systemic paradigm, there has been renewed interest in the human brain and its relationship to mental and social life. Fascination with the human brain is not new. Archeologists have found evidence of brain surgery even in primitive societies. Philosophers have speculated for centuries about the brain and its relationship to human functioning. And more recently, science and medicine have made great advances in identifying how the brain does what it does (by neurons connecting with one another), mapping its functions (brain stem, limbic system, motor cortex, etc.), and understanding how it develops (interaction of genes, environment, and self-activity).

Most of these discoveries were made under quite limiting conditions: Poking around inside a brain typically ends in serious damage or death of the organism of which it is a part. Understanding how live brains function depended upon observing the consequence of head injuries or disease. These limitations have been partially overcome during the last part of the 20th century by ingenious inventions that indicate what is going on inside a live person's skull.

The consequence has been an explosion of neuroscience research, so much so that the 1990s were declared by the United Nations to be "The Decade of the Brain." We write this book in order to share some of the most exciting and useful applications of the discoveries resulting from these efforts.

But we do need to recognize that neuroscience is still in its beginning stages. Despite the accumulation of data, neuropsychiatrist Leslie Brothers (2001) points out that there is no central theory that brings a sense of unity to the various findings. Neuroscientist Steven Rose (2005) worries that we are still locked in a 19th-century worldview — what we call a "mechanistic paradigm" — that limits our ability to conceive of the brain's complexity. And there is the question that has puzzled thinkers about thinking for centuries: "How is it that the physical brain gives rise to our subjective experience of mind?" This is called the "mind/ brain problem."

Brothers (2001) laments the tendency of neuroscience to accept underlying concepts of the individual person as an entity separate from social context. She blames this largely unexamined assumption for preventing the solution of the mind/brain problem. Brothers suggests that solving this puzzle is hampered by assumptions from realms other than neuroscience itself, such as psychology's emphasis on the individual. Brothers sees a way forward in social neuroscience, or the recognition that a major purpose of the human brain is to facilitate social communication. If neuroscientists can develop concepts and a language that is derived from brain science itself, they will be released from a major limitation on the development of the field.

Despite questions such as these, and despite how much more remains to be done, our experience indicates that there is great value in what has already been discovered about the brain. In particular, we see the resurgence of theory and research in brain science and the emergence of coaching as related: neuroscience has the potential to provide a solid platform for the practice of coaching.

Why Neuroscience and Coaching?

On the surface, a marriage between coaching and neuroscience seems incongruous. The image of the neuroscientist in a lab coat manipulating the latest imaging device is very different from that of a coach engaging with a client about how to improve relationships or performance. Yet collaboration between the two fields is expanding rapidly. The May 2007 inaugural meeting of the NeuroLeadership Summit, founded by David Rock, brought together business leaders, coaches, and neuroscientists to compare notes and plan ways to support one another. The International Consortium for Coaching in Organizations held a symposium on neuroscience and the *International Journal of Coaching in Organizations* published a special issue in 2006 on the subject. Presentations on neuroscience are becoming more common at coaching and business conferences, and organizations are offering training in brain-based coaching.

Not only can neuroscience support coaching, it is clear to us that our emerging profession has the potential to support the further development of neuroscience, for example in moving beyond the individualistic assumptions cited by Brothers (2001) as limiting the neuroscience perspective. It is our view that a coaching mind-set represents a shift from an individualistic to a contextual and social understanding that is part of a larger systemic paradigm shift, one that supports social cognitive neuroscience.

Furthermore, we believe that, in addition to being guided by curiosity and a desire to understand for its own sake, research in any field is also stimulated by questions that arise from the application of theories. Theories are "stories" that create coherent meaning from rigorous research. And, ultimately, theories are tested and proven useful (or not) when they are applied in the real world. By virtue of their common birth at the nexus of the mechanistic-to-systemic paradigm shift, coaching has the opportunity to apply neuroscience theories in practice and thus play its part in an application-research partnership. We believe that such a partnership has the potential to deepen our understanding of what it means to be human and how we can fulfill our potential. We intend with this book to make a contribution to that inquiry.

In summary, this book claims that contemporary neuroscience is beginning to provide a scientific platform to support the practice of coaching. Coaching may be seen as one application of theory arising from neuroscience research. Both owe their current incarnations to the shift from a mechanistic to a systemic paradigm.

ORGANIZATION OF *COACHING WITH THE BRAIN IN MIND*

The remainder of this book explains and expands on these claims. The five major parts are each organized around a common question we human beings ask of ourselves and others:

- Who are we?
- How can we be healthy?
- Why do we do what we do?

- How can we feel better?
- How can we get along?

Within each part, answers to the question are addressed by three chapters reflecting our metaphor for the foundation of the practice of coaching:

- "Bedrock" consists of academic or professional fields in which coaching is historically embedded.
- A "pillar" is made up of current fields or practices that lift coaching above its mechanistic foundation.
- Neuroscience planks in a "platform" provide scientific and theoretical support for coaching and concludes with guides for coaches who wish to use neuroscience principles in their coaching practices.

The chapters themselves are written in response to a series of questions. Table I.1 shows the major parts, questions, and chapters.

You can read this book as it is organized, from part I through part V. Or, particularly if you are using this book in a classroom, you may want to address chapters vertically, grouping the Bedrock chapters 1, 4, 7, 10, and 13; then the Pillars chapters 2, 5, 8, 11, and 14; and finally the Neuroscience Platform chapters 3, 6, 9, 12, and 15. This is a more historical or chronological approach.

All or many of the topics in the Bedrock and Pillars chapters are likely to be familiar to coaches, some more than others: ontology, health practices, psychology, psychotherapy, and management theory as bedrock; systems theory, performance optimization, activating the mind, accentuate the positive, and leadership as pillars. For anyone who is familiar with the historical development of any of these fields, we have placed that information in identifiable sections that may be skipped or focused on. The Neuroscience Platform material—mindfulness, neuroplasticity, thinking, emotion, and NeuroLeadership—may not be so familiar to coaches.

We have set introductory stories, historical interludes, and examples in a different typeface for ease of identification.

Table I.1 Structure and Outline of Coaching with the Brain in Mind

Preface: Who Should Read This Book?
Introduction—What Are the Questions?

PARTS	BEDROCK	PILLAR	NEUROSCIENCE PLATFORM	APPLICATION
Part I	Ch 1 Ontology	Ch 2 Social Embeddedness	Ch 3 Mindfulness	Know Yourself
Part II	Ch 4 Health Practices	Ch 5 Optimizing Performance	Ch 6 Neuroplasticity	Leverage Change
Part III	Ch 7 Psychology	Ch 8 Activating the Mind	Ch 9 Cognition	Make Decisions and Solve Problems
Part IV	Ch 10 Psychotherapy	Ch 11 Accentuate the Positive	Ch 12 Emotions	Keep Cool Under Pressure
Part V	Ch 13 Management	Ch 14 Leadership	Ch 15 NeuroLeadership	Get Along with Others

Conclusion—What Are We Doing Here?

WHAT DO WE NEED TO KNOW ABOUT NEUROSCIENCE?

Modern neuroscience both depends on and transcends the worldview that held sway until the last half of the 20th century. Technological advances that enable scientists to see inside the brain—what had been considered an impenetrable "black box"—stimulated a new understanding of the brain, which is an example of a complex system. Neuroimaging devices developed during the final decades of the 20th century have allowed researchers to confirm many speculations about how the brain works and to discover things that had scarcely been imagined before.

The idea, almost a dogma as recently as a decade ago, that brain structure is fixed and unchangeable from childhood on has been replaced. "Neuroplasticity" is the term used for what is now indisputable: Many of the very structures of the brain can be modified by experience, even in adulthood. And even more astounding is "the notion that mind is using the brain to create itself" (Siegel, 2007a, p. 32). That is, we now know that how we think can modify the brain that we use to do our thinking. Coaching clients can learn to think in ways that change their capacity to feel, think, and act—and ultimately to shift who they are in the world.

When one of us (David) explained coaching to neuroscientist Jeffrey Schwartz (personal communication, May 2007), he responded, "Oh, I see what coaching is . . . it is a way of facilitating self-directed neuroplasticity." The platform on which coaching rests is constructed from "planks" that illustrate why Schwartz made this statement.

Influenced by a computer analogy, late-20th-century researchers assumed the brain to be an information processor that does its work without reference to content or context. The brain was divided into sections, each with neuronal patterns that are specialized for their functions: seeing, hearing, talking, regulating bodily functions, or being the "executive" or boss of the brain.

Much of early brain research was concerned with identifying which parts of the brain control which functions and of finding "the seat of reason." These efforts were made under technological and ethical constraints: The only way to examine the inside of a brain was after its user was dead, and scientists had to take advantage of accidents and illness to observe the effects of damage to parts of the brain in a living person. The exceptions of electroconvulsive therapy (ECT) and lobotomies are examples of questionable experiments under the guise of treatment that nonetheless provided information about brain function.

According to a strict mechanistic interpretation, the mind is determined by brain activity, in a one-way causal direction. The extreme interpretation of this view is that the mind can be pretty much ignored, for all the responsibility it has in directing behavior. Thus, mental activity is reduced to neuronal activity. If only we could observe its 100 billion neurons, each connecting to 5,000 to 10,000 others, we could understand the mind—a daunting assignment even in a Newtonian world. Despite all these limitations, the fascination with the brain by philosophical, medical, psychological, and psychiatric researchers yielded much of the bedrock upon which today's neuroscience is founded.

Brain-shifting Discoveries

At the beginning of the 21st century, the systemic paradigm shift has combined with technological advances and interdisciplinary discoveries to create a new way of thinking about mind and brain, as stimulated by three discoveries:

1. *Neuroplasticity.* Discoveries based on new technology have revealed that adult brains are much more plastic—that is, capable of changing as a result of experience—than mechanistic assumptions previously allowed. These discoveries include:

   a. The dependence of human brain development on attachment.
   b. The capacity for adults to "earn secure attachment" even when they did not have it as children.
   c. What the human brain must have, and other species do not have, in order to create, learn, and use language as we do.
   d. The effects of successful psychotherapy and mindfulness practices on brain function and structure, not to mention mental and social life.

2. *Brains as social organs.* The idea that our thinking processes are coterminous with our own individual brains has been thoroughly

criticized by Leslie Brothers (2001) and others (Quartz & Sejnowski, 2002). Brothers attributes the difficulty in solving the "mind-brain problem"—discovering the relationship between our subjective experiences (mind) and our physical bodies (brains)— to the acceptance by the public and even by neuroscientists themselves that the mind can be explained in terms of the individual brain. Brothers (1997) has contributed to new fields of social neuroscience and social cognitive neuroscience (Lieberman, 2007; Ochsner & Lieberman, 2001) that are confirming what some previously marginalized social scientists and attachment researchers have been insisting on: that we think outside our own individual brains (Page, 2006). This development is part of a systemic shift away from limiting our concept of a human being to the extreme individualism that characterizes Western culture. As Brothers (2001) puts it, our "neural machinery" "doesn't produce mind; it enables participation" (p. 92).

3. *Rediscovery of volition.* Physics, the foundation of the mechanistic paradigm, has had to accept the alternative quantum "mechanics" because of the weight of scientific evidence. Max Planck, Neils Bohr, Werner Heisenberg, and other physicists discovered that the behavior of "stuff" at the subatomic level depended on the perspective and presence of an observer. Albert Einstein proposed a theory of relativity in which there is no such thing as absolute truth. He proved that light is both energy and matter. Mind and matter, subject and object were no longer separate.

Quantum theory is counterintuitive to the Western mind steeped in the mechanics of linear logic. How can something be true and not true, matter and not matter, at the same time? Not surprisingly, for most of the 20th century, the implications of quantum theory were largely ignored outside of physics and astronomy. Nevertheless, decades of experimentation have confirmed the predictions of quantum theorists. Physics has added its weight to the two related trends of postmodernism and globalization in bringing about a greater acceptance of systemic principles in the human sciences.

As a result of this new way of thinking about thinking, we are beginning to discover how, to paraphrase the title of Sharon Begley's book (2007), we—with an emphasis on the social "we"—can train our minds to change our brains. Coaching emerged during the last two decades of the 20th century as the change practice that embodies this new paradigm. New discoveries reveal neuroscience more and more to be an exemplar of the systemic paradigm and an evidence base for coaching. In the Neuroscience Platform chapters, we survey the beginning of what we believe will provide that theoretical platform into the future.

Energy and Information

In order to introduce the Neuroscience Platform for coaching, let us begin by thinking of our lives as a *process* rather than a thing. In an abstract sense, our life is a *flow* of energy and information. The English language does not easily express process, given its tendency to turn ongoing, dynamic activity into a static, thing-like noun: Growing becomes growth, relating becomes relationship, exploring becomes exploration, and so on. At times in this book, we will use a more verb-like form, such as "minding" instead of "mind," in order to remind ourselves that we are indeed talking about ongoing processes.

Like a river, our lives are continually changing. We are dynamic, always adjusting according to the demands of the social and physical environment, doing more or doing less, guided by the sense we make of our life, a "flowing" rather than a "flow."

What do we mean by *energy*? This is a term that we use every day, yet defining what all the uses have in common is not easy. In simple terms like those our children learn in fourth-grade science class, energy is what makes things or processes active. As energy changes, something happens or ceases to happen. As our energy wanes, we get sleepy, and as we are refreshed, we become awake and active and get things done.

Energy is related to power, though it is not the same. As a simple example, if we think of energy as the amount of water in a bottle, power is how quickly it is poured out. Energy is what enables our activity; power is how effectively we use that activity.

What is *information*? This term is also used in many different ways, some very technical, as in engineering and information processing. Robert Losee (1997) attempted to find a definition of information that could be used by journalists, linguists, and engineers as well as neuroscientists: "the characteristics of the output of a process, these being

21

informative about the process and input" (p. 254). This definition is useful, as we will see in the pages to follow, even though it leaves us wondering "What does 'informative' mean?" Siegel (2007b) provides a simplified definition by saying that information is something that stands for something else. In Losee's terms, the output, or brain signals that stand for something else, such as the bowl of ice cream we are looking at, stands for or tells us about that input to our eyes: the color, amount, and possibly flavor of the ice cream. Sometimes, of course, brain signals tell us about how *we* are feeling inside rather than about something external. That is, we can imagine ice cream even when it is not there, and that may tell us something about ourselves and our state of hunger.

What is a Brain?

Let us begin with what a scientist who has dissected an organism can see and touch: a brain. Many of us have ourselves participated in science labs where we dissected the brains of animals such as frogs, and most of us have at least seen human and other brains floating in formaldehyde. Because of its connections with its body through a relatively skinny neck, the brain is easily separated from the rest of its physical body, resulting in death of the organism, and so we think of it as central to our lives, as relatively self-contained, and thus as an organ of great interest.

The human brain is shaped vaguely like a football, and that is one reason it is difficult to represent in a book. It is definitely three-dimensional, and books are not. And there are important parts of the brain that are inside, so pictures have to illustrate a brain cut in half or peeled of its outer layer. The front of the brain (toward our face) is sometimes presented on the right on one page and on the left (facing the other way) on the next page. So which way is front when the brain is cut in half? And is the cut made horizontally or vertically?

The Brain in Our Hand

Neuroscientists have suggested (Kolb & Whishaw, 2003; Siegel, 1999; Siegel & Hartzell, 2003) that we carry a three-dimensional model of the brain with us all the time—our hand. We will borrow the idea of using the hand as a model, but adapt it to what we need for this book. If we fold our left thumb under our fingers, tucking our nails into our palm to make a fist, we can use our left hand to remind us of very general brain anatomy:

- *Cortex.* Cup your right hand over the fist you have just made with your left hand. Imagine that your eyes are in front of the two middle fingers of your left hand with your nose between the first and middle joints. Your right hand is your skull. Remove it. The top of your left fist is the top layer of your cortex, where much of what we are aware of as mental processes takes place.

- *Brain stem.* Your spinal cord is your left forearm, and it provides energy (via blood and other nutrients) and information (via nerve impulses to and from the rest of the body) to the stem of your brain represented by your left wrist. This bottom part of your brain takes care of basic processes, such as keeping you breathing and your heart beating. Around it, above your wrist and inside it and the lower part of your palm, are areas of "chemical-delivery neurons" (Zull, 2006) that have connections to all parts of the brain and that release neurotransmitters, such as adrenaline, dopamine, and serotonin. These chemicals change the quality and quantity of signaling for neurons that are immersed in them.

- *Sensory cortex.* Your fingers at the top of your fist, close to the middle joint, represent one place where sensory information is gathered from all over the body, including the sides (auditory) and back (visual) of the brain.

- *Motor cortex.* Next to the sensory cortex, also at the top of your fist, is an area that coordinates intentional muscle movement.

- *Rear association area.* The back of your hand indicates where out-of-awareness connections are made in your brain. For instance, to recognize an apple, we have to assemble separate stimuli, or incoming information, about its visual shape, color, and perhaps feel in your hand. This all happens outside our awareness. An analogy to back-end processes of a computer is relevant here. When we turn on a computer, the processing unit whirs and hums busily, although not much shows on the screen until the startup connections are made. One difference is that our brain does not shut off as long as we are alive; but otherwise, we can imagine the back part of our brain, represented in our fist analogy by the back of our hand, as a major location for putting things together outside of our awareness.

- *Front connection area.* The brain area represented by your fingers between the first and middle joints, behind what would be your forehead and eyes, is another association site. We call it a "front connection area" to differentiate it from the "rear association area" already discussed. In particular, this includes the prefrontal cortex, an area of particular importance for conscious activity, self-control, relating to others, and planning.

- *Limbic area.* The beauty of the brain-in-your-hand model is that it allows you to picture important areas inside the brain. Open the fingers of your left hand while keeping your thumb tucked against your palm. Your thumb and the places it touches are often grouped together and described as the "seat of emotion." Like a collar around the top of the brain stem, this area includes the amygdala, hippocampus, and basal ganglia. Notice its central location, with access to the top of the brain stem (the inside of your lower palm), the rear association area (the inside of the back of your hand), the motor and sensory cortices (the inside of the top part of the fingers), and the prefrontal cortex (the inside of the front-facing part of your fingers, along with your tucked-in nails and fingertips).

We can rank these areas according to speed with which they react to stimuli (Zull, 2006). The limbic area, where our amygdala is ever on guard for danger, gets top rank. It can have us running away before we even know what we are running from. Sensory input and motor output also must be fast. Conscious connections are a bit slower, and the signals to release hormones and neurotransmitters slower still. Rear association processes can be quite slow, requiring reflection and perhaps even sleep, so that competing stimuli are dampened.

The brain-in-our-hand model offers a very general overview of brain anatomy and provides a guide to references to the brain throughout this book. But what we want to examine here is not so much the physical form but the function of the brain, or what that form does. We are aware that the living, functioning brain is part of a complex whole-body system that should perhaps be called "brain-body." However, to avoid the awkwardness of that phrase, let us just remember that when we speak of the brain, we mean one element in a highly interactive embodied system. In effect, the word we use for the processes of this whole system is "living." These processes involve a flow of *information* and *energy*, two terms that we already have defined. The brain/body provides the physical structure and mechanisms for that information and energy, across the boundaries of and through the complex system that is our living self.

What is a Mind?

Next, we address the question of the mind. If we use it in everything we do, including coaching, then it is surely worthy of attention. Daniel Siegel asks audiences around the world, including scientists, academics, psychologists, and psychotherapists—all professionals who study or work with mental activity—whether they have ever learned a definition of the word "mind." Ask yourself: In all your attention to activities of the mind, including learning, change, and choice, have you ever been taught a definition of "mind"?

Siegel reports that, even among audiences whose work involves diagnosing, understanding, or changing mental processes, only a tiny percentage have ever learned what a mind is. So he provides a definition: "The mind is an embodied and relational process that regulates the flow of energy and information" (Siegel, 2007b). As we show in the chapters to come, understanding the mind from this perspective reveals what it means to be truly healthy and to "potentiate"—to engage in a process of more fully developing our potential. The regulation of information and energy is a crucial part of that flow. In effect, mind and brain are closely interrelated and dependent on one another. There can be no human brain without mind, and vice versa.

What do Relationships have to do with it?

Current neuroscience goes beyond assumptions that the mind is an addendum, an afterthought, so to speak, of brain activity. We now know that brain and mind are interdependent and necessary to each other. But that is not all that contemporary neuroscience has taught us about brain and mind. Attachment theory, trauma theory, interpersonal

25

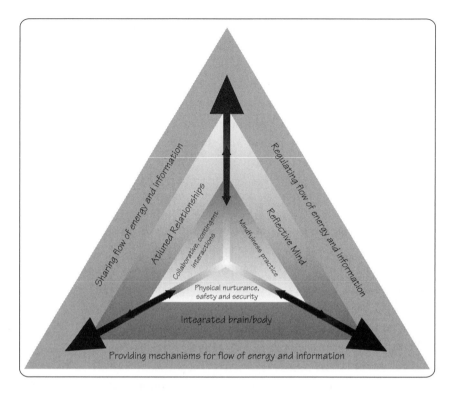

Figure I.3 Potentiating the Human System

©2008. Adler International Learninf. *Reproduced with permission.*

neurobiology, and social cognitive neuroscience have shown that nei-ther human brains nor human minds exist without social relationships. Thus, brain (body), mind, and relationships form an irreducible triad in producing the flow of information and energy that is human life. We could think of the triad as three legs on a stool. We have chosen to rep-resent them in a triangle (see Figure I.3), each side of which influences and is influenced by the other two.

Health and Well-being

In seeking a definition of human health and well-being, as opposed to an absence of disease, Siegel (2007a) suggested the optimization of these three irreducible subsystems: an integrated brain, attuned relationships, and a reflective mind. We call this "potentiating." In the pages to come, we illustrate these systems, show how they are related, and present what to do to maintain them in healthy dynamic stability: to nourish our brain/body, restore attunement in relationships, and encourage insight that draws on the mind's resources and leads to action. These processes form the basis for sharing and regulating information and energy. That is, we show how current neuroscience provides a conceptual, scientific, and theoretical foundation for coaching.

Choosing to act is not only how new ideas translate into social reality, it is how new structures are established in our brains. These methods turn the major discoveries of neuroplasticity, social neuroscience, and how the mind uses the brain to create itself into practical applications that coaches and leaders can use every day. From there, like the old joke about how to get to Carnegie Hall, the answer is practice, practice, practice.

What Are We Doing Here?

In the final chapter, we return to the story of Ishi. Globalization and communication provide the means for species-wide communication. Coaches and others are practicing using their minds to consciously create new brains and new behaviors. Will the human species be limited by its old forms and processes, like the scientists who ignored Ishi's wishes and sent his brain to be stored in a tub of formaldehyde? Or will we think about what kind of world we wish to inhabit and take steps to create it?

The Virchow quote in the preface reads, "Knowledge which is unable to support action is not genuine" (1962, p. 40). However interesting, or even fascinating, the discoveries of neuroscience may be, they become genuinely valuable only when they are put into action. For coaching and, we suspect, for much of human endeavor, the question is "How do we realize more, as much as possible, of our human potential?"

What does it take for a person to coach with the brain in mind? What guidelines support that practice? By utilizing neuroscience theory to expand on the skills of coaching, we honor the second part of Virchow's quote: "—and how unsure is activity without understanding?" (1962, p. 40). Theory and research are necessary for the development and maintenance of a profession such as coaching, yet without action in the world, they remain infertile.

27

A NOTE ABOUT THE SCIENCE OF NEUROSCIENCE

Interest in neuroscience has exploded over the past two decades, at the very time that coaching has also come into being. Advances in technology have introduced machines such as computers that simulate brain activity and others that observe the brain in action, including MEG (magnetoencephalography), PET (positron emission tomography), and fMRIs (functional magnetic resonance imaging). These have enabled researchers to observe and measure much more accurately what is happening as people process their lives. This great advance over postmortem examination has been an enormous stimulus to discoveries about brain/mind/social interaction.

However, because these findings are so new, making leaps from single studies of some particular brain activity to how people actually function in their daily lives is risky. Despite the accumulation of data and popularity of studies of the brain, neuroscientist Steven Rose (2005) worries that we are still to some extent trapped in a "mechanistic reductionist mind-set." "Imprisoned as we are," he says, "we can't find ways to think coherently in multiple levels and dimensions, to incorporate the time line and dynamics of living processes into our understanding of molecules and cells and systems" (p. 215).

Brothers (2001) insists that there is at present no central theory that makes sense of the data being produced by neuroscientists. Thus, we must recognize that we are only just beginning to understand the many potential applications of brain science to coaching. What we now think we understand is subject to revision by ongoing research and by the continuing development of our social minding processes.

But we are not satisfied with waiting until neuroscience has a fully formed discourse before we dare to make use of its findings. We take a more dialectic perspective. We say that the whole enterprise of understanding humanity is furthered by the mutual influence of theory *and* practice.

For an applied field such as coaching, the ultimate measure of the value of understanding is how useful it is. It is our experience that an understanding of neuroscience research, however new and speculative, can help coaches be better coaches and can help leaders become better leaders. As change agents whose profession arose at the same time as modern brain science, we deserve to have all the currently available knowledge that might help us do our jobs well. Therefore, we should be free to try out even preliminary neuroscience findings to see if they may be useful. We should, however, apply these caveats:

- We must be rigorous about evaluating usefulness (see Stewart, 2006).
- We should recognize that interpretations are indeed preliminary, are open to reinterpretation, and must necessarily be arrived at out of context because no central theory of the brain is yet developed.
- We may therefore discover that even well-validated useful techniques are only metaphorically related to neuroscience theory rather than being direct, accurate applications.

We ourselves are not neuroscientists, but we seek to understand the work that these pioneers are doing and to consider its implications for human well-being. Through dialogue sessions such as those at the NeuroLeadership summits, we attempt to discern the meaning of discoveries in partnership with the neuroscientists who are making them.

On that basis, we present our best suggestions as to how to apply the present understanding of the brain and how it relates to social and mental processes. We fervently hope that anyone who reads this book continues to keep informed about new findings and new interpretations, as they surely will arise.

PART I

Who Are We?

It is a universal characteristic of human beings that we ask questions about ourselves, our relationships to one another, and our place in the world. As we discussed in the introduction, answers to these questions come out of our beliefs about reality. If what is real consists of physical, material stuff, then the essence of who we are is our material bodies. Ideas, dreams, beliefs, faith, and even love are not real in the same sense. During the mechanistic era, material reality was the realm of science, and everything else belonged to philosophy or religion or fiction. The spiritual, fictional world, according to an extreme interpretation of this view, was either determined by or made entirely of different "stuff" from the material world. In either case, it could not have an effect on material reality. This interpretation was never universally accepted, but in the 20th century, even its scientific anchor in Newtonian mechanics began to come loose. The result is a new set of answers to questions about the essence of humanity. And these answers make coaching relevant.

Answering the question of who we are is not a fluffy or merely intellectual exercise, especially for coaches. Unlike plants or rocks, and like other animals, human beings move. At a very general level, we move toward reward and away from danger. That is, we move toward what we value and away from what we do not value. And values are not an isolated, individual matter. As physicist Henry Stapp (2007) puts it:

Martyrs in every age are vivid reminders of the fact that no influence upon human conduct, even the instinct for bodily self-preservation, is stronger than beliefs about

31

one's relationship to the rest of the universe and to the power that shapes it. Such beliefs form the foundation of a person's self-image, and hence, ultimately, of personal values. (p. 5)

Stapp goes on to point out that the question of values is relevant to science despite the fact that scientific endeavor sought to be value-free during the modern era of Newtonian assumptions. "What we value depends on what we believe, and what we believe is strongly influenced by science" (Stapp, 2007, p. 5). Neuroscience has the potential to confirm a basic coaching tenet: that what we choose to value makes a difference in how well we move through life. In part I, we survey paradigm shifts in how we answer a question closely related to our values: "Who are we?"

CHAPTER 1

Bedrock — Ontology

The anthropologist and her American university student had to walk for an hour after the Jeep that had brought them from Guatemala City could go no farther. They followed their native guide up and down paths through the mountains until they came to a village made up of mud huts set in a circle. In Guatemala before the civil war that made such visits too dangerous, the group would find that each village had its own typical costume, type of products that it would sell to other villages, and even its own dialect or language. The anthropologist was investigating the ravages of kwashiorkor — protein malnutrition that, in some parts of the country, left four of five toddlers dead after they switched from mother's milk to the corn gruel that was considered the best thing parents could give to a child. Centuries of mistrust of strangers, probably beginning even before the Spanish invasion, meant that people did not believe Western doctors who told them they should give their children cow's milk instead of their corn gruel. As she did not know how to resolve the problem, the anthropologist was there to listen instead of give advice.

A light mist had been falling, and the sky was overcast. One woman was brave enough to emerge from her mud-covered home, bringing two child-sized chairs for the anthropologist and her student to sit on. These seats were meant as a sign of honor. The woman, several children of different ages, and the guide hunkered down on the muddy ground. The woman spoke in her native tongue, which the guide had to translate into Spanish for the anthropologist. Then, because the student spoke very little Spanish, the anthropologist translated what was said into English.

The student had spent many hours in anthropology classes, learning about arrowheads and spear throwers and languages and cultural differences. But here she was faced with a living, breathing person who may never even have owned a book, much less taken a university class. How, the student wondered to herself, could there ever be any hope of communicating at all, given such differences?

But when the woman began to talk about her four children who had died from protein malnutrition, one after the other, the differences melted away. The woman named each child, described his or her personality, and offered precious memories. Tears filled her eyes. The student knew with sudden clarity that however different their circumstances, however little she understood the actual words that were used, she would never forget the emotional impact of that woman's experience. They looked at each other as if there were no boundaries between them. Never again could the student use the term "primitive" without putting quotation marks around it or preceding it with "so-called," as in "so-called primitive." It was not theory but lived, emotion-saturated experience shared with the woman in the village that convinced the student of their common humanity.

Ontology is what philosophers call the study of "being," of how we relate to each other and the world around us — that is, the study of who we are. Questions that philosophers classify as ontological are neither new nor limited to academic inquiry:

- What is the essential nature of human beings, physical or spiritual?
- Are we just animals with illusions that our conscious decisions have some kind of effect?
- Are people basically good and simply in need of encouragement to flourish, or are they essentially bad and in need of control?
- What part do emotions play in who we are? Are they disturbances to rational thought, or do they contribute to our ability to move through life?
- Is there such a thing as an enduring reality, or is reality a subjective creation?
- Is there such a thing as free will, or are our lives determined by heredity, environment, or both?
- If there is no free will, how can we speak of responsibility or morality?

- How independent are individual persons? Are people closely inter-related with their social and physical surroundings, or are they stand-alone entities?
- Does change happen in a line or in a circle — or in a spiral?

This initial chapter covers approaches to ontological questions that are embedded in a classical or mechanistic bedrock but that contain contributions to coaching:

Western philosophy
New Age philosophy
Anthropology
Sociology
Ontology as bedrock for coaching

WESTERN PHILOSOPHY

The word "philosophy" comes from the Greek word *philosophia*, meaning "love of wisdom." Philosophy examines the fundamental nature of knowledge, reality, and existence. Evidence of a foundation for coaching can be found in early philosophical thought. Consider whether it is better to ask a client for her ideas on how to improve her performance or to advise her based on what you think is best. Most approaches to coaching favor asking the client, based on the assumption that clients are sources of untapped wisdom. The ancient Greek philosopher Socrates pioneered this approach several thousand years ago.

HISTORICAL INTERLUDE

Socrates

Socrates (469–399 BC) is important for coaches to study. Socrates taught that each person is born with full knowledge of ultimate truth and needs only to be spurred to conscious awareness of it. He believed that people must acquire knowledge and wisdom for themselves, and so he engaged his students in a process of questioning rather than providing them with answers. His famous question, "What is the good life?" (Allen, 1991) is an

(Continued)

---

example of what is called the Socratic method. The modern interpretation of this method includes these characteristics:

- Questioning to move a person forward
- Creating a structure around the process of questioning
- Pursuing meaning and truth
- Refraining from offering advice in the belief that answers can be found inside the individual, rather than in external sources of wisdom

Augustine

The fourth-century AD monk Augustine (354–430) argued against a position that was gathering adherents in Rome. About the year 390, a cleric named Pelagius had come from Britannia in the north, claiming that people's good natures should be celebrated. According to Pelagius, by their own efforts, people could reconstitute themselves and the world around them. Augustine was a brilliant logician who had made his mark with the emperor, the pope, and other clerics by opposing heretical views. He countered the Pelagian belief in the inherent goodness of people by insisting that all human beings carry the mark of "original sin" and have to rely on the church to intervene on their behalf. The fact that Augustine is better remembered than Pelagius tells us who won the argument. Original sin became the doctrine of early Christianity and largely held sway until the authority of the church was shaken by scientific discoveries during the Renaissance. A link with Pelagian "celebration of the natural" can be traced from the Romanticism of Jean-Jacques Rousseau (1712–1778) through to today's New Age philosophies.

Descartes

Another of the enduring debates in Western philosophy is whether we observe our way to the truth (empiricism) or think our way there (rationalism). The French philosopher Renée Descartes (1596–1650), a major figure in rationalist history, proposed a materialist model of the human body. He believed that the mind was composed of different "stuff" from the physical body. In Descartes' view, called dualism, the mental and the physical influenced each other, but he never explained exactly how that happened. Subsequently, a more complete separation into different realms offered a solution to the political conflict between the church and scientists. Science could claim dominion over the physical realm while the church could rule the "soul," or mind.

This "solution" provided only a temporary truce and eroded as 19th-century scientists began to study the mind and thus encroach on the church's territory. However, as long as science assumes that the mind is simply a by-product of "real" brain activity, the battle of dualism continues to be fought, as illustrated by modern philosopher of science Daniel Dennett (1991). Dennett's claim that subjective consciousness is an illusion is in the tradition of mechanism, or the idea that human beings are reduced "to cogs in a giant machine that grinds inexorably along a preordained path in the grip of a blind causal process" (Stapp, 2007, p. 5). Such a view implies that each cog has no choice in what it will do or how it moves—that it is determined by past material causes—so how can we speak of responsibility for one's actions or indeed morality at all? What use would coaching be in such a universe? In contrast, the universe that is emerging from contemporary physics and neuroscience not only provides a home for coaching but, as we claim throughout this book, is part of why coaching has come to be.

Galileo and Newton took up the empiricist program of discovering laws of the physical world. Newtonian physics, or classical mechanics, assumed that objective truth would be discovered by reducing all events to their elementary particles and developing laws that determined how these elements interacted. This line of research proved enormously successful. However, the implication of applying these assumptions to human beings leads exactly to the cogs-in-a-giant-machine conclusion drawn by Dennett and others. Why, then, should philosophers bother to philosophize and ethicists to ethicize and coaches to coach?

Philosophers ignored the mechanistic implication that their theorizing was illusory, and they continued to wonder about such questions as whether people would be at their best if left to nature, to whom principles of equality applied, and how people make decisions—rationally or emotionally?

Western philosophy has a long tradition stretching from the ancient Greeks (Plato, Aristotle, and Socrates) to modern philosophers like Jean-Paul Sartre and Viktor Frankl. We will merely touch on those traditions that contain elements relevant to coaching.

When you coach, think of Socrates, in particular his method of questioning. New coaches often tend to violate Socratic principles by offering advice too early in the coaching dialogue. Often they do not probe deeply enough, settling for the first idea that comes up during the session. More experienced coaches follow the lead of the client and explore issues in greater depth. An experienced coach may ask 10 or more questions to elicit useful insights, whereas a new coach instead may offer interpretations.

Socratic principles suggest that coaches refrain from offering advice, understanding that the client is the expert regarding his or her life. Whitworth and colleagues, in their influential book *Co-Active Coaching*, summarize this approach by insisting that the client is naturally "creative, resourceful and whole" (Whitworth, Kinsey-House & Sandahl, 1998, p. 3).

Many philosophers influenced the development of the social sciences, which were always suspected of not being "real science" in the Newtonian universe. The social sciences in turn contributed to the emergence of coaching. In 1911, Hans Vaihinger (1852–1933), wrote *The Philosophy of "As If"* (1911, 1925), a book that influenced the sociology of knowledge and constructivism in sociology, psychology, and psychotherapy. He suggested that acting as if a belief were true has real consequences in the material world, a claim that fits the systemic paradigm and that has been confirmed by social psychology and neuroscience. The ideas of Martin Heidegger (1889–1976), who is famous for questioning "the meaning of being" (1977), were echoed in cognitive psychology, another precursor to coaching.

Existentialism

Existentialism is one of the major philosophical movements of the 20th century and one that explores territory outside the scientific objectivity demanded by logical positivism. Martin Buber (1878–1965), Jean-Paul Sartre (1905–1980), and other thinkers of the existential movement paved the way for the humanist perspective in psychotherapy (Rader & Gill, 1990).

Buber focused on people's immediate subjective experience. He was not attracted to the science of his day, a science that studied reality as a set of mechanisms. Buber was born in 1878 in Vienna but spent much of his boyhood with his grandparents in the Ukraine. His grandfather was a Jewish scholar, but young Buber was not attracted to abstract philosophy divorced from everyday life. By the time he went back to Vienna to enter university, he was exploring existential philosophy.

Perhaps he could experience true meaning in everyday existence itself, in life embedded in community rather than in the dry observations of science. He wrote the book that is translated into English as *I and Thou* in 1922 (Buber, 1970). In it he describes two basic ways of interacting with the world—not just with other people but with anything. We can hold ourselves separate from whatever is in front of us, talking to ourselves inside our heads as if we occupy one universe and the "whatever" is a thing over there in another. Even if the "whatever" is another person, we do not interact so as to open ourselves to experiencing the other's full, engaging presence. This is an "I-It" relationship. The other mode of relating is "I-Thou." We enter a living, breathing dialogue with another person where the boundary between "I" and "Thou" is fluid, and we draw upon each other's existence to enrich our own. As mystical as this description may sound, Buber's ideas of two modes of processing are remarkably like what neuroscientists have discovered almost a century later. Our thinking process alternates between a "narrative" sequence where we talk to ourselves *about* our experience and a fully present sequence of engagement, or "flow" (Farb *et al.*, 2007).

There are deep links between existentialism and coaching. Existentialists call for passion and commitment. They emphasize here-and-now experience and the influence of dialogue. They encourage choice, taking actions, and being responsible for the choices we make. They recommend approaching each day as if it might be our last, truly engaging in life and in the pursuit of excellence, and not accepting mediocrity. Self-examination and honoring individuality are also two major themes associated with existentialism.

HISTORICAL INTERLUDE

The appearance of Viktor Frankl (1905–1997) at the Evolution of Psychotherapy Conference, held every five years to bring together the most influential psychotherapists in the world and attended by thousands of therapists, would be his last public appearance. Frankl looked frail sitting on the stage in the massive conference hall, yet he held the audience in rapt attention. He described his youthful interest in psychiatry, his connection with Sigmund Freud and Alfred Adler, and his development of an

(Continued)

approach he called "logotherapy." But what moved the listeners was his story of being an inmate in a Nazi concentration camp from 1942 to 1945. It was not an abstraction for him to say that human beings can find meaning even in the most brutal circumstances imaginable. He discovered in his own experience that when all other choices have been taken away, choice remains. He reported later that when a prisoner could tolerate no more, "he found a way out in his mental life—an invaluable opportunity to dwell in the spiritual domain, the one that the SS were unable to destroy. Spiritual life strengthened the prisoner, helped him adapt, and thereby improved his chances of survival" (Frankl, 1984, p. 123). Such was true for Frankl himself. Frankl's life and work can be related to Western philosophy because of his influence on the development of existentialism; to New Age philosophy based on his emphasis on a spiritual search for meaning; and to anthropology and sociology, as well as psychology, as a result of his keen observation of human behavior under the most difficult of circumstances.

The existential themes of self-examination and honoring individuality are nowhere more evident than in the work of Frankl, the founder of logotherapy and existential analysis. His most influential book, *Man's Search for Meaning* (1984), was first published in 1946. As a concentration camp inmate in World War II, Frankl relied on his interest in human behavior and psychology to find a reason to survive. He then applied his experience to psychotherapy, stating "I had wanted to simply convey to the reader that life holds a potential meaning under any conditions, even the most miserable ones" (1984, p.12). His observation that concentration camp survivors were those who had embraced a core meaning in their lives led him to state, "I want you to listen to what your conscience commands you to do and go on to carry it out to the best of your knowledge"(Frankl, 1984, pp. 12–13). To rail against external limitations is to ignore the responsibility that comes with choice. If all we can do is create something meaningful to us, then that becomes our responsibility as human beings.

Existentialism provides rich learning for coaches. The existential concepts of following one's passion, pursuing excellence, and having choice are all relevant. Coaches help clients find their passion by following their "energy." Coaches listen closely for what is said as well as for what is not said, striving to understand what has meaning for clients, what motivates them, and what commits them to taking action. And last, coaches encourage clients to expand their thinking, to look at all possible choices rather than focusing on only one or two. As mentioned in the section on Socrates, experienced coaches do not accept as final the first idea a client articulates. Instead, they probe for deeper meaning, more elemental insights, richer connections, and more solid ground for ongoing commitment and action.

Linking Western Philosophy and Coaching

Some indications of the influence of Western philosophy on coaching include:

- The basic belief in human potential
- Placing the Socratic method at the heart of good coaching
- Acceptance of the existential emphasis on choice and taking responsibility for one's choices and actions

NEW AGE PHILOSOPHY

You may wonder why a book about science and coaching would include a section on New Age philosophy, which is rooted in spirituality rather than scientific theory. However, the philosophy behind New Age practices has influenced the evolution of coaching, more from historical perspectives than scientific ones.

The concept of "New Age" originated with astrology, which in the last part of the 20th century claimed that the planets were aligned in an "Aquarian Age," a time of increased spirituality and harmony. The term "New Age" can refer to astrology, numerology, chakras, enlightenment, reincarnation, near-death experiences, crystals, rebirthing, human potential workshops, aromatherapy, tarot cards, the *I Ching*, color therapy, yoga, reflexology, palmistry, fire-walking, channeling, kinesthesiology, witchcraft, shamanism, acupuncture, *reiki*, and many other practices. These practices have widely varying degrees of mainstream acceptance, from aromatherapy massage, which you can find in most five-star hotels around the world today, to shamanism, which is more associated with "witchcraft."

New Age philosophy draws on Buddhism, Hinduism, Taoism, Judaism, Catholicism, occultism, and paganism. Adherents include transcendentalists such as Henry David Thoreau, Ralph Waldo Emerson, and William Wordsworth in the early 1800s, and Theosophists such as Madame Helena Blavatsky (1831–1891). New Age philosophy enjoyed resurgence during the 1960s and 1970s, when traditional values were being challenged. During this time, Eastern mysticism, Yoga, Zen, transcendental meditation, and mystical writers like Carlos Castañeda gained popularity.

New Age philosophy influenced the humanist psychology of Carl Rogers (1902–1987) and Abraham Maslow (1908–1970), which focused more on human potential and less on pathology, as compared with clinical psychology. Rogers and Maslow were part of what became known as the human potential movement that emerged in the 1970s. Erhard Seminars Training, also known as EST, which became Landmark Education in 1991, continues in this tradition. Werner Erhard is one of the most-cited influencers on the development of the coaching profession (Brock, 2008). According to the Landmark Web site, over 145,000 people in 52 countries attend Landmark programs every year. There are thousands of similar, although smaller, organizations, including Insight Seminars, the Silva method, Lifespring, and many others. Visit any health food store anywhere in the world and you will find dozens of notices for workshops to help you understand your inner child, your outer mask, or your growing middle.

Some of the ideas that are common to New Age philosophy include:

- A focus on consciousness and self-awareness
- Belief in human potential
- The power of suggestion, including the use of visualization
- The illusory nature of matter
- The cyclical nature of life
- Ideas of balance and harmony
- Belief in enlightenment
- Belief in the afterlife, spirits, and ghosts (not heaven and hell)
- Meditation or contemplation
- Pacifism
- Environmental awareness

Many of these beliefs also form the core of certain coaching philosophies, in particular the emphasis on self-awareness, balance, and the belief in human potential. Some coaching models draw more heavily from New Age philosophy than from science. For example, "spiritual coaches" offer to identify the client's life mission and purpose.

Big names in New Age philosophy include Deepak Chopra, Louise Hay, Wayne Dyer, James Redfield, Tony Robbins, John Gray, Maharishi Mahesh Yogi, and Eckhart Tolle. Many coaches are fans of these thinkers. Despite their lack of scientific legitimacy, these people are influential philosophers of the present day. Millions of people read their books and follow the principles they espouse.

However, these approaches may still show the individualism of mechanistic thinking, despite their espousal of what might look like a systemic worldview. If the individual person only thought correctly or paid enough attention or spent enough time meditating, she or he could control life. However admirable it may be to encourage adherents in this way, it does leave them vulnerable to blaming themselves for difficulties, even when those difficulties are out of their control as individuals. Therefore, coaches would be wise to temper their admiration of New Age thinkers with the skepticism of a scientist. Contemporary science does not ignore the physical world; rather, it includes human beings as participants rather than as predetermined cogs.

Linking New Age Philosophy and Coaching

A common theme in New Age philosophy is the belief in human potential and in innate human goodness. Coaches and New Age adherents both tend to agree with Theory Y (people need nurturing to develop) rather than Theory X (people need discipline to develop) (McGregor, 1960). It is advisable, however, for coaches to temper the New Age proposition that an individual's belief can accomplish anything, so as to protect clients from being vulnerable to self-blame when things do not work out as desired.

Most coaches do look and listen for the client's potential, in keeping with the view that clients are naturally creative and resourceful and that they are the expert in their life, not the coach. New Age philosophy agrees with the Socratic principle that coaches do not tell clients what to do but rather believe in their potential to come up with the answers that work for them.

ANTHROPOLOGY

The word "anthropology" literally means the study of human beings (in Greek, *anthropos* means "human beings" and *logia* means "the study of"). Therefore, it is directly relevant to the question "Who are we?"

Anthropology is made up of different subfields in different areas. In North America, anthropology includes cultural anthropology, archaeology, physical anthropology (or sometimes biological anthropology), and linguistics. In Britain, anthropology is limited to social anthropology. We will focus on cultural or social anthropology because its subject matter necessitates a subjective, value-focused, and community approach, and thus it is most useful to coaching.

Cultural anthropologists of the late 19th and first half of the 20th centuries focused on documenting the many cultures that were disappearing as expanding empires decimated their populations, as happened for many of Ishi's compatriots in California, or absorbed them into the modern industrial economy. The underlying attitude was similar to that of biologists who wish to catalog endangered species. Although anthropologists such as Alfred Kroeber, Ishi's benefactor, held these cultures in great esteem, they nonetheless treated the people as objects of scientific interest rather than as subjects who had their own perspectives and rights. As part of the social movements of the second half of the 20th century, native people demanded their own role in determining their importance to science.

To be fair, anthropological fieldwork meant that anthropologists got to know their "informants" as fellow human beings, and their experience formed a strong counterbalance to 19th-century beliefs that "primitive" people were somehow inferior and incapable of becoming "civilized." Anthropology has shown racial categories to be social creations; has established all human beings alive today as members of the same species; and has recognized the fact that any infant of our species will fully take on the language and customs of the culture in which it is raised, whatever its inheritance. Anthropological evidence supports the growing insistence of all people on the validity of their own culture, countering the ideology of "natural superiority" that has justified slavery and genocide.

In recent times, anthropology has turned its methods toward studying human behavior wherever it occurs, not just among "primitives." The culture of contemporary organizations, the structure of modern families, the evolution of behavior, and the relationship of culture and personality have become of more central concern to anthropologists.

American anthropologist Clyde Kluckhohn (1948, p. 35) made these three statements in discussing personality:

All people are the same.

Some people are the same.

No people are the same.

All three statements are true, so which perspective a coach takes depends on the needs of a particular client at a particular time.

Example: "I Still Feel Humiliated"

Harold was an energetic and successful salesman who had just been promoted to national sales manager of a retail electronics chain. Shortly after the very public announcement of his promotion, the chain was acquired by an international conglomerate that brought in a new management structure, and Harold was out of a job. "I got a great severance package," he said in coaching, "but I still feel humiliated. What's that about?" His coach explained the neuroscience finding that all people are sensitive to a loss in status. "Does this apply in any way to your situation?" the coach asked. Recognizing that the general finding applied to him helped Harold "normalize" and accept his feelings.

In many cases, people are comforted by learning they are not alone in their suffering. Yet people can feel resentful when they think that their uniqueness as an individual is being disregarded. Many psychological assessments can be interpreted so as to treat the person being assessed as just a number or category. This experience of "ignoring who I am"—an example of "nomothetic" or all-or-some-people-are-the-same approach (Page, 2001), can motivate a person to seek a coach.

Clients sometimes bring their assessment results to a coach hoping that the coach's one-of-a-kind ("ideographic" or no-people-are-the-same) approach will reaffirm their unique characteristics and circumstances.

It is also true that the habits, ways of behaving, and the language that we share with some other people help us feel "at home" in a social group. That is, we share a culture with some other people. Culture is the "sets of learned behaviors and ideas that human beings acquire as members of society" (Lavenda & Schultz, 2003, p. 4). Cultural anthropology is concerned with how culture affects the belief systems and behavioral patterns of people living in different social groups.

Methods of Anthropologists

A major characteristic of cultural anthropology is its emphasis on fieldwork. A cultural anthropologist may immerse herself in a community for years in order to learn about a group of people, participating as much as possible in their daily life. The anthropologist's goal is to study the behaviors and norms that occur within a living community rather than in a laboratory. In such a situation, "objectivity" is a hindrance to understanding.

"Holism" refers to the anthropological practice of observing all of the factors that influence human experience. Economics, religion, politics, biology, and customs are a few examples of the many different perspectives an anthropologist will consider when getting to know a culture. Thus, anthropologists have long recognized the necessity of considering context and diverse perspectives in their work, a decidedly systemic approach.

Anthropological practices of ethnology and ethnography, both introduced in the late 19th century, are particularly relevant to coaching.

> [E]thnology is the attempt to develop rigorous and scientifically grounded explanations of cultural phenomena by comparing and contrasting many human cultures. By contrast, ethnography is the systematic description of a single contemporary culture, often through ethnographic fieldwork. (Barfield, 1997, p. 157)

Ethnographic fieldwork recognizes different subjective experiences as valid and valuable in order to understand the meaning people give to their activities. As in coaching, ethnographers listen for what their subjects *mean*, not just for what they say.

Culture

It is useful for coaches to be aware of how culture affects our clients' behaviors, thinking, and values. Different cultures have different values. For example, North American culture places great value on individual independence and initiative while Asian culture values considering the collective. Compare the North American expression "The squeaky wheel gets the grease" to the Japanese expression "The nail that stands out gets pounded."

Helping our clients identify the religious, economic, political, linguistic, value, gender, and behavioral systems in which they are embedded enables them to understand themselves better. It also helps identify the pressures that result when personal beliefs and practices differ from those of the dominant culture, whether in an organization or the larger society. This understanding is particularly useful in coaching a globally mobile workforce.

Gathering cultural information at the start of a coaching engagement can be very useful, although we must always ensure that it is the client who is being served rather than the curiosity or cultural education of the coach.

One application of anthropological principles to organizational coaching is the 360-degree feedback process. By interviewing several of the client's coworkers, the coach can get a more contextual picture of the client and illuminate blind spots he or she does not see. How work group or team members respond to a client's leadership, relationship skills, or delegation practices—or even the decision to conduct an assessment— can also reveal the organization's culture.

This list of general questions can help elicit information about a client's culture:

- What culture do you identify with?
- What are the some of the cultural beliefs, values, habits, and customs that are unique to your culture?
- To what extent are you a typical member of your cultural group?
- What is the culture of the environment in which you work?
- How well or poorly does your cultural background fit with the environment in which you work? With the personal culture of the individuals you work with?

Another link with anthropology is the concept of shadowing. In order for an anthropologist to understand a culture, he or she will build trust and rapport with people by living among them for an extended period of time, paying close attention to every aspect of their lives. Shadowing, or literally following a client through the workday, is an effective way to obtain a more holistic view of clients and their environment. Shadow coaches spend considerable time observing the way their clients run meetings, manage projects, and go about their daily routines in order to identify the patterns they may wish to change, once they become aware of them.

If shadowing a client is not an option, a coach can gather information about daily life patterns by asking more specific questions, such as these:

- Tell me specifically what is involved in your workday, as if I were viewing a videotape: When and how do you arrive at work? Are you usually early, on time, or late? How do you greet your coworkers? How do they respond? What's the first thing you do when you get to your desk? And so forth.
- What language(s) did you speak growing up? What language(s) do you speak now? At home? At work?
- How do people socialize at work?
- What do you and your coworkers do to relax?
- What are the rules for business or work in your family? Your culture?
- How do you think that people should treat one another at work?
- How do you refer to your boss? To your supervisees?

Again, a coach must be careful not to spend the client's time on information that is merely interesting to the coach. But if a client is being coached about relationships and issues of "fit" at work, looking for patterns in the information just listed may reveal helpful approaches.

Values

The word "values" appears many times in this section and indeed throughout this book. A value is a belief, mission, or philosophy that means something to an individual or group. Values, goals, meaning, purpose, engagement, passion, and motivation are interrelated concepts. When we value something, we move toward it. Our goals, or what we move toward or away from, reveal our values. Goals and values have to mean something to us, or we are unlikely even to notice them. Subjectively, we feel that striving for or reaching our goals is what gives our lives a sense of purpose. When our work provides an opportunity to fulfill a life purpose, we are highly motivated and engaged.

Every individual has a core set of personal values, whether aware of them or not. Anthropologists have discovered universal values in all societies they have studied, such as reciprocity and the importance of family. However, there are wide variations, for example, in the definition of family, in who is included in "family," and in beliefs about how families should function.

For instance, a Hindu teacher told one of us (Linda) that he did not consider his son to be an adult until he was 30 years old. In India, preserving the family unit is valued more highly than in North America, where grown children are encouraged to seek independence. While anthropology emphasizes the values of social groups, psychotherapy and coaching have tended to focus more on individual values.

Values can be a central theme in coaching. Values are the unconscious filters used to make choices. Identifying, getting clear about, or crystallizing our personal values can help us make better decisions. A clear understanding of our values can even reduce stress. A study by UCLA psychologists (Creswell et al., 2005) found that "[r]eflecting on meaningful values provides biological and psychological protection from the adverse effects of stress" (p. 841).

Values assessments are often done in career counseling to help people identify career choices. For example, someone who values care giving might do better as a nurse than as an investment banker. Consulting firms, career firms, recruitment companies, and the like provide many values assessment tools. They are also used in leadership development programs to help leaders better understand themselves and others. Many of these tests have been carefully validated to provide dependable guidance.

Linking Anthropology and Coaching

- To understand the individual, study the culture.
- Observe people in their natural habitat.

- Gather data from a wide range of sources to understand a client holistically.
- Do your best to see the world through the client's eyes.
- Investigate subjective meaning and values for a better understanding of clients' lives and motivation.

SOCIOLOGY

Sociology is the study of human social interactions among individuals, groups, and societies. Sociology explores how human beings live together and are affected by economic, cultural, political, and religious factors. Sociologists focus on how social structures (class, family), institutions (education, military), and problems (crime, divorce) affect the individual and society.

HISTORICAL INTERLUDE

In 1838 in France, Auguste Comte (1798–1857) invented the term "sociology." This new science developed during the 19th century, when everything, including human behavior, was coming under scientific scrutiny. Comte analyzed the influence of cultural, political, and economic factors on human social development.

Herbert Spencer (1820–1903), an early British sociologist, adapted Darwinian evolutionary principles to human society, coining the phrase "survival of the fittest."

German sociologist Max Weber (1864–1920) combined economics with sociology, describing and predicting the spread of a bureaucratic class. His contributions ran counter to those of fellow German Karl Marx (1818–1883), whose analysis of capitalism had a major influence on sociology. Marx developed a materialist interpretation of the more idealistic "dialectic" of Georg Wilhelm Friedrich Hegel (1770–1831). Marx's revision represents, according to British scientist Steven Rose, the only nonreductionist approach to science in Western history (2005, note, p. 189) and thus is a contribution to a systemic paradigm shift.

Most sociologists are concerned with an overall "macro" perspective, examining the forces that impact a whole social system, while anthropologists take a more "micro" look at what is happening within a specific culture. However, some sociologists have discovered patterns in two-person (dyads) and three-person (triads) groups that can inform coaching. For instance, a two-person group has the potential for greater intimacy than a larger group, while the pressure to conform is greatest in three-person as compared with larger and smaller groups.

Sociology studies specific jobs and professions. Its high-level perspective can help clients understand their career. Sociologists are also helping coaching define what characteristics would make it a full profession.

In their seminal work, *The Social Construction of Reality* (1966), Peter Berger and Thomas Luckmann borrowed from the philosophy of William James and of Hans Vaihinger (mentioned in the Western philosophy section above) that human beings create reality by acting "as if" it were true. Through such tacit agreements, we create a social environment that becomes real in its consequences despite its origin as a mere concept, idea, or "fiction." As Berger and Luckmann state:

> Just as it is impossible for man [sic] to develop as Man in isolation, so it is impossible for man in isolation to produce a human environment. . . . Man's specific humanity and his sociality are inextricably intertwined. *Homo sapiens* is always, and in the same measure, *homo socius*. (1966, p. 51)

This emphasis on the interdependence of individual and society informs systems theory, constructivist strands in psychology and psychotherapy, and the circular causality of the systemic paradigm. The idea of the brain as a social organ is gaining influence in neuroscience. Both coach and client benefit from the understanding that, while it may *seem* impossible to change the way a social group operates, nonetheless all social group norms are created by human beings and can be changed by them.

Methods of Sociologists

The methods that sociologists use to gather empirical evidence include quantitative surveys that are statistically analyzed and qualitative interviews and observations, much like anthropological fieldwork. The resulting information is then summarized using rigorous techniques to discern underlying patterns. Coaches can use variations of these methods with clients. To understand the forces operating within a team, a leader might interview each team member to gather information from various perspectives. Knowing team members' hopes, fears, goals, and constraints can help identify roadblocks to improving the team's performance.

Sociology is particularly relevant to organizational coaching. Clients operate within complex social webs at work and in their communities. Understanding the nature of these webs can help clients navigate barriers and achieve their goals. For example, a client who wants a promotion may need to address complex political issues in the workplace, including hidden issues of status and power. These factors have been intensely studied. In *The 48 Laws of Power* (1998), Robert Greene explains how a leader can acquire and hold power.

Sociology can help clients realize that their problems are not unique but shared with much of humanity. Some argue that even the personal impact of gender, race, and class inequalities can be better understood and remedied by taking a macro view. By stepping back from immediate examples of discrimination or prejudice, clients may see patterns that will help them deal more objectively with the effects they experience personally. Sociological studies can also provide information to help overcome stereotypes. Although they come from different academic traditions, sociologists share with social psychologists the recognition of the importance of social embeddedness.

Sociology teaches us that social forces have an impact on how people believe they should behave. One of most important gifts that coaches give their clients is helping them to be authentic, even when that goes

Example: "Not Feel Defensive or Apologetic"

One coaching client, Maria, is an ambitious lawyer and mother of three young children. After taking several years off to start a family, she decided to return to work four days a week. However, she met resistance from some members of her family and community, where women were expected to stay home to care for their children. Maria needed a coach to support her goal of returning to work. She told her coach that she received tremendous value from the coaching sessions because she could show up as the career person she wanted to be and not feel defensive or apologetic. Furthermore, the coach kept her new vision in focus, offering her needed support and structure until her intention became a reality.

against social expectations. A coach can offer clients support to break free from the preconceptions that others may have of them.

Linking Sociology and Coaching

- Gather information from a number of sources, both quantitative and qualitative.
- Identify the social expectations that shape client beliefs and behaviors.
- Identify behavior patterns that present as unalterable givens in any social situation.
- Consider the social context in any coaching scenario, and be sensitive to issues of power and status.
- Remember that reality is socially constructed and can be reconstructed through coaching support and other co-constructive social relationships.
- Stereotypes are generalizations that must be verified before applying them to any particular person or group.

ONTOLOGY AS BEDROCK FOR COACHING

Essentially, coaching is a series of conversations, a mutually respectful dialogue between a coach and a client for the purpose of producing identifiable results. Coaches help clients solve their problems by asking a series of questions and supporting and encouraging clients to formulate answers. Coaches examine and challenge their clients' basic assumptions (paradigms) with a view to what more is possible. Clearly, coaches assume that what people think makes a difference.

Coaching is a form of learning, but a coach is not a teacher and does not need to know how to do things better than the client. A coach observes patterns, sets the stage for new actions, and supports the client to put new, more successful actions into practice. Through various coaching techniques, including listening, reflecting, asking questions, and providing information, coaches help clients to become self-generating (to come up with their own questions and answers) and self-correcting (to identify and change their own ineffective behaviors).

Clients seek coaching when their paradigms no longer produce the desired results. Essentially, they seek a paradigm shift that will enable them to move more effectively toward their goals. However, this new paradigm must also be compatible with the network of paradigms imposed by the client's community, culture, and the larger society.

To work with clients in all these ways, coaching must tackle the question of what it means to be human. Its examination of this question is informed by a shift from Western and New Age emphasis on the individual to anthropological and sociological recognition of the importance of community and social context. Thus, the story of ontology can be told as the beginning of a shift in emphasis from individualism to community and context. Coaches reap the benefit of this shift by connecting personal beliefs with how individuals, groups, and organizations interact with each other and with society.

In summary, coaching has roots in Western philosophy, New Age philosophy, and the social sciences. Like bedrock that is composed of different geological deposits, these schools of thought provide part of the foundation for coaching. Each in its own way, these elements have struggled with the reductionism that predominated beginning in the 16th century. In the next chapter, we examine how three important developments of the 20th century provided a bridge or a pillar to uphold contemporary neuroscience: Globalization has introduced Eastern philosophy to Westerners steeped in individualism. Systems theory stresses how people are connected to one another and how their interactions relate to change. And quantum mechanics provides a scientific basis for the importance of human choice and activity. We continue our quest for understanding "Who are we?" by considering these developments and explaining how they serve as a bridge between mechanistic and systemic thinking.

CHAPTER 2

Pillar — Social Embeddedness

The farmer's horse, on which he was dependent for his family's liveli-hood, ran away. "Oh," cried his neighbors, "you are ruined!"

"We'll see," said the farmer. "Who knows what fortune is?" A few days later, the family horse returned, bringing with it a wild horse.

"Congratulations," said the neighbors. "Your fortune is assured!"

"We'll see," said the farmer. "Who knows what fortune is?" Not long after, during harvest time, the farmer's son fell and broke his leg when he was training the wild horse.

"Oh, woe," said the neighbors. "Your harvest will rot in the fields!"

"We'll see," said the farmer. "Who knows what fortune is?" Not long after, the military came to the village to conscript all able-bodied young men. The farmer's son was left behind because of his broken leg.

"Oh, you are a fortunate family," said the neighbors. "We may never see our sons again!"

"We'll see," said the farmer. "Who knows what fortune is?"

This story, which appears in many forms in Eastern philoso-phies, illustrates a perspective that transcends short-term accounting principles. Philosophers struggled against mechanistic limitations in understanding the meaning of life. New Age philosophy developed in opposition to many materialist tenets. And sociology and anthropology have had to operate largely without being accepted as "true sciences" by proponents of classical mechanics. Many questions are left unanswered by a strictly mechanistic approach.

- Certainly there are individual differences, but it seems that there are vast areas of the world in which people simply explain things differently. Is this true? If so, how come?
- What is it about a system that makes it more than the sum of its parts?
- Although we complain when the weather report predicts sunshine and we get rain, predictions of overall weather patterns are quite surprisingly accurate. How can apparently random events show such regular patterns?
- How do complex systems manage change in a sustainable and "healthy" way?
- Quantum physics provides a new way of looking at the world, one that allows for the effects of an observer on physical events. Does this mean that we can think anything into existence?

Increasing globalization during the 20th century has shown that the question "Who are we?" is answered quite differently in Western and Eastern philosophies. As the global economy becomes more integrated, and now that the entire world can be viewed from space, traditional barriers that once separated East and West are breaking down. This is good news for coaching, which is a global enterprise. It also supports the shift to a less reductionistic, more holistic paradigm that takes context and community into account.

"Social embeddedness" is the phrase we use to describe a pillar linking ontology with a neuroscience platform that supports the future of coaching. Social embeddedness consists of these perspectives:

- Globalization
- Systems theory
- Quantum theory
- Social embeddedness as a coaching pillar

GLOBALIZATION

Asking "Who are we?" generates fierce debate because the question asks us to consider the nature of life itself. Many such questions cannot be answered definitively by science. For instance, we cannot raise some people without heredity and others without environment in order to compare the effects of nature and nurture. Science may try to approximate these experiments — for example, through twin studies and by comparing very large groupings of people across space and time. In practice, we answer these questions according to how the people around us behave and explain events. In Western society, particularly in North America, individualism reigns. In other societies, the idea that our individual "self" is part of the community is unquestioned. In both cases, the alternate explanation often simply disappears, like the air we breathe, because it is so pervasive. We do not question what we do not perceive.

It is true that neither individuals nor societies can be aware of everything. Each culture tends to focus on the assumptions that have best advanced its survival. It is not surprising that hunting and gathering societies, which rely on cooperation for survival, exalt reciprocity and respect for the natural world. In the harsh desert climate of the American Southwest, indigenous people who take a portion of a medicinal plant make a ritual offering in exchange. Reciprocity is reinforced constantly, with tales of woe befalling those who violate this sacred principle. It is no wonder that competitive exploitation of the environment seems foreign to such a culture.

While the "aware territory" of a culture is well explored, the "unaware territory" is overlooked, often until there is contact with a very different culture. At that point, what had been out of awareness is revealed, with the potential result of rich learning.

Richard Nisbett is a social psychologist at the University of Michigan who built his reputation studying how ordinary people think about the world. Nisbett described himself as a "lifelong universalist concerning the nature of thought" (2003, p. xiii). He assumed that what he found to be true about thinking applied to everyone everywhere, as implied by the title of his book, *Human Inference* (1985). For that reason, he was surprised when his new graduate student, a brilliant young man from

57

China, said, "You know, the difference between you and me is that I think the world is a circle and you think it is a line" (Nisbett, 2003, p. xiii).

Nisbett was skeptical that there was such a difference. He had spent years studying principles that he and most other Westerners assumed were universal, such as the mechanistic principle of one-way causality. For example, a cause may create an effect, but the effect does not then create the cause, as would be expected in a circular world. But he was fascinated enough to investigate his graduate student's claim.

Nisbett worked with colleagues in North America, China, Korea, and Japan to compare characteristics of Westerners and Asians. They found quite dramatic differences in how the two groups perceived the world, what they recognized as problems, how they solved those problems, and what they thought of themselves and the concept of "self" in general.

Nisbett reports the results of this research in *The Geography of Thought: How Westerners and Asians Think Differently—and Why* (2003). He recognizes that putting "Westerners" and "Asians" in separate groups ignores the considerable differences among subgroups and individuals. Furthermore, these are not the only two broad groupings that would be expected to show differences. But, Nisbett insists, "My research has led me to the conviction that two utterly different approaches to the world have maintained themselves for thousands of years" (p. xx). Previously, Nisbett the Westerner had been unaware of these differences, unaware of the territory revealed by listening more carefully to how "Asians" think. In telling us what he heard when he became more aware and began to listen differently, Nisbett provides an example of the creativity that is unleashed when previously unaware territories are brought into awareness.

Yiyuan Tang is a neuroscientist at Dalian Medical University in China and his government's representative on the Human Brain Project. He is also a visiting professor in the Oregon laboratory of Dr. Michael Posner, one of the leading neuroscientists of our time. The two are working on several studies involving attention. Tang (2007) participated in the first Global NeuroLeadership Summit in 2007 in Asolo, Italy. He and other scientists presented research that had practical implications for business leaders and coaches.

In his presentation, Tang showed a slide of two photographs. One was of a jet plane flying over a mountain range. The other was of a tiger at the edge of a rain forest. He asked us, the audience, to look at the photographs and then to think about what it was that we were looking at. He explained that he shows these pictures to people in his laboratory, where he is able to observe where they focus their visual attention. What he found was a real eye-opener, so to speak.

"In general," he said, "there is a difference between what Chinese people look at as compared to what North Americans or Europeans focus on. On average, Chinese subjects look more at the background—the mountains or the rain forest and stream. Westerners spend more time looking at the plane and the tiger." That is, Asians spent more time looking at context. A greater emphasis on context is one element that Nisbett found characterized Asian as compared with Western approaches.

As an illustration, reread our description of Dr. Tang's photographs. As Westerners, we labeled the photographs "a jet plane" and "a tiger," with descriptions of mountain and forest as secondary. Would it be any less true to label those photographs "a mountain range with a jet plane flying over it" or "a stream in a rain forest with a tiger at the edge"? These two different perspectives are equally true. This realization is a small but important aspect of the shift from mechanistic to systemic worldview. Awareness of the validity of diverse perspectives is contributing to this shift.

According to Nisbett, Chinese philosophers value reason over linear logic. Western philosophers search for logical rules that maintain the truth of assertions. Chinese philosophers search for the reason things are as they are by observing an ever-changing environment in which all events are dialectically related to their opposites. Every happening implies its opposite, and that opposite holds the seeds of its opposite, in a circular fashion. This perspective is reinforced by stories like the tale of the old farmer that began this chapter, variations of which we have heard many times in our studies of Eastern philosophy.

The story goes on and on, with every happening portending its opposite. In this worldview, the meaning of any event or object can be understood only in relation to what else is going on, to what came before and what will come after. The ability to *reason*, to understand that true fortune has to do with recognizing the impermanence and connection of all things, is as important to Asian thought as *linear logic* is to Westerners.

As Eastern philosophy has become more familiar in the West, it has increasingly influenced philosophical, psychological, and even medical inquiry. In this chapter, we briefly explore Buddhism, Hinduism, Taoism, and Confucianism. Note that while some of these are considered religions, we explore only their philosophical bases.

Buddhism

Buddhism, like coaching, focuses on how we experience the world and, in particular, how we strive to improve our lives by choosing alternative ways of thinking and acting.

Buddhism began around 500 BCE when Siddhartha Gautama, also known as the Buddha, abandoned the life of a wealthy prince and devoted himself to meditation in order to understand the suffering of the world. He is said to have experienced "enlightenment" and developed a large group of followers in India, who then traveled throughout Asia to spread his teachings. Although there are hundreds of varieties of Buddhism, the basic principles include meditation and other rituals and practices, such as chanting, a specific code of conduct, and an overall philosophy about the world and the role of human beings in it.

Buddhism has influenced coaching in many areas. The concept of mindfulness is a central theme in coaching and is becoming an important element of neuroscience research. In *The Mindful Coach*, Douglas Silsbee (2004) defines mindfulness as "the state of awareness in which we are conscious of our feelings, thoughts, and habits of mind, and able to let unhelpful ones go so that they no longer limit us" (p. 27). Silsbee describes the profound influence of Buddhism on his work as a coach:

> Buddhism has provided an integration of everything that I have learned in decades of focused personal growth and development work. No other framework I have run across provides the same lucidity in describing what I observe as I seek to live fully and intentionally, and to be as effective as I can be as a coach in helping others develop their own skills and capacities. (Silsbee, 2004, p. 29)

Buddhist principles have brought several concepts to coaching:

- Self-awareness
- Self-observation

- Heightened consciousness
- Not judging
- Letting go of attachments and aversions
- Honoring oneself and others
- Being connected to everything

Over the last decade, the Dalai Lama and many high-profile celebrities have contributed to a renewed interest in Buddhism (see Begley, 2007; Houshmand, Livingston, & Wallace, 1999). Daisaku Ikeda, the leader of a Japanese Buddhist layperson's group, has published dialogues with intellectual leaders including Arnold Toynbee, Linus Pauling, Norman Cousins, Mikhail Gorbachov, and Majid Tehranian.

Coaching researcher Barbara Braham interviewed seven executive coaches, all of whom had been practicing vipassana meditation (from the Theravada Buddhist tradition) for 10 to 20 years. She found that "all of the vipassana practicing coaches stated that they felt the philosophy of the Dharma was completely aligned with the theory, practice and goals of executive coaching" (Braham, 2006, p. 2).

Hinduism

Hinduism originated in India, with roots that stretch back at least to 1500 BC. The "religion of a million and one gods," Hinduism is a fusion of religions and ideologies. Like Buddhism, its aim is to help individuals achieve enlightenment and connect with "ultimate reality." Hinduism believes that there are many paths to "the truth."

Key ideas in Hinduism include:

- *Bhakti*: devotion
- *Dharma*: doing what is right
- *Yoga*: discipline
- *Karma*: the consequences of the choices we make
- *Samsara*: reincarnation
- *Moksha*: salvation
- *Jnana*: knowledge

Hinduism advocates nonviolence, truthfulness, friendship, compassion, fortitude, self-control, purity, and generosity. While sharing many values with Buddhism and other Eastern philosophies, Hinduism also promotes idol worship and reincarnation. In Hinduism, the soul follows a cycle of birth and death until it attains *moksha*, which is determined by one's *karma*, or past actions.

Some of the people influenced by Hinduism include the German philosopher Arthur Schopenhauer, Ralph Waldo Emerson, and Henry David Thoreau, whose philosophy of transcendentalism is based partly on Hinduism. Mohandas Gandhi and Martin Luther King, Jr., were influenced by Hinduism. The beat poets and the Beatles, who influenced the beat generation of the 1950s and the social movements of the 1960s, based much of their thinking on Hindu philosophy. Hinduism's influence on the modern psyche can be traced through New Age music, poetry, and art, as well as philosophy and wellness theory. It remains an active religion, with an estimated 650 million followers, not far behind the Catholic Church with 840 million.

Many aspects of Hinduism relate to coaching. Here we will focus on two:

1. *Generosity*. Coaches should take a generous approach with clients, focusing on what they are doing right and acknowledging their efforts. The generous coach notices how the client is learning, growing, and changing and reflects these observations back to the client in an encouraging manner.

2. *Yoga*. This practice emphasizes the importance of the mind-body connection, of mindfulness, of being grounded and connected to others, and of being compassionate toward them. The yogic greeting, *namaste* (pronounced "nah-mah-stay") means "I honor the person within you," an appropriate stance for any coach.

Taoism

Lao Tzu, the founder of Taoism, lived in China during the sixth century BC. As with Buddhism, the goal of Taoism is to help people live happier, healthier lives by understanding the true nature of the world.

Loosely translated, *tao* means "the path" or "the way." Lao Tzu taught that human beings and their activities are blights on the otherwise perfect order of life. Believing that all striving is counterproductive, he counseled people to reject human pursuits. Instead, he urged them to move with the shape and flow of events. Although this attitude may seem to be at odds with coaching that focuses on performance and results, it does underline the importance of becoming aware of what we have control over rather than railing against what we do not.

Taoist philosophy includes physical exercises using the breath, called *chi quong*; mental exercise using meditation and contemplation; and the study of poetry to build greater awareness. Taoist philosophy gave us the *yin-yang* symbol, which represents the balance of opposites in the universe. This symbol is basic to the Chinese martial art of *tai chi*, a moving meditation, where the emphasis is on going with the flow of energy in any conflict.

Coaches can learn from the Taoist emphasis on spontaneity, self-transformation, balance, and compassion.

Many individuals hire a coach because they want a confidential sounding board, someone to whom they can be accountable as they establish and complete small action steps toward achieving their ultimate goal. Based on Taoist aphorisms, scholar Deng (1992) emphasizes the importance of a relationship such as this, even for experts or people at the top of their field, recognizing that no one can be right all the time: "That is why we need a parent for a parent, a master for a master, and leaders for the leaders. This prevents errors of power. In the past, even kings had wise advisers. Every person who would be a leader should have such assistance" (p. 28).

Deng also emphasizes treating every experience as a process of exploration. "For those who follow the Tao, travel is every bit important as the destination. One step after another: That is so central to the wisdom of Tao. . . . Reduce your problems into smaller, more manageable packages, and you can make measurable progress toward achievement" (Deng, 1992, p. 295).

Rick Carson, present-day coach and author of *Taming Your Gremlin* (1986) states, "Over 2,500 years ago Lao Tzu brushed with picture symbols the *Tao Te Ching*, which included this wisdom: Simply notice the natural order of things. Work with it rather than against it. For to try to change what *is* only sets up resistance" (p. 10).

The observations of the Tao are surprisingly consistent with discoveries of neuroscience and brain plasticity that also support coaching. Especially noteworthy are the notions of moving attention away from the "problem," which only breeds "resistance," and focusing instead on resources, strengths, and competencies to achieve desired change (Cooperrider & Whitney, 1999).

Confucianism

Confucianism is based on the teachings of Confucius, the Chinese philosopher who lived from 551 to 479 BC. Confucianism is a complex system of moral, social, political, and religious ideas that continue to exert a major influence on Chinese thinking. In many parts of Asia today, elements of Confucianism are blended with Taoism and Buddhism to form a set of coexistent and almost secular religious traditions. In some ways, Confucianism can be seen as a set of ethical guidelines for living rather than a philosophy about the nature of existence itself.

Confucian ideas are based on these values:

- *Jen*: benevolence; the highest virtue
- *Yi*: righteousness
- *Li*: etiquette and ritual
- *Xin*: honesty and trustworthiness
- *Hsiao*: love, generally within the family unit
- *Chung*: loyalty to the state

Several Confucian values apply to coaching, including benevolence, honesty, and trustworthiness. And many coaches use ritual (such as closing one's eyes and relaxing, taking a deep breath, or arranging the phone and coaching chair) to prepare themselves for a client session. The coaching principle of accountability can be related to the Confucian emphasis on self-discipline that promotes harmonious social life.

Linking Eastern Philosophy and Coaching

Elements common to most Eastern philosophies are the desire to understand ourselves as individuals and as participants in society and the desire to become more self-aware, more "conscious" of who we are and how we impact the world around us.

Coaching shares with Eastern philosophy an interest in deepening awareness and contemplation. While Eastern philosophies recommend specific practices, coaching uses many different methods to help clients become more "self-aware." The ideas of "self-actualization," popularized by humanists in the 1960s, were heavily influenced by Eastern philosophies.

Although Eastern philosophies and coaching diverge regarding moral codes and specific spiritual beliefs, neuroscience research provides increasing evidence that mindfulness practices yield benefits for coaches and their clients. Chapter 3 examines the neurobiology of consciousness and the ability of "mindful meditation" to improve brain function. So that we do not think of "mind" in "mindfulness" as a reversion to a dualistic separation of thinking and feeling, or of mind and body, Jon Kabat-Zinn (2005) points out that in all Asian languages, the word that is translated into English as "mind" could also be translated as "heart." That is, in accepting the influence of globalization, we could just as well speak of "heartfulness meditation."

SYSTEMS THEORY

Karl Ludwig von Bertalanffy (1901–1972) was a biologist who was born and studied in Austria and then moved to North America. Although he is barely known outside scientific circles, his work on General System Theory (von Bertalanffy, 1968) provided a cross-disciplinary model that has been applied beyond biology to ecology, cybernetics, education, history, philosophy, psychotherapy, psychology, sociology, and neuroscience — nearly every field mentioned in this book. His theory is one among many that resulted from focusing on context and relationships among elements rather than on the individual elements themselves.

A system is simply "anything that is not chaos" or "any structure that exhibits order and pattern" (Boulding, 1985, p. 9). Generally, a system is defined as a set of elements and the relationships between those elements (Weinberg, 1975). More technically, a system is an "organized whole made up of components that interact in a way distinct from their interaction with other entities and which endures over some period of time" (Schriver, 1995, p. 51).

There are many types of systems, often grouped into physical, biological, or social systems. Systems can be mechanical, reproductive, ecological, evolutionary, or human. One can even think of the world as composed of physical, biological, social, economic, political, communication, and evaluative systems (Boulding, 1985).

Von Bertalanffy questioned reductionism as early as the 1920s, preferring holism and organismic approaches. If a system includes its elements—molecules, matter, thoughts, people, actions—and their relationships, holism means that the elements cannot be understood without reference to their relationships with one another, just as understanding the relationships requires taking into account the properties of the elements that are in relationship.

Over time, systems develop (they are dynamic). That is, both the elements and the relationships change, and they do so through a process of mutual influence and influence from outside the system. Yet if the system remains a coherent system, it is the "same" system. After enough generations, none of the students, professors, or staff (elements) who were at a university during a student's tenure will still remain, but it is still considered the same university. The university may have gotten rid of some departments, instituted coeducation, or changed dormitory rules (relationships), but it is still in some sense the same system.

Different types of systems stay the same in different ways. Physical systems, such as our bodies, maintain a balance through homeostasis, or instituting balancing mechanisms to keep our temperature or our need for nourishment within optimal limits. Our bodies cannot operate for long outside these limits without risking permanent injury or death. But some systems are able to reconstruct themselves quite thoroughly despite being thrown into chaos. They do so by a process of dynamic stability, a term that has been applied to processes of neuroplasticity by neuropsychiatrist Jeffrey Schwartz. The rest of this section explains and illustrates this concept. Part of chapter 3: Neuroscience Platform applies dynamic stability concepts to the search for human health and wellness.

Von Bertalanffy's emphasis on organisms as opposed to mechanisms yielded his proposal of open systems. Newtonian theory did not ignore systems. After all, a steam engine must take into account the relationships of its parts. But the underlying model assumed the system was closed and could not renew its source of energy without outside intervention. Ultimately, the engine will run out of steam. In a very simple form, this is called entropy, and according to what scientists formulated as the Second Law of Thermodynamics, entropy increases. That is why the search for perpetual motion machines is doomed. If we think big and assume the universe is a closed system, eventually it will wind down and no longer have the energy to keep its elements in relationship. It will cease to exist as a system.

Von Bertalanffy was not satisfied with applying the assumption of a closed system to organisms. He claimed:

> The conventional [mechanistic] formulations of physics are, in principle, inapplicable to the living organism, being an open system having a steady state. We may well suspect that many characteristics of living systems which are paradoxical in view of the laws of physics are a consequence of this fact. (von Bertalanffy, 1968, pp. 39–40)

As we shall see, the "laws of physics" that von Bertalanffy is referring to are those of Newtonian mechanics. The characteristics of human systems do not yield paradoxes when viewed from the perspective of contemporary quantum mechanics.

In preparation for this discussion, we reveal some exciting and surprising findings about the way that complex systems develop, evolve, and interact. These findings can be very useful for coaching individuals, who themselves are complex systems, as well as for understanding how clients interact with other complex systems, such as personal or work groups or organizations. The ability to think in systems terms is considered a necessary discipline for organizational leaders (Senge, 1990).

We are applying the term "systems theory" to a wide range of models across disparate fields, from mathematics, to engineering, to biology, to family therapy, to neuroscience. To explain these ideas and understand their relevance to coaching, we must convey some technical information at a high level of generality. The ideas we explore come from chaos theory and complexity theory.

Chaos Theory

Chaos theory is a multidisciplinary field that has its roots in the sciences, particularly in physics and mathematics. In a sense, the name of the field is paradoxical because investigators are not ultimately looking for disorder, as is commonly associated with the word "chaos," but for the order that underlies what may seem to be unpredictable, disorderly systems.

HISTORICAL INTERLUDE

The first known exploration of chaos occurred in 19th-century France, when mathematics professor Henri Poincaré (1854–1912) described chaotic behavior in the interaction of the planets in the solar system.

George David Birkhoff (1884–1944) continued Poincaré's work in the United States, and discovered the first "strange attractor" in 1916 (published 1932), although his work remained mostly unknown (Kellert, 1993). Strange attractors are points in a chaotic system around which elements form to produce stable patterns. Margaret Wheatley (1992) refers to strange attractors as "the order inherent in chaos" and "a basin of attraction" (p. 122). The concept of a strange attractor is a metaphor for seemingly natural forces that impose a semblance of order on a loosely controlled system, such as the "invisible hand," an economic concept that is posited to account for the appearance of order in the marketplace.

In short, strange attractors can be thought of as patterns that indicate the evolution of a system, ones that we can visualize almost like a fingerprint. Strange attractors show us that even the "most chaotic of systems never goes beyond certain boundaries; it stays contained within a shape that we can recognize as the system's strange attractor" (Wheatley, 1992, p. 21).

If we stand on a high balcony overlooking a crowded railway station, for example, the individuals below look like they are moving around in random ways. But watching more carefully, we see patterns in this seemingly chaotic behavior. People are bunched together around a screen that tells whether trains are delayed. There is a line where tickets are sold and another at the snack bar. Someone giving away free samples has attracted another crowd. By observing these patterns, we can predict the overall behavior of crowds, whether they are made up of people or fish or birds or water molecules or microscopic cells. Computing technology has contributed to our ability to make these predictions.

According to Stephen Kellert (1993), formal chaos theory did not begin to develop until the early 1960s, when Benoit Mandelbrot discovered fractals, an example of strange attractors, while working at IBM. A fractal is a complicated pattern, with the same theme repeated infinitely from smallest to largest magnification. A fractal is produced when, for example, a computer applies a certain relatively simple equation to the results of that same equation and does this over and over (iteration). Mandelbrot's discovery of how simple inputs can produce immensely complicated outputs and the recognition of this process in nature eventually caught the attention of the scholarly world. The history below draws from James Gleick (1987).

In 1961, Edward Lorenz was researching weather systems at the Massachusetts Institute of Technology. He was one of the first scientists to have his own computer, and he used it to create and test a simple weather model. It would print out data showing air cycling clockwise, then counter-clockwise, then clockwise again, changing at apparently random intervals. One day he wanted to rerun a test starting from the middle instead of the beginning. But the results were startling:

> This new run should have exactly duplicated the old. Lorenz had cop-ied the numbers into the machine himself. . . . Yet as he stared at the new printout, Lorenz saw his weather diverging so rapidly from the pattern of the last run that, within just a few months, all resem-blance had disappeared. (Gleick, 1987, p. 16).

Lorenz checked his numbers and made sure the program had not changed. What had happened to create such a different result? Then he realized that the computer stored six decimal places, but the printout showed only three. And it was the printout that Lorenz had used to copy the numbers for the new run. There was a difference of only 1 part in 1,000. But such a small difference in input made a big difference in the eventual output. He had expected a very orderly repetition of the pattern he had seen before. Instead, he got chaos.

Lorenz had discovered that the principle of nonlinearity, as shown by Mandelbrot for the computer iteration of mathematical equations, also applied to natural phenomena. In dynamic, or ever-developing (one might say ever-iterating) systems, small changes in inputs, magnified by system feedback, resulted in huge changes in outputs over time. This is the non-linearity principle. Lorenz asked himself, "Does the flap of a butterfly's wings in Brazil set off a tornado in Texas?" He called this the butterfly effect. Lorenz's discovery shows that nonlinearity is a characteristic of sys-tems we are familiar with every day.

Lorenz determined that long-term weather forecasting or any long-term prediction of a dynamic nonlinear system was impossible because of the magnified effects of small changes in input. In 1963 his results were pub-lished in his now-famous paper "Deterministic Aperiodic Flow," which

(Continued)

---

appeared in the *Journal of Atmospheric Science*. The meteorologists did not understand it, and physicists and mathematicians do not read meteorology journals. Lorenz's discovery went unnoticed for a decade.

Chaos theory gained traction in 1976, after Michael Feigenbaum (1978) discovered "universality" while at Los Alamos Laboratory in New Mexico. He found that very different chaotic (nonlinear dynamic) systems exhibited the same quantitative features. At this point, other researchers began to take notice and were soon able to use computers to explore and build on the earlier findings of Poincaré, Birkhoff, Mandelbrot, and Lorenz. Chaos theory quickly developed into its own interdisciplinary field.

In 1987 James Gleick's book *Chaos: Making a New Science* brought chaos theory to the general public. Before examining the links be tween chaos theory and coaching, including a number of models that can be directly applied to coaching, we explore some of the basic principles of chaos theory.

Chaos theory refers to the many systems that cannot be predicted— that is, they are nonlinear and dynamic. For example, the effects of the weather cannot be predicted in the same way that the behavior of a mechanical device such as a power saw can be. The so-called butterfly effect is one reason for this unpredictability. Although chaos implies randomness to many of us, the fascination with chaos theory is that it reveals an orderly system hidden behind what appears to be random. As John Briggs and David Peat (1999) put it, there is a "hidden order within the chaos" (p. 5). Chaos theory "focuses on hidden patterns . . . and the 'rules' for how the unpredictable leads to the new." It is "an attempt to understand the movements that create . . . complex patterns of all sorts" (p. 2).

For example, the "rule" of nonlinearity means that a very small change in input may produce an unpredictably large change in the system's behavior—butterfly flap to hurricane.

According to Garnett Williams (1997), chaos theory "deals with long-term evolution" (p. 7). That is, it focuses on how a system behaves over the long run, as there must be enough iterations in order to discern patterns. Gleick (1987) credits scientist Joseph Ford with the description of evolution as "chaos with feedback" (p. 314). For example, random (chaotic) genetic mutations create differences in a population of birds. Some of those differences are better adapted to the environment. The feedback mechanism is that individuals with ill-adaptive differences do not survive to pass their genes to the next generations. With many iterations, over time, changes accumulate and appear to "spread" to the whole population. As a result of chaos with feedback, we see bright red cardinals, which are very different from black crows or, indeed, from penguins.

When scientists talk about chaos theory, they are talking about systems. As we indicated, a system is made up of parts or elements and their relationships. An open system receives external inputs and produces outputs and exists over time. The output from this moment may be input, or feedback, for the next moment. In chaos theory, the systems studied may be simple or complex, but they share three properties: they are nonlinear, dynamic, and deterministic.

NONLINEAR SYSTEMS   As we have pointed out, nonlinearity means that a small change in the initial conditions (input) may result in a disproportionately large change in the result (output). That is the principle behind the butterfly effect. Similarly, a large change in input may result in almost no change, as corporations that have spent millions on change initiatives can often attest. It may be helpful to think of linearity first in the mathematical sense: Draw a straight line and put your finger on a point on the line. If you move your finger along the line, the movement in the horizontal x direction is proportional to the movement in the vertical y direction. This is linear behavior, as the change in input (x) is proportional to the change in output (y). Nonlinear behavior occurs when the change in input results in an output change that is not proportional.

DYNAMIC SYSTEMS   A dynamic system is one that moves or changes or evolves over time. If its elements and their relationships do not stay the same, the system is dynamic. Not surprisingly, most natural systems are dynamic. This is often painfully true for organizations. All dynamic systems face twin challenges: If their elements and relationships are too inflexible, they risk being unable to adapt to changing circumstances. If, however, they are so ill defined or lacking in energy as to lose coherence or

Example: "Sensitive Dependence on Initial Conditions"

If you place a marble at the top of a bowling ball and let it go, it will roll down in a particular direction. If you try to do the same thing again, the marble will almost surely roll down in a different direction, because you probably will place the marble in a spot very close to, but not exactly the same as, the spot where you put it the first time. A very small change in your placement of the marble results in a very large change in where the marble goes. This nonlinear behavior is also called sensitive dependence on initial conditions.

It turns out that many naturally occurring systems have this property, including a coaching engagement. This is one reason why a seasoned coach pays particular attention to the initial interview with a client and clarifies the conditions for a successful relationship up front. It is also why coaching cannot be conducted by formula, in a cookbook fashion.

identity, the system ceases to exist as a system. Profit is what enables a business (system) to cohere. When it is no longer profitable, the business loses its identity and declares bankruptcy.

DETERMINISTIC SYSTEMS   A deterministic system is ruled by cause and effect, but with an important difference from mechanistic determinism, where causality moves in only one direction. The behavior of a deterministic system appears random but is not. Its future state depends on its present state, inputs, and the rules for inputting those variables. One of the rules is that output from one time step may be input for the next step, modeling feedback within the system. Effects now become causes in the future. Causality thus becomes circular.

One of the surprises in chaos theory is that there are more deterministic systems than originally thought. Behavior that scientists once attributed to noise, error, or randomness often results from the interaction of simple principles that can be observed or determined. Chaos theory has disproved long-held, fundamental beliefs: Simple systems behave in simple ways; complex behavior implies complex causes; and different types of systems behave differently (Gleick, 1987).

Chaos theory has contributed to our understanding of systems behavior in numerous ways by letting us understand old events in new ways and by showing us that what appears to be random may not be. As Williams (1997) explains, "Chaos theory shows that such behavior can be attributable to the nonlinear nature of the system rather than to other causes" (p. 15). In addition, "studying chaos has revealed circumstances under which we might want to avoid chaos, . . . stabilize or control it, encourage or enhance it, or even exploit it" (p. 17).

As Wheatley (1992) observes, chaos theory has resulted in

> a new appreciation of the relationship between order and chaos. These two forces are now understood as mirror images, one containing the other, a continual process where a system can leap into chaos and unpredictability, yet within that state be held within parameters that are well-ordered and predictable. (p. 11)

Complexity Theory

Complexity theory evolved over the last two decades in response to chaos theory. Chaos emphasizes the underlying order of nonlinear dynamic systems whose behavior is deterministic but unpredictable over the long run because of circular causality. These principles apply in general to people and societies just as they do to rain clouds and fractal equations. Complexity theory emphasizes the criteria for orderly change and sustainability in nonlinear dynamic systems that have the additional characteristic of being self-organizing. Such systems have a capacity for *emergence*, or results that could not have been predicted from knowing the present state of elements and their relationships, inputs, and the rules for inputting those variables.

Human beings are examples of such systems. We could program a computer with the present state of a person, add in all his or her considerations regarding taking a next action, and prescribe rules for how those choices are made, just as with a fractal equation. Over time, the computer's predictions about that person's behavior often might be correct. But there would also be a chance that the person would do something entirely unexpected, unpredicted, not determined—emergent. This is the property that enables coaching clients, leaders, and organizations to take truly innovative leaps.

In his 1988 book, *The Dreams of Reason*, Rockefeller University professor Heinz Pagels stated, "I am convinced that the nations and people who master the new science of Complexity will become the economic, cultural, and political superpowers of the next century" (p. 10).

Next we add to our definitions of systems and chaos the definition of complex systems, and then discuss complexity in general.

Georges Anderla, Anthony Dunning, and Simon Forge (1997) define complex systems as "networks of myriads of independent agents interacting with each other, without any central control, in a multitude of ways" (p. 210). Our immune system, ecosystems, families, and workplaces all fit this definition. Complexity theory attempts to "understand the often unpredictable but self-organizing nature of complex clusters of entities functioning as a system" (Siegel, 1999, p. 7). Of great relevance to this book, the brain is a complex system and a subsystem of a larger, emergent complex system consisting of brain, mind, and social relationships. Chapter 3 builds on the elements of complexity theory to explain that larger system of which the brain is an element.

Anderla and colleagues explain the essence of complexity theory as applying to situations of chaos plus. That is, at first, complexity reveals itself as general trends and behavior with observable patterns over time. We see this when observing neurons in the brain, an ant colony, the market economy, a neighborhood, or a couple married with children. As with chaos theory, the elements that make up each are produced by their mutual interactions across different levels, space, and time.

However, in a complex system, each element is an active agent, or influencer, as well as a passive recipient of influences. Any coherence that we see or think we see in the system is "due solely to the competition and/or cooperation among the agents. Such self-organizing systems are often highly adaptive. They can also be stratified into levels of increasing complexity, with agents at one level serving as building-blocks for those at a higher level" (Anderla et al., 1997, p. 211). That our cells and immune system are said to have a kind of active "intelligence" is recognition that they are agents serving as building blocks for our bodies.

As with "chaos," the use of the word "complexity" can cause some confusion. Peter Senge (1999) points out that we are not interested in complexity as in the intricate details of something, which we might better describe as "complicated." We are interested in what he calls *dynamic* complexity, the complexity of a system's behavior over time. The first two principles of complexity theory, nonlinearity and dynamic, are ones we are already familiar with. The third, nondeterministic, is in contrast to chaotic systems and relates to the characteristic of emergence.

NONLINEAR SYSTEMS Nonlinearity, a concept introduced in the "Chaos Theory" section, also applies to complex systems, but with some additional considerations. Regarding the human brain, Siegel (1999) explains that "small changes in the microcomponents of the system can lead to large changes in the macro-behavior of the organism" (p. 220).

The moment when a small change precipitates a large effect is called a tipping point. For example, if you begin with warm water and slowly cool it, you will not see any significant change until, suddenly, it freezes. It has reached a tipping point.

While systems can tip into chaos without warning, psychiatrist John Ratey (2003) points out an advantage: The direction of the surprising tip can be positive rather than negative.

> Critics sometimes claim that "ordinary" measures like exercise and diet may be too simplistic to affect unordinary behavior. Not so. [Complexity theory shows] how powerful universal factors can be in affecting the brain-body system. . . . Small and seemingly inconsequential action may lead to successful treatment of a disorder. (pp. 357–358)

As discussed earlier, any response (output) that itself becomes input is feedback. Feedback accounts for nonlinearity in systems but takes on special meaning in a system where the elements are agents with goals. *Each element* in such a system takes the feedback in as input and uses this

Example: "An Ordinary Walk"

Despite his depression, Joel followed his therapist's advice and took a walk. The next day he took another, and then another. Soon he found himself jogging. He realized he felt better and had more energy. When his neighbor mentioned a job opportunity, he decided to try for it. He started going out with colleagues after work and began to make friends. "The man's

(Continued)

extraordinary metamorphosis began with an ordinary walk. There are many tools right at our fingertips for changing our mental health, both in correcting our problems and simply becoming the kind of person we want to be" (Ratey, 2003, p. 358). This is an example of how, in coaching, a small change in thinking can create substantial change in a person's life.

information to adjust its behavior. As Williams (1997) eloquently explains, "Feedback is that part of the past that influences the present, or that part of the present that influences the future" (p. 12). For Joe Schriver (1995), feedback is "information received by systems about the progress toward goals and the system's response to that information" (p. 62).

We are all familiar with the terms "positive" and "negative" feedback. In regard to feedback, these terms do not refer to whether feedback is nice; they refer to the effect of the feedback. Positive feedback results in more of the same behavior, and negative feedback results in less. In systems terms, "positive feedback amplifies or accelerates the output. It causes an event to be magnified over time. Negative feedback dampens or inhibits output, or causes an event to die away over time" (Williams, 1997, p. 12).

DYNAMIC SYSTEMS A dynamic system is one that must continually adapt or adjust to its context. The concept of an open system was introduced at the beginning of this chapter. A closed system changes only according to its internal conditions. When running experiments, scientists try to create closed systems that are self-contained and not influenced by any "variables" outside of the experiment itself. This isolation allows scientists to reproduce results and understand basic scientific laws, but it is not a situation that represents the real world. Even in the laboratory, as Gerald Weinberg (1975) points out, and despite scientists' best efforts, they may still see unexpected "randomness" in their experiments. There is no way for them to tell if the randomness is inside the system or is getting in through "leaks" or unintended openness between the outside world and the system.

By contrast, open systems "engage with their environment and continue to grow and evolve" (Wheatley, 1992, p. 77). The boundary between the system and its environment is not a barrier but more like a border crossing that allows some things to pass in or out. The more easily things can pass through, the more open the border and the system. This crossing of the border can be an energy exchange, feedback, or communication. An organism may import energy resources and output waste products. An organization may import staff or corporate culture or raw materials and output products or services for sale.

There is a relationship between a system's openness and its need to maintain a healthy balance between too much and too little change. According to Ervin László (1972), "Openness refers to the import-export activities of the system, which it needs to 'stay in the same place,' that is, to maintain its own dynamic steady-state" (p. 37). Naturally occurring complex systems tend to exist in a steady state; they are not frozen in a particular form but undergoing a dynamic cycle of change that is stable over time. László explains that the particular configuration of parts and their relationships

> maintained in a self-maintaining and repairing system is called a "steady-state." It is a state in which energies are continually used to maintain the relationship of the parts and keep them from collapsing in decay. This is a dynamic state, not a dead and inert one. (p. 37)

This state is what we refer to as *dynamic stability*.

Complex systems can be stable over a long period of time despite considerable changes that occur within them. As Wheatley (1992) says: "The system allows for many levels of autonomy within itself, and for small fluctuations and changes. By tolerating these, it is able to preserve its global stability and integrity in the environment" (p. 95).

As the system responds to the environment and seeks to maintain a steady state, it may reconfigure itself internally. Social scientist Joe Schriver (1995) refers to this as the redistribution of power, where "power" is defined as the ability to influence progress toward goals. As a power conflict develops within a system, an effective system "self-rights" by making adjustments to reduce conflict and get back to a balanced state. Sometimes, however, the adjustments are resisted.

Relationship therapist Harriet Lerner (1989) calls this a "change-back" reaction. She "inoculates" clients who are making changes in their relationship behavior by letting them know that their partners may pressure them to change back to their old ways in order to reestablish a balance that is at least familiar. This concept is important to consider in coaching. When a client is changing behavior, he or she can expect that some forces in the system will resist this change. Normalizing this resistance for clients and supporting them through it is an important role for the coach.

The nonlinear and dynamic characteristics of complex systems are variations on chaos principles of nonlinearity and dynamic. The next, emergence, is different from chaos's deterministic principle. Emergence is closely related to the fourth principle of complexity, self-organization, and is important to the fifth, co-evolution.

EMERGENT SYSTEMS   Emergence is one of the most fascinating aspects of complex systems. A system as a whole may have properties that do not exist in their parts nor could they be predicted from knowing determinants of elements, their relationships, inputs, and rules for inputting. These properties of complex systems are described as "emergent" based on the idea that "properties will 'emerge' when we put together more and more complex systems" (Weinberg, 1975, p. 60). Examples of emergence include consciousness arising from the aggregate behavior of neurons, the global stability of ecosystems, and the "invisible hand" of economics, which arises from the behavior of companies, consumers, and markets.

SELF-ORGANIZING SYSTEMS   Emergence is possible because agents in complex systems effectively organize themselves rather than being controlled by some central authority. An example is our immune system, which consists of agents throughout our body that identify, communicate about, and respond to threats to our physical dynamic stability.

The discovery of self-organizing behavior seems to contradict the Second Law of Thermodynamics, which says that systems tend toward disorder, or entropy. Self-organization is defined as "matter's incessant attempts to organize itself into ever more complex structures despite the ever-present forces of decay and dissolution" (Anderla et al., 1997, p. 34). A self-organizing system can readily respond to its environment, adapting if possible. According to complexity theorists, this adaptation generally leads to increased complexity in the system.

John Holland, an expert in self-organization and emergence and professor in the University of Michigan's Center for the Study of Complex Systems, identified in 1998 these self-organizing characteristics:

- *Tagging*—recognizing, naming, or labeling entities. Examples include pricing, job titles, and the immune system's ability to identify foreign cells.
- *Internal models*—simplified representations of the environment. There is some disagreement among experts about whether these models are implicit (embedded in the system) or explicit.
- *Building blocks*—components that can be recombined to make new components (e.g., the four proteins of DNA).

CO-EVOLVING SYSTEMS   Open systems not only adapt to the environment, they also influence the environment by importing and exporting across the system boundary. The environment is changed as a result, and so it also evolves over time as the systems within it evolve. For example, Wheatley (1992) cites James Lovelock's "Daisyland" model, which showed that daisies help to regulate Earth's temperature. This concept is called co-evolution. "In this view of evolution, the system changes, the environment changes, and, some scientists argue, even the rules of evolution change" (Wheatley, 1992, p. 97).

As a more recent example, Apple produced the iPod, which has profoundly impacted both consumers' music purchasing and listening behavior as well as other companies' product offerings. "Organizations and their environments are evolving simultaneously toward better fitness for each other" (Wheatley, 1992, p. 98).

SELF-REFERENCE SYSTEMS   Closely tied to the concept of evolution as a property of complex systems is the idea of self-reference, meaning that complex systems evolve in ways that are consistent with their current form. Wheatley (1992) explains: "The presence of this guiding rule allows for both creativity and boundaries, for evolution and coherence, for determinism and free will" (p. 135). Human consciousness is an important aid to self-reference. When members of an organization or team commit to a vision or mission as defining who they are as a group, they set boundaries within which their problem-solving can be operate freely.

Self-reference is a sort of strange attractor (a concept from chaos theory), a pattern that makes change more orderly in the face of turbulence. "Instead of whirling off in different directions, each part of the system must remain consistent with itself and with all other parts of the system as it changes" (Wheatley, 1992, p. 146). An exception to the principle of self-reference is Prigogine's (1996) discovery of dissipative systems, which can re-create themselves to a significant degree when faced with extreme environmental disturbances.

Linking Systems Theory and Coaching

Coaching is not an analytical practice that seeks to understand people by examining their individual parts in a reductionist process. Instead, coaches observe people as systems that are part of and that are trying to influence other systems. In coaching, as in systems theory, we are concerned with the evolution of behaviors and activities over time and the use of feedback in that process.

Coaches look for patterns in order to understand events and behavior. In chaos theory, unlike other fields of science, "patterns are substitutes for laws." Coaching is about "finding patterns in observed data, patterns that give insight and meaning" (Anderla et al., 1997, p. 45). As coaches, we may see a pattern in a small setting, such as an individual coaching session, and suspect that what we have witnessed could be representative of behavior happening more generally, like a fractal that repeats itself in small as well as large magnification.

An analogy may help explain this principle, called "self-similarity," and its relationship to coaching: If we remove a section of a regular photographic negative and then shine light through the portion we have cut out, we see only that portion of the original image. A holographic "negative" is different. Shining a laser through a small portion of a holographic image yields the full holograph, but in less detail. That is, every portion of a holograph, and every portion of a nonlinear dynamic system, yields information about the whole. In coaching, a client's behavior in a session may reflect patterns that hold true at work.

In *Seven Life Lessons of Chaos: Timeless Wisdom from the Science of Change*, Briggs and Peat (1999) view chaos theory as a metaphor for life, with our world as one big system. They evoke the image of a mountain stream that is continually changing but remains stable as a whole and is interconnected with the natural world of which it is a part.

> Similarly, each of us as an individual is inter-connected to the systems of nature, society, and thought that surround and flow through us. We live within movements constantly affecting each other and creating an unpredictable chaos at many levels. Yet within this same chaos is born all the physical and psychological order that we know. (p. 4)

The main thesis of the Briggs and Peat book is that chaos theory teaches us, just as it teaches scientists, to question our long-held assumptions. It encourages us to look at our lives and the world in new ways. Next is a high-level summary of the seven ways Briggs and Peat (1999) suggest for doing this, with the addition of a few supporting comments from Wheatley (1992):

1. *Approach life with creativity, not control.* "Making a pact with chaos gives us the possibility of living not as controllers of nature but as creative participators" (p. 8). The butterfly effect shows us how much we cannot know or control. Briggs and Peat encourage us to flow like the stream, to awake each morning "open to the possibility that we can make our lives afresh" (p. 10) and to be open to the subtlety and nuances around us.

2. *One individual, or subtle influence, can make a difference.* The butterfly effect and Mahatma Gandhi show us this. "We can never be sure how important our own individual contribution will be. . . . The best we can do is act with truth, sincerity, and sensitivity, remembering that it is never one person who brings about change but the feedback of change within the entire system" (p. 51). Along these same lines, Wheatley (1992) observes that, when it comes to seemingly small acts, "the world is far more sensitive than we had ever thought" (p. 127).

3. *Self-organized communities can be powerful.* Communities can go with the flow and spontaneously respond to chaos in a self-organizing and collectively creative way without a lot of formal structure. The World Wide Web is an example of this. In facilitating groups, one of us (Linda) developed a rule of thumb: "When in doubt,

trust the group." She has never been disappointed with the results of applying this rule.

4. *Simplicity and complexity are two sides of a coin.* Chaos theory shows us that what seems complex may have simple causes and that simple patterns can be found amidst chaos. We are capable of finding order beyond the chaos. "Our brains have evolved to spot the patterns within complex and ever-changing situations, while at the same time uncovering the nuances within these patterns" (p. 97).

5. *Be open to seeing the art of the world.* We are surrounded by nature's patterns (fractals), which are beautiful and energizing. Compare this to the often mechanical and constricting patterns that we create for ourselves (schedules, subdivisions, and streets).

6. *Time is fractal and elastic.* We feel constrained by a lack of time, but many different meditative practices demonstrate the immense satisfaction that comes from relaxed absorption in the moment. Time passes quickly when we are engaged and slowly when we are bored. Despite this, we often fill our time with activities that are not challenging enough to create that optimal condition.

7. *We are part of a whole.* We operate holistically, on biological, individual, and societal levels. Wheatley (1992) believes that by studying the universe in pieces rather than holistically, we create uncertainty.

Briggs and Peat's list is by no means exhaustive, and other sources describe additional life lessons (see Boulding, 1985; László, 1972; Lewin, 1992; Prigogine, 1996). Wheatley (1992) offers an eloquent idea tied to "meaning" as a strange attractor:

> By the end of our lifetime, we are able to discern our individual basins of attraction. What has been the shape of our life? What has made seemingly random events now appear purposeful? What has made "chance" meetings fit smoothly into the movements of our lives? We discover that we have been influenced by a meaning that is wholly and uniquely our own. We experience a deeper knowledge of the purpose that structured all of our activities, many times invisibly and without our awareness. Whether we believe that we create this meaning in a retrospective attempt

to make sense of our lives, or that we discover meaning as the preexistent creation of a purposeful universe, it is, at the end, only meaning that we seek. Nothing else is attractive, nothing else has the power to cohere an entire lifetime of activity. (p. 137)

Ian Stewart (1989) concludes his book *Does God Play Dice?: The Mathematics of Chaos* with a similar observation: "What controls the relationship of equation to solution, of model to behavior, is not form, but meaning" (p. 301). Viktor Frankl's (1984) work, as discussed in chapter 1, strongly supports the observations of Wheatley and Stewart.

Attractors may be thought of as values, not espoused values, but the actual guiding principles that result in the "typical behavior" of a system. Although we know that systems may be dynamic and chaotic—that they change and sometimes behave in surprising ways—attractors (values) create relatively stable and recognizable patterns. In a coaching context, attractors could be clients' values, attitudes, beliefs, strengths, and unconscious perceptions that underlie their thoughts and decision-making processes. Understanding attractors within a system and raising awareness of them help clients understand and perhaps change their patterns.

Tools for working with values as attractors include:

- Seligman's VIA Strengths Inventory (University of Pennsylvania, 2008b): values exercises
- Cognitive-behavior therapy exercises around exploring beliefs
- Personality profile assessments (e.g., Myers et al., 1998)
- Visual-Auditory-Kinesthetic (VAK) preferences (see chapter 3 in American College of Sports Medicine, 2006)
- The "Discovery" phase of Appreciative Inquiry (Orem, Binkert, & Clancy, 2007)

There may be other attractors present, such as the leadership style within an organization, cultural influences, policies, and processes.

Working with clients to understand their internal attractors and develop a clear vision of their "ideal self" into the future provides a foundation for change. Our ideal self is an image of the person we want to be and a reflection of our intrinsic values. Daniel Goleman (1995) provides evidence of the potency of focusing on the desired end state. Numerous studies have shown that intrinsic motives have more enduring impact on a person's behavior than extrinsic motives (Deci & Ryan, 1985).

When adults change their behavior, they engage in a series of epiphanies, or discoveries, that make up what Richard Boyatzis has called the Intentional Change Model (Boyatzis & McKee, 2005a), one of the action-reflection models we discuss more fully in chapter 5. He provides a model based on two key attractors: an individual's strengths and the gap between the real self and the ideal self. Strange attractors may pull us unconsciously, or they may be created consciously as a means to change our behavior. Research shows that coaching toward aspirations, dreams, and desired states such as our ideal self can access and engage deep emotional commitment and psychic energy.

In coaching, minor events may lead to dramatic results, as with the butterfly effect. If a system is chaotic, it is unpredictable over the long term, but shorter-term or more general attractor like predictions still may be possible. For example, in a group or team context, if the leader is demonstrating certain behaviors, other individuals in the team are likely to behave in the same way. This relates to the biblical admonition to search out the mote in one's own eye before demanding that someone else remove their imperfection.

We may discover with our clients that a few simple principles or factors are keys to addressing difficult situations, so that what appears complex on the surface ultimately has a simple solution. Surface chaos may cover underlying patterns.

Wheatley (1992) also sees the voluntary introduction of chaos into a situation or project as a useful tool, despite the uncomfortable uncertainty that comes with it. We have a natural tendency to try to move from confusion to certainty as quickly as we can. She explains that "science is helping me understand, among many things, the uses of chaos and its role in self-organization. I think I not only expect chaos now, but I've grown more trusting of it as a necessary stage to greater organization" (p. 149). As a result, she has started to introduce more chaos, in the form of less formal guidance and more freedom, into her projects. Coaches may recognize the use of chaos, and the associated discomfort and uncertainty, as a creative force in their coaching work. This idea has links to the change theory models that propose a need to go through a stage of chaos and uncertainty before something new is created.

Self-reference is a concept from complexity theory that has particular relevance to leadership. Wheatley suggests that if a leader can identify a core of values and vision, and can refresh this core through dialogue, she or he can reference this in order to maintain personal integrity through difficult times. "When I look at the shape and meaning of my own life, and how it has evolved with change, I understand the workings of this principle in intimate detail" (Wheatley, 1992, p. 147).

The principle of self-reference applies also at the organizational level, especially during turbulence. A strong corporate identity can provide independence from environmental change and can serve as a guide to the organization's evolution. "When the environment demands a new response, there is a reference point for change. This prevents the vacillations and the random search for new customers and new ventures that have destroyed so many businesses over the past several years" (Wheatley, 1992, p. 94).

A well-developed organizational identity includes a strong sense of purpose. When they have a purpose to refer to, staff members are able to work more independently and effectively. "Employees can be trusted to move freely, drawn in many directions by their energy and creativity. There is no need to insist through regimentation or supervision, that any two individuals act in precisely the same way" (Wheatley, 1992, p. 136).

This same idea can be applied to the development of an individual's personality. Self-reference is the systems theory explanation of having clear values, a purpose, and established goals. The clearer we are about our own values, the easier we can build a system around ourselves that is in line with these values. This concept is at the core of coaching. Often a key piece of the coaching journey has to do with raising a client's awareness of his or her own values, beliefs, and behaviors. A coach's role is to facilitate the client's clarity in these ways, therefore empowering future decisions.

Biologists and physicists have published research in journals dedicated to complex systems. Nonlinear dynamics have also been studied in all fields of psychology. For a survey of findings, see Stephen Guastello's (2000) summary of perception, learning, memory, cognition, development, motivation, social cognition, attraction, creative problem solving, leadership emergence, work group coordination, and management research.

Linking Systems Theory and Coaching

In summary, the coach's job is to help the client, a complex, chaotic system, boost functioning and performance within complex, chaotic systems. The science tells us that:

- We are drawn to certain attractors, creating patterns of meaning and regularities amidst seeming chaos.
- Existing patterns indicate strong attractors such that a client may experience resistance or push back when trying to influence change.
- Understanding patterns is a key step to being able to influence systems effectively.
- What we cannot control, we may nonetheless be able to influence in small ways.
- Small things can make a big difference, and sometimes big things make no difference.
- Systems made up of self-organizing agents with shared values and good communication can maintain dynamic stability in the face of challenges.

QUANTUM THEORY

In 1900, Max Planck discovered a constant that is one of three basic quantities woven into the structure of the universe. The others are the gravitational constant, as described by Newton, and Einstein's speed of light. Einstein's discovery required a rethinking of Newtonian principles, but Planck's "quantum of action" required a full rewrite of physics theory.

There was considerable resistance to rewriting what had stood the test of three centuries. However, experiment after experiment to test Planck's work has revealed classical mechanics to be merely a special case of quantum principles. This is because Planck's constant is very small, and including it in a mathematical prediction of big events, such as how fast something falls from a fifth-story balcony or a planet's orbit around a star, makes very little difference. As a result, and as history and experience have shown, quantum principles can be ignored when we are predicting how long to leave our cake in the oven. But at the very smallest level, at the level of interactions of atoms and particles and ions, Planck's constant makes a big difference.

Whether these differences need to be taken into account in the "Who are we?" inquiry depends on the answer to this question: Does classical mechanics apply well enough to understanding human beings, or must we take quantum theory into account? Physicist Henry Stapp wrote *Mindful Universe* (2007) partly to answer that very question. In doing so, he closes a gap that has puzzled philosophers and scientists for centuries: How do the objectively measurable physical processes of the brain give rise to the subjectively experienced ephemeral processes of the mind?

We have discussed the consequences of a deterministic materialist view of human beings. If all that we think or do is predetermined by a clocklike mechanism that is merely playing out past causes, then responsibility or morality is an oxymoron. An ethical code for coaches makes no sense if control over our behavior is an illusion. But we continue to insist on the importance of choice, awareness, and accountability in many areas of life, not just in coaching. To a great extent, this is because we *experience* having to make choices among alternatives that we *experience* as being equally likely of being chosen. Classical mechanics demands that we ignore subjective experience and instead put our faith in the claim of classical mechanics, bolstered until the mid-20th century by a united scientific establishment, that objectivity is attainable and that all would be understood if we could completely describe each constituent piece of reality.

As Stapp (2007) explains, quantum mechanics closes the gap between subjective and objective and places human activity at the center of what we can know about the world. Here is our simplified, seven-step understanding of his argument:

1. All that we can perceive, anything in nature, *everything* is, in actuality, constantly flowing and changing. Dynamic. In development.
2. If we want to know anything about anything, we have to capture that thing at a moment in time.
3. We accomplish this capture by some measure or other. Especially for tiny, tiny things that make up atoms, we cannot see their activities directly, so we place an instrument such as a Geiger counter next to them. If the Geiger counter pings, we take that as evidence

that the "thing" we are studying exists. At that moment, our knowledge takes a big leap, from zero to 100%. It is there!

4. But remember that "it" is a flowing process, not a thing. The process itself is what Stapp calls a "smear" of possibilities. There are many possible answers to the question "Is it there?" (i.e., will the Geiger counter ping?) The ping is almost triggered by this or that or the other aspect of the process . . . or not even close . . . or would have pinged except the timing was off or. . . . Statistically speaking, there are only probabilities for a ping or not. But those probabilities turn into certainty, into facts once we get the results of the experiment.

5. The questions we pose and the methods we use to answer them are an integral part of the facts we observe. Our questions do not determine what the answers will be. We ask and nature responds. But with every answer, the smear of possibilities collapses momentarily into a certainty that has been set up by the question and measurement. And that is the ground on which we stand to ask our next question: If there's no ping, "Would there be a ping if I moved it over here?" No ping. "What about here?" Ping. "Oh, it's here! Is this the only place it is? . . ." The actual ongoing process gets divided by human activity into packets of question answered, question answered, question answered. In this way, we participate in organizing our experience into what we call "knowledge."

6. Is there anything about human activity to which this smear of possibilities can be applied? Stapp notes that the activity of neurons in the human brain depends on a flow of tiny ions that fits quantum principles exactly. Whether a neuron will fire is a matter of probabilities. But by paying attention to our thoughts, we are essentially asking questions and setting a subjective measure to test the answer. "Did he disapprove?" "Am I upset?" "Did that feel good?" Ping. "Oh, he must like me." Each question answered, question answered, question answered represents connections among neurons that are strengthened with each repetition. Stronger connections mean the question/answer combination is more likely to be repeated in the future. "He likes me" becomes more and more an assumption, a certainty that we act on automatically. Not only are the connections between neurons strengthened by repetition, there

is evidence that new neurons are formed. The very physical structure of our brains is affected by what started as attention, as being conscious of what we are thinking and feeling, as asking a question and then noticing, or measuring, how the environment responds.

7. Therefore, by the conscious mental activity of paying attention, we can affect our physical brains. Siegel's "notion that mind is using the brain to create itself" (2007a, p. 32) is no longer preposterous.

Stapp's *Mindful Universe* (2007) explains in much more detail how quantum theory demands participation of the observer, replaces the study of reality with the study of knowing, and shifts inquiry from observing to doing, from stasis to process, and from being to becoming.

Linking Quantum Theory to Coaching

Coaches must assume that change is possible and that clients can make choices rather than being predetermined by a mechanistic universe. Quantum theory explains and supports our subjective experience of making decisions in the face of indeterminacy. The quantum principle of entanglement, or the capacity of particles to be coordinated over impossibly long distances, supports the idea that all entities in the universe are connected. Specifically, human beings are socially embedded and connected to one another in ways we can scarcely understand.

SOCIAL EMBEDDEDNESS AS A COACHING PILLAR

In the coaching relationship, we are inviting people to do things differently, recognizing that one new decision can open up a whole new world. Doing a simple exercise for only minutes every day can change the way people think of themselves.

In any system, some things are in clients' control and some are out of their control. Clients always have the choice as to how to interpret what happens. Clients can utilize "life lessons of chaos" and approach life with creativity rather than control. With creativity, clients are more likely to influence the system. Using the concept of self-organizing communities, clients can focus on values and purpose and allow the system to organize itself, to evolve and reveal a deeper source of collaborative power.

The recurring thoughts that we have are attractors. Unless we consciously change these patterns, they will keep bringing us back to the same place. Coaching can be useful in raising awareness of these thoughts, in naming and in categorizing them. This is important in being able to move past them. Neuroscience is further revealing the mechanisms behind these principles.

An individual is a complex system and is part of other complex systems—families, social groups, organizations, and so on. As coaches, we are helping our clients see the patterns in these systems and make desired changes.

It must be clear by now that one answer to the question "Who are we?" is this: Human beings are nonlinear dynamic complex self-organizing systems that display quantum principles. We are embedded in larger systems that are also nonlinear, dynamic, complex, self-organizing, and quantum. This systemic understanding provides a bridge to the emerging characterization of the brain, mind, and relationships as mutually interdependent subsystems of the human system.

Next we turn to the contemporary platform of neuroscience, specifically the topic of mindfulness, in our attempt to answer the question "Who are we?"

CHAPTER 3

Neuroscience Platform — Mindfulness

Claims for the advantages of years of mindfulness training are pretty impressive. But our clients walk in the door without those many years of meditation practice. They are concerned with how to change now, not having to wait for 10 years of sitting or chanting or yoga. Dalian University professor Yi-Yuan Tang and his colleagues (Tang & Posner, 2008; Tang et al., 2007) wondered if a program that integrated several body-mind aspects of meditation, including body relaxation, breath adjustment, mental imagery, and mindfulness training, might produce results that show up more quickly. Faster is not necessarily better in and of itself, but Tang argued that it is important to apply the same testing standards to mindfulness as to drugs or other change interventions. This is difficult to do when results do not show up for years and only then after unceasing compliance.

Tang and his group recruited 80 undergraduates from the university and gave half of them relaxation training only. He gave the other half the full integrated body-mind training (IBMT) recorded along with selected music. Both groups met with a trained coach whose job was "to create a harmonious and relaxed atmosphere for effective practice." Both groups, relaxation and IBMT, practiced for 20 minutes a day for 5 days.

Long-term meditators tend to be able to notice and calm themselves when they are about to fly off the handle. This is called self-regulation.

They also are better at paying attention and at being present. If you were in the IBMT group, you would have filled out questionnaires and taken tests before any training to show that you were pretty much the same as your compatriots in the relaxation group when it comes to self-regulation, attention, and being present.

After the training was a different matter. On average, you and your 40 IBMT colleagues would show better self-regulation, attention, and ability to be present in the moment as compared to the group that only got relaxation training. Even your baseline cortisol levels, a measure of stress levels when at rest, would be reduced significantly for you who had done IBMT training. And remember that this was after only 5 days of training. As the authors wrote, "Our study is consistent with the idea that attention, affective processes, and the quality of moment-to-moment awareness are flexible skills that can be trained" (Tang et al., 2007, p. 17155).

We have pursued the question of who we are as human beings partly by looking at Western philosophical traditions. Over the past four centuries, these have been steeped in Newtonian assumptions, particularly those that reduce individuals to objects trapped in a clockwork universe, suffering from an illusion of choice but determined by past events. Increasing global interconnections and scientific discoveries have accelerated a shift in that perspective toward a more contextual, community-oriented worldview. Interest in New Age philosophy during the last half century has combined with social science traditions that focus on holism and social systems to strengthen a shift to a systemic paradigm.

Systems and quantum theory bridge the two paradigms and bring us to an understanding of dynamic stability as a measure of a well-functioning nonlinear dynamic self-organizing complex system. Neuroscience tells us that the brain is such a system.

- How does modern neuroscience respond to age-old questions about how the brain relates to who we are as human beings?
- What is consciousness, the very capacity that allows us to ask "Who are we?"
- What are the characteristics of a brain that indicate it is a system?
- How can we get to know ourselves better so as to answer some of these questions?
- What constitutes healthy brain processes?

- What is mindfulness, and how does it relate to mind and brain?
- What should coaches know and do in order to understand their own brains and to help develop those capacities for leaders and others they are coaching?

For centuries, philosophers and scientists have questioned how the mind and the brain relate to one another. Western culture tells us that we think with our brains and feel with our hearts. In other societies, other organs may be presumed to be the emotional or thinking center. The radical materialist aspect of the mechanistic worldview reduces mind to brain activity.

During the 18th and 19th centuries, many educated people believed in phrenology, the practice of determining personal character and ability from the shapes and bumps on people's heads. This practice has been thoroughly discredited. Today, some critics of modern neuroscience dismiss efforts to correlate brain measurements with ability as "modern phrenology" (Begley, 2007). Such skepticism is understandable considering that past experience teaches us to treat the discoveries of any science as preliminary until thoroughly tested.

Enormous debate continues to surround the study of consciousness. What is consciousness? Where is it located? From the mechanistic perspective, only the material world is real, and mental activity is reduced to brain activity. Causality moves in only one direction; therefore, the brain gives rise to the mind, not vice versa. Mental phenomena, including consciousness, are considered to be products, or epiphenomena, of brain activity.

Until recently, it was impossible to view a live brain in action in order to gather information that might bring into question the mechanistic paradigm. Technological advances have now made it possible for scientists to study consciousness more directly, with shocking results.

Quantum mechanics tells us that the nonmaterial attention of an observer can shift how subatomic particles decay (Stapp, 2007). Since our brains are made up of atoms, which are vulnerable to influence from mental events, it can no longer be claimed that the brain creates the mind in a linear causal fashion. Daniel Siegel's claim that our "mind is using the brain to create itself" (2007a, p. 32) indicates the extent to which our ideas about what it means to be human are changing as an aspect of the systemic paradigm shift.

Even the debate between free will and determinism has been affected. According to mechanistic determinism, free will is an illusion. The brain does its thing and the mind rationalizes along. However, people subjectively experience making choices. How do we reconcile "objective" reality with "subjective" experience? Quantum mechanics has rescued free will from its deterministic graveyard by uncovering the dynamic relationship between brain and mind. If we are to answer the question "Who are we?" we must understand the system of which the brain is a part. We must know ourselves.

We discuss these topics under these headings:

- The potentiating brain
- Thinking processes
- Mindfulness practices
- Practice guide for coaching with the brain in mind—know yourself

THE POTENTIATING BRAIN

Based on what we have covered up to now in this book, we conclude that a key purpose of any kind of coaching is to develop the potential of the beings who engage in it. Coaching clients may arrive at coaching, or may be referred to it, in order to deal with a particular skill or issue, but coaches generally are trained to look always for that person's greater potential, even in very short coaching interventions. Eliciting that potential means, ultimately, that people learn how to change their brains. But what is the limit to this? At what point do we reach our full potential, the state where we there are no more changes to be made?

Our death represents one clear limit, and there are degenerative diseases such as Alzheimer's and injuries from accidents or strokes that limit our brain's abilities. Neuroscientist James Zull (2006) also recognizes that, compared to children, there are some changes that are more difficult, or impossible, for adults to make, such as learning to speak a new language like a native. "However," says Zull, "the neurological nature of learning strongly suggests that there is no age of finality for any learning" (p. 7). That is, even though *some* types of changes cannot be counted as part of our potential, as long as our brain is functioning at all, we can still learn.

Brain as a Complex System

As one of the most complex systems known, the brain is an excellent systems case study. It clearly fits our definition of a complex system. The brain is composed of neurons, which are the independent agents or elements in the system. The neurons are related to one another and are grouped into specialized components, such as the visual cortex, which pass information among them. The brain exhibits other properties of complex systems presented earlier.

As an open system, the brain responds to input from its environment (stimulation from the body or elsewhere) and outputs signals to the body as a response.

EMERGENT SYSTEM   Consciousness, state of mind, thinking, and personality emerge from the interaction of the brain's neurons. "A system like the brain functions the way it does, not because of the nature of the pieces out of which it is made, but because of the way these elements are self-organized and interact. It is their collective behavior that is important" (Anderla, Dunning, & Forge, 1997, p. 43).

Psychologists agree that personality, for example,

> is not the mere sum of our feelings, volitions, instincts, and conceptions. It constitutes an integrated unity of all these in mutual relation. . . .[Our personality traits] interact and constitute an integrated "personality syndrome" which acts as a whole and has properties as a whole. (László, 1972, p. 32)

SELF-ORGANIZING SYSTEM   Ervin László (1972) points out that "while a genius must have more gray matter than a sparrow, the idiot may have just as much as the genius. The difference between them must be explained in terms of how those substances are organized" (p. 32). The processes within the brain actually organize how the brain functions. No single component controls how the brain is organized. Rather, as the neurons fire, the activated neural pathways are strengthened, thereby increasing the likelihood that the particular pattern will be activated in the future.

Building on this idea, Siegel (1999) describes how the brain's activity results in self-organization that creates certain common states of

95

mind within an individual, in a self-referencing manner. These states can be seen as attractors. "The probability of activation of a state is determined by both the history and present context or environmental conditions. . . .With repeated activation, the state of mind becomes more deeply engrained, and the state is remembered" (pp. 218–219). The remembered state then serves as a reference point for further organization.

Robert Post and Susan Weiss captured this phenomenon by slightly modifying Hebb's axiom: "Neurons which fire together, survive together, and wire together" (Siegel, 1999, p. 219). This is the basis for neuroplasticity, or the capacity of the brain to change.

CO-EVOLVING SYSTEM   Through feedback and self-organization, the brain develops and becomes more complex over time. This is consistent with the evolution of complex systems discussed earlier. In the brain's feedback process, the effects of a state of mind become an input into future behavior. This is a systems explanation for the effects of behaviorist reinforcement. In human development, we can see that an individual is able to develop significant new and much more complex skills between infancy and adulthood.

For each of us, and for clients, the movement from simplicity toward complexity is another way of saying "development." Children develop increasingly complex interactions with their social and physical environments. As they mature, they not only run and jump, they dance and make subtle gestures and change their stance depending on a myriad of contexts. They vary old patterns in new situations and create new patterns in old situations.

> Stability of the system is achieved by the movement toward maximizing complexity. Complexity does not come from random activation, but instead is enhanced by a balance between continuity [probability of repeating past states] and flexibility [sensitivity to environment] of the system. (Siegel, 1999, p. 219)

The brain's movement toward complexity is somewhat counterintuitive, since we know that some neurons will not be used and will atrophy. For instance, children at birth can differentiate all possible meaningful sounds in human languages, whereas by two years of age, they have

96

already "specialized" in the sounds of the language(s) spoken at home. Those neurons that have not been stimulated have atrophied, or been "pruned." Is this really a move toward complexity?

Siegel (1999) says yes, explaining that changes such as this are part of creating a more integrated system:

> [A]s the system or organism evolves, it develops a more limited set of possible states. This increase in the system's differentiation, this specialization in the patterns of activation, is based on the coordination of basic elements into a more highly coupled, integrated system. (p. 221)

Even though a reduction in what one part of the brain is capable of may seem at first glance to yield less complexity, it means that different parts can specialize for different functions. Integration in a system requires a linkage of differentiated elements. Specialization means that different parts of the brain are truly different. Therefore, linking them, as in dividing the labor so more can be accomplished, provides for much more complexity than could be achieved if every part did all the same things.

This system integration idea can be taken even further, beyond a single brain to integrating the activities of multiple individuals. "Maximal complexity is achieved by the combination of individual differentiation and interpersonal integration" (Siegel, 1999, p. 225). Being either totally independent from or overly dependent on others decreases complexity. "As a dynamical system, the mind may be restricted in its balanced movement toward complexity either by excessive responsiveness to others or by an intense autonomy and resistance to joining with others' states" (Siegel, 1999, p. 226).

NONLINEAR SYSTEM   Small changes, say, in the chemistry of neurotransmitters, can lead to big changes in behavior, such as less anxiety. As Siegel (1999) explains, "Viewing the mind as a complex system, we can see that the 'dysfunction' at one level or organization may produce large changes in the functioning of other levels and of the system as a whole" (p. 220). For example, obsessive-compulsive disorder may be triggered by activity within a small region of the brain, but ultimately it has a significant impact on whole brain function and resulting behavior. Siegel (1999) notes that nonlinearity also has its benefits, in that "small changes in a person's perspective, beliefs, or associations of particular forms of information processing can suddenly lead to large changes in state of mind and behavior" (p. 221). Of course, the trick is to figure out exactly which small changes will result in those larger changes that are desired.

With this description of the brain's movement toward increased integration and complexity, we arrive at a definition of "dynamic stability" for the complex system that includes the human brain.

The Process of Potentiating

Systems theory shows that even a small input into an open, nonlinear, self-organizing system such as a brain can result in a dramatic transformation. For that reason, we have concluded that we never reach our full potential as long as we are alive and have any brain function at all. We have been seeking the right word or phrase that captures this important goal of coaching. Do we say that coaches help clients develop their full potential? No, because there is no such state. We never achieve our full potential, except perhaps momentarily, but then we and our environment change. That is, achieving potential is a *process*, not a destination or *thing* we *have*. This is consistent with the shift in quantum theory from product to process.

We could say that we help clients develop "fuller" or "greater" potential, but those are still nouns and adjectives that treat potential as a *thing* rather than as a process. In seeking the right term, we hope to avoid the tendency in Western languages to name ongoing, changing processes as if they are static, immutable (noun like) objects (Nisbett, 2003). This is the problem with "potential." The term "potentiate," however, is a verb that is used generally for a process of increasing power and effect. It is applied specifically to the effects of transmitters on the likelihood of a neuron firing. This is good company for a word to be in. We have chosen to borrow it to describe the ever-developing capacity of the human mind. We dare to introduce such a term because current language simply does not convey what we mean to get across. We suggest it as a possible contribution to finding "ways to think coherently in multiple levels and dimensions, to incorporate the time line and dynamics of living processes into our understanding of molecules and cells and systems" (Rose, 2005, p. 215).

Coaches help clients potentiate, or engage in an ongoing process of developing their potential. It is the potentiating process in the context of our thoroughly embodied brains and social minds that makes something new possible. In the chapters to follow, we examine neuroscience research for clues as to how potentiating, as we use it here, happens and can happen more reliably. Thus we will be prepared to examine a brain-based definition of human health and wellness and a formula for arriving at that state.

Bottom-up Brain

What is the brain for? As we have said, one crucial function is to gather, sort, integrate, and provide information about what is "out there." "Sensation" is the term that philosophers, physiologists, and psychologists use to refer to input from our senses, commonly listed as touch, sight, sound, smell, and taste. We also sense the position and movement of our bodies, balance, and internal states of pain, discomfort, hunger, thirst, and so forth.

Common mechanistic assumptions informed past studies of our senses. That is, sensory systems were seen to convey information in much the same way as a radio picks up signals and conveys them to the processor that converts them to sound. Input from our senses informs our brain about changes "out there." From this linear perspective, the process of hearing begins with an input of air waves that is transformed by our inner ear and auditory nerves into electrochemical impulses that are transmitted to the part of the brain that interprets the signal as sound. This is called "bottom-up," or sensory, processing. The bottom part is the brain/body; only after it does its processing does the "top" processor, the mind, come into play.

In this linear model, the mental activity of perception, or our interpretation of sensation, does not begin until the auditory signal reaches the brain area specialized for sound. It is at this point, according to this model, that the minding process kicks in to create "top-down" meaning or perception. The mind draws on past experience (memory) to interpret the changes in auditory input and therefore (and only then) to "recognize" what is being heard.

We now know that this linear view is vastly oversimplified and that top-down and bottom-up processing are always mixed. Our meaning-making minds are interacting constantly with our brain-body sensory systems. In short, we "mind" at the very same time that we "sense," and in some cases before.

Mirror Neurons

The discovery of mirror neurons by Giaccomo Rizzolatti (Rizzolatti et al., 1996), Vittorio Gallese (Gallese et al.,1996), and their colleagues at the University of Parma in Italy added support to the growing understanding of how perception is not a sequential after-effect of sensation. Rizzolatti and Gallese are neurophysiologists who were working with a team of scientists in the 1980s and 1990s to study the firing of neurons when macaque monkeys moved their hands.

The scientists placed an electrode in a single neuron in the motor cortex, the part of the brain in primates (including humans—roughly the top of the fingers in our brain-in-the-hand model) that controls the movements of our limbs and bodies. They recorded what happened when the monkey reached for a piece of food. The monkey grasped the food and the neuron fired. But there was an additional discovery for some neurons: The neuron fired not only when the monkey picked up food but also when it saw one of the researchers pick up food. That is, the brain of the monkey reacted to the observation of a person's action just as it would if it were itself performing that action. For obvious reasons, these specific cells were named "mirror neurons." Further investigation showed that some 10% of neurons in the motor cortex of these monkeys' brains are of the mirror type (Rizzolatti & Craighero, 2004).

Although research ethics do not allow implanting electrodes in individual neurons of human brains, functional magnetic resonance imaging (fMRI) and other neuroimaging evidence indicate that certain regions in our brains become active when we see other people experience an emotion or take an action of some sort (Rizzolatti, Sinigaglia, & Anderson, 2008). It is expected that individual mirror neurons will be identified in the motor cortex of the human brain.

Of even greater interest is the fact that this neuronal firing occurs only when the actions of the person being observed are intentional. In the old linear paradigm, the motor cortex was thought of as the region that receives orders to move only after sensations have been

100

gathered, meaning added, perceptions drawn, and decisions made as to what to do about it. The amazing discovery is that only when Person A *intends* to reach for a coffee cup does Observer B's mirror neurons fire. A chance gesture toward an object where there is no likely goal (say just lifting your arm), however similar it might seem to an intentional reach, does not cause the neuron to fire. Thus, at the level of a single neuron in the case of monkeys, and presumably also for human apes, some differentiation must be made right there in the motor cortex as to what Person A is intending to do. We make meaning at a level that was previously thought to be simply carrying out orders. This brings the formerly assumed sequence of sensation-then-perception into question.

Contrary to the model of brain processing that prevailed during much of the mechanistic era, our sensing and interpreting functions are intertwined. However, much of the interpreting that is connected to sensing is in the nature of the neurons and the brain itself, as with mirror neurons, and thus does not occur consciously. In chapter 6, we discuss how we can intervene somewhat in these processes by setting our intentions and exercising "veto power."

Mirror neurons also bring into question the assumption that our brain and mind processes are limited to our own individual, skin-wrapped bodies. Just as brain processes such as hearing a sound cannot be separated from mental processes such as anticipating it, inputs from other people cannot be entirely separated from our outputs and inputs within ourselves or with them. We can also share information and energy with others, thus borrowing from their experiences and perspective. This process of sharing is not only gratifying but necessary for our development as human beings.

Sensation versus Narrative

As we have seen, brain and mind are thoroughly intertwined. From research done by neuroscientists such as Norman Farb and his colleagues (2007), it appears that the default process of our brains is to engage in an inner "narrative" mental process, much of it to do with imagined or remembered social interaction. Rather than registering the input of immediate sensations—the wind on our skin, the taste of a mouthful of casserole, the sound of her voice as she is speaking, the whiff of a rose in a vase on the table next to us—we instead are "somewhere else." We are not present here and now but rather "in our heads" planning the assignment or reliving the argument. We call it "daydreaming" or, in the extreme, "dissociation."

Linking the Potentiating Brain and Coaching

Having the capacity to ignore present inputs and to create our own narrative reality depends on our brain's ability to create patterns of connections that are often called *mental maps*. Making such linkages, especially novel ones, is something the brain does automatically. Doing so has the advantage of increasing the number of differentiated maps that are linked, thus increasing brain and mind complexity. Increasing complexity is, after all, the measure of development of a nonlinear dynamic system. Before discussing the advantages and disadvantages of "living in the narrative," let us examine the brain and mind processes that result in mental maps.

THINKING PROCESSES

Daniel Siegel (2007a) draws on several scientific disciplines for his definition of mind: "a process that regulates the flow of energy and information" (p. 5). Note the word "process." If we take this definition seriously, we should use a verb form and speak of "minding" instead of "the mind": Minding is a process of regulating the flow of energy and information. However, because this usage is unusual in English, we suggest keeping in mind, so to speak, that when we speak of "mind," we mean a set of processes rather than a thing.

The mind is also "embodied." Yes, it is centered in the brain, but as we have emphasized, the human brain is mutually dependent on and distributed throughout the whole body.

The human mind is also "relational." The flow of energy and information occurs among people as well as within an individual. It is a repeated theme in this book that our thinking process incorporates the mental activity of other people. This is another dramatic break from the focus on the self-contained individual that has characterized Western philosophy and science.

Development of Mind

How does subjective mind arise from physical brain and social relationships? One aspect of this intertwined genesis has to do with two cells that combine and divide to become the billions of neurons and other cells that make up a human body-with-brain. Each of those neurons forms up to 10,000 connections in response to genetic information and environmental stimuli, especially those from the social environment.

But this is not a passive process. Steven Rose (2005) emphasizes the self-creating, or "autopoietic," nature of the human embryo. "Autopoietic" is a term formed from the Greek words for "self" and "production" and is closely related to the "self-organizing" characteristic of complex systems. "Autopoiesis" refers to a system that produces and replaces its own elements. "It is through autopoiesis that the to-be-born human embryo constructs herself" (p. 63). After birth, the human being continues to be "an active player in its own destiny."

Rose explains that while the brain is forming during gestation in the human womb, genes from the original combination of two cells convey some information about where neurons should be located in the brain, but the voyaging neurons also interact and help each other along the way. Around 200 billion neurons go to the right point, traveling some 200 miles across each person's brain. Many die along the way, their destination and function to be taken over by others. Over the first few years of life, the brain reduces to about one 100 billion neurons; much of this loss is based on pruning those neurons that have not made connections.

From even before we are born, our brain interacts with the world to try to make sense of what might otherwise be senseless noise. We identify patterns in light and shade that become our parents, patterns in sound that become language from which we build conscious meaning. We find patterns in the way our muscles interact with the world, which builds our motor skills, getting us from crawling, to walking, to running and to finer skills like playing music or typing.

Some of this interaction comes "preprogrammed" by our genes. For example, a newborn immediately takes a breath when it encounters oxygen at birth. However, most of what we learn comes from experience, from interacting with the world, in particular the social world. Even "inborn" activities, such as eating, are shaped by how that activity happens in connection with others. The patterns that are formed in the brain as a result of repeated neural firing from our mind and relationship processes are called schemas or maps by cognitive researchers. Following neuroscientist Gerald Edelman, we will use the term "map" here.

Neural Darwinism

Neural Darwinism is a concept developed by Edelman. Its meaning is captured by the phrase "Use it or lose it." Edelman was a Noble laureate in biology who made the leap to neuroscience later in his career. In *Neural Darwinism* (1987), he applied some of the ideas of Darwinian selection and survival of the fittest to the brain. He established a now widely accepted model for what occurs in the brain in relation to the physiology of our thoughts, or the physical consequences of how we think.

Edelman's theory was that every memory—every piece of data, idea, habit, thought—is made up of a set of connections among neurons, like a map of connecting highways in our brain. Each map or set of connections involves some 10,000 to 50,000 neurons. We create maps for every sight, sound, word, face, person, idea, and memory that we remember, whether consciously or not. Everything that stays with us forms a map that is part of our brain.

We sometimes form temporary maps. For example, we do not hold in mind the number of every automobile license plate that we pass on the way to work. But after taking that journey even once, we will have formed a rudimentary map of the route. After taking it many times, we will easily remember it; with enough repetitions, we will follow it even when we are not consciously attending to it. The map of the plate number is lost, while the map of the route becomes engrained, automatic, or what we often refer to as "hardwired."

There are maps of maps and the map of maps, and so forth. For example, the word "car" energizes many maps connected to it: the sound of our car, the sound of other cars we know, the sound of the word "car" in other languages that we know, related words in English such as "automobile," the memory of cars we have driven or owned or desired, different types of cars, all the designs and colors of cars we have seen, the smell of cars, how to drive a standard versus an automatic transmission . . . all these maps are connected to that higher-order map for "car."

We build up these layers of maps for experiences throughout our lives. We have maps for the feel of blocks in our hand, if we played with them when young. Maps of when to use the word "they" versus "them" in a sentence. Maps for the difference between irony and sarcasm; for every song we know; for the faces of everyone we have paid attention to. The brain rapidly accesses and updates these each second as we interact with the world.

Even at birth, there is evidence that children have already begun to form these maps of the world—that is, cognitive (although not conscious) expectations of what is familiar and what is likely to come next. Research has shown that infants recognize the language their mother speaks, presumably through hearing sounds spoken during gestation. One-year-old babies also prefer music that was played while they were in the womb, even though they had not heard that music during their first year after birth (Levitin, 2006).

Each map is a set of connections among points in our brain, among our neurons, which are the primary cells in the brain. The neurons are connected by axons and dendrites, like the roots and branches of a tree, respectively. The dendrites, or branches, from one neuron accept neural signals from the axons, or roots, of many others, thus forming connections among thousands and hundreds of thousand of neurons. A map is a set of these connections that makes it possible to know what we know, think what we think, and do what we do.

According to Edelman, maps are internal representations of the way the external world works. These enable us to understand and interact with that world. The maps that are most utilized in this way get the most energy. Another way of saying this is that the maps that convey information that is most accessed get further hardwired into our brain and become more likely to be activated in the future.

These maps are constantly competing for resources, as there is not enough energy for every neuron to connect with every other possible one from moment to moment. So the brain also "prunes" neurons, thus erasing unused connections, as we go along. This is a fundamental principle of the way our thinking works at a physical level: Our models of the world are constantly changing and reconnecting. Our ideas, models, thoughts and interpretations are hypotheses about the world that are, to anthropomorphize the process, competing with each other for survival in the brain moment to moment.

However, early in life, neurons are not yet as well connected as they will be later. It is as if the houses in the subdivision are built but without extensive roads, power lines, or phone lines. These connections are created moment to moment by a dialectic relationship of experience, genes, and self-determined activity. Rose (2005) suggests that the volume of activity is such that some 30,000 new synapses per second are made over every square centimeter of a newborn's cortical surface. This explains why identical twins in the same house, with the same parents, eating the same diet can end up with quite different personalities. As with any nonlinear dynamic system, imperceptible differences in experience, combined with individual choice, can result in surprisingly large differences as people grow up. Given such rapid development, this is true even when genomes are identical. Consider how much truer it is when genomes are different.

One of the implications of how different our brains and minds become has to do with differences in these maps. At a general level, it may seem easy to understand how someone else's mind works. For example, different people use pretty much the same parts of their brain to walk. Telling someone the best way to get up out of a chair and walk out the door should be straightforward: "Use your motor cortex to activate muscles in the legs, and out you go."

The similarity of how we operate at this gross level tempts us to tell others what to do. (Giving advice also has status implications, as we will see in chapter 15.) However, if you consider the question of what motivates someone to get up and walk in the context of that individual's history of attempts in the past, the process becomes much more complex. It is unlikely that one person can guess exactly how others get themselves moving, given all the unique developmental histories. The neuronal patterns John Doe uses to regulate his flow of energy and information are just too different from those used by Jane Smith. Because of the limits of working memory that we discuss later, John's working memory cannot possibly encompass all the aspects of Jane's mental map or neuronal patterns in order to understand what she should do next. This is a neuroscientific explanation for why advice giving is not an effective way to coach others.

Constructing Meaning

To the brain, all the senses are the same: Data enter the brain and immediately are subject to sorting and interpreting and attempts to identify patterns, to make meaning. As we have learned, sensing of data and the perceiving of meaning are not separable in the brain. When you first hear a song on the radio, it may sound like noise, depending on your past experience with music. In *This Is Your Brain on Music*, Daniel Levitin (2006) describes how the whole brain is involved in the musical

Example: "How Did You Know It?"

This happened recently to one of us (Linda), who was exposed in graduate school to the West African language Yoruba. Decades later, in a cab, she overheard the driver speaking to a friend on the phone.

"Are you speaking Yoruba?" she asked the cabbie.

"Yes. How do you know it?" the driver asked.

"It just sounded familiar," answered Linda. Her brain had connected patterns of sounds that characterize Yoruba and stored this as a map that remained dormant until it was activated many years later.

experience. Our brains are built to make sense out of otherwise random noise. Have you noticed, for example, that after a few days in a new place where a language you do not know is spoken, the overall sound patterns take on some familiarity? Later, when you hear that language spoken, you may recognize what language it is, even if you still cannot understand a word.

Linking Thinking Processes and Coaching

Our brain, mind, and relationship processing never stops. Our mental maps are continually being activated, even while we are sleeping. But being awake does not mean that we are present and registering here and now sensory input. We have said that the default activity of our brains and minds seems to be telling ourselves stories, especially ones to do with people. The great advantage of this is the human capacity to "live" in the past and future as well as in the present.

MINDFULNESS PRACTICES

If, as physician Craig Hassed suggests in his book, *The Essence of Health* (2008), mindfulness meditation is simply focusing our attention on a particular thing or thought, then we spend much of our lives meditating. The problem is that we often meditate on worries, anger, regrets, resentments, or depressing thoughts. Because of the interdependency of mind and brain/body, these all have effects on our bodies, increasing our stress levels and decreasing our resiliency. To be mindful, to be able to direct our attention to the here and now, is a crucial capacity for coaches. We must be present for our clients if we hope to work with *them* rather than with our imagined stories *about* them.

Mindfulness training has many advantages for us as coaches, in addition to helping us coach. Evidence is mounting that mindfulness practice contributes to health and well-being. And as Yi-Yuan Tang and his colleagues have shown (Tang et al., 2007), we do not have to spend 10 cloistered years at it for broad-spectrum meditation training to show measurable results.

For example, we are limited as to how much we can attend to. Thank goodness we can continue to operate on automatic mental maps that we are not presently attending to. We arrive at home unaware of driving there. We find the dishwasher empty having thought through tomorrow's schedule while putting the dishes away without being aware of lifting the plates and cutlery.

But what if we want to change that automatic behavior? What if we find ourselves locked into inflexibility, the other side of chaos? What if acting on the same mental map is a threat to our well-being? Obsessive-compulsive disorder (OCD) is the name applied to people who have this experience. Treating OCD is not part of what coaches do, but successful treatment of the disorder helps us all understand more about how to manage dynamic stability in our lives and about the place of mindfulness in this process (Schwartz & Begley, 2002).

Use of Mindfulness

We have described the formation of mental maps and shown how they enable us to live in a "narrative" rather than to be present in the immediate flow of sensory experience. Examples are accumulating that show mindfulness practices as crucial to utilizing this knowledge to make changes in our lives.

Daniel Siegel (2007a) documents his exploration of mindfulness practices following his 1999 book that showed the effects of attuned interactions on the brains and minds of both children and adults. Previously, Siegel had sought to expand the boundaries of physiologically oriented psychiatry but found it difficult to compare research from related fields, such as cognitive and developmental psychology, philosophy, linguistics, sociology, anthropology, and neuroscience, because of differences in history and terminology. He invited scholars, practitioners, and scientists from these and other fields to form an interdisciplinary inquiry they called interpersonal neurobiology.

With growing interest in neuroscience by figures such as the Dalai Lama (Begley, 2007) and the acceleration of scientific research into mindfulness (Kabat-Zinn, 2005), Siegel decided to experience mindfulness practices firsthand (2007a). He went on silent retreats, practiced yoga, and interviewed proponents of various approaches. As a result, he came to see mindfulness practices as ways to develop a better relationship with oneself. Attuned relationships with other people are characterized by accepting that the other has thoughts and desires, just as we do, and by taking those unique qualities into account in our interactions. Similarly, developing a reflective mind means that part of us becomes an "other," or what Schwartz and Begley (2002) call an "Impartial Spectator," to ourselves.

Siegel (2007a) uses a metaphor to describe this relationship with ourselves. He suggests that we imagine a wheel with a rim, a hub, and spokes connecting the rim and hub. The rim consists of our senses, our conscious and unconscious memories, our physiological reactions—all the components of the moods and reactions we are subject to. The hub can be a passive victim of whatever thought or sensation happens to travel along one of the spokes to capture it momentarily. Or the hub can simply observe, or be a spectator to the many signals traveling from the rim down one or another spoke.

Jeffrey Schwartz and Sharon Begley (2002) credit Buddhist mindfulness practice with providing insights to help obsessive-compulsive patients. Buddhist teachings emphasize that human beings are capable of "inhabiting" any of 10 subjective states, or "worlds," that range from intense suffering to anger to enlightenment. That is, when we are in a state yet unaware of that fact, it can seem that we *are* anger and that everything in our environment upholds that interpretation. Each of those 10 states can be viewed through the perspective of 10 aspects, such as its cause or consequence, and each of those 100 combinations has within it the potential to change into any other of the 10 states in an instant. These 1,000 state-aspect combinations exist in the three realms of living beings: their physical and mental components, and the environment in which they exist. All together, this yields 3,000 conditions in a single moment of time.

The point of all this is simple. The bad news is that if we are not aware of it, we are continually at the mercy of ever-changing conditions. We can be happily sitting down to work on our laptop in a comfortable seat at the corner coffee shop and *bam!* an angry coffee shop owner insists that we leave since we have not bought anything. Our insistence that we were *intending* to buy makes no difference to him, and we find ourselves in a state of vengefulness. "I'll never come back here, and I'll tell all my friends, too!"

The good news is that, to the extent that we are aware of the state, to the extent that we can be a spectator to what just happened, we have any of the other 2,999 conditions inherent in the present state as options for us to move into. Awareness of, or enlightenment to, this fact provides the freedom to veto the thoughts that lead down a path to an unhappy or unhealthy or unhelpful state and instead choose which state to occupy in this next moment.

Various mindfulness practices use different techniques, but in general, they all help us "practice" for those moments when we are catapulted into a state that is unpleasant or not in our interest. Or when we discover that we are meditating on worries, anger, resentment, or other unhelpful thoughts. Learning about enlightenment is very different from being able to put it into practice. We learn to consciously manage our internal states by recognizing that the noise being transmitted from the rim is not us. It is information about sensory and memory and external inputs or about the processes of our brains, but we ourselves are not those messages; we are the ones receiving them.

When we identify with the hub that is doing the receiving rather than to the messages being sent down the spokes, we strengthen our Impartial Spectator. The more we connect with our self as the hub, the stronger those connections become. At that point, we realize that we can choose what messages coming down the spokes to attend to. We can compare messages and see patterns. We have a metaperspective that enables us to use the full potential of our minds to create our brains and invite healthy responses from others that then reinforce our own more fulfilling states of mind.

Choosing and Attending

Earlier we asked whether human beings really have free will—whether our subjective experience of choice is illusory. In chapter 6, we will present arguments based on brain science, as supported by quantum theory, that whereas the impulse for our actions arises from unconscious processes, we do have the choice to veto those impulses. We also present a formula that relies on this capacity.

Here we examine the question of why we are so attached to being able to choose. Why is choice so important in day-to-day life? One answer is that when people are allowed to make their own choices, they feel empowered and alive. When we have no choice, but must simply follow directions without any input, our energy ebbs. This claim is based on a good deal of evidence, some of which is listed next:

- In Norway, workers in the Norway Postal Service who had more decision-making authority and more learning options scored higher on measures of psychological function and overall health (Mikkelsen, Saksvik, Eriksen, & Ursin, 1999).
- Studies of franchisees (Baron & Schmidt, 1991; Knight, 1986) show that the desire to make their own choices appears among the top three reasons for purchasing a franchise. This is despite the fact that franchisees tend to work harder for less money than those in the corporate world.
- Residents in nursing homes who took part in making the decision to enter the home showed better post admission adjustment, scored higher on measures of health and well-being, and were more likely eventually to be discharged (Reinardy, 1992). Geriatrician Bill Thomas (1996) founded a movement in nursing homes called the Eden Alternative. He found that giving residents choices increased their life expectancy.

- Studies on how exercise builds new brain cells (van Praag et al., 2005) show the benefits accrue only when the exercise is voluntary (Olson, Eadie, Ernst, & Christie, 2006).

The applications to coaching are obvious. When clients are told what to do — by bosses, spouses, or coaches — not only are they likely to react to a status threat, as we discuss in chapter 15, they may actually suffer psychologically and physically. When any of us becomes more mindful of our own mental processes (thoughts, sensations, emotions), we increase the possibility of choosing something different. Our self-awareness, and that of our clients, is what enables us to recognize that we want to change. The potentiation of a new brain requires a self-reflective mind.

Linking Mindfulness and Coaching

Let us imagine a group of people who share these nine characteristics:

1. They use their physical energy well, being able to marshal tremendous effort but also to rest and relax. They are energized by challenges and love their work.
2. They experience both heights and depths of emotion but express it appropriately.
3. It is not that they do not feel fear, but they are able to recognize it and still do what the situation requires. We sometimes think of them as courageous, but they think of themselves as just doing what has to be done.
4. When we meet them, we feel that they are really present and engaged with us and that they treat us respectfully, as fellow human beings.
5. They seem to keep their friends and loved ones "in mind" even when they are apart, and they both give and receive support from others. They easily take the perspective of others, and we often have the sense that they can feel what we feel.
6. They are creative, coming up with solutions that seem to come from nowhere.
7. They often surprise us, doing something we would not have expected of them, but it certainly fits what is required.

8. They are self-aware and do not get defensive when we point out a mistake or a way they could improve. They are certainly not perfect, but they do grow. It is as if everything that happens to them serves as a springboard for becoming even more highly functioning.
9. They do not have to be reminded to do the right thing—they do it to maintain a sense of their own integrity.

Would you be likely to hire such people or follow them if they were leaders or seek them out if they were coaches?

Siegel (2007a) surveyed research regarding the effects of mindfulness practice on mental functions, specifically focusing on those coordinated by the prefrontal cortex. He found that the listed functions were enhanced and, in several cases, the relevant brain structures actually were denser and more connected for meditators as compared to non-meditators:

- Brain/body regulation
- Emotion balancing
- Fear modulation
- Attuned communication
- Empathy
- Intuition
- Response flexibility
- (Self) insight
- Morality

You may note that these nine functions correlate with the nine characteristics of the group of people described in the previous list. It is no wonder that regular practice of a mindfulness technique can be seen as a foundation for all the brain-based coaching knowledge and skills we offer in this book.

PRACTICE GUIDE FOR COACHING WITH THE BRAIN IN MIND—KNOW YOURSELF

The first step in coaching with the brain in mind is to know ourselves. That makes it imperative for coaches to consider the question

"Who are we?" not only for humankind as a whole and for our particular clients, but starting with ourselves.

Ontology is the branch of philosophy that considers this question. With the Enlightenment came an answer based on Newtonian physics — that people are cogs playing out their predetermined parts in a mechanistic universe. This answer did not match with the human experience of choice and agency. Quantum physics is in the process of expanding the explanation of the physical universe to include the participation of human activity. Both coaching and current neuroscience have taken a place on this expanded stage.

Western philosophy's emphasis on the individual has been widened by globalization and systems theory to include the importance of community and context, or the systems in which the individual is embedded.

Mindfulness practices help us develop the capacity to be self-observers. Specifically, coaching that takes neuroscience into account requires coaches to be able to:

- Experience others directly through the senses, in the moment, rather than through narrative circuitry (stories coaches tell themselves *about* clients).
- Develop and engage their own "Impartial Spectator" or self-observer so as to reflect on and come to know themselves better.
- Support clients in becoming more self-aware and self-appreciative.

We now turn to a question that often follows "Who are we?" and often relates to coaching: "How can we be healthy?" In exploring answers to this question, we examine the history of medical and health practices that form a bedrock for coaching, the developments in wellness and change theories that form pillars to raise coaching above its bedrock, and current neuroscience findings regarding neuroplasticity that form a theoretical platform for coaching.

PART II

How Can We Be Healthy?

In part I, we discussed the shift that leveraged Eastern philosophy and the study of other cultures and societies into a growing acceptance of a systemic worldview. We learned that social context and community are more important than the principle of "the supreme individual." Western medicine, being influenced by dualism and mechanistic science, has made great strides in healing or preventing disorders that fit with assumptions of individualism and the separation of body and mind. But health concerns in the last century have stimulated a shift toward systems thinking and holism. Coaching has been shaped by a trend to reconnect body and mind in health practices and to rediscover health promotion, in addition to disease treatment and prevention.

Concerns about how to stay healthy sooner or later are reflected in questions about change: "How can I keep doing healthy activities or stop doing unhealthy ones, or in other ways change what I am doing?"

It is no surprise that change is hard. At one time, beliefs about the brain were not encouraging, as it was assumed that brain development reached a peak in youth and then declined over the rest of our lives. However, the discovery of adult neuroplasticity has changed what scientists and human change practitioners assume is possible. We hinted at some of the elements of neuroplasticity earlier and will take up the topic more fully in this part.

CHAPTER 4

Bedrock — Health Practices

Recently, one of us (Linda) was speaking about brain development to a gathering of coaches. In referring to age-related effects, she said, "For those of us who are getting older, we are concerned about possible cognitive decline." She meant to make the point that there are certain practices, such as mindfulness, that could delay loss of cognitive function. However, someone in the audience paid attention to something different. "Is there anyone here," he asked, "who is *not* getting older?"

The audience member's point is well taken. It may be possible to ignore aging when we are young and even to fervently hope for it when we are very young, but we are all getting older. Our physical system may display large effects that accumulate over time from seemingly small inputs, such as poor nutrition or repetitive stress. Disease and accidents also trigger the question: What can we do to improve health and functioning? Over the centuries, various health practitioners have attempted to answer this question.

This bedrock chapter focuses on applications of research and theory in medicine and other health practices. Health is a resource that we often take for granted until we no longer have it. Today more attention is being paid to connections between mental and physical health, between mind and body, and between caring for ourselves and caring for others, yet in a real sense, our bodies remain an anchor to our overall well-being.

- If ontology helps us understand what it means to be a human being, what does it take to be a *healthy* human being?
- How can we use our bodies in concert with our minds to achieve optimal functioning of the whole?
- How can we strive for achievement and at the same time reduce stress?
- What practices and approaches are truly healthy and life-giving as opposed to passing fads, misguided advice, and even frauds?
- How can we develop our bodies to support achieving greater potential and higher performance?

As with ontological inquiry, none of these questions is new. In ancient and Asian traditions, community and preventive health practices and spiritual healing are integral to the study of medicine. Medical historian Henry Sigerist (1951) suggested that medicine has four goals:

1. Promotion of health
2. Prevention of illness
3. Restoration of health
4. Rehabilitation

Although these tasks overlap, Western medicine attends primarily to the third and fourth goals, with the first and second relegated to public health educators and governments, if they are considered at all. Furthermore, for Western medicine, restoration of health is mainly conceived as treating physical disease without taking mental health, social context, or even the whole body into account. This leaves the promotion of health, as well as a holistic conception of all the other tasks, to alternative health practitioners, media, and others on the outskirts of currently defined medical practice. Despite the impressive achievements of Western medicine, the expansion of holistic mind/body practices indicates that not all our health concerns are being met. Similar trends have contributed to the emergence of coaching at this time. If we take mind/body holism seriously, then brain health is part and parcel of body health, and vice versa.

It is important for coaches to understand the relationship between human physiology and stress, a relationship discovered by mainstream medicine. It is also necessary for coaches to judiciously support clients

118

who wish to explore more preventive and holistic ways of achieving optimum health. This chapter covers several holistic health and wellness approaches that have direct applications to coaching. From a broad history and vast set of traditions, we have selected these topics:

- Western medicine
- Physiology
- Stress
- Wellness theory
- Health practices as bedrock for coaching

Alongside well-established alternative health practices such as yoga and acupuncture, there are some practices that are harmless but not health-promoting and others that are downright fraudulent and dangerous. There is also a growing media trend to distort and sensationalize legitimate research. To assist coaches in helping their clients to make informed choices, this chapter concludes by presenting principles for identifying unreasonable claims regarding health products and practices.

WESTERN MEDICINE

In introducing her medical history text, Lois Magner (1992) states:

> One of our most appealing and persistent myths is that of the Golden Age, a time before the discovery of good and evil, when death and disease were unknown. But scientific evidence—meagre, fragmentary, and tantalizing though it often is—proves that disease is older than the human race. (p. 1)

In contrast to Magner's claim, the founder of modern pathology, Rudolf Virchow (1962), stressed that it is human values that label something a disease: Invading organisms or malfunctions of body parts are simply various forms of life going through natural functions and changes. Human beings judge some changes to be undesirable, label them disease, and seek treatment in the form of a further change that reverses or relieves them. This process is a particularly human activity generally considered to fall in the domain of medicine.

Archaeological evidence—"meagre, fragmentary, and tantalizing" as it may be—shows that forms of medicine have been practiced for as long as humans have existed. Hunting and gathering societies, organized in small, mobile bands, left traces of ingesting medicinal herbs, of surgery to remove frozen fingers or toes, and of rituals that were likely intended to promote health or treat illness (Magner, 1992). In subsistence economies such as these, knowledgeable elders or shamans undoubtedly combined religious rituals, magical practices, and empirical knowledge to both promote health and treat disease (Sigerist, 1951).

When the practice of sedentary agricultural life began its global spread some 10,000 years ago, the picture of health and disease changed dramatically. Population density provided greater opportunity for the spread of infectious diseases, unsanitary conditions allowed for parasites and other illnesses, and wars to protect and extend agricultural land meant more battle injuries. Populations that depended on one or a few crops risked missing necessary nutrients or starvation in the case of crop failure (Magner, 1992). Thus, both the need for more specialized medical knowledge and care and the resources to provide them increased.

Everywhere that "civilizations" developed—first in the Near East, India, Asia, and Central and South America—populations were divided vertically into sedentary geographical territories and horizontally into classes. Privileged classes consisted of priests whose power was based on presumed ability to control forces of nature and rulers whose power came from military prowess. These classes had the resources to pursue health and avoid disease, to the extent that knowledge in their time permitted. Pursuing such knowledge was a priority, and achieving it bestowed privilege and power.

Among these early civilizations, Sigerist (1961) described Greek and Indian medicine as particularly advanced because of the emphasis on drawing conclusions from observations: "Both civilizations had forms of religious medicine, had magic, but on the basis of empiricism developed philosophical systems of medicine which looked beyond the sick man for universal laws." Thus, Greek and Indian medicine became more effective, both in promoting health and in treating illness, "because the Greeks and the Indians acquired a much more profound knowledge of nature and of man within nature, in health and in illness" (p. 3).

Remember that medicine from a historical perspective does not separate treatment of illness from health promotion. For example, in common with the practice of other early civilizations, Greek and Indian medicine placed a high value on physical exercise: "Physical education, athletics, and sports were at all times powerful measures in the promotion of health, in the development of a concept of positive health as a joyful attitude toward life" (Sigerist, 1961, p. 9). Indian medicine never lost its ability to incorporate both health promotion and disease treatment. Western European medicine borrowed and built on Greek traditions but did not maintain that more well-rounded approach. It is only within the past few decades that Western medicine has returned to a holistic emphasis on physical exercise and other health-promoting practices and their mental and spiritual connections.

HISTORICAL INTERLUDE

Health Promotion versus Illness Prevention and Treatment

Roman civilization drew on Greek medical practices and added to them the resources to build public health infrastructure: baths, sanitation, and clean water supplies. Personal hygiene was part of daily ritual, and "purity" of the human body was of great concern—for the upper classes, that is. However, with the ascent of Christianity in the early centuries of the the first millennium, a very different attitude toward the human body was introduced: "The Christian conception was strictly dualistic; mind and body are in opposition, and what matters is the soul. Why, then, care for the body that is the earthly, sinful part of man?" (Sigerist, 1960, p. 20).

Holistic Greek and Roman attitudes and practices were seen as pagan, and Christian monks inherited the tradition of healing, but within the confines of religious practice: Healing the physical body became an opportunity to practice the suffering that Christ had modeled. Even though it was difficult to enforce, Christians were forbidden to seek the superior services of Jewish or Arabic physicians. Public hygiene practices all but disappeared. From 1131 on, edicts were passed forbidding priests and ministers to practice medicine, especially surgery, as it was seen as a worldly art (Sigerist, 1960). At the same time, folk

(Continued)

traditions of medicine were labeled witchcraft, and practitioners were burned at the stake. Thus, both magical and empirical medical traditions were banned in favor of religious ones. As mentioned in the introduction to this book, consulting authoritative texts such as the Bible was the only acceptable "way of knowing," and this applied to medical ways of knowing.

With the Renaissance, roughly spanning the 14th through the 17th centuries, came interest in Greek and Roman ideas, but only regarding developing mental qualities and rhetorical abilities; the interest in hygiene and a balanced life characteristic of upper-class Greek and Roman societies was not renewed. To the extent that positive hygiene or health measures existed, they tended to be decreed by absolutist rulers practicing *noblesse oblige* rather than as a response to human need. Books, in this case classical texts, remained the authoritative sources for knowledge. As a result, diseases and plagues were rampant in the 17th century, especially among children.

Jean-Jacques Rousseau's *Contrat Social* in 1762 rejected absolutist government and introduced the concept that human beings are naturally good and reasonable and can therefore help themselves become better. Thus, "hygiene from below" accompanied democratic political ideas such as were fought for in the American and French revolutions. This democratization also opened the possibility of accepting Galileo's insistence on observing the solar system and Newton's observations regarding gravity, not just as revealing bits of knowledge but as representing a new way of knowing. Thus, empirical science as we know it was born.

But the old authoritarian influence was not erased easily. A sort of uneasy truce was struck between the authority of the church and classical texts on one hand and scientific inquiry on the other. This truce relied on the dualism of mind and body, as elaborated on by René Descartes (1596–1650). The physical body was admitted to be part of the natural world, and thus available for scientific inquiry. But the church maintained its dominion over the mind, which was considered a different kind of "stuff," spiritual and not material, the seat of the soul. The scientific practice of medicine was limited to treating the physical body, not the immaterial mind.

The next development came in the 18th and 19th centuries with capitalism and industrial manufacturing. Driven by the profit motive, factory owners literally worked people — men, women, and children — to death. The life span of the average factory worker in England in the 18th century was 18 years (Labonté, 1983). In response, workers protested and formed labor unions, in turn stimulating employers, who were further motivated by a fear of killing off their workforce, to give in to some of the demands for shorter workdays and prohibitions on the worst practices of child labor. A public commission in England was appointed to study sanitary conditions, leading to the Public Health Act of 1848 and the spread of a new hygiene movement around the world. Governments took on the role of providing for sanitation and clean water and of regulating the worst of workplace practices.

We tend to point to scientific discoveries such as penicillin and technological inventions such as defibrillators as reasons for the astounding increase in life span between the 18th and 20th centuries, but public health and hygiene measures deserve most of the credit. As Sigerist (1961) concludes: "There can be no doubt that it was in the field of prevention of diseases that modern medicine attained its greatest achievements" (p. 16).

Thus, of the four concerns of medicine that Sigerist listed—promotion of health, prevention of disease, restoration of health, and rehabilitation—Western medicine narrowed its attention primarily to the restoration of health in the physical body, primarily by diagnosing and treating disease, and, to the extent that it was profitable, to rehabilitation after accident or disease. Government took on the task of prevention of disease through public hygiene measures and by working with medical researchers and pharmaceutical firms to develop and require vaccinations for common diseases.

Answers to "How can we be healthy?" were provided in the 20th century partly by religious and spiritual practices, many of them borrowed from Eastern traditions that had not separated mind and body. Alternative health practices, such as chiropractic, naturopathy, therapeutic massage, herbology, and acupuncture, bridged all four medical concerns but were not accepted in traditional medical circles.

In addition, toward the end of the 20th century, postmodern intellectual trends, theory in physics, global connections with societies that have maintained a more holistic outlook, and neuroscience findings brought into question the idea that mind and body can be treated as separate. Part of what has called forth coaching, with its whole-person approach, is this understanding of the necessary interaction of mind and body.

At the same time, formerly faraway places on the planet are becoming effectively closer. As Magner (1992) points out, in the history of medicine, there exist extremes of, on one hand, caring *for* the patient as a means of providing care *to* the patient and, on the other, assuming that following the gospel of specific etiology and understanding the underlying cause and mechanism of a specific disease will enable us to control it.

> This view fails to take into account the complex social, ethical, economic, and geopolitical aspects of disease in a world drawn closer together by modern communications and transportation while simultaneously being torn apart by vast and growing differences between wealth and poverty. (p. xi)

Coaching is called to fill a gap that demands both a holistic and caring approach to clients and a very broad knowledge and experience base, especially when it comes to helping people change. Knowledge from health practices help coaches fill that gap.

PHYSIOLOGY

Physiology is the study of how living biological organisms function. Physiology differs from anatomy, which is the study of the form or structure of an organism. However, function and structure are clearly integrated.

Physiology has been intensely researched in Western societies since 17th century anatomist William Harvey (1578–1657) described blood circulation. It is a highly developed discipline with many applications including nutrition, exercise, and medicine.

Physiology provides a link between coaching and human health and well-being. Clients want coaches to help them excel in their lives and push their limits. Individuals who want to reach their potential need to be as physically healthy as possible so they can push their limits without compromising their health. A balanced diet, the right exercise program, enough sleep, and a manageable level of stress improve health and life expectancy.

Coaches who lack health training should not provide health-related advice. Instead, they may help clients identify their own goals and values for improved health, then help them find information about and live according to those goals. Keep in mind that many coaching clients are high achievers who may ignore the needs of their body and thereby undermine their ability to achieve their goals. Often, mindfulness exercises put us in touch with important messages from our body about how to keep healthy.

While coaches typically are not hired to improve clients' diet or sleep patterns, issues such as these often come up in coaching. Coaches should therefore understand the basics of health and well-being and be willing to refer clients to health practitioners when issues beyond the coach's expertise are identified.

Example: "How to Get It Together"

Consider the case of Lois, a high-level executive who could not focus on what she wanted. "I'm having a really lousy day. Nothing's working. I can't seem to figure out how to get it together." Her coach listened to her description of a hectic workweek that included a heavy travel schedule, not enough sleep, and the fact that she was on a 1,200-calorie-a-day diet.

"Do you see any connections between your lack of sleep and restricted diet on one hand and your fatigue and confusion on the other?" the coach asked.

The ensuing conversation led to Lois's commitment to build better physical self-care into her schedule.

The healthcare industry is massive, and the media often report research findings that are compelling but less than complete, particularly regarding diet and nutrition. Rather than being caught up in momentary fads, it is important that the coach focus on basic concepts that are tried and true. Keep in mind that even concepts that are statistically "proven" work differently for each individual ("no person is the same"), and a coach can help a client become aware of how a particular diet or exercise pattern works *for that person.*

Diet and Nutrition

A new "breakthrough finding" about diet and nutrition is reported almost every week in the media. Often these findings contradict one another. However, some basics do seem to stay the same. For example, a well-balanced diet that includes a variety of whole foods, especially fruits, vegetables, fiber, and quality protein, strengthens our minds and bodies and keeps our energy levels high. Avoiding sugary, highly processed and deep fried foods is also advised. As the Mayo Clinic literature (2006) states: "Research has shown and clinical experience has confirmed that what you eat directly affects your health" (p. 47).

A healthful diet can provide protection from chronic diseases such as cardiovascular, diabetes, and cancer: "The American Cancer Society and the American Institute for Cancer Research agree that diet contributes significantly to various types of cancer—30 percent to 40 percent of cancers are directly linked to dietary choices" (Mayo Clinic, 2006, p. 5).

Reduced food intake has a profound impact on mental abilities. One British study reported in *The New York Times* (O'Connor, 2006) examined 44 healthy adults who fasted overnight. Those who ate nothing in the morning scored lowest on memory tests and experienced the highest levels of fatigue four hours after waking.

A more extreme study conducted in the 1930s found that the psychological impact of hunger is profound and long-lasting (Keys et al., 1950). Forty adult male volunteers, who had been screened for exceptional physical and psychological health, were subjected to six months of semi starvation. During the study, four dropped out because they could not tolerate the hunger, three developed binge-eating, two began to steal food, one developed depression, and two were admitted to hospital with symptoms of psychosis. A follow-up study done 50 years later found that abnormal eating behaviors and food-related concerns persisted in all 25 volunteers who agreed to be interviewed (Crow & Eckert, 2000).

Sharing a healthy meal with friends and family not only provides nutritious benefits, it is a pleasure that traditional cultures cherish. A shared meal provides connection, which leads to enjoyment and an increased sense of well-being. Research has shown that social isolation can be almost twice as dangerous to health as smoking (Goleman, 1995).

Many coaching clients realize that their diet is inadequate for their needs. They may be seeking to gain more day-to-day energy or wanting to lose weight. In either case, it is advisable for coaches to refer their clients to dieticians. Encouraging clients to seek professional help in any health-related area is a wise principle to follow.

While encouraging clients to seek professional help, coaches can also provide these valuable health-related supports:

- Accountability—that is, having someone to report to
- Pacing—Helping clients take small steps and acknowledging their progress as they do so.

Water

Almost 80% of the human body is water, and we are constantly losing or excreting moisture. It is crucial that we drink enough to function properly. Dehydration can contribute to medical problems, including kidney stones, headaches, fatigue, and poor concentration. However, according to a recent review of research by doctors at the Renal, Electrolyte, and Hypertension Division of the University of Pennsylvania (Negoianu & Goldfarb, 2008), there is little support for claims of improved kidney and other organ function, reduced toxicity, management of obesity, prevention of headaches, and better skin tone from drinking water beyond what is guided by thirst. Clearly, under circumstances of extreme heat or exercise, proper hydration is a concern. But the idea that everyone must drink eight glasses of 8 ounces of liquid each day seems to be an urban myth.

Water plays an important role in how our bodies function. It "regulates body temperature, carries nutrients and oxygen to cells via the blood stream and helps carry away waste. Water also helps cushion joints and protects organs and tissues" (Mayo Clinic, 2006, p. 49 n.). Although "we obtain water through food, it is important to drink enough water or other liquids to keep our bodies functioning optimally" (Beers, 2004, pp. 927–929 n.).

Fortunately, our bodies have evolved so that we feel thirsty when we need water. However, it is possible to override or disregard that bodily signal, especially if we are concentrating on a goal or task. Coaches can help clients identify ways to make drinking enough water easier, or more "automatic." For example, keeping a jug of water and a glass in the office or keeping a cup of herbal tea on the desk can prevent dehydration and make it easier to respond to thirst without interrupting a task.

Exercise

Exercise is part of any healthy lifestyle and can do wonders for our quality of life and well-being. Exercise can help us live longer, give us more energy, delay the effects of aging, help us sleep better, and even help combat depression. A German study (United Press International, 2001) reported that half of patients suffering from long-term depression felt substantial improvement after a 10-day exercise program. This compares well with the 50% improvement for patients treated with drugs

(Vedantam, 2006). Duke University researchers found that the anti-depressive effects of exercise are long-lasting, preventing the return of depression for clients who have suffered for years (Duke University Medical Center, 2000). Exercise helps strengthen the immune system and is recommended to prevent or treat cardiovascular disease, high blood pressure, obesity, diabetes, and osteoporosis.

Exercise is also linked to enhanced psychological well-being, greater self-confidence, and healthier self-esteem. Exercise releases mood-elevating hormones called endorphins, which help us to relax and feel better. Exercise also reduces stress. In *The User's Guide to the Brain* (2003), John Ratey explores the finding that exercise helps our thoughts organize themselves. He says that the brain utilizes similar circuits for organizing thoughts as it does for moving, so physical movement can help us solve problems. Have you ever been stuck on a problem and had the solution pop into your head after you gave up and went for a walk?

Ideally, one should engage in some form of physical activity that elevates heart rate for at least 30 to 60 minutes each day. Walking, jogging, cycling, swimming, dancing, hiking, yoga, climbing stairs, gardening, or even doing chores such as cleaning and raking are some examples of recommended physical exercise.

Exercise can be a daunting assignment for many clients; for them, exercising just once or twice a week might be a breakthrough. It is important for a coach to encourage small steps in the knowledge that regular exercise takes effort and requires the development of habitual behaviors, ones that we engage in without having to tax our limited ability to pay attention. Helping our clients build on small gains is the essence of developing good habits.

Some clients find it is helpful to link their interest in improved health with their desire for more social contact. Exercising with a friend increases social interactions, making it more likely we will turn up for those early-morning runs. Taking up a team sport can provide even greater benefits. Our connectedness with others has a direct link to wellness, as we explain later in this book.

More to the point for a book on the brain, exercise helps build new brain cells. Salk Institute neuroscientist Fred Gage and his colleagues reported in 1998 that exercise contributes to the generation of new neurons in mice (Kempermann, Kuhn, & Gage, 1997). Subsequently, other researchers have confirmed that this finding applies to humans (Olson, Eadie, Ernst, & Christie, 2006). Coaches and their clients would be wise to take these results as seriously as the scientists do. As Columbia University neurologist Scott Small said, "I constantly get asked at cocktail parties what someone can do to protect their mental functioning. I tell them, 'Put down that glass and go for a run'" (Reynolds, 2007).

Sleep

While scientists are not exactly sure why we need sleep, it is well established that a lack of sleep has a significant impact on the human mind and body. Think about the last time you missed a significant amount of sleep. Were you able to think clearly? Were you able to perform at your best, physically and mentally? Numerous scientific studies show that lack of sleep inhibits performance.

According to Dr. James B. Maas (2001), "[Sleep] restores, rejuvenates, and energizes the body and the brain. . . . [Sleep] has profound effects . . . in terms of alertness, energy, mood, body weight, perception, memory, thinking, reaction time, productivity, performance, communication skills, creativity, safety, and good health" (pp. 6–7 n.).

Not only does sleep help our nervous system perform properly; some experts even link a good night's sleep to improved brain functioning because it gives our neurons a chance to rest and rejuvenate, which leads to optimal emotional, social, and physical functioning during awake hours (Marshall & Born, 2007). Sleep also provides the opportunity for our brains to consolidate new learning, as found by one study linking sleep to "restructuring new memory representations" which in turn "facilitates extraction of explicit knowledge and insightful behaviour" (Wagner et al., 2004, p. 355).

A lack of sleep can affect our mood, impair our memory, inhibit our physical performance, and decrease our ability to think clearly. Sleep is, in fact, so essential that a lack of sleep can kill a human being faster than a lack of food. Long-term studies of thousands of subjects indicate that lower mortality is associated with an average of seven hours of sleep per night (Hassed, 2008).

Although the average for adults is 7 to 8 hours per night of quality sleep, individuals require different amounts of sleep, and the amount needed also tends to vary throughout life. Albert Einstein required 10 hours of sleep a night to function well; President Coolidge required 11; President Clinton needed only 6; and Martha Stewart needs 4 to 5 (Maas, 2001, p. 3).

It is very common for clients to skimp on sleep or for their sleep quality to be poor. Millions of North Americans suffer from a lack of sleep. Travel, long hours of work, inactivity, and stress can all have an impact on sleep. "Sleep quality" is a function of the time we spend in different stages of sleep and the amount of time we spend sleeping without interruption. Older people may need 7 to 8 hours, with one period of deep sleep early in the night. After this period, they may wake easily and have trouble getting back to sleep. Therefore, if sleep is an issue in coaching, it is important to talk about how long, how well, and when the client sleeps.

Coaches can find useful resources about how to improve sleep in books and on the Internet. (See, e.g., Mercola, 2008.)

In summary, performance is not optimal if we skimp on sleep. Coaches can help clients identify their sleep needs and design their lives to obtain the right quality and quantity of sleep.

Balance

The term "homeostasis" is applied to the tendency of living organisms to maintain equilibrium. This process can be seen in the metabolism of a cell or physical body, and it has also been applied to group, social, and individual biological and psychological processes.

The human body is constantly working to maintain equilibrium in many different systems. Regardless of external temperature or climate, our internal temperature remains constant. Whether lying, standing, walking, or running, the healthy person's blood pressure and heart rate are continually adjusted to maintain optimal functions. In addition, the quantity of minerals and electrolytes in our bloodstreams is continually monitored and adjusted.

Using an elaborate and complex feedback system, the body attempts to balance the need to respond to changing circumstances with the need to maintain stability. The tension between change and stability creates mental and physical rhythms or patterns that repeat in various forms.

These patterns can be observed if we pay attention to them. There is the rapid rhythm of our heart beating and the slower rhythm of our breathing. There are rhythms of exertion and rest, of hunger and digestion. There are "ultradian" (meaning more than once a day) rhythms of approximately 90 minutes that alternate between an active focus on external stimuli and a more passive, internal focus on one's own thoughts and feelings (Rossi, 1991). These 90-minute rhythms also apply to sleep cycles. Coaches learn to be sensitive to the increases and decreases in energy that occur during client sessions.

There are longer rhythms of sleeping and waking, of work versus holidays, and of concentrating on a project or career before retirement. During the waking day, some people exhibit a pattern of being better able to focus on work first thing in the morning, others in the evening. Many people work harder when they are younger and slow down as they age. A big expenditure of energy on a project usually requires some downtime afterward in order to bring various systems into balance. An intense workweek may require a deeply quiet weekend to reduce demands and let the mind recover.

It is only when we notice a pattern that we are able to interact with it consciously. Noticing that we do our best work at the start of the day or year or season might allow us to schedule a writing project for this time rather than later. Noticing that we think more clearly after exercise can help us to improve output by scheduling demanding work more appropriately.

Research shows that the brain makes unexpected connections, "aha!" moments, when we take a break from a problem to do other things (see Rock, 2006). Taking this into account, we may be more effective if we work on a difficult mental task for 45 minutes of each hour and do something else for the other 15.

Building on a recurring theme in this chapter, balance is not only about taking time off work. Balance can be achieved by noticing how we operate and reorganizing our efforts to maximize output. Many good books are available to help identify more effective habits (e.g., D. Allen, 2001). They cover issues such as when to schedule difficult work, how to organize and tackle complex projects, how not to spend all day on e-mail, and so forth.

The human brain has a significantly larger prefrontal cortex than other animals have. This part of the brain is believed to be involved in "executive functions," or the ability to monitor and manage activities. These functions include goal setting, planning, and pattern recognition. From this perspective, having a coach is like adding an extra prefrontal cortex onto your brain. In other words, the coach's brain supports the client's brain to plan, set goals, notice patterns, and better manage overall functioning.

Having use of the coach's brain enables us to step out of the details of everyday experience and observe how we function from a meta-level, or a higher perspective. Being outside the client's individual system, the coach can observe and discern patterns that the client is too close to see.

Mind-Body Connection

Despite popular views to the contrary, science has thoroughly discredited the dualistic view that mind and body are separate and made of different "stuff" (Rose, 2005). When we are preoccupied, stressed, depressed, or consumed with fear or anxiety, our bodies will suffer, and we run the risk of physical ailments (Beers, 2004, p. 7 n.). When we are physically sick, it is difficult to concentrate or think clearly. Our general mood and outlook (optimism or pessimism) also affect our overall health and longevity, and this realization has strengthened the shift away from separating mind and body.

Strong social ties are known to increase health and resilience. Schwartzer and Leppin (1992) analyzed 80 studies that together included over 70,000 subjects. They found that as social support and quality of social connections increase, incidents of illness decrease and life expectancy improves.

In a related study, Gatchel and his colleagues (Gatchel, Polantin, & Mayer, 1995) found that in 91% of the cases, psychological factors predicted which back pain patients would recover from an injury and which would go on to become disabled. Another study found that psychological variables alone predicted delayed recovery in 76% of back pain cases (Burton et al., 1996). Steven Sanders (2000) provides an overview of research on risk factors for disability from back pain that extends these findings.

132

These studies show that our state of mind has a dramatic impact on our physical well-being, which in turn impacts our ability to think, make decisions, and perform at our peak. It is a circular feedback system: an improvement or difficulty in either mind or body affects and is affected by the system as a whole. It has become more and more clear that our minds and bodies, including our brains, are part of a whole system rather than being in separate categories of "stuff," as assumed by dualism. Neuroscience is beginning to uncover the actual mechanisms that link mind and body.

Linking Physiology to Coaching

Coaches should be on the lookout for how clients can improve their performance through nurturing their physical health. Because bodies and minds are dynamically linked, improving the functioning of one tends to improve the functioning of the other.

The human body is a complex system; therefore, a small change can have a big impact.

Encouraging clients to exercise just twice a week or make other health-related changes might dramatically improve their energy and work performance.

Example: "Maybe I'm Just Losing It"

Harold noticed that his memory for details was slipping, and he was sure that he might as well not be in the office between 3 and 5 P.M., for all he was able to accomplish. He was the chief executive officer of a large-market media company and was well respected because of his accomplishments during 30 years in the business. "Maybe I'm just getting old. I've been reading about age-related cognitive decline. Maybe I'm just losing it."

Harold's coach asked about eating and sleeping patterns and discovered that his problems had started about the same time as he and his wife moved into a new condominium. He was not sleeping as well in their new bedroom, and after further discussion it became clear that the early-morning sun flooding into their east-facing windows woke Harold earlier than he was accustomed to. After installing blackout curtains that made the bedroom darker, Harold found he was able to get a full night's rest. Within a few weeks, his memory and performance at work improved dramatically.

Coaches can help clients notice the patterns that their performance reveals. As a result, coaching may involve helping a client:

- *Manage a daily schedule* — for example, planning what time of day to do certain types of work
- *Manage a weekly, monthly, or annual schedule* — for example, setting time for big projects to coincide with high-energy periods
- *Balance work with leisure* — for example, choosing a daily schedule that allows for rest or exercise or taking shorter annual holidays in order to have more three-day weekends during the year
- *Think about longer-term patterns* — for example, taking a longer sabbatical after an intense period of work or planning for retirement

Every individual has unique needs when it comes to the rhythms of life. Coaches can help clients improve their performance by generating awareness of their needs and improving their ability to manage their own rhythms to create a more healthful balance.

While coaches should not provide specific health advice, an awareness of the importance of diet, water intake, exercise, and sleep patterns can be highly beneficial for clients.

Cultivating a referral network of trusted health specialists is advisable, as is developing lists of information resources that can be recommended to clients. However, the most important resource is a client's awareness of his or her own unique body signals.

STRESS

Stress in this context is what causes bodily or mental tension. Stress is related to physical, chemical, or emotional factors and may contribute to illness.

We tend to think of stress as negative. However, Hans Selye (1907–1982), the researcher who brought the term "stress" into our everyday vocabulary, divided stress into two categories: positive stress, called "Eustress," and negative stress, called "Distress" (1956, 1974). Eustress gets us out of bed in the morning, helps us meet deadlines, and reminds us to pay the mortgage. Without this positive stress, we might never even attempt to fulfill our potential. Distress, however, is damaging or pathological.

Coaching clients tend to be high achievers who deal with large amounts of both types of stress. Coaches can help helping clients find their optimal levels of stress. Mihaly Csikszentmihalyi (1991) refers to this as "flow" and says that this enjoyable state occurs when demands are just beyond what people believe they can attain:

> [A] piece of music that is too simple relative to one's listening skills will be boring, while music that is too complex will be frustrating. Enjoyment appears at the boundary between boredom and anxiety, when the challenges are just balanced with the person's capacity to act. (p. 52)

Coaches would do well to inquire about the amount of stress their clients are under and to find out how it is being dealt with. Too much stress, especially negative stress over a long period of time, is associated with physical and mental health problems, such as high blood pressure, heart disease, shortness of breath, tightened muscles, headaches, body aches, anxiety, and depression. Suzanne Segerstrom and Gregory Miller (2004) analyzed over 300 empirical studies showing that stress also affects our immune system: If we are experiencing too much stress, we may be more likely to develop a cold, flu, or other virus. Excessive stress can also contribute to allergies and autoimmune diseases.

Coaches should help clients stretch themselves in order to produce more personal growth, but not so much that it leads to undue stress. Prioritizing schedules, learning to say no to activities that do not contribute to overall goals, and including activities like exercising, yoga, and meditation are good ways to help clients manage their stress levels. These and other approaches can prevent stressful challenges from compromising health and well-being.

Boyatzis, Smith, and Blaise (2006) introduced some important links between coaching and stress in the paper "Developing Sustainable Leaders through Coaching and Compassion." They describe the physical, mental, and emotional impact of what they call "power stress," a type of stress that leaders in organizations experience. Power stress results from three major stress inducers:

1. Being seen by others
2. Dealing with ambiguity
3. Having to deliver results under pressure

As Boyatzis and his colleagues put it, "Leader sustainability is adversely affected by the psychological and physiological effects of chronic power stress associated with the performance of the leadership role" (2006, p. 8).

These collaborators also propose that coaching others is one way to reverse, not just halt, the damaging impact of long-term stress. Thus, they go beyond the concept of coaching as just a way to develop leaders, suggesting that "the process of coaching others may actually allow leaders to increase their own sustainability as a result of the physiological effects of experiencing compassion, which can serve as an antidote to stress" (Boyatzis et al., 2006, p. 12).

Linking Stress Theory to Coaching

- When it comes to dealing with stress, the role of the coach is not to be an expert but to encourage clients to develop greater awareness of their patterns and to pay more attention to their needs.
- Once a client has identified stress as a possible source of interference with goals, the coach provides support, accountability, and encouragement for the client to take actions that reduce stress to manageable levels.
- Many helpful resources—books, journals, and the Internet—deal with stress management.
- Many clients are functioning below their potential because of excess stress that can be mitigated with simple practices. Exercising a few times a week with friends might be all it takes to reduce stress significantly.
- Leaders experiencing "power stress" can ameliorate its effects by developing coaching skills and utilizing compassion in coaching others. The recent findings in neuroscience on the importance of social connection support this suggestion.

WELLNESS THEORY

As dualistic assumptions have eroded, holistic medicine has become more popular. Enter the phrase "wellness center" on any Internet search engine, and you will access hundreds of community agencies, hospitals, universities, and medical centers around the world. The Web site for the Wellness Center at Howard Community College in Maryland, states:

> Wellness is a state of optimal well-being. It means achieving balance and harmony in all aspects of your life. Wellness is achieved through the integration of physical, social, emotional, intellectual, spiritual, and environmental health. Wellness is a conscious commitment for continued growth and improvement. (Howard Community College, 2007)

Wellness theory addresses the "health promotion" aspect of Sigerist's (1951) four goals of medicine, discussed earlier in the chapter. Today, wellness theory is applied in many health professions, including chiropractic and naturopathy. It has also become a field of study within social work, with special relevance to the needs of people living with disabilities. Wellness theory also provides a holistic approach to promoting well-being within corporations and communities.

Wellness theory encompasses the biological, psychological, social, and spiritual aspects of human functioning. It looks at the relationships among individuals and their families, communities, physical environment, and society. It is studied by social workers, sociologists, social psychologists, and medical and alternative health workers, all with the goal of improving health and well-being at all levels of society.

Wellness theory is strongly linked with positive psychology, which is examined in chapter 11 as one of the pillars of modern coaching. In both cases, the aim is to improve quality of life, going beyond the task of treating disease and dysfunction to the whole system rather than focusing on isolated aspects of the system.

Wellness practice includes nutrition, physical exercise, mental imagery, relaxation and stress management techniques, and even letter writing and journaling. Finding wellness experts can be difficult because formal research on wellness is limited and much of what passes for research is anecdotal. Part of the problem is the interdisciplinary nature of the field; different experts may be unfamiliar with one another's research results and specialized language. Another problem is the bias toward funding research only on diseases that can be profitably treated with drugs and other medical interventions. A wellness practitioner may have trained as a chiropractor, naturopath, nutritionist, physical trainer, or counselor but practices as part social worker, part therapist, part health practitioner, and part coach.

Many coaching programs use assessments that draw on wellness theory as a base for developing goals and objectives. "Lifestyle assessments" and the "wheel of balance" help clients assess their intellectual, physical, financial, social, and spiritual health in order to identify strengths and areas needing development. Definitive research on the value and use of these assessments is not yet available, but growing interest will likely stimulate more research in wellness, as it has with coaching.

The next list summarizes some common indicators of wellness from a variety of Internet and print sources which the authors have compiled. Although it is neither definitive nor based on research, coaches and their clients may find it useful as an awareness tool:

- Social wellness is indicated when a person . . .
  - relates and connects well with a variety of people.
  - participates in community and social activities.
  - develops and builds lasting friendships.
  - experiences intimacy.
  - cares for others and allows others to care in return.
  - maintains meaningful relationships with family, friends, and coworkers.
  - values diversity and treats others with respect.
  - maintains the same values and beliefs when interacting with a single individual or with a group.
- Emotional wellness is indicated when a person . . .
  - can manage strong emotions.
  - can share feelings and talk about emotional concerns.
  - can say no when appropriate without feeling guilty.
  - feels happy much of the time.
  - has people in life who care and who can be called on when needed.
  - feels good about him- or herself.
  - values time alone.
  - perceives him- or herself as liked and respected by others.
- Intellectual wellness is indicated when a person . . .
  - reads widely.

- enjoys thinking about ideas and discussing them with others.
- is open to new ideas and thinks critically.
- is creative and curious to learn.
- seeks new challenges.
- Environmental wellness is indicated when a person . . .
  - has a conscious relationship with the natural world.
  - is aware of the limits of natural resources.
  - conserves energy (e.g., by shutting off unused lights).
  - recycles paper, cans, and glass as much as possible.
  - avoids polluting the environment.
- Occupational wellness is indicated when a person . . .
  - engages in meaningful work.
  - pursues hobbies/interests/activities that are pleasurable outside of work/academics.
  - can accurately assess his or her strengths and weaknesses on the job.
  - believes he or she has the qualities of a valuable and valued employee.
  - is proceeding toward his or her life goals.
- Spiritual wellness is indicated when a person . . .
  - has dreams and goals.
  - takes time for spiritual growth and exploration.
  - has a life philosophy.
  - takes time to think about the meaning of experiences.
  - has a moral code of right and wrong, and acts accordingly.

In the Introduction, we presented Figure I.3 as a model of optimal human functioning that incorporates discoveries from brain science. We invite you to compare these everyday indicators of wellness with the "Potentiating the Human System" categories supported by brain research.

Linking Wellness Theory to Coaching

- It is assumed that mind and body are connected.
- The client is assumed to know more about his or her situation than the practitioner.
- Practitioners are seen as having important skills, especially the ability to recognize patterns that the client may not see.

- Change occurs when the client alters his or her narrative from despair and helplessness to hope and empowerment.
- The client defines the problem and then client and practitioner collaborate to create the solution.
- Both coaches and wellness practitioners often participate in collaborative teams to enhance solutions.

Resource Section: How to Recognize and Avoid Unsupported Claims of Health Benefits

The mass media use hyperbole to attract readers and customers. Jason Daley wrote an article for *Popular Science* (April, 2007) that investigated the truth behind this newspaper headline: "Are You Drinking Enough Coffee? Get Health Up to Speed." The article implied that scientists recommend drinking coffee to prevent Type 2 diabetes.

Daley looked up the original study and found that the preventive benefit came only after drinking the equivalent of six or seven cups of coffee. Side effects of ingesting this much coffee were not investigated. Taking this example as an illustration, Daley urged readers to rely on common sense: "overdosing on caffeine isn't the best way to lower your diabetes risk" (p. 74).

Skepticism is a skill that coaches need to practice, as our training tends to focus on believing (as in believing in a client's potential) rather than on doubting. Here are four "Skills of the Skeptic" to help you avoid misleading health and science claims:

1. *Read more deeply.* Track down the original scientific or medical report. The Internet is an invaluable resource for such research. If an original article is accessible only via an expensive online journal or database, look elsewhere. Copies may be available in more accessible publications or on the scientist's own Web site or blog.

   Note: In most scientific articles, the first few paragraphs summarize the results and may discuss past research and current controversies on the subject. The middle sections describe the methods and findings in great detail and often are so technical that only highly specialized scientists can understand them. The last section discusses the results and their implications. In order to avoid being overwhelmed by technical details, consider reading only the first and last sections. If you need to decipher the middle sections, you can always consult a local physician or science teacher.

2. *Trust your instincts.* Just because a scientist believes his or her own conclusions, it does not mean that you should. Do not be bamboozled by scientific jargon or the alphabet after a scientist's name.

3. *Check the dosage.* Like the coffee example, think about how much we would have to consume of some "miracle food" to gain any benefit. Scientists often feed laboratory animals excessive amounts of foods or chemical compounds to test the limits of the effects. And there are many other considerations—what else is and is not being eaten or done—that could make all the difference.

4. *Delay action.* Before you throw out your vegetables and stock up on chocolate (after another headline in Daley's article: "Chocolate's Better than Broccoli"), remember that a single health claim is just that—one claim that must be retested and proven. Do what wise scientists do: Wait for the evidence to accumulate. By the way, the chocolate used in the chocolate research was not the garden-variety chocolate most of us eat. And there is no evidence that the flavonoids in chocolate are better at protecting our health than flavonoids found in other foods. High-cocoa-content dark chocolate may be beneficial in small amounts, but it cannot replace whole foods.

HEALTH PRACTICES AS BEDROCK FOR COACHING

Ambitious individuals can become so focused on their end goal that they ignore their well-being. They may skimp on the nutrition, sleep, exercise, and downtime they need to function best. Over time, such ill treatment can interfere with achieving the end goal.

Good coaches recognize that every individual is unique, with her or his own requirements for achieving maximum performance. One client might prefer to work 80-hour weeks, eight months a year, and take the other four months off for vacation or travel. Another might prefer to work 30 hours a week, most of the year, and take shorter vacations once a quarter. The important thing is to ask clients the right questions, without being attached to what answers might come, to get a sense of what works for specific clients, what sustains them, and what keeps their energy and motivation levels high.

Good coaches help their clients see their patterns and rhythms and identify their own needs. Unmet needs can create problems, such as poor health, mood swings, lack of focus, or other distractions, that prevent clients from achieving their goals. When clients become more aware of how well they are caring for themselves, they are more likely to achieve their ambitions without sacrificing their health.

Coaches help clients focus on their whole life—not just on their jobs or finances, but on every area of their life. Areas that are out of balance may show up as health issues. But people who are rewarded for being single-mindedly goal-oriented may ignore their body's signals. Even becoming ill or being threatened with ill health may not be enough to motivate them to change, as Alan Deutschman (2006) and many smokers have discovered. Fortunately, coaches have resources that reach beyond facts, fear, and force to motivate change. We now turn to pillars that optimize performance.

CHAPTER 5

Pillar — Optimizing Performance

Linda's mother spent most of her life working in the health industry, so she knew the facts about smoking. She had also seen her husband die from smoking-related complications, and it was clear she feared a similar fate. Her family hid her cigarettes and lighter, but she would replace them and keep on smoking. They all knew there was no way to force her to stop until she literally couldn't draw enough breath to inhale a cigarette. She died not long after.

All the advances of medicine and its willingness to incorporate non-traditional approaches have not solved the problem of compliance. Not the government, public health officials, alternative health practitioners, or licensed medical practitioners know how to overcome resistance to keeping ourselves healthy. Even the threat of death is not enough to motivate many of us to do what we are told we must. Alan Deutschman (2006) says chances are only 1 in 9 that we will make a significant change, even when we are told our life's at stake, as in Linda's mother's case. Deutschman says this is because the three techniques usually relied upon to create change — facts, fear, and force — do not work. He has taken on the mission of replacing these with three approaches that work better: relate, repeat, reframe. Not surprisingly, these are built into the coach approach. They are part of the shift from a top-down control approach to a more systemic understanding of what triggers a person's own motivation to change.

Beyond being healthy, people want to know how to get better at doing the things they value most. These concerns link with the previous theme of "dynamic stability" in systems theory. Ongoing psychological change can be compared to the metaphor of "flow" as a flexible river between banks of rigidity on one side and chaos on the other. Flow indicates a balance between unyielding sameness experienced as boredom on one hand and constant, overwhelmingly chaotic upheaval on the other.

The two extremes represent the limits of desirable change, of dynamic stability that is part of our emerging definition of mental and physical wellness.

This idea of flow is one that will recur in this and chapters to come. High-performance athletes speak of flow, as an indication of peak performance. Page (2005) suggests that flow is the subjective experience of "expertising." In all these cases, dynamic stability or flow has to do with changing in ways we desire. Change is not always desirable, as we discover in the case of individual illness or aging or societal and organizational upheaval.

- How can we achieve the changes we want without changing the things we want to keep?
- Why are some changes so difficult while others happen in spite of our efforts to stop them?
- How can we deal with the fact that change is inevitable?
- How is change related to loss?
- Can we predict the stages of change?
- Does change start with behavior or with feelings or with thought?
- What context or conditions are most conducive to positive change?

Change is at the heart of coaching. Coaches fall in the category of human change agents or facilitators. In the presence of a coach, change may happen faster or more easily or be more desirable. Knowledge of change can help coaches fulfill this potential. We explore these questions in the sections to come:

- Sports psychology
- Change theory
- Models of change
- Optimizing performance as a coaching pillar

SPORTS PSYCHOLOGY

Sports psychology was accepted as a subdiscipline of psychology by the American Psychological Association (APA) in 1986. Like coaching, sports psychology has yet to establish itself in the academic world, having few doctoral-level programs. The APA allows professionals to call themselves sports psychologists based on experience and related professional training rather than on any specific academic degree.

Kinesiology is a related field that developed out of medicine and physical education and encompasses human anatomy, physiology, biomechanics, exercise physiology, exercise psychology, and the sociology, history, and philosophy of sport. Most of the research that informs sports coaching is generated by these disciplines.

There are hundreds of sports coaching books on the market, with the work of Timothy Gallwey being prominent. Gallwey's books include *The Inner Game of Golf* (1981), *The Inner Game of Tennis* (1987), and *The Inner Game of Skiing* (1997). They demonstrate the power of coaching more than they teach the novice how to acquire new skills in sports.

Gallwey's more recent *Inner Game of Work* (2001) shows how coaching skills can be applied to the occupational world. Gallwey coaches people to be successful by suggesting that they simplify their thinking and believe in themselves. He developed the formula $p = P - I$, meaning performance equals potential less any interference.

The idea that our minds can interfere to limit our performance is central to sports psychology. Finding the right mental zone when under pressure requires removing mental distractions. The neuroscience behind this principle is that each neuron has a limited capacity for electrical signals (about 2,000 per second) so that the brain can be literally flooded by internally generated signals, making it harder to process external information.

The Foundations of Sport and Exercise Psychology by Schoenfeld and colleagues (2003) examines the field of sports psychology in some detail and offers excellent resources for coaches of all types.

Three central concepts from sports psychology that are relevant to coaching include:

1. Goal setting
2. Visualization
3. Achieving the zone—the right state of mind for peak performance

A brief summary of each concept follows, along with some key findings.

Goal Setting

Research has shown that people who set goals:

- Perform better
- Exhibit increased self-confidence
- Are happier with their performance
- Suffer less stress and anxiety

There is substantial research on why and how goal setting works, the right types of goals to set, and how to set them. The *Coaching Science Abstracts* Web site developed by Brent Rushall (1996) is an excellent resource. He reports research indicating that effective goals are:

- Specific so action can be targeted
- Time-defined rather than stretching vaguely into the future
- Measurable to provide for clear evaluation of success
- Challenging enough to provide stretch but not so challenging as to induce distress

Visualization

Research in sports psychology and other fields has verified that imagining an experience in detail can dramatically affect performance. This principle is used to mentally prepare Olympic athletes, racecar drivers, jet pilots, parachutists, and participants in other high-risk activities. Visualization helps to resolve fears. For example, a salesperson who fears rejection can visualize various ways to manage a disgruntled client.

The science behind visualization is this: The pathways in the brain that we use to undertake an activity—for example, throwing a basketball into a hoop—are the same pathways used when we merely picture this activity. In both instances, the visual cortex—the part of the brain that sees—is activated. Because use of any circuit strengthens that circuit, rehearsing a performance in the imagination can prepare mental circuits in ways similar to the real performance.

However, effective visualization must be correct, precise, and repeated.

- *Correct.* Visualizing an activity incorrectly will only reinforce the incorrect behavior.
- *Precise.* The more vivid and detailed the visualization, the more connections are created in the brain. Precise visualization has become a standard tool in training Olympic athletes.
- *Repeated.* Visualization is most effective when it is done in short segments over time. It is more effective to practice visualizing delivering a great speech for 3 minutes every day for 5 days rather than practicing for 20 minutes in 1 day.

The Zone

Athletes often describe peak performance as occurring in an ideal mental zone. Finding this zone is a central goal of sports psychology, as it encompasses an attitude of engagement in the task at hand. It is common knowledge that attitude plays a tremendous role in sports and in many other endeavors. Sports psychology offers helpful advice for maintaining the right attitude when facing challenging situations—that is, when the stakes are high and the pressure is on. For many people in the workplace, and certainly for many coaching clients, this describes their day-to-day existence. Some principles that relate to both sports and coaching include:

- Finding flow
- Controlling our thoughts
- Preperformance strategies

FINDING FLOW   The concept of flow (Csikszentmihalyi, 1991; Page, 2005) was mentioned earlier in this chapter and elsewhere in this book. Flow can be achieved by creating enough challenge to demand complete attention to the task at hand, but not so much challenge that the individual becomes overwhelmed and unable to proceed. Identifying goals that provide the right amount of stretch is a task for all coaches.

CONTROLLING OUR THOUGHTS   Brain studies of top athletes show that, compared to amateurs, professionals use minimal mental resources when performing a complex activity. There are two aspects to this phenomenon:

1. Through repetition, they have hardwired an activity so that it has become automatic and therefore requires less conscious effort to execute.
2. They have developed the discipline to keep out unwanted thoughts and remain focused on the task at hand. The ability to prevent fears, doubts, and distractions from getting in the way of performance is essential for peak performance. There is a similarity between this capacity and the results of mindfulness practices as discussed in chapter 3.

PREPERFORMANCE STRATEGIES   Top athletes develop preperformance rituals to help them establish an optimal state of mind and engage in flow. Examples include specific warm-up exercises, mental imagery, or even dressing in a certain order. These rituals serve to quiet the mind and help it focus.

Linking Sports Psychology to Coaching

Professional coaches can learn a good deal from the research and techniques of sports coaching, a field that, like coaching, is dedicated to improving performance. Utilizing the power of high-quality goals, visualization and mental preparedness can make a difference to any client.

In some ways, coaching a top executive is similar to coaching a top athlete. In *The Psychology of Executive Coaching*, Bruce Peltier (2001) summarizes the similarities between coaching athletes and coaching executives. Both types of coaches are exhorted to:

- Take the high road—create honest relationships and value integrity.
- Establish clear working contracts.
- Focus on the fundamentals, even with peak performers.
- Treat each client as unique.
- Utilize audio and video feedback techniques.
- Start with a plan, but do not let your plan get in the way. Be ready to adjust.

CHANGE THEORY

There is a common misconception that human prehistory was a time of stability, with changes coming about only very gradually. Early anthropologists, themselves caught up in the Industrial Revolution and the political upheavals that accompanied the ascendance of capitalism, contrasted their current experience with the societies of indigenous peoples who were portrayed as living in idyllic, unchanging paradises. Robert Redfield wrote *The Primitive World and Its Transformations* (1953) to dispel this notion. Change, sometimes dramatic change, has always been part of human experience, and not all of it has been triggered by climate or other environmental events.

We have discussed basic principles of change that hold true at different levels as a part of systems theory. Here we focus on information about barriers to change that create conflict with new initiatives, especially in

---

HISTORICAL INTERLUDE

In European history, the Middle Ages are also thought of as centuries where nothing happened, sandwiched between the dynamic periods of Classical Greece and Rome on one hand and the Enlightenment on the other. This, too, is mistaken, as it was the accumulation of technological and cultural changes, along with the introduction of what had been ongoing scientific developments in the Middle East and Asia, that made the Enlightenment possible.

Post-Enlightenment philosopher Auguste Comte (1798–1857) developed a three-stage conception of social evolution, starting with "Theology," or belief in spirits and gods and eventually in a single God; proceeding through "Metaphysics," or abstract philosophy; and culminating in "Positivism," or a scientific understanding of the world. His goal of arriving at social practices that are based on science was influential in expanding the reach of the mechanistic paradigm into the human sciences. Herbert Spencer (1820–1903) was stimulated by Charles Darwin's description of evolution to apply this biological concept to human mind and society. It was Spencer, not Darwin, who coined the term "survival of the fittest."

In his efforts to understand the inner workings of the human psyche, Sigmund Freud (1856–1939) utilized the dominant metaphor of technology

(Continued)

to represent psychological processes (1995). To summarize, the machine metaphor of the steam engine represents the pressure of the unconscious, held in check by the cylinders of civilized forces, the power of which may be transmitted toward socially acceptable ends by an effective clutch, the ego.

One political principle at both the social and the individual level is that whether one promotes or opposes change depends on whether that change is perceived to result in a gain or a loss. For Karl Marx (1818–1883), this principle showed itself as class interest—that the ruling class had most to gain from preventing change, while the working class had most to gain from a revolutionary change that put the majority in power. Whether one agrees with Marx's unqualified championing of the latter or not, his analysis of the dynamics of power in capitalist organizations certainly informs the work of coaches in organizations.

Max Weber (1864–1920), a major figure in the history of sociology, developed his theory of bureaucracy as a corrective to Marx's emphasis on revolutionary change. Bureaucratic tendencies may be seen, at their base, as ways of slowing down and introducing change as a rationalized process that ultimately maintains existing power relations. After the transformation of the Russian Revolution in 1917 threatened (or promised, depending on one's class interest) systemic change throughout the capitalist world, Joseph Stalin's counterrevolution utilized bureaucratic means as part of establishing and maintaining the power of a new ruling class.

In North America, the biological metaphor of homeostasis was applied to social change, accompanied by the assumption that a conflict-free society was a healthy society. This application reached its apex with functionalism in American sociology at mid-20th century. Talcott Parsons (1902–1979) developed a paradigm to aid in describing both simple and complex societies at the "macro" level (1968). The goal of removing conflict from human interaction was brought into question by the turmoil of the 1960s and the introduction of postmodern analysis that revealed whose interests were being served by such prescriptions.

In fact, change does not occur without conflict. As we shall see, the very process of change itself arouses powerful emotions for an individual. The systemic paradigm allows for dialectical clashes of seeming opposites. Current research guided by that paradigm has shown that, however useful a metaphor from biology may be in revealing a partial truth, change cannot fully be understood at one level (molecular, chemical, biological, individual, social) by applying models from another.

organizations. We present models that can help coaches facilitate changes that a client desires.

Why Is Change So Hard?

In the last few years, scientists from a range of fields, including neuroscience, sociology, and management, have confirmed what many of us know all too well: Change is hard. This is as true for unintended change as it is for those things we are trying to change. Change is also delicate and fragile, chaotic and complex. Some people think of coaches as midwives, helping people through the difficult and often painful process of change. If indeed coaches are one of many types of "psychosocial change agents," as proposed by David Orlinsky (2007), it is important for us to understand why change is so difficult.

One major reason is the homeostatic tendency of complex systems such as human minds and organizations to balance movement in one direction with compensatory movement in the opposite direction. Other reasons are to be found in discoveries from psychology and from neuroscience.

Cognitive Dissonance

Cognitive dissonance is a concept first described by American social psychologist Leon Festinger (1919–1989). Festinger noticed that measures of anxiety increased when people were asked to behave in ways that were contrary to their beliefs. When they modified their beliefs to be more in line with their behavior, the anxiety abated (1957). Extensive follow-up research has explained this phenomenon as an aspect of motivation: Dissonance produces anxiety that moves us to change. On another level, cognitive dissonance may be seen as the tendency of parts of a complex system to cohere or influence one another.

Bruce Peltier (2001) describes the link between the theory of cognitive dissonance and why individuals resist change. Individuals are comfortable when their thoughts, feelings, and behaviors are consistent, and they are uncomfortable when they are in conflict (dissonant). Changing often means admitting that our past behavior was wrong or in some way making a break from the past. Cognitive dissonance suggests that admitting we were wrong triggers anxiety from the inconsistency between past behavior and current beliefs about it. In fact, for some individuals whose core belief is "I must always be right," it may be more important to be "right" than to be happy or accepted by one's colleagues.

Example: "I'm Sure I Was Right Before"

In his annual 360 assessment, Fred was presented with a challenge to change his onboarding process for new hires. His coach probes Fred's resistance, and the two discover a thinking pattern that is not limited to how Fred relates to new employees:

"If I admit that I need to change, I'd have to admit I was wrong before. I don't like to be in the wrong. In fact, I'm sure I was right before." [Notice the adjustment that gets rid of dissonance.] "Therefore, I'm not going to change."

When Fred became aware of his tendency to adjust his beliefs to fit his desire to be right, he redefined what it meant to "be right" according to the perspective of cognitive dissonance. He decided it was wrong to allow himself to be controlled by such a pattern, however "right" it might feel in the moment. In this case, a theoretical understanding of cognitive dissonance helped Fred free himself from an unconscious imperative.

Questioning and Thinking

As a psychotherapist, Marilee Goldberg (1998) in *The Art of the Question: A Guide to Short-Term Question-Centered Therapy*, described thinking as in internal question-and-answer phenomenon. She considers questions as virtually programming thoughts, feelings, behaviors, and outcomes, even though people typically are not aware of their internal questions or of the profound power they exert in shaping and directing their experiences and lives. By changing those questions, one can set in motion a different process leading to a different result.

In 2004, now as Marilee Adams, she integrated her question-based theory of change into a business fable, *Change Your Questions, Change Your Life: 7 Powerful Tools for Life and Work*, to illustrate the process she had discovered. Adams noticed that change agents such as coaches, organizational development consultants, human relations professionals, and mediators have been as responsive to her theory of change as psychotherapists.

From a brain perspective, it is not surprising that our inner questions and internal conversations frame and impact how we perceive the world and therefore how we act in that subjective reality. We noted in chapter 3 that our default mental process is to engage in an inner narrative, especially involving posing questions and seeking answers about our social environment. This sets up expectations which, we will learn in chapter 6, orient our senses to notice and process information matching the expectations we set or inner questions we ask. We act on what we notice. Even what we see as a possibility for action is influenced by our mindset or state of mind. Thus, becoming conscious of and changing our self-questioning is a powerful way to take control of changing our behavior.

The Brain's Error Detection Function

Our brains have functions to detect changes in the environment and to send strong signals to alert us to anything unusual. These error detection signals are generated by a part of the brain called the orbital cortex (located right over the eyeballs, or orbits) that is closely connected to the brain's fear circuitry in a structure called the amygdala. These two areas compete with and direct brain resources away from the prefrontal region that promotes and supports higher intellectual functions. As a result of error detection and amygdala activation, we act more emotionally and more impulsively: Our animal instincts start to "take over."

When our error detection machinery goes into overdrive, we end up with the problem we mentioned earlier: obsessive-compulsive disorder (OCD). Our brain sends a constant, incorrect message that something is wrong, so we keep trying to fix what we *think* is the source of the problem (out there), but because it is the (internal) message itself that is incorrect, the problem never gets fixed by what we keep doing.

Even for people without OCD, trying to change a routine behavior triggers messages in our brain that something is not right. These messages are designed to demand our attention, and they can readily overpower rational thoughts. But, as we have mentioned, psychiatrist Jeffrey Schwartz (Schwartz & Begley, 2002) found that even the extremely resistant disorder of OCD could be changed by the application of what he calls "mental force," one aspect of which is "veto power," which we will explain in detail in chapter 6.

The Tendency to "Hardwire" Habitual Activities

Brain physiology provides another key to why change is hard. A set of deep structures located near the brain's core, called the basal ganglia, functions exceedingly well without conscious thought, as long as what we are doing is a habitual, routine activity. In contrast, our working memory, based in the prefrontal cortex and used for learning new activities, has quite limited resources. This area fatigues much more easily than the automatic pilot basal ganglia. It requires more energy, and it is able to hold only a limited number of elements "in mind" at one time.

We are fortunate that practice results in repeated activities being taken on by deeper structures that are more efficient and leave our working memory free to deal with novel happenings. For instance, after just a few months of learning to drive a car, we begin to do it without thinking. Once that happens, changing to drive on the other side of the road requires full conscious attention. It does not feel natural. Many people who swap continents prefer never to have to undergo this experience.

Most of what we do every day is habitual, including how we get out of bed, shower and dress, plan our day, get to work, and deal with challenges. Trying to change any of this takes a lot more energy, in the form of attention, than many people are willing to invest. Just as we prefer not to learn to drive on the other side of the road, we do what we can to avoid change in many situations.

There are more explanations and models for how and why change is challenging. Much of this book is about how to make change easier. The previous points are just some of the reasons that change is harder than is generally understood. We have been led to believe by the behaviorist view that people will change if they are given the right incentives. This may be the case with animals and children in relation to basic behaviors, but when it comes to creating change in high-functioning adults, there is far more resistance and complexity than can be addressed simply through a carrot-or-stick approach. There are physiological forces that resist change. Even folding our arms the other way—with the opposite forearm on top—triggers discomfort that signals us to return to the "right" way of doing things.

Linking Theories of Change to Coaching

Rather than being judgmental of ourselves or others for failing to change, which only serves to further stimulate the error response, we can normalize the difficulty of change. Even when we are willing to change, our brain is triggered to be on guard when changes are introduced. One reason mindfulness practices are useful to coaches is that they help us avoid judgment and be patient as clients learn to identify and calm their reactions to change.

MODELS OF CHANGE

Whereas change is hard, it is also unavoidable. Not only that, thousands of self-help messages suggest that we should embrace change and consciously create or guide it toward the goals we set rather than allowing it to guide us passively. In this section, we explore several major change models that developed as part of a broad self-help movement over the last century, looking briefly at how these models can help a coach support change processes:

- Kurt Lewin's three-step process of change
- Elizabeth Kübler-Ross's stage theory
- James Prochaska's transtheoretical model
- William Bridges's three processes of transition
- W. C. Howell's four phases of learning
- John Kotter's eight steps to change
- Peter Senge's systems approach
- Richard Boyatzis's action-reflection cycle

These models provide options to support clients through change in any given situation.

All change models have two things in common:

1. They help coaches put language to the undistinguished emotional state that change triggers—in other words, to name what is going on.
2. They help to normalize that emotional state, letting people know that what they are experiencing is normal or even to be expected.

Naming and normalizing serve to assist people through change.

KURT LEWIN'S THREE-STEP PROCESS OF CHANGE   Kurt Lewin (1890–1947) was an influential psychologist we have mentioned several times. Lewin's contribution to group dynamics and sensitivity training, his work on action research, and his field theory model are all contributions to coaching. Here we are most interested in his studies of change.

Lewin wrote "Group Decision and Social Change" (1947) after World War II. His theories were applied in the military as well as in education and are often referred to as strategies for brainwashing. He describes a "three-step process of change":

1. *Unfreezing.* This is a process in which groups or people must be convinced that their former beliefs were incorrect. People need to let go of restricting attitudes.
2. *Change to the new level of belief.* This involves altering one's perceptions of oneself and changing one's way of thinking.
3. *Freezing of a new level.* This step ensures that the new change is permanent. It involves developing hardwired new mental pathways so new behaviors become long-term habits.

According to this model, change proceeds in stages, and people will need to complete one stage before moving to the next.

Example: "I Don't Know Why People Aren't Knocking Down My Door"

Alex comes to coaching wanting to achieve greater success in his retail business. "I have the best-quality products available. I don't know why people aren't knocking down my door to buy them."

After some exploration, it becomes obvious that Alex expects customers to seek him out. He needs to become more outgoing if he expects people to even know his products exist. But the work of change will not start until an unfreezing occurs and Alex becomes aware of how his current way of blaming clients for his flagging sales is not effective. Only after this unfreezing has occurred can Alex move to generating new options. Reading all the sales manuals in the world will not "get through" to him before that first step.

After the coach asks questions that helped in unfreezing, Alex says, "I guess I could practice talking to everyone who comes into the store, even if they don't come up to me and ask about something."

Once Alex tests the new behavior and finds that it works, the stage of "change" has occurred. Coaching then moves to the refreezing stage, consisting of practice often and in enough situations that the desired behavior becomes more automatic. A coach who understands that the three stages need to occur in this order can help a client moves through them more easily.

Elizabeth Kübler-Ross's Stage Theory

Elizabeth Kübler-Ross (1926–2004) wrote *On Death and Dying* in 1969. In the research she did for this book, she identified a pattern in dealing with death that she believed to be universal. This pattern can also be applied to large-scale change processes:

- *Denial and isolation.* This step is used by almost everyone when any sort of change is first presented.
- *Anger.* This emotion is expressed through anger at people or things.
- *Bargaining.* Bargaining is a brief stage in which a person says, "Just let me live to see my son graduate" or "If I can get through this, I'll dedicate my life to good deeds."
- *Depression.* This stage consists of a feeling of sadness for the loss. How deeply depressed a person becomes can depend on vulnerability due to predisposition, circumstances, or previous losses.
- *Acceptance.* This stage is not so much a happy stage as simply the realization that death or change is inevitable.

Although Kübler-Ross calls this a "stage theory," these stages are not linear. Clients can skip over some or stay stuck in one. It is important to recognize that, for some clients, change feels like death. Most coaches and their clients will have experienced this kind of emotional cycle around any major change. Events like a relationship breakup, a large business loss, or a serious illness could bring on any or all of these stages. And, in our experience, the only "mistake" that clients make is assuming that they can avoid this process entirely.

The Kübler-Ross model is useful in a number of ways. Coaches may help clients:

- Recognize that a change process may involve strong emotions.
- Identify which stage they are in by recognizing their current feelings.
- Be aware of stages they may move into or through.

When clients understand that their reactions to change are normal and to be expected, their anxiety and fear are reduced. Although the emotions themselves may continue to be strongly felt, disturbing thoughts about the emotions, such as "I must be going crazy" or "This will never stop," may be relieved.

Example: "I Know I Just Have to Go Back to the Basics"

Cornelia was facing the close of her department due to technological changes. The product line she had helped to develop was simply outdated.

At first, Cornelia denied that anything would change, even though she knew deep inside what was going to happen: "I know I just have to go back to the basics that have brought us success in the past: find better suppliers who can provide us with competitive product. Develop a better marketing strategy. Bring in new training for the sales force."

Cornelia's coach asked if she was familiar with the Kübler-Ross Stage Theory. In putting together what she knew of the model with what the coach added, Cornelia was able to recognize that her emotions were similar to those she had experienced during another big change process she had gone through, namely the loss of her husband. As a result, she allowed herself to accept that the change was inevitable and move into the other stages more quickly.

James Prochaska's Transtheoretical Model

Psychologist James Prochaska introduced this model in 1979 in his book *Systems of Psychotherapy: A Transtheoretical Analysis* (Prochaska, 1979). Prochaska was trying to understand why psychotherapy could not help his father, who had died from alcoholism and depression. He analyzed over 18 major theories of psychotherapy and behavioral change, thus his use of the term "transtheoretical." Prochaska studied smokers and alcoholics who were in psychotherapy as well as those who were attempting to change on their own. His work has been internationally recognized and widely applied, especially in the health and health promotion fields.

In 1994, Prochaska and two colleagues wrote *Changing for Good: A Revolutionary Six-Stage Program for Overcoming Bad Habits and Moving Your Life Positively Forward*. The authors studied over 1,000 people who had positively and permanently altered their lives without psychotherapy, thus making his model of particular interest to coaches. Here is the model they developed:

- *Pre-contemplation.* Does not intend to take action or change in the next 6 months.
- *Contemplation.* Intends to take action within the next 6 months or so.
- *Preparation.* Intends to take action within the next 30 days and has taken some behavioral steps in this direction.
- *Action.* Has changed the overt behavior for less than 6 months.
- *Maintenance.* Has changed the behavior for more than 6 months.
- *Termination.* Believes that overt behavior will never return and has complete confidence in coping without fear of relapse.

These stages are not necessarily linear. A client could start at any of the earlier stages and could move up and down the stages as well.

Example: "I'll Practice until I Get It Right"

After several months of contemplation, Clinton prepares to stop smoking and finishes off his last pack without buying another. He does not smoke (action stage) for 3 months, but then takes a cigarette while on vacation and thus moves back to the contemplation stage. With the help of his coach, Clinton sees this as part of the process of change, not as a failure that indicates he should give up. "I guess I was just practicing quitting. I'll practice until I get it right and actually quit for good."

The model helps clients see their change process from a higher perspective. It also can be seen as an elaboration of Lewin's three-step model. In understanding this, clients can get some distance from the process of changing their smoking or other behavior, as recommended by David Rock's "clarity of distance" approach (2006). Or, from a solutions-focused perspective, it is the smoking that is the problem, not the person.

Coaches often feel a responsibility to hold clients accountable for their actions, but clients should not be rushed into changes until they have done sufficient contemplation and preparation. The ability to balance accountability and preparation is the mark of an experienced coach. The model also indicates that a maintenance program may be required to ensure that the change is not just short term.

An effective way of using this model in coaching is to help clients spend time at each step in the process, identifying activities to deepen their experience in each stage.

Example: "Will I Actually Be Able to Do It This Time?"

Continuing with Clinton and his desire to stop smoking, he and his coach developed a list of ways to get the most out of the contemplation stage. These included writing a list of all the reasons to make this change, discussing the list with others, and reading some books on the topic. When Clinton worried, "Yeah, but will I actually be able to do it this time?" the coach redirected him to the task at hand. "We'll deal with that question when we get to that stage. Right now, are you still learning things in this contemplation stage?"

During the preparation stage, Clinton investigated how to best stop smoking, gathering information about what to expect. Eventually, when he felt ready, Clinton made a decision about how he would take action.

As a result of the careful focus on the two previous steps, Clinton's action phase was more effective than it had been previously. He carefully chose what he considered was the best course for him, and he knew what to expect. In this case, Clinton chose to use nicotine patches. He weaned himself off the patch after one month and remained smoking-free for the next five months.

The action and maintenance phases received the same degree of attention during coaching. Clinton invited his friends to his house rather than going with them to smoky bars and in other ways stayed away from situations that would make it easy to accept the offer of a cigarette. The maintenance phase was a delicate one, but the coach helped Clinton predict the times when he might be attracted to his old habit so that he could plan and prepare. He made sure he went to a smoke-free resort for his next vacation.

The coach arranged for a six-month follow-up session at which Clinton expressed his conviction that he would not smoke again.

With an understanding of this change model, coaches can better help their clients complete any change they want to undergo. The process is similar for changing a health-related behavior or developing a new skill or habit.

The transtheoretical model is directly relevant to coaching and deserves the attention of any student or practicing coach.

William Bridges's Three Processes of Transition

William Bridges (2003) is best known as a consultant on transitions at work. He has helped many individuals and organizations deal more effectively with change.

Bridges makes a distinction between transition and change: Transition is internal, while change is external. Transition is the psychological reorientation that an individual must go through before the external change can take effect. Some examples of external changes include a different policy, practice, or structure that a leader is trying to introduce. Transition takes longer because it requires three separate processes, all of which are emotionally unsettling. These can also be referred to as phases because the process is not linear, and individuals may move back and forth among the phases:

1. *Ending.* Leaving something behind and saying good-bye. In this phase, people are being asked to let go of the way they were; they can feel they are losing their identity.
2. *Shifting into the neutral zone.* A state of limbo that is full of uncertainty and confusion for most people. Bridges considers this the most difficult phase. Because it is in between the old reality and the new one, it is sometimes referred to as a psychological no-man's land. It is an uncomfortable, chaotic time accompanied by feelings of

confusion and loneliness. Some people escape this phase by rushing ahead, and others retreat into the past. The upside is that it is the most creative phase, when innovation is most possible. It is comparable to Wheatley's (1992) introduction of chaos during a change process.

3. *New beginning.* Moving forward and adopting new ways of behavior. Some people may not be able to move into this phase until they have seen that others will not be punished for their new behavior.

In his book *Transitions: Making Sense of Life's Changes* (2004), Bridges outlines this "Checklist of Change":

- Take your time.
- Arrange temporary structures.
- Don't act for the sake of action.
- Recognize why you are uncomfortable.
- Take care of yourself in little ways.
- Explore the other side of change.
- Get someone to talk to.
- Find out what is waiting in the wings of your life.
- Use this transition as the impetus to a new kind of learning.
- Recognize that transition has a characteristic shape.

Bridges believes that in order for leaders to coach others through a transition, they must be coached first. Leaders must understand the transition phases in order to help their employees through them, and a good coach can help leaders discover their own unique best approaches.

Clients can easily identify with the simplicity of William Bridges' three-phase model and the emotions associated with each phase. It is especially important to understand the middle phase of fear and uncertainty and that many clients will hold on to their current ways of thinking to avoid the emotions in this stage.

Example: Stuck in the Neutral Zone

Hélène found herself not at all motivated to look for a new job. She had recently moved with her husband to San Francisco from France and felt that something was holding her back from finding a new position in international trade. Her coach introduced the Bridges model and asked if she saw any connections with her situation. She quickly recognized that she had not "let go of" her old life and was stuck in the middle, the neutral zone. She was resisting the idea of looking for new work because she was longing to be home with her family and friends in France. Her feelings of turmoil became more manageable once she understood how normal they were. She was then able to let go, bit by bit, of who she used to be (a woman living and working in France) and focus more on moving into a new beginning (a woman living and working in the United States).

W. C. Howell's Four Phases of Learning

William Howell is an industrial and organizational psychologist who studies people at work. In *Information Processing and Decision Making* (Howell & Fleishman, 1982), he described a four-stage model that is so widespread that there is debate over its origin:

1. *Unconscious incompetence.* We do not know what we do not know. We are incompetent at something but do not even know this to be the case. Emotions at this phase are generally blissful and positive.
2. *Conscious incompetence.* We try a new skill and realize we are not able to do it. At this phase, we immediately feel much worse than before we tried and failed. Emotions include frustration, annoyance, and stress.
3. *Conscious competence.* We can manage to execute a new skill, but it requires conscious attention. If we are distracted, we make mistakes. Strong positive emotions accompany our accomplishment, but those can be mixed with frustration when we "slip back."
4. *Unconscious competence.* The new skill comes naturally and thoughtlessly. We have mastered a new habit and no longer have to use our conscious mind to focus on it.

This model has links to the discussion earlier and in subsequent chapters about hardwiring well-practiced habits. The model can be helpful for clients who are trying to change a habit or learn a new skill. It is easy for people to become disheartened and quit as they enter stage 2, so it will be useful for clients to know it is normal to feel worse, not better, after they start attempting a new skill. An easy way to explain this model is with the analogy of learning to drive, a common skill today. Most people are now able to drive a car without thinking about it. When they were first learning (conscious incompetence and conscious competence), they usually felt incompetent and stressed about it.

In the business environment, a number of new skills challenge people, especially new hires and people in new positions.

Example: Selling Is Not the Same as Managing

Christine had built quite a reputation as a territory sales rep. She seemed to be a natural successor to the sales manager when he retired. However, the chief executive realized that selling was not the same as managing salespeople, so he made sure Christine had a coach to help her through the transition.

After the first two 70-hour weeks of rushing around trying to do everything, Christine was left with a sense of overwhelm and annoyance. She and her coach realized she needed to stop doing the work herself and start leading others to do it. Her unconscious incompetence at motivating others was the other side of her well-practiced ability to motivate herself. The Howell model helped her understand her feelings so she could focus her self-management skills on consciously developing ways to help her sales staff become as competent at that level as she had been.

In other situations, newly minted senior leaders may need to learn to delegate better, or empower others more, or build consensus more effectively. In any of these situations, clients may experience considerable discomfort when they first try a new skill, and it may take some time and focus to get them to the place of unconscious competence. Coaches can help again by naming and normalizing the experiences their clients are going through.

Howell's model can also be useful in learning to coach, as this requires new habits and skills that we want to be automatic, or unconscious, so we can apply our conscious attention to the needs of the client. For example, self-managing (detaching from the client's emotions), listening for the client's positive energy instead of for problems, and learning to let the client do the thinking about their issues are all necessary to our work as coaches, and they all may take time and practice before becoming unconscious competencies.

John Kotter's Eight Steps to Change

John Kotter's *Leading Change* (1996) has become one of the most important texts in the field of organizational change management. In *The Heart of Change: Real-Life Stories of How People Change Their Organizations* (2002), Kotter and Cohen defined eight key steps to a successful change initiative. Although these steps were written about organizational change initiatives, the insights in this work can be directly translated to personal change initiatives as well:

Step 1. Create a sense of urgency: This is needed for any change process to start. Without urgency, people will not focus on changing.

Step 2. Put together a guiding team. Any difficult change can benefit from a team of people working together to guide the change. In personal coaching, this might involve a team of experts or the support of a family unit.

Step 3. Create visions and strategies. Any change process needs to be supported by a clear vision. Without a vision driving the change, we can easily forget why we are changing.

Step 4. Communicate for buy-in. Kotter talks about the need for repetition here, to produce change we need to keep the change top of mind, for ourselves as much as others.

Step 5. Empower people. This step is not as directly transferable to coaching one on one but is very relevant in trying to bring about change in a group. In this case, individuals need to be empowered to drive the change, to act on the vision. Otherwise there may be no movement.

Step 6. Produce short-term wins. These are critical. Short-term wins make the change initiative real. They provide credibility and momentum and build confidence.

Step 7. Build momentum. It's important to use the opportunity of any small wins to build momentum. Carefully choose next steps that can also be wins, to increase confidence and momentum.

Step 8. Nurture a new culture. This step is about ensuring the change is long lasting, similar to the maintenance phase in Prochaska's model. We need to stay aware of the change for some time.

Kotter's model is one of the most useful for executing successful change programs, as, unlike other models that focus on the challenges or map the change process, it points to what to do more of. Kotter's model can be directly applied to goals that a client wants to achieve.

Example: 60% of Employees Looking to Be Transferred

Michael was a human resources executive who discovered that some 60% of employees in one department of his financial services firm were looking to be transferred or to find new employment. Michael had been working with his coach on using Kotter's model for a change initiative in another department, so he knew the steps well. He began with showing the metrics and cost of the potential loss of personnel at his next meeting with the chief executive, and the two came up with a plan to build a team to deal with the crisis, including the department manager and key informal leaders.

With support from Michael, the team analyzed the problem as one of morale, developed a strategy for introducing coaching skills training to improve the morale, and went about selling it to the department and senior executives. Michael investigated and presented options for training to the team, and they made the final decision on the supplier. At critical stages, Michael suggested that the chief executive check in with the team and the department, taking every opportunity to acknowledge each small step.

A new sense of accomplishment began to knit the department together, as much because of the process as of the actual training they received. After just six months, the next performance reviews showed a complete turnaround in the department's satisfaction level, and personnel from other departments were asking for transfers into it. The team continued to meet occasionally to make sure the changes were maintained.

Peter Senge's Systems Approach

Peter M. Senge is a senior lecturer at the Massachusetts Institute of Technology and the founding chair of SOL, the Society for Organizational Learning. His book *The Fifth Discipline* (1990) introduced the influential concept of the learning organization as a response to increasing complexity and pace of change in business. Senge's model focuses on the organization but again may be applied to an individual.

The fifth discipline is systems thinking, which fuses other leadership attributes into a whole that supports business goals. Senge's ideas about change come out of his systems theory perspective:

- Start small.
- Grow steadily.
- Don't plan everything.
- Expect challenges.

Senge encourages managers to think like biologists or ecologists when approaching organizational change, considering the whole system and how that system will evolve over time through interactions with other systems. Because of the complexity of an organizational system, trying to plan every step in detail actually constrains a leader's capacity to respond to the unexpected. We have already discussed the systems perspective and related concepts of complexity and chaos in chapter 3.

Richard Boyatzis's Action-Reflection Cycle

We will discuss the concept of mastery, or "expertising," in chapter 8 as one of the topics studied by cognitive psychology. The development of mastery involves an ongoing process of bringing one's experience and knowledge to bear on a new attempt at a task and then allowing that action to inform the further development of knowledge and skills (Page, 2005). We will also discuss action research, the approach pioneered by Kurt Lewin that has influenced community organizing. These approaches are further developed in the action-reflection ideas of Boyatzis and colleagues (Boyatzis & McKee, 2005a) that change theory should be represented not in a linear stage model but as a circular spiral that fits more appropriately with the systemic paradigm.

Many versions of this model exist, all of which share the difficulty of representing in two-dimensional space the development over time of ever more complex concepts or knowledge or skills. Figure 5.1 is a simple example. The process cycles clockwise from action to reflection and back, as represented by the arrows. Experience and experimentation transform what is observed and reflected upon, just as observation and reflection transform the concepts and plans for the next action. The arrows the next time around are never at the same point as the last time around. This spiral into increasing complexity is what differentiates expertise building from mere repetition of the same experience. That is why some people can spend many years driving a car and yet not be expert drivers, as compared to those who consciously attend to the

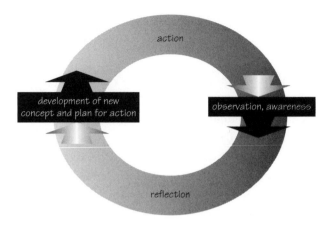

Figure 5.1   Action-Reflection Cycle

experience of driving and utilize what they learn to improve their next actions behind the wheel.

Linking Change Models to Coaching

Coaching clients live in a world that is constantly changing. On top of this, clients come to coaching because they want to speed up or deepen a process of change they are going through, whether it is learning a way to get "in the zone," changing a negative health habit, taking on a new position at work, or approaching a relationship without triggering conflict.

Coaches play an important role for clients, in that they offer the necessary support and structure to deal effectively with change. Understanding the different models discussed in this chapter is important because the issue of change will be part of almost every coaching session. By sharing the models of change with clients, we can help them feel "normalized" and not so alone in their emotional state. The next general principles apply no matter which specific model the coach (or client) may choose:

- Any change may be deeply challenging.
- Intended change requires support, focus, and dedication.
- Identifying the stage of change clients are going through, have already passed through, or are heading toward reduces their fear.
- Describing a relevant change model that applies to many other people or organizations serves to normalize a client's experience.

OPTIMIZING PERFORMANCE AS A COACHING PILLAR

Consider just a few of the types of changes that people and organizations face:

- Cycles of abstract time—days, months, quarters, years (both fiscal and calendar)
- Physical seasons (summer, winter, spring, fall) and life cycles (birth, aging, death, disease)
- The broad sweep of historical eras and changing interpretations of history
- Effects of wars, natural disasters, and epidemics
- Emigration and immigration
- Shifts in social mores, values, prejudice, discrimination
- Social and political movements and their effects
- Moving offices, homes, work, or school location
- Personal illness, separation, and death
- Organizational mergers, acquisitions, bankruptcy

It is not surprising that nearly every book or article on change begins with the claim that change is inevitable and that individuals or organizations resist change at their own peril. Systems do fail, and change that overwhelms our capacity to maintain some sort of solid footing is usually the culprit. This is certainly the case with our brains. Although human beings display considerable neural resilience in recovering from or working around disease or injury to the brain, this becomes impossible when the traumatic change is too severe.

Mental disorders may be categorized as indicating either too much chaos and changeability (e.g., bipolar disorder) or too much rigidity and lack of change (e.g., obsessive-compulsive disorder). The space between these two extremes is a healthy state of dynamic stability. In order to build an understanding of how to achieve that state, we turn next to exploring the relationship between changing our minds and changing our brains.

CHAPTER 6

Neuroscience Platform — Neuroplasticity

It had rained overnight in the foothills of the Dolomite Mountains in northern Italy. Early-morning sun glistened on cobblestones in streets barely wide enough for a small car. Cyclists who had pitted their strength against steep inclines breathed a thrill of victory in reaching the ancient town of Asolo. NeuroLeadership Summit participants threaded their way among the cyclists and townspeople to gather in the 500-year-old convent that had become the headquarters for CIMBA, an international business school and conference center. Jeffrey Schwartz was about to unveil a formula for consciously managing brain changes that he and David Rock had developed:

$$DS = (exptn + exprnce) \times AD^+ \times VP$$

In other words, dynamic stability equals a combination of expectation and experience multiplied by positive attention density multiplied by veto power. Dynamic stability is another way of saying "positive change," change that allows a system to adapt and develop, rather than remaining inflexible and unable to respond, and to do this without becoming overwhelmed by chaos.

For most of the 20th century, assumptions of mechanistic science, added to limitations on observing the inner workings of live brains, led to several conclusions:

1. Damaged brains cannot regenerate.
2. Human brains at birth have all the neurons they will ever have.
3. Human brain structure is fixed by the beginning of adulthood.
4. From adulthood on, loss of neurons and thus of mental function is the best that can be expected.

Any contrary examples, such as people regaining the use of limbs after a stroke or of becoming accomplished pianists or athletes as adults, were dismissed as anomalies at best and hoaxes at worst. During the last decades of the century, however, several lines of inquiry shook those assumptions.

Attachment research established the importance of a secure relationship between a child and a parent. Not having that security was correlated with a number of mental health problems, including difficulty in establishing a secure relationship with one's own children. But in his book *The Developing Mind*, Daniel Siegel (1999) reported research showing exceptions. Some parents whose insecure attachments had been identified when they were children ended up as adults being able to establish secure relationships with their children. This was very different from what should have been true based on the assumption that adult brain structure is immutable. Furthermore, psychotherapists were discovering treatments that at least relieved the symptoms of trauma, despite the belief that traumatic experiences created untreatable brain damage.

In a compelling series of stories, Jeffrey Schwartz and Sharon Begley (2002; Begley, 2007) describe more direct evidence of brain plasticity. Edward Taub showed that monkeys' brains are able to rewire and return function to a limb whose nerves had been severed. Michael Merzenich and his colleagues applied this finding to helping human stroke victims regain function. Fred Gage and others discovered not only that adult brains can form new neurons but that this is possible at least into the eighth decade of life.

172

As a result, it is clear that our brains can grow to an extent never thought possible even 30 years ago. But questions remain.

- How can we keep from introducing so many changes so fast that our systems just cannot keep up?
- What are the limits of neuroplasticity?
- How does our new knowledge of the brain help us know how to change when we want to?
- What kinds of experiences are more likely to stimulate brain growth?
- What can we do consciously to encourage our brains to develop?
- How can we stop doing what we do not want to do?
- How hard is it and how long does it take to create a structural change in the brain?
- How does brain change relate to systems theory?
- Do we have free will?

We examine these and other questions under the next headings:

- Dynamic stability
- Placebo effect
- Experience and hardwiring
- Attention
- Veto power
- Applying the Schwartz-Rock Formula for Dynamic Stability
- Practice Guide for Coaching with the Brain in Mind—Leverage Change

DYNAMIC STABILITY

We examine each of the terms in the Schwartz and Rock formula for dynamic stability in order to understand neuroplasticity in some detail. Earlier we looked at dynamic stability from the perspective of systems theory as well as quantum mechanics. We know that healthy self-directed (autopoietic) systems are changing continuously but maintain a stable identity, neither inflexible nor disintegrated. Quantum theory tells us that an observer's attention can hold subatomic particles in a stable state.

Systems in dynamic stability develop over time by becoming more complex. A child's first steps may be awkward, but over time her brain and body develop so that she can execute complex ballet or hip-hop moves. A child's brain may be subject to pruning, but the remaining neurons form complex networks of connections stimulated by the changing environment, especially social interactions. An organization that manages to survive through difficulties usually does so by developing complex skills and systems that enable it to meet future challenges more easily. Through dynamic stability, a skilled athlete or math expert develops abilities that can be nothing less than amazing.

Linking Dynamic Stability to Coaching

The development of advanced skills requires ongoing calibration. Taking on an overwhelming challenge may end in frustration and a sense of failure. Being asked to repeat something we have already mastered may be accompanied by boredom or lack of engagement. Coaches can help clients be aware of the characteristics of flow that create a sense of engagement and build expertise.

PLACEBO EFFECT

In medicine, the placebo effect, or the tendency for people to experience relief from a sugar pill just because the doctor recommends it, has long been recognized. But what is this phenomenon from a neuroscience perspective, and what is its relationship to neuroplasticity?

Robert Coghill is a scientist who studies pain and its representation in the brain. At the First Global NeuroLeadership Summit, Coghill (2007) reported that pain triggered by the same outside event was experienced quite uniquely by different people. This finding has implications for how people's mental processes work. The objectively identical pain stimulus (e.g., heat) can be "felt" or rated by some people as 1.5 on a 10-point scale and by others as 8.5 on the same scale. This is not a matter of some people reporting less experienced pain just to appear brave or others reporting greater pain as a dramatic gesture. In functional magnetic resonance imaging (fMRI) studies that indirectly measure changes in cerebral blood flow, different reported pain levels were correlated with different cortical activity. So people who reported pain of 1.5 actually had a different measure of brain activity from people who reported pain of 8.5.

But why is this work relevant to a gathering of coaches and business leaders? Coghill explained that listeners could replace the word "pain" in his studies with the word "information." We have already defined information as output that tells us about input as well as the process involved in conveying the input.

As we argued earlier, information that comes from a painful stimulus is not delivered by our sensory apparatus bare and unadorned by our minds. Rather, the painful output that registers in our consciousness tells us not only about the original input or stimulus but also about the mechanism and process that regulates that flow of information. Coghill's research indicates that the parts of the brain that are most active in regulating our unique perception of pain are the "higher levels," which include past history, present context, and future implications.

As for what pain research can tell us about expectations, Coghill developed an "expectation paradigm" in which subjects learned to expect a mildly painful heat stimulus after a short time interval, a medium stimulus after a middle time interval, and a severely painful stimulus after a long interval:

- Mild: After 7.5 seconds, a stimulus of 46° Celsius
- Medium: After 15 seconds, a stimulus of 48° Celsius
- Severe: After 30 seconds, a stimulus of 50° Celsius

After enough trials that people knew what to expect, Coghill varied the stimulus, sometimes delivering a severely painful stimulus after only a short interval. That is, people expected a mild pain but received a severe one. The results were surprising. Not only did the subjects report experiencing less pain than when the severe stimulus was delivered after the expected long interval, their brain activity was similar to what occurred when they actually received a mild stimulus. The fMRI measures showed similar brain activity when people expected a mild pain but received a severe one as compared to when they both expected and received a mild pain. To put it another way, when people expected a weak pain but received a severe one, they experienced the pain as weak.

The difference is significant. It is comparable to the pain relief experienced when a person is given a shot of morphine. Conclusion: Expectation alters our experience of pain. And, more generally, mental activity alters whether we experience incoming information as positive or negative. Coghill suggested that he had discovered the brain traces of the placebo effect, the well-established tendency for a person's expectations about treatment to affect his or her recovery. In psychotherapy, for example, Hubble, Duncan, and Miller (1999) marshal evidence that approximately 15% of variance in psychotherapy outcome is attributable to the placebo effect.

But expectation is not the whole story behind the placebo effect. Coghill's experiment does not work the other way. People who expect a severely painful stimulus but receive a mild one report the pain as mild. Coghill explains this as the interaction of desire and expectation: We *want* a mild stimulus. Our expectations of what is severe are tempered by the desire for mild, with the result that we perceive mild as mild, even when we expect severe. This may be an example of confirmation bias, or ignoring negative information that does not suit our purposes. We are more likely to pay attention to information that matches our intentions.

Coghill's studies support his claim that we are constantly constructing expectations and intentions and then testing them against incoming sensory data. That is, neither experience nor expectations alone account for phenomena like the placebo effect. It is the combination of expectation and experience that creates an important element in managing the human system that makes up our existence.

Linking Placebo Effect to Coaching

How can coaches help clients construct their expectations to take advantage of the placebo effect, especially in a situation that may have painful consequences? First of all, it is important for clients to be aware of their intentions. The coaching question "What do you want?" is repeated so often because it both clarifies and activates our desires and intentions. When we can help clients expect the best, they may be able to produce an effect similar to the placebo.

Example: "Another Chance to Design My Own Job"

Adele's job in upper management at a government agency required her to retire at age 60, and she was not ready for retirement.

"What do you want?" asked her coach.

"I want to be able to use my experience and not have it just lost or forgotten, but I have no idea how or where to use it."

"When in the past have you successfully figured out questions like that?" (This is an approach from solution-focused techniques discussed in chapter 10.)

"Oh, right. When I was transferred to a new department and had to create a new position for myself, I had no idea what to do. I went into a learning frenzy, taking courses and talking to people and gathering information about what was required. I designed a position that's now been duplicated in several other departments. That came out great!"

"What can you apply from that experience to this retirement opportunity?"

"I can see it as another chance to design my own new job."

Adele signed her first consulting contract with her former agency the week after she retired. By clarifying her intention, she became more likely to notice opportunities that matched what she wanted. Then, by activating her positive memories of a similar change in the past, she shaped an expectation that helped her bypass negative or discouraging feedback. Even if she got a painful response to her inquiries, she experienced it as a mild setback because of her positive expectations. As Coghill suggested in his NeuroLeadership Summit presentation (2007), "Change through aspiration is more effective than change through desperation."

However, Coghill also warns us that our ability to think our way to positive experiences is limited. Believable expectations can alter reality (such as objectively measured painful stimuli), but when our expectations cross into unbelievable territory, the effect breaks down. By expecting a mildly hot stimulus, we may be able to experience a hotter stimulus as being mild, but only if the stimulus is not so hot as to cause physical damage. Expecting a truck to go around us when we stand in front of it is not likely to result in a positive experience. However, there is a large territory within which coaching our expectations effectively changes our experience and resulting maps of the world.

EXPERIENCE AND HARDWIRING

Coaches can use the power of awareness to help clients perceive and move toward their intentions. Repetition of this movement can result in hardwiring, or the shift of conscious intention to automatic processing, that enables us to act on information without requiring the limited resources of attention.

But human capacity to make this shift raises other problems: What if we react automatically, either because of implicit or explicitly practiced hardwiring, and that reaction is no longer appropriate in a new situation? Consider the experience of the new chief executive officer (CEO) of a resources company who wanted managers to offer their ideas about new processes and markets. But the managers had been trained by the previous command-and-control CEO to keep their ideas to themselves. The new CEO could not understand why brainstorming sessions were more like funerals. Issues like this are frequent challenges for leaders and are common fare for coaches. Understanding techniques for encouraging and guiding such changes requires recognizing how expectations fit into the larger picture of the brain and mind.

Linking Experience and Hardwiring to Coaching

Once a habit or emotional reaction or train of thought has been hardwired, it is useless to try to erase it. That is not a choice we have. It is, however, possible to pay attention to what we want to replace it with. Jeffrey Schwartz (Schwartz & Begley, 2002) does not underestimate the effort it takes to consciously redirect our attention, especially in the face of signals of danger. His experience with treating patients with obsessive-compulsive disorder (OCD) gave him tremendous respect for their courage and tenacity. However, it becomes easier to persist in this task when we understand that quantum physics supports the possibility of using our minds (and the minds of others) to change our brains (see Begley, 2007).

ATTENTION

One aspect of our mental lives in which we exercise choice has to do with where we direct our attention. By exerting conscious energy, we decide what to pay attention to. Over time, the connections we make because we are paying attention become hardwired, and the basis for further actions. This fact has enormous importance in change management in general and in coaching, which Jeffrey Schwartz (Rock & Schwartz, 2006) has called "self-directed neuroplasticity," (p. 32) in particular. After all, "self-directed" implies choice.

The collaboration of Jeffrey Schwartz with physicist Henry Stapp (Schwartz, Stapp, & Beauregard, 2004) has provided the foundation for our recognition of the importance of the systemic paradigm for both coaching and neuroscience. Schwartz (Rock & Schwartz, 2006; Schwartz & Begley, 2002; see also Stapp, 2007) explains that, in order to communicate with one another, the neurons in the brain require individual chemical ions to travel across channels that are, at some points, not much more than an ion wide. Ions are atoms or molecules that have an electric charge because they have either gained or lost an electron. According to quantum physics, this makes the brain a quantum environment subject to the laws that apply at this subatomic level. One of those laws is this: The questions you ask influence the results you see.

Applying this to the quantum brain, asking one question rather than another, or focusing our attention on one item or another, influences the connections the brain makes and "profoundly alters the patterns and timings of the connections the brain generates in each fraction of a second" (Rock & Schwartz, 2006, p. 36). Applying this concept to the principle of change, if we shine our spotlight on something new that represents the change we wish to make, our brain makes new connections. This is not just a theoretical possibility: That the brain makes new connections in this way "has shown to be true through studies of neuroplasticity, where focused attention plays a critical role in creating physical changes in the brain" (Rock & Schwartz, 2006, p. 36).

We have discussed the research by Fred Gage and others (Eriksson et al., 1998; Olson et al., 2006; van Praag et al., 2005) showing that the adult brain changes in response to stimulating environments and voluntary exercise. Schwartz (Schwartz & Begley, 2002) extended this in his psychiatric practice to people suffering from OCD. Remember that this is a very troubling affliction that its victims experience as having no control over. A popular depiction of this disorder is the detective *Monk* in the television series of the same name. The lead character, played by actor Tony Shalub, uses his obsession with detail to solve crimes.

Even so, part of the show's appeal lies in Monk's difficulty with everyday interactions. Because most people with this disorder are not able to make good use of their compulsive behavior, they are simply left with the suffering and isolation it entails.

Schwartz trained OCD patients to become mindful of their compulsive impulses and to attribute these to false messages from the brain's error-detection systems. When they experienced an impulse, for example, to wash their hands after having just done so, Schwartz helped them say to themselves, "This is not a signal of danger, this is just my brain sending a mistaken signal." They then practiced choosing to do something else, for instance playing the piano or watering their plants. After just two weeks of training in this method, not only did the patients report behavioral change, Schwartz was able to see systematic changes in neural structure in positron emission tomography scans of the patients' brains. This is an example of what Schwartz calls "self-directed neuroplasticity," the very term he also applies to coaching.

Quantum Zeno Effect

Looking more closely at the science behind this process, what accounts for such changes? At the first NeuroLeadership Summit in Asolo, Italy, in May 2006, physicist Henry Stapp explained the Quantum Zeno Effect. He drew a random pattern of dots and said that this could be a picture of how atomic particles decay. They are dynamic, or in motion, but they are not stable, or orderly. If an observer fixes attention on *that* decaying particle — Stapp pointed to one of the dots he had drawn — the pattern becomes orderly. Attention creates a "strange attractor" phenomenon around which decaying particles group. In this way, the atom achieves dynamic stability — moving, but in an orderly fashion.

Schwartz (Schwartz & Begley, 2002) points out that, at the molecular level, repeated observation holds a molecule in place, slowing the rate of fluctuation it exhibits when unobserved. Some scientists do not believe this effect is applicable to phenomena of the human brain, but if we accept, as Stapp and Schwartz do (Schwartz et al., 2004; Stapp, 2007) that the brain is a quantum environment, then our ability to focus our attention on newly connecting brain circuits should eventually hardwire them. That is, by choosing what to shine the spotlight of attention on, we can effect changes in the very structure of our brain.

In other words, our minds are not just a side show for what our brains, as nurtured by social interactions, are doing. To paraphrase Daniel Siegel (2007b), our minds use our brains to create themselves.

The key word to take note of in the description in the last paragraph is "repeated." Focusing once on a new connection, say, remembering the name of a new employee, will not hold in place the brain circuit that represents that information and create an instant map. We must manage the flow of energy such that we pay intense attention to the change we want to make, and we must do it over and over. If our working memory gets exhausted or overwhelmed or distracted, we simply repeat the effort of paying attention as soon and as often as we are able. Rock and Schwartz state this concept in this way: "It is Attention Density that brings Quantum Zeno Effect into play and causes the proper brain circuitry to be held in place in a stable dynamic way" (2006, p. 37). When we pay sufficient attention to certain patterns over time, they become part of who we are and how we perceive the world.

It follows, then, that what we pay attention to is crucially important. If we pay attention to the problem or to the negative qualities of a situation or person, that is what will become hardwired. If we rehearse in our minds how embarrassed we will be if we do not remember the new employee's name, what result can we expect?

Attention Density

Attention density is the quantity and quality of attention paid to a particular circuit consisting of connections among neurons in the brain. As we explained in chapter 3 on mapping, our brains structure information as mental maps, or circuits, for every word, picture, experience or concept for which we have any associations. One word or idea may trigger responses in visual, emotional, kinesthetic, auditory, motor, memory, and language centers. Attention density is either the sum or the product of the quality and quantity of focus. We say "or" because no studies have yet been done to verify whether the two elements are multiplicative. We look forward to studies that will provide this information.

Quality of Focus. The number of other circuits that are activated in connection to the original circuit and the amount of energy coursing through that circuit comprise quality of attention. For example, you will generate more energy if you have an emotional reaction to a topic.

Questions are more powerful the more that they increase attention density. For example, a coach may ask, "What did your boss tell you in your performance review?" Auditory memory circuits are likely activated, along with a visual picture of the scene, memories of whatever emotional reaction the client had, and an inner rehearsal of what might be said in response.

If, however, the coach asks, "What went well in your performance review?" the client has a much broader series of circuits to choose from: all those from the previous question, but additionally overall evaluation of the effects of the interaction, comparison with other performance reviews and other times when the client was evaluated, hopes and fears going into the review, reactions afterward, conclusions, questions. As a result, the client's attention is held longer, more richly, and more positively.

Quantity of Focus. This is the number of times focus is directed to the desired circuit. If the coach made a request and the client agreed to journal about the review and her insights from coaching, more circuits would be involved and held active for even longer. The client would have to spend time summoning memories, conclusions, comparisons, insights, and emotional reactions and putting these into writing. This might take several sessions. If the coach asks her about her journal experience at the next session, the focus is repeated. This increases the client's focus on lessons to be derived from coaching around her performance review from perhaps several hours or days to possibly weeks and months. That focus is now also linked to many more centers of her brain. Both the quantity and the quality of attention have gone up, as many more circuits were activated many more times.

Linking Attention to Coaching

As coaches, we need to help our clients pay more attention, for longer, in order to make connections with new ways of thinking that align with their goals. We need to increase their attention density to the right circuits. Often the best way to find out how to achieve this is to ask clients themselves.

The quality and quantity of attention determine the strength of connections in our brain. But to achieve dynamic stability, it matters what we pay attention to. Remember that we get more of what we pay attention to. To pay constant attention to fears, regrets, worries, or vengeful thoughts means that we will increase these undesirable aspects in our lives. Eventually, we may have trouble avoiding one or the other of disintegration or rigidity, the two shoals between which dynamic stability flows. This is as true for organizations as it is for individuals. The plus (+) sign in the dynamic stability formula is a reminder to focus on strengths such as the ones we discuss in chapter 11 on positive psychology (Seligman, 2002).

But let us examine the final element in the formula for dynamic stability.

VETO POWER

Earlier we emphasized the self-creating nature of each human being and how unique that makes us. Drawing on the work of physicist Henry Stapp (2007), we claimed that our minds are not determined by the structure of our brains or by our genetic inheritance, although both set material limits to our growth and accomplishments.

As Schwartz et al. (2004) argue, quantum discoveries have breathed new life into previously discarded concepts, such as those of William James. Will power or volition was a topic of debate among philosophers and early psychologists such as James. Both psychoanalysis and behaviorism ignored volition in the interest of promoting unconscious drives and stimulus response, respectively, as explanatory models. But quantum discoveries have revived the question of whether the subjectively experiencing person can exert free will or whether she or he is at the deterministic mercy of environment or heredity (or of seemingly intractable disorders such as OCD).

Subjectively, we have the experience of sitting at a desk and then, without any sense of being "made" to do so, voluntarily "deciding" to take a sip of tea. This feels like free will. However, many of our behaviors, such as shopping selections, can be predicted so well that there is a science of product placement. Can neuroscience help to reconcile this experience of free choice with decades of evidence that behavior can be controlled?

Neuroscientists Libet, Gleason, Wright, and Pearl (1983) came up with good news and bad news regarding free will.

Bad News. They found that the brain generates a signal, a "readiness potential," to pick up our teacup about five-tenths of a second before we actually pick up the cup. We are not conscious of this signal until about three-tenths of a second later. The bad news is that if we define free will as the ability to consciously generate readiness potentials, we don't have it. In chapter 13, we discuss the fact that the brain is constantly in processing mode. The subjective manifestation is that thoughts are constantly appearing and disappearing. Some of those thoughts have to do with "voluntary" actions. We do not voluntarily think these up, as we do not even become aware of them until three-tenths of a second after they register on instruments in the lab. So we do not freely *will* our options for action to appear in our brains.

Good News. But that is not the whole story. There is a lag of about two-tenths of a second between the time we become aware of a readiness potential and our taking the unconsciously proposed action. The sequence is this:

- At 0.5 second before an action, instruments register our brain's (unconscious) readiness potential.
- At 0.2 second before the action, we become aware of the urge to act.
- At 0 second, we act.

It is in that gap of two-tenths of a second between awareness and action that we can decide *not* to do what we have unconsciously generated as an option for action. We can decide *not* to reach for the teacup or make a snide remark or cut another piece of cake. Schwartz and Begley (2002) call this "veto power." We do not have free will when it comes to voluntarily creating our brain's readiness potential, but we have "free won't" when it comes to performing the acts that we become aware of.

As part of his treatment, Schwartz helps his OCD patients recognize the signal to wash their hands or check the lock as coming from their brain, not from danger "out there." This is an example of input not about the outside world but about the functioning of the brain system itself. Patients learn to recognize this and to use the two-tenths of a second after becoming aware of the faulty brain signal to veto it. They can choose instead to do something else. In doing some other desirable action, they are creating new maps and recruiting the principle of neural Darwinism to, eventually, reduce the strength of the old compulsion.

Linking Veto Power to Coaching

As we have seen, the concept of free will has its limitations. Understanding this fact helps us understand one reason why changing old habits to new ones is so difficult. We have noted that the brain makes connections based on use. When we have repeated a behavior often enough, it becomes automatic, a potential that often and easily comes to mind, a habit. The more often we perform that action, the stronger the connection and likelihood that it will present itself as a readiness potential.

However, every time we exercise veto power and do something other than the habit we are attempting to break, the more we reinforce alternative actions. Schwartz and Begley (2002) recognize the immense courage and energy this takes, but Schwartz knows it is possible because of his successful treatment of OCD patients. Discovering that people can do something other than wash their hands (again) or check to see if the door is locked (again) is why, when David explained coaching to him, Schwartz called it "self-directed neuroplasticity."

How else can we increase the probability that a person's insight from a coaching session will end up becoming reliably hardwired? All the techniques that coaches learn to help clients be accountable to themselves apply here: journaling about insights, setting up physical reminders, celebrating small victories, exercising "veto power" when the old pattern emerges, and so forth.

But that is not all. We do need to recognize that our working memory, the equipment that turns on and focuses our attention, is limited and vulnerable to internal and external distractions, as we discussed earlier. That is, our individual minds have these limitations. By "borrowing" the attention power of other minds, we can extend our capacity for attention density enormously. After all, that is surely a major ingredient in the success of coaching. The coach has the responsibility to, first, make sure the client is paying attention to what is positive—his or her strengths, what has worked well in the past, the upside of the problem. Second, the coach steadies the spotlight on the intended change, not by issuing orders but by asking questions that will direct the client's attention to the brain circuits to be hardwired. In this way, the relationship with the coach supports attention density.

APPLYING THE SCHWARTZ-ROCK FORMULA FOR DYNAMIC STABILITY

Systems theory indicates that a healthy human or organizational system is one that exhibits dynamic stability. We have now examined each of the elements presented at the beginning of the chapter in the formula for dynamic stability:

$$DS = (exptn + exprnce) \times AD^+ \times VP$$

Dynamic stability may be enhanced by a combination of expectation and experience. Our expectations can have a substantial and measurable effect on our experience. The dynamic, or changeful, aspect of dynamic stability is made possible by neuroplasticity, or the fact that experience can change the brain. Positive experiences are more likely to be system sustaining. More specifically for changes we consciously desire, if the Quantum Zeno Effect holds true, it is attention that changes the brain. Because the brain is a social organ, dynamic stability will be enhanced by relationships that are also positive and dynamically stable.

The formula for attaining dynamic stability of human systems is to add expectation for our desired outcome to experience, multiply that by quantity and quality of positive attention, and multiply that by saying no to those impulses that either lead us to repeat what has not worked or to do something other than what we have determined will work.

Example: Distracted by Her Own Feelings

Anne is an external coach for a broadcasting company. A producer requested that she coach him about his difficulties in working with his production team. He had met Anne through her facilitation of leadership workshops and recognized her capacity for appreciating "creative" (read "volatile") temperaments.

Their sessions soon turned to his loneliness and lack of intimacy. Anne, who had lost her husband just four months previously, found herself emotionally upset by her client's suffering. She felt like her client did—lonely and alone. There was no question of romantic involvement, but she found herself distracted by her own feelings. The more she berated herself for getting upset, the more upset she got. The client's state of mind was clearly triggering her own, but not to the benefit of the coaching.

Anne's own coach recognized that Anne's usual ability to stay tuned to her client's experience was in jeopardy. After making sure that Anne was paying attention to her own grieving process outside her work, the coach suggested using the dynamic stability formula and explained its elements. The two began by setting Anne's intention to take note of every instance where the client reported a positive interaction with anyone—colleagues, friends, family, salespeople—anyone.

This expectation on Anne's part led to her experience of the client as being more connected with people. She consciously paid attention to those moments of positive interaction, showing her interest by asking questions and remembering details about them from one session to the next. The producer also found himself paying more attention to his positive interactions.

When a thought of her own grief appeared in her mind, rather than focusing on it, Anne said to herself, "Veto that," and directed her attention back to the client. Over time, she found it easier to stay attuned in sessions. The fact that feedback from his production team indicated his relationships were improving showed that her newfound stability was helping the client as well as being more comfortable for her. In this way, both the producer in his circle of relationships and Anne in her relationship with her client began to experience an upward spiral of dynamic stability.

Over time, refocusing our attention on the combination of positive expectations and corroborating experience while practicing veto power over and over will produce new mental habits and new hardwiring.

Capacities such as brain/body regulation, fear modulation, and emotion balancing are generally associated with the prefrontal cortex, or PFC, which we mentioned as part of our brain-in-the-hand model. The PFC is located behind the hard bone of our forehead and behind our eyes. Different areas of the PFC seem to perform tasks similar to an orchestra conductor: integrating, coordinating, and modulating energy and information that come from all parts of the brain. However, we must remember that, as with an orchestra conductor, the PFC does not itself produce the energy and information. The whole brain/body is required for that.

Our brains consist of neurons and their innumerable connections, plus other cells and substances such as neurotransmitters. This system makes it possible for us to gather information from "out there," beyond our brain/body; to coordinate our different brain/body functions; to participate in sharing information; and to link past, present, and future. The capacity to predict the future not only means we can act rather than react, but, as quantum physics suggests, the very nature of that action can actually shape the future.

PRACTICE GUIDE FOR COACHING WITH THE BRAIN IN MIND — LEVERAGE CHANGE

Coaches who keep the brain in mind treat clients as whole persons (mental, physical, social, spiritual) who are embedded in systems with wide repercussions. They know the basics of several models of change and collaborate with clients to match model to situation. Besides understanding the elements of the formula for dynamic stability, such coaches know how to encourage client expectations, attention density, and veto power.

Three specific guides are particularly relevant to the question "How can we be healthy?" Keeping the brain in mind helps coaches:

- Recognize and balance the needs of physical brain/body, mind, and relationships.
- Pay attention to attention (their own and others'), including metaphors, energy levels, signs of being stuck, and unconscious signals.
- Catch themselves when they are about to repeat an unwanted pattern, veto that, choose a more beneficial path, and learn from the experience — and help clients do the same.

Asking how we can change and do better begs a consideration of why we do what we do in the first place. This is the question we consider in part III.

Why Do We Do What We Do?

At the beginning of the 20th century, psychologists took on the mantle of objective observers of human behavior. As a scientific endeavor, psychology systematically studies and attempts to explain observable behavior and its relationship to unseen mental processes and to external events in the environment. However, from a bedrock mechanistic perspective, can anything that studies "unseen mental processes" qualify as a science? Struggles over that question ended with the first shift in 20th-century psychology, from objective to subjective perspectives as part of the cognitive revolution in the 1950s.

With the "rediscovery" of the mind by psychology, the topic of learning took on more importance in understanding why we do what we do. Based on earlier perspectives, learners were passive recipients of teaching. As an emerging pillar supporting coaching, adult learning theory took the lead in shifting the emphasis from a passive to an active, participating learner. During the last part of the 20th century, the teacher became more a facilitator or guide or encourager—more like a coach. Students were encouraged to bring their own experience to the classroom and to take responsibility for setting goals and proactively moving toward them rather than reacting to or merely taking in a predetermined curriculum.

With the neuroscience platform taking shape, this shift continues toward making it possible for coaches and leaders to understand how the brain makes connections, makes decisions, and solves what may sometimes seem to be intractable problems.

Before we begin, we want to make an important point. Many people confuse psychology with psychotherapy. Like biology and medicine, the two fields are related. However, psychology and biology are scientific disciplines. Their adherents conduct research and develop theories to explain their subject matter. Psychotherapy and medicine are applications of those sciences, plus others. Understanding how and why people behave as they do, as in psychology, is not the same as being able to treat a person's mental illness, as in psychotherapy. There are many psychologists (clinical or counseling psychologists) who practice psychotherapy, just as many physicians, social workers, psychiatric nurses, clinical counselors, and people who call themselves "psychotherapists" do. The practice of psychotherapy has its own history, research, and theory, rooted as much in medicine as in psychology. Therefore, psychotherapy is discussed on its own in part IV.

CHAPTER 7

Bedrock — Psychology

In 1920, John Watson (1878–1958) conducted an experiment in his laboratory at Johns Hopkins University. He placed a rabbit next to a 9-month-old boy named Albert, who immediately was attracted and reached out to the furry animal. Then, out of sight of the boy, Watson made a very loud sound by hitting a steel bar with a hammer.

Innumerable introductory psychology students have witnessed the heart-wrenching film of what happens next: "Little Albert" jerks back suddenly at the loud sound and begins to cry. After seven repetitions, the boy began to cry as soon as the rabbit was presented to him, even without the sound. Little Albert had been conditioned to fear rabbits. Watson was engaged in establishing behaviorism as a major theory to explain human behavior, and it all had to do with observable and objectively measurable behavior, exactly what the science of the day required. Watson had introduced behaviorism to North American psychology.

Psychology is a modern attempt to apply scientific methods to questions that have interested philosophers for centuries:

- Can we predict what other people will do?
- Can we influence how they behave?
- Are there "natural laws" that underlie our actions?
- How can we observe and measure behavior so as to discover those laws?
- Is there a role for subjective experience in studying people's actions?

- How much can we understand about an individual divorced from context?
- What are personalities and how do we get them?
- How can we explain the similarities and differences among people?

Psychology finds its roots in the ancient philosophers we explored in chapter 2. Understanding the "psyche," the Greek word for "soul" or "spirit," was an inseparable part of religious, spiritual, and health teachings throughout most of human history, but the physical and mental were separated in Western thought after medieval times.

HISTORICAL INTERLUDE

The separation between physical and spiritual (including mind) began to be challenged in the 16th century when the name "psychology"— putting together "psyche" or "soul" and the Greek word for study or knowledge—was first used (Green, 2007). The newly named psychology became a rich topic for philosophers over the next three centuries, but scientists mainly busied themselves discovering laws of the physical world, leaving the "soul" or "psyche" to the church and philosophers.

The increasing secularization of the 19th century allowed science to bring its methods to bear on the psyche. The "scientizing" of psychology can be traced to 1879, when Wilhelm Wundt (1832–1920) established the first psychology laboratory at Germany's University of Leipzig. In keeping with scientific procedures of the time, Wundt carefully measured human abilities and perception, such as the perceived heaviness of different levels of weight, and called his studies "psychophysics." Wundt's laboratory promised to apply the same principles of objectivity to psychological phenomena that had led to the advances of industrialization. Thus, it attracted scholars from all over the world, who then went back to their home countries to introduce the work to others. One of these was the American philosopher William James (1842–1910).

James founded the first psychology laboratory in the United States at Harvard University. He followed Wundt's model in the laboratory, but James retained an interest in topics beyond what could be measured in laboratories of the day. James is best known for his work *The Principles*

---

of Psychology (1950), a huge two-volume encyclopedia of psychological topics of interest in his era. These included brain function, stream of thought, the self, habit, perception, attention, voluntary movement, and the will.

James's approach to psychology, now over 100 years old, has remarkable parallels to coaching and eventually to neuroscience and quantum theory.

At the beginning of the 20th century in North America, psychology stood at a crossroads between the subjective, introspective exploration of "unseen mental processes" typified by James and the emphasis on measurement that characterized Wundt's experimental approach. Wundt himself engaged in introspective inquiry, but it was the experiments conducted in his laboratory that fit best with an attempt to conform to "hard" science. Careful measurement and experimentation had met with enormous success in providing technological solutions for manufacture and transportation, and it therefore enjoyed great prestige. Why not apply those methods to the psyche?

As the 19th century changed to the 20th century, problems of business, education, government, and the military were presenting challenges for the emerging dominance of the United States. As psychological critic Isaac Prilleltensky (1994) wrote, psychology "did not hesitate to volunteer its services in exchange for recognition as the 'master' science of human affairs" (p. 28).

Psychology was successful in negotiating this exchange. It fulfilled its part of the bargain by assuming the mantle of value-free seeker of objective truth. According to Prilleltensky (1994), "By portraying itself as a strictly 'objective' endeavor, psychology erroneously interprets many of its *prescriptive* biases as merely *descriptive* assertions about human behavior" (p. 25, emphases in original).

Psychology also adopted a pillar of Western capitalist ideology: that self-interest is the primary route for the promotion of well-being. In this view, "the self is conceived of as a supreme entity with magnificent powers" (Prilleltensky, 1994, p. 17). Once it is assumed that the self supersedes the system, change can come only from the self, and not the organization or society. This assumption relates not only to understanding behavior but also to how we go about changing it. The shift to recognizing social context as a crucial aspect of maintaining and creating change is a theme of great relevance to coaching. It appears in nearly every chapter of this book.

But the beginning of the 20th century was the heyday of mechanistic science. In taking on the mantle of science, psychology rejected the subjective approach of James, the holistic perspective of classical healers, the dialectic and historical traditions of Hegel and Marx, and the willingness to admit and examine underlying values. These "systemic" elements lay fallow, to be rediscovered in North America at the very time when coaching emerged. How psychology lost and then began to recover these elements is the story that underlies the topics in this chapter.

Psychology is divided into a number of subdisciplines, most of which have applications to various areas of human or social endeavor, and many of which have direct relevance to coaching. Because of the breadth of psychological inquiry, other subdisciplines will be examined in subsequent chapters. These four bedrock areas and a summary will be presented in order to discover their usefulness in a coaching context:

- Behaviorism
- Psychometrics
- Developmental psychology
- Evolutionary psychology
- Psychology as bedrock for coaching

BEHAVIORISM

The subjective effect of James Watson's experiment with Little Albert appeared to be of no concern to the experimenters. It is not known what happened to the boy as a result of this experiment, and it should be noted that treating people as experimental subjects without considering possible ill effects is no longer permitted in psychology laboratories. Strict ethical guidelines regarding the use of human beings in psychological and other research are now in place (see American Psychological Association website).

However, in his time, Watson was in a line of eminent researchers including the famous Ivan Pavlov (1849–1936) in Russia. Pavlov conditioned dogs to salivate to a bell after it had been rung time and again just before the introduction of meat powder into the dogs' mouths. Pavlov's careful documentation and Wundt's measurement of human sensory abilities combined with Watson's experiments, such as those with Little Albert, to make it seem possible to develop a science of mind that was as objective and rigorous as any of the natural sciences.

HISTORICAL INTERLUDE

It was not long before applications of the new behaviorist science spread outside the laboratory. In the very year of the Little Albert experiment, Watson's affair with his lab assistant was discovered, and he was asked to resign from his professorship at Johns Hopkins.

After divorcing his wife, Watson married his former lab assistant and took a job at the V. Walter Thompson advertising agency. Promoted to vice president in 1924, he put to work the psychological principles he had developed in the laboratory, selling such products as Pond's Cold Cream, Maxwell House coffee, and Johnson's Baby Powder.

Many of the techniques that advertisers use to this day were developed during Watson's years in advertising. For example, he translated the Little Albert experiment into a positive frame. If you show or tell us over and over about something we react to positively (a sexy model, desirable clothes, delicious food), then follow that immediately with a product, consumers will "associate" that positive reaction with the product and buy more of it. We may complain about the incessant repetition of ads on TV, the radio, the Internet, or billboards, but early "scientific" research showed repetition to be effective. If variety was proved to be the key to sales, you can bet we would never see the same ad twice.

The most influential figure in the history of behaviorism is B. F. Skinner (1904–1990). Reading a description of Watson's behaviorist philosophy changed his life. As a doctoral student in psychology at Harvard University, he invented equipment (known popularly as the Skinner Box) to time and measure reinforcement and responses. As a professor at several universities and then back at Harvard, Skinner developed the theory of operant conditioning: We behave the way we do because of certain consequences we have experienced. Skinner denied that feelings or intentions play any part in determining behavior. These were "unseen mental processes" that occurred in the "black box" of the mind, not

(Continued)

---

directly observable (at least not back then) and therefore not admissible as scientific data. In the spirit of the mechanistic paradigm, only the conditions, termed "stimuli," and consequences of behavior, termed "reinforcers," were of interest.

Skinner claimed to have found a new version of psychology, which he called behavior analysis, based on his philosophy of radical behaviorism. According to this approach, human actions are always really reactions that can be studied in a laboratory the same as reactions of any animal might be studied. Behaviorists equated children with the rats, monkeys, fish, cats, and chickens on which they experimented, and then applied learning from these experiments to the classroom, to the training of teachers, to military training, and thus to the world. People were assumed to have been born as "blank slates." Obtaining whatever behavior one might desire from them was a matter of arranging proper conditions and consequences. Steven Pinker (2002) more recently argues vigorously against this approach, but in the 1950s, introductory psychology courses primarily focused on behaviorism as the core of scientific psychology.

The impact of behaviorist thought on our daily lives cannot be underestimated. Watson wrote articles for popular magazines of the time, insisting, for example, that parents who show their children too much affection run the risk of ruining their child's healthy development. He contributed to the development of the self-help movement, one that continues to be guided by whatever psychological or pseudoscientific finding is popular at the moment. Skinner did not hesitate to apply the results of his laboratory research to human life and society in general. The government of the United States used "scientific" principles to sell the public on entering World War I (further discussed in chapter 13 in the section on social psychology). Hitler and the Nazis did the same to garner support for their war efforts. Psychological research has been used to enhance police and military techniques of intimidation and torture and allegedly even political and economic control (Klein, 2007).

The enormous influence of behaviorism on psychotherapy is covered in part IV. While some applications of behaviorism are reprehensible, the field has also left a legacy that has contributed to society in many ways. Behaviorism was behind the growth of the animal research field, which led to a better understanding of issues such as our relationship to drug dependence, motivational systems, learning processes, and how we cope with stress, not to mention a number of neuroscience discoveries.

In terms of research, behaviorist literature is enormous. Some of the specific principles that have emerged include:

- The law of exercise: repetition strengthens learning.
- The law of effect: the effect of reward is to strengthen learning.
- The principle of fast feedback: the optimum time between response and reinforcement is about half a second. In other words, for positive feedback to have an impact, it should be immediate.
- Punishment tends to be less effective than positive reinforcement combined with no reinforcement. Punishment may have unintended consequences and, rather than inhibiting the targeted behavior, often results in continuing the behavior when the punisher is not present.

Behavioral psychology's impact on coaching is also substantial. From this field, we learned that people can change and that we—and they—can arrange consequences to impact that change.

For example, Skinner introduced a three-stage behavior training method:

1. Define the goal or terminal behavior desired.
2. Define the starting point (the current behavior).
3. Positively reinforce each step in the desired direction while ignoring all other behavior.

Example: "Train the Professor"

University students prove the efficacy of these steps every time they pull the "train the professor" prank. Before a class, students decide on a goal (terminal behavior). For example, they may decide to have the professor stand close to the left side of the chalkboard. The professor begins the class, say, behind the lectern on the right of the board (current behavior). Students look down and away—whatever might indicate a lack of interest or attention (ignoring behavior that does not lead toward the goal). Whenever the professor makes a move toward the left of the chalkboard, the students sit up and pay attention (positively reinforcing goal-related behavior). After many repetitions, to the delight of budding behavioral scientists in the room, the professor is standing close to and on the left of the chalkboard.

Dog owners and parents will recognize these steps. The fact that attention, treats, or praise work only when the professor, dog, or child is "hungry" for that particular reinforcement brings up cognitive questions of expectation, motivation, personality, and context. For reasons such as that, both coaching and neuroscience have moved beyond behaviorism while retaining its useful elements.

Coaches can help clients develop behavioral methods to manage and improve their results. For example, if we break a large project into smaller steps and then reward ourselves for completing each step, or if we allow ourselves dessert when we exercise three times a week, we are engaging the principles of operant conditioning. Behaviorism has a reputation of being manipulative, but when a client is involved in the development of an action plan, it becomes behavioral self-control rather than manipulation.

The behaviorist approach also contributed significantly to the development of "competencies" to capture observable performance standards. Professional regulatory or licensing bodies, such as for accounting, management, counseling, and coaching, have attempted to specify competencies (see, for example, the International Coach Federation website in Internet Links). Organizations identify specific behaviors that employees should be exhibiting in their various roles. Leadership competencies, for example, are now common in many organizations, with behavioral coaching made available to executives to help them improve competencies identified as less than optimal.

One of the proponents of "behavioral coaching" is Marshall Goldsmith (2003), an organizational coach who begins a coaching engagement by establishing an agreement with the client and his or her manager. The agreement defines the behaviors that are seen to be most likely to improve leadership effectiveness (establishing a goal or terminal behavior). A further agreement sets out who in the organization will determine whether the change has occurred after a year of step-by-step work with Goldsmith (comparing current behavior with desired future goal).

Overall, the behavioral approach is very much alive and well in organizational settings. When business leaders want to change the behaviors of large numbers of people, they often look first to behaviorism. Most managers swear by the principle of rewarding good behavior (e.g., with bonuses) in order to get more of it. This is the basis of the field of performance management. Managers also tend to believe in some form of punishment for behaviors that are not desired, though their options for delivery of punishment are increasingly limited by legal restrictions, union contracts, and an emphasis on promoting respectful relationships that has helped to fuel the popularity of coaching. How management is moving beyond this paradigm to a model that relies on "leadership" is covered in part V.

Even before technology provided the means for neuroscientists to observe events inside the black box of the brain, cognitive psychology had broken through the behaviorists' objections to the scientific investigation of thought, emotion, meaning, and intentions. More on that in chapter 8. Meanwhile, it is important for coaches to realize that there are aspects of behaviorist discoveries that are difficult to ignore and that form part of the bedrock for both coaching and neuroscience.

Linking Behaviorism to Coaching

The overall behaviorist philosophy is something that sits well with some coaches and not with others. In summary, these three principles may be useful to coaches:

1. Provide carefully timed carrots and do not ignore the stick.
2. Either positive rewards or punishment accounts for the motivation to change.
3. Change comes from identifying a goal as defined in behavioral terms, building a step-by-step action plan, and providing reinforcement as motivation.

PSYCHOMETRICS

HISTORICAL INTERLUDE

The subdiscipline of psychological testing, or psychometrics, arose very early in the history of scientific psychology. In the 1890s at the University of Pennsylvania, if you were an experimental psychology student of Professor James Cattell, himself a student of Wundt, you would have

(Continued)

taken a series of tests to measure the strength of your grip, how fast you could move your arm, how quickly you reacted to sound, and other simple functions. Cattell hoped to find easily measurable abilities (none involving any complex thinking skills) that would correlate with your grades and would be an indication of "intelligence." He and colleagues at other universities of the time failed to find any such correlations, and the testing movement in North America stalled for a while.

But in France, Alfred Binet (1875–1911) was closely observing the intellectual development of his two daughters, and he concluded that complex mental processes such as abstract reasoning, not simple physiological abilities, were what marked intelligence. At the same time, Theodore Simon (1873–1961), also in France, was working with children who were then described as "retarded," and he and other educators and psychologists such as Binet convinced the French government that educational opportunities for such children needed to be improved. But how to identify these children? Simon proposed to Binet a testing program based on the theories Binet had developed.

Based on trial and error with both "normal" and "retarded" children, the two men devised a test that in its final version in 1911 included five tasks for each year of childhood from age 3 to 12. Children who could perform all tasks up to and including the ones for their actual age would have a "mental age" that was the same as their chronological age.

For example, a child of 4 can typically copy a square but not a diamond. If a 4-year-old were able to copy a diamond (as normally only a 7-year-old can do), the chronological 4-year-old would have a mental age of 7, according to the original Binet test. In order to have measures that could be easily compared, psychometrists developed a quotient by dividing the mental age by the chronological age and then multiplying the result by 100. Thus, our 4-year-old diamond copier would have an intelligence quotient of 175 — a genius indeed.

The intelligence quotient of a 7-year-old who could at best perform tasks typical of a 4-year-old would be 57, indicating eligibility for Simon's special educational program. When word of the success of the Binet-Simon test reached the United States, a resurgence of interest in psychometrics resulted.

Assessment for such things as "intelligence" did not strictly fit the behaviorist paradigm, as the traits being tested were often "unseen mental processes." However, because psychometrists dealt with measurement and statistics, many saw this as qualifying what they were doing as "real" science. Thus, psychometrics lent its weight to the growing acceptance among policy makers and social institutions of psychology as a science:

- Business wanted to know how to select workers who fit their jobs and expectations.
- Public education policy makers wondered how to select students for different types of educational opportunities. Lewis M. Terman (1877–1956) translated Binet's work into English in 1916, extended it to age 15 and to adults, and developed what would become the Stanford-Binet intelligence test. Others followed, the most influential being the Wechsler Adult Intelligence Scale (WAIS) and the Wechsler Intelligence Scale for Children (WISC) developed by David Wechsler (1896–1981) and still in use today, primarily in clinical and school psychology practice.
- The U.S. military faced the problem of sorting huge numbers of draftees and enlistees into World War I–related duties. Binet-type tests were difficult to administer to large numbers of subjects, so Robert Yerkes (1876–1956), who was president of the American Psychological Association at the time, headed a team that devised two paper-and-pencil tests: Army Alpha for those who could read and Army Beta for those who could not. The involvement of nearly 2 million men in this testing program supported the acceptance of psychometrics and the legitimacy of scientific psychology.
- The Thematic Apperception Test (TAT), a personality assessment developed by Henry A. Murray (1893–1988), was also used during the World War II efforts (OSS Assessment Staff, 1948) for selecting and assigning duties to soldiers. The TAT was an exception to behaviorist trends and utilized Murray's long-standing relationship with Carl Jung for theoretical underpinnings.
- Psychiatrists wondered how to diagnose pathology in people who seemed to function well most or some of the time, so Starke R. Hathaway and J. C. Mckinley at the University of Minnesota hospitals developed the Minnesota Multiphasic Personality Inventory

(MMPI) in 1942. Current versions are still widely in use. Administration and interpretation of the MMPI are restricted to trained physicians and clinical psychologists, and its emphasis on psychopathology makes it of little relevance to coaches.

- Less clinically oriented personality tests have proliferated as self-help and self-awareness movements stimulated widespread curiosity about one's "personality." Many of these assessments are used by coaches to provide a framework for thinking about a client's approach to problem-solving, relationships, work, stress, and just about anything else in life.

Psychological tests are used extensively in nearly every other subdiscipline of psychology, and assessments have been developed to identify almost every conceivable trait or skill or attitude or potential. The computer has made it possible to conduct much more complex statistical analyses than were possible in the early attempts to determine school achievement, job fit, or military readiness. However "scientific" or "statistically valid" a test is, the question our clients ask is "What does it mean for me?"

In chapter 1, we referred to Clyde Kluckhohn's quote:

All people are the same.

Some people are the same.

No people are the same. (Kluckhohn & Murray, 1948, p. 35)

These statements yield three different frameworks for thinking about and dealing with people. When comparative psychologists and linguists ask about how human empathy or language ability compares with that of apes or other animals, they are engaging the first framework and focusing on ways in which all people are the same.

Typically, psychometrists are interested in the second of Kluckhohn's frameworks: the ways in which some people are the same. They devise measures that put people into categories based on the similarity of their responses.

The process of one-on-one coaching utilizes the third framework. A coaching engagement is, after all, a relationship between unique, one-of-a-kind individuals, and effective team or organizational coaching also honors this principle. Using "objective" assessments to ignore the uniqueness of clients (i.e., treating them as test scores or labels) is destructive of the respect and intimacy that is at the core of coaching. It may be useful to conceive of coaching about assessments as an opportunity to translate from the second to the third of Kluckhohn's frameworks: to explore how assessment scores or categories are revealed or modified in this person's unique life and context.

Many coaches consider it important to become trained in administering, or at least interpreting, the assessment instruments that are most often used in their context.

Whatever the specific assessment instrument that a coach uses or that a client brings to us for interpretation, certain principles apply:

- Knowing the category that describes how "some people are the same" can be very useful.

Example: "Slow and Deliberate"

Marilyn was required to complete an assessment as part of deciding on a career. She was categorized as being "slow and deliberate" rather than "quick and impetuous." Her career counselor knew better than to suggest a job that required speed and suggested instead a position in which accuracy was valued.

- Treating the results of assessments as the final word on a person can lead to two errors: (1) the category (in Marilyn's case, speed) is taken out of the person's full social and historical context; and (2) the person may be treated as if she or he *is* the category.

Example: From Slow to Careful

When Marilyn brought the assessment to her coach because she had been asked in a performance review to improve the speed of her work, the coach shifted the framework to one that avoids these two potential errors. Rather than taking the category of "slow and deliberate" as being true at all times in all circumstances, the coach wondered when it was

(Continued)

that Marilyn completed tasks more quickly. The coach discovered that anxiety caused Marilyn to slow down and check her work over and over. When Marilyn identified those circumstances in which she felt anxious, she was able to take steps to reduce their effects.

In addition, the coach wondered what meaning the speed of her work had for Marilyn—not for anyone else, not even for someone who scored exactly the same on the assessment. This framework stresses the individual uniqueness of each person—how "no people are the same." Marilyn discovered the "slowness" that might have meant a lack of motivation for another employee actually was a sign of her commitment to her company and to her job. She wanted to make sure that she did her work exactly right.

When she reframed her "slowness" as "engagement," Marilyn was able to negotiate new expectations with her boss. Even for her own self-image, she was able to think of herself as a person who sometimes did things slowly and carefully when she was unsure and when the outcome was very important. Marilyn felt very differently about this, as compared to thinking of herself as being slow.

- Many times clients bring assessments to coaches not because they misunderstand the content of interpretations they have been given but because they want to be treated as whole, unique human beings in exploring those interpretations.
- It is necessary to keep in mind what it is that the assessment is measuring. For example, if a test shows that a person is anxious, is that because the setting in which the test was administered is anxiety-producing? That is, if your job depends on how you do on a test, it would not be surprising to find that your state of anxiety goes up when you take it. That is different from an enduring trait of anxiety that a person might demonstrate whatever the setting.
- Another problem occurs when an assessment is seen as the personality or pattern or trait itself. The assessment is merely an indicator, a finger pointing to a personality or pattern or trait, not the actual trait. This is a variation of "the map is not the territory." Thus, feedback from the coach must always be verified by the client if the results of an assessment are to be truly useful.
- Finally, all psychometric assessments are based on averages or other statistics about *groups* of people (some people who score the same). The tests indicate only *probabilities* regarding any individual person.

Linking Psychometrics to Coaching

The development of psychometric tests is a highly technical field far beyond the scope of this book. However, we do not have to be experts to understand that a particular client's test scores are only as good as the quality of the assessment instrument itself. We see assessments in popular magazines—like "Four Questions to Tell if You're a Really Cool Person." Any of us can make up an assessment. We can assess the popularity of television shows by asking a dozen of our friends which ones they like. But then we may be surprised when our favorite show gets canceled. The assessments that give clients the most useful information are ones that were developed:

- By analyzing ("norming") responses from a large number of different people (not just our friends, who tend to be like us).
- By making sure they measure what they say they measure ("validity").
- By ensuring they come up with essentially the same results from test to test or over time ("reliability").

The development and distribution of assessments is an industry in itself. Coaches who consider administering or interpreting a particular test are fortunate to have the resources of the Internet as an aid to due diligence. Many assessments and their scoring are also available on the Internet. Courses on how to deliver and interpret testing instruments abound. But we should never hesitate to ask test distributors for a plain-language explanation of how the assessment was developed and where and how others have used it.

In summary, coaches would do well to remember that:

- Formal, written assessments are simply different lenses for gathering information about people.
- People are so complex that their full richness cannot be conveyed by a single perspective, no matter how carefully designed the assessment instrument may be.
- "Objective" assessments and subjective conversations with clients can serve as two poles between which an increasingly rich understanding of our clients can cycle and emerge.

Developmental Psychology

As universal public education became policy during the 19th century, governments sought ways to determine whether schooling was effective. To do this, they needed to understand what could reasonably be expected of children at different ages. Psychology was called on to provide the answer, and the field of developmental psychology was born.

HISTORICAL INTERLUDE

At the time in North America when behaviorism insisted on ignoring unseen mental processes, Jean Piaget (1896–1980) in Switzerland was making enormous strides in understanding how those processes develop. Early in his career, Piaget taught at the school in France run by Alfred Binet, the developer of intelligence testing introduced earlier in the section on psychometrics. Piaget noticed that students of a certain age tended to make the same mistakes in answering questions on the test. He was fascinated by the pattern of these errors and began to wonder if that and similar patterns characterized cognitive capacities at different ages. He and his wife, Valentine, had three children whom he studied from infancy. As a result of these observations, Piaget (1928) organized cognitive development into a series of stages—levels of development corresponding to infancy, childhood, and adolescence.

In Piaget's scheme, from birth to age 2 is called the Sensorimotor Stage. From age 2 to age 7 is the Preoperational Stage, when motor skills are acquired. The Concrete Operational Stage occurs from age 7 to age 11, when children become able to think logically about concrete events. After age 11, they go through what Piaget termed the Formal Operational Stage, when they develop abstract reasoning. These stages have proven to be extremely important in education as well as in psychological development studies.

Piaget also developed a theory of "schemas," another name for mental maps. He defined schemas as building blocks of simple ideas that we from into more complex ones. He proposed that in childhood we learn through "assimilation," meaning that we take in information from our surroundings to form new schemas. As adults we learn through "accommodation,"

---

which means using new information to change existing knowledge or schemas.

Piaget can be seen as contributing to constructivism in psychology, a stream of thought that developed outside of behaviorism and came into its own with the cognitive revolution to be discussed in chapter 8 in the section on cognitive psychology. Constructivist ideas have roots in the philosophy of Hans Vaihinger (1921) and in the sociological theory of Peter Berger and Thomas Luckmann (1966). Piaget influenced Lev Vygotsky (1896–1934), a Russian researcher whose ideas became known in the West in the 1960s; and Lawrence Kohlberg (1927–1987), who focused on the moral development of children and adolescents.

Developmental psychology studies age-related changes in behavior across the life span. Whereas behaviorists claimed that "we are whatever our conditioning makes us," developmental psychologists said that "we are our stage of life."

It must also be noted that some theorists, such as Alfred Adler, downplayed the assumption that every person went through the same stages in the same order. This matched with his focus on the uniqueness and creativity of each individual. More recently, feminist and postmodern theorists have questioned whether stages of personality, cognition, or moral development apply universally or only to the men or specific ethnic or cultural group on which the theory was based. When a certain developmental pattern is accepted as "normal," then people who differ (remember, "no people are the same") may think of themselves or be treated pejoratively as "abnormal."

Despite these criticisms, the major emphasis of developmental psychology has been on understanding the characteristic changes in appearance, behavior, interests, and goals from one developmental period to another. Early research concentrated on schoolchildren. Later, interest spread to preschool, then infancy. Shortly after World War I, research studies of the adolescent years began. Between then and World War II, there were some studies of the early adult years, but they concentrated mainly on specific problems. Adulthood, middle age, and old age were ignored; it was as if no changes took place between adolescence and death. In the 1970s, books and journals began to appear that indicated stages in adult life that were as important as the stages in a child's life.

With the exceptions of parent coaching and coaching with educators, coaches are more likely to use theories of development focused on adults.

Erik Erikson (1902–1994) was one theorist who emphasized developmental change throughout the human life span, not just in childhood or adolescence. In Erikson's theory (Coles, 1970), eight stages of development unfold as we go through life. Each stage consists of a crisis that must be faced. According to Erikson, this crisis is not a catastrophe but a turning point of increased vulnerability and enhanced potential. The more successfully an individual resolves the crises, the healthier his or her development will be.

The stages include:

1. *Trust versus mistrust*, experienced in the first year of life.
2. *Autonomy versus shame and doubt*, occurring in late infancy and toddlerhood (1 to 3 years).
3. *Initiative versus guilt*, occurring during the preschool years.
4. *Industry versus inferiority*, which takes place from age 6 to age 11 and involves the shift from whimsical play to a desire for achievement and completion.
5. *Identity versus identity confusion*, when adolescents begin to seek their true identities and a sense of self (Erikson coined the phrase "identity crisis").
6. *Intimacy versus isolation*, experienced during the early adulthood years.
7. *Generativity versus stagnation*, a crisis of middle adulthood.
8. *Integrity versus despair*, faced during late adulthood.

It can be enormously helpful for a coach to reframe a client's midcareer questions as an opportunity to generate new goals or to confirm forgotten values.

Frederic Hudson has also contributed to the theoretical understanding of adult development (Hudson, 1999; Murphy & Hudson, 1995). Called "Dr. Midlife" by the *LA Times*, Hudson has brought a welcome theoretical depth to pioneering work in coaching.

Otto Laske based his Interdevelopmental (IDM) Institute coach training on what he calls a "Constructive Developmental Framework" (Laske, 2007). Laske claims that coaches must themselves pay attention to their own developmental level. Laske claims that "Interventions are developmentally counter-productive wherever the coach resides at a lower stage than does the client" (p. 239). Laske's emphasis on values and his appreciation of constructivism and dialectic method are indications of developmental psychology's contribution to the shift to a systemic worldview.

Linking Developmental Psychology to Coaching

- Developmental changes, crises, and urges can be important motivators, and coaches should keep developmental stages in mind when dealing with clients. A woman of 25 may well have different goals and a different opportunity for development from a woman of 50.
- It may be helpful for clients to reframe issues in their lives as opportunities to explore the next developmental phase.
- When facing the crisis of generativity versus stagnation, many organizational leaders begin to ask about their legacy, and legacy coaching can be of tremendous value at this point in their lives.
- However, just as we pointed out in the discussion of psychometrics, the essence of a coaching relationship is one in which two unique human beings collaborate in conversations that respect that uniqueness. No person—adult or child—is fully represented by a description of his or her developmental stage, however much people may benefit from exploring whether that stage applies to them and what it may mean specifically to them.
- An argument for coaches having their own coach and continuing to develop professionally is that we may inhibit our clients' development by not continuing to grow beyond our own limits, what we call in this book "potentiating."

EVOLUTIONARY PSYCHOLOGY

Charles Darwin (1809–1882) was a British naturalist who shocked the 19th century with his book *On the Origin of Species by Means of Natural Selection*, first published in 1859. He proposed that through millions of years, all species of plants and animals had evolved from a few common ancestors. Natural selection theory rests on the assumption of inherited variations within a species. Certain variations aid those who have them in adapting to their environment, especially when the environment changes. The offspring of these individuals produce more offspring than others. Traits that hinder adaptation for the individual who carries them are eventually eliminated. Over time, these changes accumulate and the species evolves.

HISTORICAL INTERLUDE

Herbert Spencer (1820–1903) was an influential force for social psychological thought at the end of the 19th century. Spencer extended Darwin's notions from the biological realm into the social. It was Spencer, not Darwin, who coined the phrase "survival of the fittest." His espousal of Social Darwinism became quite influential in the thought of many early American psychologists, including William James.

The social Darwinist idea that behavior (not just physical traits) could be influenced by heredity was in direct opposition to Watson's idea that environment, or conditioning, accounted entirely for personality and other psychological traits. Watson's position that nurture trumped nature did not go unchallenged. William McDougall (1871–1938), a British psychologist who became professor of psychology at Harvard University, emphasized the role of instincts in human behavior and made it clear that he had little use for behaviorism or its resulting radical emphasis on nurture.

In 1924, the Psychology Club, a group of amateurs and professionals who were interested in psychological questions, took advantage of the enmity between the two theorists and arranged for a debate in Washington, DC, that was billed as "The Battle of Behaviorism." McDougall and Watson each presented his argument, pulling out all the stops to convince the audience. The vote was taken, and McDougall won. But not only was his victory narrowly won, he ended up losing the war for popular and even academic influence. It was Watson's behaviorism that fit with early-20th-century North American assumptions that science and technology could cure all social ills.

But the nature side of the dichotomy did not disappear. As part of the ideology that justified racism in the United States, "eugenics" was proposed as a way to maintain inherited physical and mental advantages. Nazism applied the theory systematically, first by eliminating political opponents, such as union leaders and socialists, and then by extending

---

the policy to Jews and Gypsies. Along with the defeat of Nazi Germany in World War II, eugenics was discredited.

However, similar underlying assumptions and further discoveries in genetics fueled the development of sociobiology, a field that fell to perhaps its lowest point with the publication of The Bell Curve (Herrnstein & Murray, 1994). This book cited questionable statistics to revive the theory of racial inferiorities.

Konrad Lorenz (1903–1989) was an Austrian ornithologist and animal psychologist whose work on imprinting, modeling, and comparing animal and human psychology was influential in bringing biology and psychology into the same realm. He was awarded the 1973 Nobel Prize in Physiology and Medicine (sharing it with Nikolaas Tinbergen and Karl von Frisch) for discoveries in ethology.

Michael T. Ghiselin, an American philosopher and historian of biology, renewed the use of the term "evolutionary psychology" in a Science article published in 1973. Leda Cosmides from the Department of Psychology and John Tooby from the Department of Anthropology at the University of California Santa Barbara, began the Center for Evolutionary Psychology in the 1990s. In their online publication, Evolutionary Psychology: A Primer (1997) they quote Darwin's Origin of Species: "In the distant future I see open fields for far more important researches. Psychology will be based on a new foundation, that of the necessary acquirement of each mental power and capacity by gradation" (in Cosmides & Tooby, 1997, p. 1). Cosmides and Tooby rely on this quote to support their claim that psychological traits, as well as physical traits, are governed by the scientific principles of evolution.

Evolutionary psychology understands human behavior as a result of the human brain's evolution via natural selection. According to Cosmides and Tooby (1997), "Psychology is that branch of biology that studies (1) brains, (2) how brains process information, and (3) how the brain's information-processing programs generate behavior." They define the mind as "a set of information-processing machines" (p. 1). Their reduction of the mind to activities of the brain and their identification of the brain with a machine, albeit a computer, locates evolutionary psychologists firmly in the mechanistic paradigm.

Matt Ridley attempts to step beyond mechanism by resolving the nature/nurture debate. In *Genome: The Autobiography of a Species in 23 Chapters* (1999), Ridley celebrates the mapping of the human genome, comparing it to our species discovering its own recipe, with genes as the active ingredient. But Steven Quartz and Terry Sejnowski (2002) point out that experience, such as seeing different sights, turns on genes that build our visual pathways. A parent's touch stimulates the development of genes that protect offspring against stress. "Genes, then, are the tools experience uses to change the brain's response to new demands in new environments" (Quartz & Sejnowsky, 2002, p. 46). Nature and nurture cannot be disconnected.

What human beings inherit is the potential to produce a brain. Our brains are much more adaptable than was once believed, so adaptable that we cannot be said to "inherit" them. Rather, we inherit the capacity to participate, as Leslie Brothers (2001) puts it, to reformulate the details of the recipe as we are putting the socially derived ingredients together. The mind, unlike what would be possible in a purely Newtonian universe, is able to take a conscious and influential part in the mixing and making. In their book *Mean Genes* (2001), authors Terry Burnham and Jay Phelan argue that to understand human behavior, we need to stop looking at Freud and start looking at Darwin. Modern neuroscience suggests that we need to look beyond both Freud and Darwin to a new paradigm.

This is not easy to do, since the claims of evolutionary psychologists often seem so commonsense. One of these claims is that our brains have evolved little since we left the African savannah. Cosmides and Tooby (1997) state a major principle of evolutionary psychology: "Our modern skulls house a stone age mind" (p. 1). The claim is that many of our current everyday mental habits were created in response to environments that we no longer live in. Steven Rose (2005) lists several problems with this claim:

- The characterization of "Stone Age" life in the writing of evolutionary psychologists, while couched in scientific language, is often based more on Flintstone comic strip portrayals than on science.
- The idea that certain traits were fixed "back then" (whenever that might be) and could not possibly have changed is questionable because we do not know how fast it is possible for natural selection to operate.

212

- The hindsight conclusion that the fittest members of a species are the ones whose genes appear in subsequent generations is tautological—the very definition of "fitness" depends on whether genes "determining" that trait show up in a later gene pool.
- Because human minds and activity may affect inheritance, we cannot attribute fitness to genetics alone.
- The modular computer analogy ignores the importance of integration, which is increasingly the focus of neuroscience theory.
- Brains/minds do not just process information; they are concerned with meaning.
- Anthropologists among so-called primitive peoples from the 1970s report very different behavior as compared with the 1990s. Thus, how can we assume that the 1970s behavior represents ancient Stone Age traits?
- The one thing we know for sure is that the human brain is enormously adaptable. It is also highly social, with a vast potential for cooperation.

How can we who are not experts in these fields evaluate the claims and counter claims that surround evolutionary psychology? First of all, we can recognize that the new scientific paradigm that forms a theme throughout this book transcends either-or, nature-nurture, genes-environment dichotomies. That is, brains and physical bodies, minds, and environment have co-evolved. As brains and bodies have adapted to changing environments, minds have changed in response, and environments have changed as a result of the evolving behavior. In a linear sentence, there is no way to show the arrows of influence and adaptation going in all directions. Even the most complex graphic illustration, with bidirectional arrows connecting every element, is still just a snapshot of a moment in time that cannot capture the dynamism of an interacting system over time. It may be that the next challenge faced by our evolving thinking processes is how to conceptualize such complexity.

Linking Evolutionary Psychology to Coaching

Coaches have immediate concerns of how to help clients achieve their goals in the material world as it (temporarily) exists. Evolutionary psychology is popular because it seems to explain some of the difficulties human beings have with change.

For example, Burnham and Phelan (2000) ascribe modern tendencies to eat the wrong food to "powerful, instinctual hunger" that enabled Stone Age ancestors to survive by eating as much as they could any time that they could. We can leave aside possible contrary examples of plentitude illustrated by "potlatches" on the North American West Coast in more recent history. Certainly anyone who has tried to maintain a strict diet knows the feeling of "powerful, instinctual hunger." If attributing this to our "Stone Age mind" helps us eat more healthful meals, then perhaps it is a harmless misapprehension.

Evolutionary psychology suggestions on diet can be applied to being served food on a plane that includes a brownie for dessert. Our Stone Age "instinctual hunger" for the brownie can be overcome by immediately opening a package of mustard and smearing it over the brownie so as not to be tempted.

As the section on change theory in this book has shown, rather than attributing our behavior to genetic inheritance from the Stone Age, modern neuroscience suggests other ways to explain difficulty with change, ways that are being directly tested and proved rather than surmised in hindsight.

The rediscovery of Darwinian principles has helped speed a resolution to the dualistic conflict that arises from the question "Are we determined by nature or by nurture?" In short, the answer is both and neither. As evidence of Alfred Adler's forward thinking, he got it right nearly a century ago when he wrote, in awkward English,

> Do not forget the most important fact that not heredity and not environment are determining factors — Both are giving only the frame and the influences which are answered by the individual in regard to his styled creative power. (Ansbacher & Ansbacher, 1956, p. xxiv)

The discovery of neuroplasticity means that neither nature, or heredity, nor environment, or nurture, determines who we are. Seeing the two as linked in a dialectic process is part of a shift to a systemic paradigm. Both nature and nurture set limits and contribute influences, but complex self-determining systems such as human beings and their societies are capable of demonstrating emergent properties. Evolutionary psychologists tend to see the mind as "caused" by an information-processing machinelike brain.

Attributing modern-day difficulties to having inherited a "Stone Age" brain and behavior may help clients avoid self-blame, but the scientific basis for this claim is questionable.

PSYCHOLOGY AS BEDROCK FOR COACHING

The attempt to establish a scientific study of human behavior serves as part of the bedrock for coaching. Although much of psychological research, especially in the early part of the 20th century, has been limited by the requirement for objectivity that comes from the mechanistic worldview, many principles continue to be valid:

- Behaviorist principles guide many coaching programs and contribute to the attempt to define competencies in behavioral terms.
- Psychometric assessments are a major focus of the change strategies for many coaches.
- Developmental psychology has provided concepts for exploring client issues over their life span.
- The claims of evolutionary psychology can be seen as warnings to stick close to evidence rather than taking speculative leaps.

In 1956, a new cognitive approach replaced the association of stimulus and response that guided Skinner and his predecessors. Learning theory grew beyond its assumptions of passive receivers of knowledge. These new approaches assumed an active mind and provided a pillar to support the systemic paradigm, coaching, and neuroscience.

CHAPTER 8

Pillar — Activating the Mind

The "cognitive revolution" is said to have begun in 1956. "Revolution" in the scientific world does not occur as the result of a popular uprising and fall of governments but something seemingly much tamer: the publication of books and articles and presentations at academic conferences. Jerome Bruner, Jackie Goodenough, and George Austin took on the decidedly unbehaviorist topic of cognitive strategies in their 1956 book, A Study of Thinking. George Miller published "The Magical Number Seven" (1956) as an exploration of the limitations of working memory. Other articles applied information and communications theory to psychological issues that had not been resolved by behaviorism and in so doing brought together developments in psychology, linguistics, neuroscience, computer science, anthropology, and philosophy. It was in 1956 that the term "artificial intelligence" was used for the first time, as the topic of a conference of computer scientists at Dartmouth University.

This "revolution" had many precursors, some of which have been referred to in previous chapters. But Miller points to one specific day that, for him, marks the birth of cognitive psychology and cognitive science as an interdisciplinary effort: September 11, 1956. The Special Interest Group in Information Technology at the Massachusetts Institute of Technology had organized a symposium, with the first day devoted to coding theory. September 11 was the second day of the symposium, and participants presented a series of papers that could have been seen as just a hodge-podge of unrelated research topics.

On that day in 1956, however, Miller and others exercised their very human capacity for meaning making by seeing the various papers as part of a larger whole. In Miller's words:

> I left the symposium with a conviction, more intuitive than rational, that experimental psychology, theoretical linguistics, and the computer simulation of cognitive processes were all pieces from a larger whole and that the future would see a progressive elaboration and coordination of their shared concerns. (2003, p. 143)

Thus, in putting mental activity back into psychology, cognitive psychology restored creating subjective meaning to the list of human functions. In a revolutionary stroke for the academic world, the mind became an active part of psychology.

By 1956, "Behaviorism was an exciting adventure for experimental psychology but by the mid-1950s it had become apparent that it could not succeed" (Miller, 2003, p. 142). Along with this rediscovery of the mind by cognitive psychologists and advances in developmental psychology, educational theorists were making discoveries that are closely related. The question "Why do we do what we do?" began to be answered in ways that broke away from mechanistic assumptions.

- Do thoughts cause feelings or do feelings cause thoughts? And which of those causes actions?
- How do people get to be really good at what they do?
- Why can't we just tell people what they need to know?
- Why do they not seem to get it even when we tell them?
- How can we motivate people to find out how to do something themselves rather than complaining and expecting someone else to do it for them?
- Why do we spend so much on training when people seem to forget whatever they have learned days or even hours after the session?
- How can I control the anxiety that gets in the way of learning what I need to know?
- How can we learn other things than just skills or knowledge?
- What are the best conditions for learning?
- Is learning best done alone?

- Can people learn how to learn better?
- What parts do other people play in learning?

Rather than treating learning as a product or outcome, recent thinkers see it as a process (Knowles, Holton, & Swanson, 1998). Knowing about the process of learning is crucial for coaches. And, since most coaches work with adults, it is important for us to know that adult learning has specific characteristics, specifically that adults learn best when they are actively engaged as part of the process.

This chapter covers the next topics:

- Cognitive psychology
- Learning theory
- Activating the mind as a coaching pillar

COGNITIVE PSYCHOLOGY

HISTORICAL INTERLUDE

The first decade after the "revolution" was heavily influenced by applying the computer metaphor to mental processes (gardner, 1985). noam chomsky astounded linguistic scholars by suggesting that people's brains had to be hardwired with certain capacities in order to learn a language — that the "blank slate" assumption of radical environmentalist behaviorism was simply wrong. computer scientists called on cognitive psychologists to model the human thinking and problem-solving process so they could build computers that could make decisions and win chess games against experts.

Using the computer as a model for the human brain provided for useful discoveries (e.g., about language learning) and applications (e.g., Neuro-Linguistic Programming). However, as cognitive psychology pioneer Michael J. Mahoney (1991) pointed out, by the 1980s, cognitive psychologists had discovered that modeling human thinking required understanding the flesh-and-blood organism that embodied that thinking, the social and relational context that surrounded and supported it, and the emotions

(*Continued*)

and values that guided it. Psychologist Ulric Neisser (1976) championed and then abandoned laboratory experiments as not being applicable in the "naturalistic" setting of the real world. Philosophers became fascinated with the mind and began to engage in quasi-psychological experiments. That is, psychology began to discover its holistic, contextual, socially embedded, interdisciplinary, and values-oriented "soul" at the very time that coaching was being born.

During the half century since 1956, great strides have been made to understand what goes on in the black box of the brain. At first, this was based on an analogy with a computer: The brain was seen to be a "general-purpose, symbol-processing system of limited capacity" (Eysenck & Keane, 2005, p. 28). Several different approaches have contributed to a broadening of this understanding: laboratory experiments, studying the results of brain damage, attempts to model human brain activity on computers, and the use of functional imaging and other technologies. The integration of these approaches is now referred to broadly as cognitive neuroscience and forms part of what we are including in chapter 9 and other aspects of the Neuroscience Platform for coaching.

The cognitive revolution, located mainly in mid-20th-century North America, stimulated an explosion of interest in topics that had been considered "merely" philosophical or speculative or on the sidelines of "real" behaviorist research.

- *Sensation and perception.* Early behaviorist assumptions were that people learn to put specific bits of sensory information together so they can recognize objects and people. Simply put, this was "bottom-up" processing. Gestalt theorists, however, emphasized native capacity to see the whole, that is, to process from the "top down." We now know that sensation and perception, visual and otherwise, is a much more complex activity than previously thought. One important finding, harking back to the visualization exercises in sports psychology, is that the brain areas that process something we actually see are very similar to the ones activated when we imagine that something.
- *Accuracy in noticing.* Surely you would notice the gorilla-suited actor walking into the middle of the film you are watching, turning to look

at the camera, pounding its chest, then walking off. But 50% of participants in the study by Daniel Simons and Christopher Chabris (1999)
were so involved with their assigned task (counting the number of
times that a basketball was passed back and forth) that they never
noticed the gorilla. This phenomenon is labeled "inattentional change
blindness" and can best be avoided by setting one's mind ahead of
time to be aware of important details. A coach can help in this planning function and also in noticing what the client misses.

- *Attention.* The limits of working memory, or what we pay attention
  to, have been of interest to cognitive researchers since Miller's 1956
  article, "The Magical Number 7." Studies have focused on what
  happens when people concentrate on listening to or looking at
  just one thing and what happens when they try to pay attention to
  more than one input. The results show that attention is more complex than Miller imagined. For instance, when people are asked to
  listen carefully to a voice in one earphone, they generally cannot
  report anything about what was spoken into the other, unattended,
  ear. However, if they are later asked the meaning of an ambiguous
  word, like "bank," they are much more likely to refer to a financial
  institution if the message in the unattended ear was about money
  rather than fishing.

- *Automatic (hardwired) and controlled processing.* The research on attention
  has resulted in the proposition that our conscious attempt to control
  what we pay attention to is much more limited than what we process
  without being aware. Thus, we can know more than we are conscious
  of knowing. Coaches who are comfortable with silence are more
  likely to allow clients to become aware of knowledge just outside
  their present consciousness. This is also a factor in the process of
  insight that is presented in chapter 9.

- *Short-term memory.* Early theorists said that, in order to remember
  something, we need to pay attention to a sensation that lasts only a
  few seconds. Attention puts that item in a "short-term store" that is
  of limited capacity and vulnerable to distraction. Miller (1956) put
  the limitation at 7 items plus or minus 2. More recently, cognitive
  neuroscientists have replaced this simple model with a more complex working memory model, but the idea of the limitation of attentional short-term memory seems to hold true.

- *Rehearsal.* Practice, practice, practice is the secret to getting memory from short to long term. The immense potential of our long-term memory was illustrated early in cognitive psychology, with subjects in experiments able to recognize thousands of pictures they had seen before.

- *Implicit versus explicit learning.* Our ability to learn without verbalizing, or being conscious of, what we have learned exists, not surprisingly, from birth and probably before. However, explicit memory appears not to come on line for human infants until around the time they learn a language. What they remember is then influenced by their cognitive development, as we discussed in the section on developmental psychology.

- *Remembering.* Whereas our recall of explicit memories is accompanied by a sense that we are remembering, we can have implicit memories without any sense that they are memories — they seem like here-and-now experiences. In chapter 9, we further discuss the mental maps that we lay down implicitly and how awareness of them can free clients from unhelpful reactions in similar but different situations. The coach's role is often to point out how doing the same thing (or interpreting a situation in the same way) cannot be expected to lead to different results.

- *Remembering to remember.* One issue that is often discussed in coaching is that of how to remember to do something in the future. Cognitive psychologists call this "prospective memory." There are two general strategies for reminding ourselves to remember: time based and event based. If we promise ourselves to do something two hours or two days in the future, that is time-based reminding. If we use a reminder such as the dog barking at the mail carrier to remember to check our mailbox, that is event-based prospective memory. According to Eysenck and Keane (2005), event-based reminders are more effective.

- *Mastery.* Research on people in various fields who are considered experts at what they do supports the importance of practice. For a complex activity such as musical performance, sports, or computer programming, about 10 years, or 10,000 hours, of practice are considered necessary to develop expertise. But the usual conception of the word expertise, as a product or achievement that one possesses, is quite wrong from the perspective of how it is achieved. Expertise is a dialectical *process* of continually testing one's store of skills and knowledge against challenges or issues that arise (Bereiter & Scardamalia, 1993). Much of cognitive psychology has morphed seamlessly into cognitive neuroscience. These themes are revisited in chapter 9 from the perspective of brain research.

Linking Cognitive Psychology to Coaching

Coaches may find these ideas from cognitive psychology particularly useful:

- Our inner expectations influence what information we take in and notice from the outside world.
- Reminding ourselves of what is important to look out for helps us to notice changes rather than being blind to them.
- Even when we do not pay attention, we may take in information that can be accessed in quiet times or as vague feelings or "intuition."
- Short-term memory that requires attention is limited. Rehearsal or practice is what puts information in almost unlimited long-term memory.
- Reminder techniques can help us remember to remember in the future.
- Expertise is an ongoing process that requires thousands of hours of practice and reflection.

LEARNING THEORY

In part II, we discussed models for change that have direct relevance to coaching. When clients want to achieve a change, they usually must learn something new, and thus coaches are called on to be experts in learning. Because of this, it may appear that all change is learning. But that is not the case. Is it learning if you change in these ways?

- Hunch your shoulders when you step outside into a snowstorm?
- Move your leg when the doctor taps just below your knee?
- Grow half an inch between grades 6 and 7?

- Sleep more than usual when you are ill?
- Gain inches on your biceps following a period of physical training?

None of these changes is a direct example of learning. Learning refers to those changes in a person's capacity that last longer than immediate reflexes and that are not attributable to growth, illness or accidents, or physiological processes (Tight, 1996). As Malcolm Knowles (Knowles et al., 1998) points out, learning results when individuals interact with their environment to fulfill a need, resulting in a greater ability of those individuals to adapt to their environment.

Clearly, this ability to improve how we deal with our environment is a major factor in the survival of the human species, so learning has been important since well before written history began. For most of that history, learning occurred unconsciously—a child watching his father fashion an arrowhead from volcanic glass; an apprentice working alongside a blacksmith; a group of women carding wool, weaving, and sewing together. After the invention of writing and books, conscious learning often was seen as the purview of a select few: first monks in monasteries and then government officials or scholars in universities. But the pace of change has accelerated to the point where Peter Senge (1990) asserts that every organization should be a learning organization and every person a lifelong learner.

When we first started writing this chapter, we titled it "Adult Learning." Our friends in the education field laughed and insisted that learning was learning, whatever one's age, and that the same principles applied. As we will see, this is true with very few exceptions.

Research on formal learning in the Western world was at first focused on young people in school. More recently, research has shown that learning is different in some ways for different age groups. Theories have arisen that account for how people gain knowledge when they are beyond what used to be called "school age" and are "independent," as defined by societal norms. The interest in this topic has been so intense that no single theory covers the field. In the introduction to the canonical book *The Adult Learner*, Knowles and colleagues (1998) acknowledge that the subject is too complex to be covered by a single theory or set of principles. Instead, they cite the story of the blind men describing an elephant—each one touching a different part of the animal and claiming that it is like a rope (when touching the tail), a pillar (when feeling a leg), or a snake (after contact with the trunk). Because of the differing perspectives on adult learning, the authors call for a multifaceted conception.

HISTORICAL INTERLUDE

We can see the beginnings of Western European adult learning models in classical Greece and Rome, with Plato and Aristotle, when learning was considered a process of mental inquiry among adults and was accomplished via the case method, Socratic dialogue, and debate.

This changed during medieval times when learning was either experiential and happened without conscious theories or was handed down from authorities, mainly the church. The revival of observation, debate, and empirical inquiry was part of the 18th-century Enlightenment's rediscovery of Greek and Roman traditions. But outside of serving philosophical inquiry, learning did not become a topic on its own until the public school movement of the late 19th century. The need to educate the young of a whole society and to educate teachers to fulfill this function stimulated the development of theory regarding how to teach children.

The term "andragogy" refers to the teaching of adults, as contrasted with "pedagogy," the teaching of children (Cross, 1981). Malcolm Knowles is considered the father of andragogy, which he pioneered in the 1960s and 1970s. He is best known for his core adult learning principles, the use of learning contracts, and the book *The Adult Learner*, which is now in its sixth edition (Knowles et al., 1998). This book provides an extensive listing of people who contributed to the field of adult learning from 1885 to 1986, either through original research and models or through the reflection and consolidation of others' ideas. The list includes many pioneers in psychology, including Pavlov, Freud, Skinner, Lewin, Maslow, and Rogers. Because coaches work mainly with adults, the principles of andragogy certainly apply to coaching.

David Kolb (1984) and Robert Gagne (1965, 1974) are two of the most prominent learning theorists of the past 40 years. Kolb's work built on that of Kurt Lewin, American educator John Dewey (1859–1952), and Jean Piaget and promotes experiential learning and more recent "learning to learn"

(Continued)

ideas. Kolb (1984) refers to Lewin's four-stage feedback model for learning that is similar to the many "action-reflection cycle" models summarized in chapter 5:

- Experience
- Observation and reflection
- Abstraction and generalization
- Testing implications in new circumstances

Gagne (1965, 1974) developed a systems approach to learning that includes an information processing model and hierarchical levels of learning.

Additional theoretical models of interest to coaches include those of Gerald Grow and Dan Pratt.

Gerald Grow (1991) proposed four stages in learning autonomy and suggested that the facilitator tailor his or her style to match the learner's stage of autonomy. A learner's stage is determined by self-teaching skills and personal autonomy, as they relate to the learning at hand.

Dan Pratt (1998) described adult learners' need for varying degrees of direction and support, depending on their individual personalities, past experiences, and what they are trying to learn. He proposed a four-quadrant model for understanding a learner's level of self-direction. This model is useful to help coaches understand how to adapt their style depending upon the how self-directive the client is able to be.

Tight (1996) traces the development of andragogy through succeeding additions to the theory by Knowles. Knowles's initial core principles about how adults learn expanded on Lindeman's (1926) work from the 1920s in which he stated that, as a person matures, he or she becomes more:

1. Self-directed rather than dependent or passive
2. Experienced, providing more resources
3. Ready to learn what his social roles require
4. Focused on application to immediate problems rather than being subject focused on what may be useful in the future

In the 1980s, Knowles added two more principles that are of particular importance to the adult learner:

5. Knowing ahead of time what is to be learned, why, and how the learning will be accomplished

6. Understanding how the learning will be of value to her or him personally so as to stimulate internal (rather than external) motivation

In the 1998 edition of *The Adult Learner*, Knowles and his colleagues complemented these six core principles with a claim that andragogy must take into account these two dimensions:

1. Individual and situational differences
2. Goals and purposes for learning

These six principles and two dimensions remain basic and commonly accepted tenets of adult learning despite being sharply criticized from some quarters, since they imply that children do not learn this way. Most of these concepts have been demonstrated to apply to pedagogy as well, to the benefit of that field. The only principle that stands unchallenged by this criticism is the second: that adults have more experience from which to learn. Tight (1996) states that adult learning differs from educating children primarily in "the extent to which the former involves negotiation, recognition of experience and some kind of partnership between learner and teacher, trainer, facilitator, or whatever" (p. 26). Clearly, the "whatever" in this statement would include a coach.

A typical coaching engagement can be seen as a form of adult learning, and coaches may benefit from understanding the rich heritage that learning theories provide. For instance, Carl Rogers (1951) proposed that we cannot actually teach another person directly; all we can do is facilitate the learning. Tight (1996) agrees that what was once seen as imparting knowledge or doing things to passive students is now defined as facilitating self-directed learning.

Tight (1996) criticizes the commonly accepted definitions of learning because they focus on the individual learner without acknowledging the importance, especially for adults, of the learner's social context and interactions—that is, their experience—whether in an organization or a community. In essence, he sees learning as being influenced by the learner's social systems. He also describes the current approaches to adult learning as more trial and error, in keeping with the fact that both individuals and organizations are unique in many ways and thus may not be well served by a cookbook approach to learning. "[T]he business of adult learning comes down to a largely rule-of-thumb or heuristic approach. In other words, if it works, do it again; if it doesn't, modify it or try another approach altogether" (Tight, 1996, p. 24). Thus, the issue for learning theory today is how to facilitate learning in unique situations.

A coach benefits from having theoretical principles that can serve as guides. Even more important is the coach's ability to creatively devise ways of working with clients that match the particular needs of each client and his or her situation.

Constructivism, or creativity, has also had a powerful influence on learning theory. Like andragogy in general, constructivism stresses personal autonomy, experiential learning, and problem solving. Constructivism also highlights the need to connect new learning to old in order to retain it and the importance of the learning context, which cannot be separated from the learning itself. Constructivism has contributed to a mechanistic-to-systemic shift in many fields, including sociology, anthropology, psychology, and psychotherapy. Savery and Duffy (1995) describe principles of constructivism in learning theory, many of which apply to coaching quite directly.

Current learning theory is multidimensional, emphasizes the subjective experience of the learner, and recognizes the importance of context. For those reasons, we consider learning theory to be one of the pillars that lifts coaching above the mechanistic bedrock of the early 20th century.

The next sections discuss the main principles of adult learning.

Individual and Situational Differences

Certain aspects of learners' personalities affect how they learn (Knowles et al., 1998; Jonassen and Grabowski, 1993):

- *Field dependence and independence.* Patterns of thinking, sometimes called cognitive controls, determine how the learner reasons about and processes information. The learner's level of dependence or independence on cues from his or her environment is perhaps the most relevant and extensively researched cognitive control for adult learning. Jonassen and Grabowski's research (1993) showed that these two types of learners have distinct preferences for learning processes and activities.

- *Learning style.* All people have different ways that they prefer to learn, and this changes as each individual develops. There are four dimensions of learning style to consider:
  1. Analytic and impersonal versus global and social
  2. Cognitive complexity and abstraction versus cognitive simplicity and concreteness
  3. Impulsivity (talking while thinking) versus reflection (think first, talk later)
  4. Convergent thinking (logical, conventional) versus divergent thinking (creativity and variety)
- *Learning contracts.* Knowles advocates using learning contracts for both formal classes and informal learning projects. Learning contracts specify the learning objectives, learning resources and strategies, evidence that the learner has met objectives, and ways to validate such evidence. More detail and examples can be found in chapter 13 of *The Adult Learner* (Knowles et al., 1998) and *Using Learning Contracts* (Knowles, 1986).

Flexibility and Opportunities for Self-Direction

Flexibility and self-direction are adult learning characteristics that are part of the heritage of coaching. Popular in the United Kingdom, flexible learning has been defined by the U.K.'s Further Education Unit as "the adaptation of available learning opportunities to meet the needs of the learner in a way that optimizes the autonomy of the learner as well as the effectiveness of the process of learning" (quoted in Tight, 1996, p. 97).

Self-directed learning, pioneered by Alan Tough (1971, 1982) in the 1970s and 1980s, is learning in which "the responsibility for, and control of, the learning experience—its planning, delivery and assessment—is largely transferred from the institution to the individual learner" (Tight, 1996, p. 101). Ideally, coaching is both flexible and self-directed, as the client determines the direction of and is responsible for the learning, and the coaching process is customized to meet the client's needs.

Self-directed learning is a composite of two distinct dimensions: self-teaching (the ability to teach oneself something) and personal autonomy (assuming ownership and control of one's learning). A person may self-teach without personal autonomy, or vice versa, depending on the circumstances and the learner's abilities.

- *Self-teaching.* Adults need to be convinced of the value of learning something before they undertake learning it. In his learning project research in the 1970s, Tough (1971, 1982) found that when adults initiate their own learning, they spend considerable time and energy analyzing the benefits of learning and the costs of not learning. As learning facilitators, it becomes our responsibility to ensure that learners understand the learning program's benefits, such as improved quality of life or performance.

  By collaborating with the coach to develop a coaching engagement, the learner will spend time thinking about the "why" and have a deeper understanding of this as the coaching engagement proceeds. In addition, the coach and learner can craft learning activities that identify the gap between the current reality and the desired level of mastery.

- *Autonomy.* Adult learning experts agree that adults prefer to be in control of their own learning experiences, which stems from a self-concept of being responsible for their own lives and decisions and a need to be seen as capable of self-direction. This often conflicts with learners' expectations of training and education programs, in which learners may assume a passive role of being "dependent" on the facilitator to learn. In response, effective adult educators offer opportunities for learning experiences that help transition learners from dependency to self-direction (Knowles et al., 1998). Whether a learner chooses to learn in a self-directed way depends on many factors, including efficiency, learning style, previous experience with the subject being learned, previous learning socialization, social orientation, and locus of control.

- *Locus of control.* Locus of control is a primary factor in personal autonomy, based on Julian Rotter's social learning theory (1954). A person may perceive his or her locus of control as internal or external. This is a fairly stable personality trait that the facilitator may not be able to influence significantly. Internals believe that they have control over events, and externals believe that outside forces control them. Internals are more likely to choose tasks that require skill, and externals are more likely to choose tasks that require luck.

- Knowles explains that internals are more likely to take control of their learning situation, to seek out new information and focus on the learning itself rather than on what other people are thinking or requiring. The quality of their learning tends to be better. Externals, however, are more likely to be anxious about learning. "Thus, internals do not need as much help when it comes to learning and externals, even after given help, tend to not take control" (Knowles et al., 1998, p.138).

Patrick Penland (1979) asked a sample of adult learners why they preferred to learn on their own instead of taking a course. These same reasons may also explain why adults choose coaching. The listed percentages of adults indicated the response that was "most important" to them:

46.8%	Desire to set my own learning pace
37.4%	Desire to use my own style of learning
36.2%	Wanted to learn right away rather than waiting for a class
31.0%	Desire to keep learning strategy flexible and changeable
29.8%	No class taught what I wanted to learn
27.8%	Desire to structure the learning project myself
17.9%	Lack of time for group learning program
14.0%	Don't like formal classroom situation with teacher
5.3%	Transportation to class too hard or expensive
5.2%	Course or class too expensive

Taking Prior Experience of the Learner into Account

PRIOR EXPERIENCE AS LEARNING ACCELERATOR Connecting with learners' experience is an excellent way to increase the value, meaning, and retention of new learning. Knowles and colleagues (1998) suggest that experience provides a "rich resource for learning" (p. 139). Experiential learning activities include simulations, problem solving, case studies, experimentation, group discussion, and peer-helping activities.

Experience has a major influence on how new learning is retained and stored in long-term memory. Ormrod (1990) offers four principles:

1. Experience acts as a selector or filter, determining what is remembered and what is not.
2. We are more likely to remember the underlying meaning than the actual details.
3. We use our existing knowledge to help us understand new information.
4. We may add existing knowledge to the new information, thereby modifying it.

PRIOR EXPERIENCE AS LEARNING BARRIER   The variety of experiences that a person has over time leads to greater diversity among adult learners compared to child learners. Thus, adult education stresses individualization in order to accommodate a wide variety of learners. While such individualization may be difficult to achieve in the classroom, it is expected in a coaching relationship.

Children view experience as something that happens to them, while adults view experience as part and parcel of their own identities and as something they *do*. Adult learners may consider any learning situation that goes counter to their experience as a personal rejection or devaluation.

In addition, our experiences help us to develop schemas, habits, and biases that may be productive in our daily lives but may prevent us from learning new ways of thinking. To address this, adult learning facilitators look for ways to help learners become aware of and examine their existing mindsets and become more open-minded. When new learning significantly challenges our current thinking, unlearning may be necessary before new learning can be integrated.

SINGLE- AND DOUBLE-LOOP LEARNING   Both Argyris (1982) and Schön (1987) have worked extensively on how to overcome our tendency to resist learning that challenges our current thinking. Argyris distinguishes between single-loop learning, which is consistent with our current thinking and thus easily learned and integrated, and double-loop learning, which requires a fundamental change in our thinking (first loop) before we can accept and integrate it (second loop).

Schön defines two different forms of action learning: knowing-in-action and reflection-in-action. The former is similar to single-loop learning, in that nothing is challenging our current thinking, and we continue operating much as we did before. Reflection-in-action is similar to double-loop learning. It is a process of thinking while doing, and requires not only reflection to discover challenges to our current thinking but also effort to evolve our thinking accordingly.

Not surprisingly, effective facilitators and learners are able to engage both reflection-in-action and double-loop learning.

ORIENTING TO WHAT IS RELEVANT TO THE LEARNER   Adults are more committed to learning when they believe that what they will learn will be highly relevant and useful to them immediately or in the near future. Given that, adult learners need to know what will be learned and how they can apply that learning. To maximize the learning,the facilitator should assess learners' needs and develop the learning objectives collaboratively with the learners.

Adult learning experts advocate performing a needs assessment and a context analysis prior to setting learning objectives. The learner and facilitator should work together to determine how to best go about doing the needs assessment. Needs assessment methods include doing a gap analysis between current and desired proficiencies, looking at performance reviews, looking at best practices, administering formal assessments, and soliciting information from others (such as family, friends, and coworkers). Learners may not want to include others in the needs assessment, but it has the additional benefit of increasing commitment of others to the success of the learning process.

In addition, the facilitator should analyze the context of the learning. This means understanding "the major influences in the setting where learners are likely to apply what they learn" (Knox, 1986, p. 67). This is similar to a systems approach and helps learners use learning strategies that take advantage of encouraging factors in the learning environment and that combat discouraging environmental factors.

In other words, in order to take prior learning into account, the facilitator must conduct:

1. A needs assessment that includes understanding preferred style, relevant experience, and purpose for learning.

2. An analysis of the learning context including encouraging and discouraging factors.

Types of Learning

Application of these principles to particular adult learners requires selecting appropriate approaches.

ACTIVE LEARNING Adult learning experts strongly recommend active learning opportunities, in which learners take an active rather than a passive role. These activities include discussion, practice, and problem solving. Active learning helps learners in their search for meaning by establishing the validity of the learning. It helps them build cognitive relationships with old learning and desired proficiencies and helps them retain the learning as well.

Active learning is both supportive and challenging. It serves as a model for learning, exploration, and self-directed learning. It helps learners gain confidence in their learning abilities, provide each other with feedback, and gives them empowering flexibility that can lead to serendipitous discoveries (Knox, 1986).

EXPERIENTIAL LEARNING Kolb and Fry (1975) proposed an experiential learning model built on Lewin's action research. Kolb stresses the importance of experiential learning and reflection in the learning process, both key components of coaching. The Kolb and Fry model has a four-step experiential learning cycle that is similar to the action-reflection models discussed earlier:

1. Become fully involved in the concrete experience.
2. Observe and reflect from multiple perspectives.
3. Form of abstract concepts and generalizations; integrate observations into reasonable theories.
4. Test implications of new concepts in new situations. (Go back to step 1.)

Regarding step 2, Tight (1996) explains that some researchers consider critically reflecting on a learning experience to be the crucial element in gaining the greatest benefit from the experience. This element

234

could be conceived of as a "learning conversation" where the reflection takes place initially with the assistance of a teacher or facilitator but, with practice, is carried out by learners on their own. For coaches, the ability to help a client reflect on his or her experience is crucial for maximizing the learning from coaching.

FOCUSING ON GOALS   Following the needs assessment and analysis of learning context, the facilitator and learner(s) develop objectives together, just as happens in coaching. Working together to develop the objectives gives learners an increased understanding of and commitment to achieving the objectives. This and further understanding of the relationship between current and desired proficiencies helps them to learn how to learn (Knox, 1986).

The needs assessment and context analysis are likely to result in too many learning objectives. To narrow them down, the learner selects those objectives that are desirable, feasible, productive, satisfying, and efficient, and that have brief and clear expected outcomes. This is similar to S.M.A.R.T. (Specific, Measurable, Attainable, Realistic, Timely) goals often used in coaching. The resulting set of learning objectives are likely to evolve over time (Knox, 1986).

ENHANCING PROFICIENCIES   Adult learning may be undertaken to advance personal, societal, or institutional (corporate) growth. While most people will learn in order to increase their proficiencies at work or in their personal lives, others will have developed further and seek learning for self-fulfillment or out of social concern (Knox, 1986). We are reminded here of Maslow's hierarchy of needs, where self-actualization is at the top of the pyramid, more likely pursued when other, more "basic" needs have been met. When improving the targeted proficiency requires learning how to function at a higher level, the most effective learning process is very similar to coaching.

In such instances, teaching entails helping learners process ideas more deeply, confront discrepancies between current and desired proficiencies, recognize differing perspectives, examine assumptions and values, and consider higher-level reasoning. Such a transformation is more likely when adults gain a broad view of "themselves as learners with goals to pursue and efficacy in the learning process" (Knox, 1986, p. 25).

INTERNAL MOTIVATORS   In the workplace in particular, managers assume that external factors, such as salary and promotion, are what motivate their employees. In actuality, these external factors can be demotivating, or at best not provide significant motivation in and of themselves. For this reason, they sometimes are referred to as hygienic factors. It turns out that the most powerful motivators are internal, such as the desire for increased self-esteem, personal growth and satisfaction, and quality of life.

Victor Vroom's (1995) expectancy theory of adult motivation in the workplace proposes that an adult's motivation to learn is based on three factors:

1. Probability of success
2. Value of the outcome
3. Expectation that the learning effort will lead to the desired outcome

Raymond Wlodowski (1985) asserts that an adult's motivation to learn is based on four factors (the first two of which are variants of factors in expectancy theory):

1. Wanting to be a successful learner
2. Learning something he or she values
3. Choice in learning
4. Having an enjoyable learning experience

In summary, learners are most motivated when they believe that they can succeed at learning and that the learning is personally valuable (i.e., important and helpful with a problem or task in their lives).

FEEDBACK AND REINFORCEMENT   Feedback, meaning the information a learner receives about his or her progress, is a familiar concept for coaches. Feedback influences the learner's commitment to learning and indicates how to adjust one's efforts in order to reach goals. It can also trigger fears based on negative experiences from the past that interfere with learning (Perry, 2006).

Adult learning experts (Knox, 1986) suggest several guidelines for providing effective feedback, though these are often meant for more formal feedback processes, such as grading and assessment:

- Learners are not always receptive to feedback, so it is wise to include them in planning or selecting how it will happen. Understanding why and how feedback is delivered makes it less likely that the learner will distort, deny, or defend against it.
- Formal evaluation and feedback instruments must be reliable, validated, and applicable to the client. See chapter 7 on psychometrics for further discussion.
- When most people hear the word "feedback," they assume criticism or judgment. It is reassuring when objectives are clear and feedback helps learners compare their performance with their own expectations rather than with other people's performances or unstated standards.
- Timeliness and specificity are keys to effective feedback. When learners get specific information immediately, they can adjust quickly and prepare for the next learning opportunity.

Positive feedback (designed to encourage more of the same) is one way to reinforce a newly learned behavior. Other means of reinforcement include praise, recognition, rewards, role models, best practice standards and, perhaps most important, the successful use of learning in the actual performance setting (work, home, etc).

In what may be a surprising suggestion, Knox (1986) recommends that feedback and external reinforcement be used only some of the time, and on an irregular schedule, so that the learner becomes self-directing and self-correcting rather than dependent on the instructor or coach.

Role of the Facilitator

Wlodowski (1985) described a set of characteristics of those who motivate learners. Such facilitators demonstrate empathy and enthusiasm while communicating with clarity and drawing on their expertise. As coaches, our expertise is in the process of facilitating learning and change rather than in the content of the client's interests. However, having expertise in the area being learned may help reassure and motivate the learner.

FACILITATION STYLE   Three modes of helping adults learn are instruction, inquiry, and performance. Since coaching avoids direct instruction but encourages questioning and an action focus, we concentrate on inquiry and performance modes.

The inquiry mode of instruction involves the instructor and learner working together to solve problems that neither has previously mastered. Knox's (1986) explanation of inquiry reveals that this is the mode most commonly used in coaching.

In the inquiry mode, the learner and facilitator focus on problem solving. By practicing this process, the learner discovers and formulates satisfactory solutions at the same time as drawing general meaning out of the learning experience. "The instructor's contribution emphasizes helping participants use inquiry procedures so that they learn how to learn. Typically instructors help learners discover major rules and concepts" (Knox, 1986, p. 143).

In the performance mode, performance is used as a learning vehicle. Coaches, especially those with a behavioral focus, often use this mode. The goal is for the learner to achieve a repeatable, high level of performance through doing "real" work. The instructor encourages the learner to gain practical experience that is both successful and encourages growth while also providing feedback and encouraging reflection about the learner's performance.

USING QUESTIONS   Coaches already know that questioning is a powerful learning tool, and adult learning experts agree. Knox (1986) notes that questions can be used for many purposes:

- To understand the learner's current proficiencies
- To guide learning by focusing on important concepts, relationships, or processes
- To formulate problem-solving strategies that take into account recent learning
- To understand meaning by questioning assumptions, values, interpretations, and implications
- To evaluate the application of learning to the learner's situation, life, beliefs, and plans

- To keep the discussion on track
- To summarize progress (pp. 145–147)

Knox offers three recommendations for effective questioning:

1. Ensure that there is sufficient rapport that the learner feels secure in responding thoughtfully to the questions.
2. Carefully prepare questions (especially initially) that connect the learner's situation and interests with the learning objectives.
3. Follow the learner's thinking, using questions that will help him or her move forward and understand meaning.

Knox (1986) notes that being able to follow a learner's thought process "is the highest art of teaching, and doing it well depends on great understanding of both content and learners. The outstanding teachers of history have asked thought-providing and insight-producing questions" (p. 146). In coaching, it is often argued that powerful questioning is still possible without the coach having mastered the content. Nonetheless, most coaches would agree that powerful questioning that follows the learner's thinking is the highest art of coaching. In chapter 15, we discuss the concept of collaborative, contingent conversations and how engaging with another in this way actually can have salutary effects on brain development.

With regard to questions, we also refer to the discussion of the "Learner/ Judger" mindset as taught by Marilee Adams (2004). According to Adams, questions we ask ourselves trigger states of mind that guide our actions and interactions with others. Helping a client become aware of those questions and develop the ability to ask herself or himself those questions that trigger a learner mindset can be a powerful support.

W-P-W LEARNING MODEL   The Whole-Part-Whole (W-P-W) learning model was proposed by Swanson and Law in 1993. It can be considered an elaboration on "tell them what you're going to tell them, then tell them, then tell them what you told them." Basically, the W-P-W model suggests that learning activities have three sequential parts— whole, part, and whole again.

For coaching sessions, a W-P-W approach can be effective by providing focus and motivation at the beginning of a session and reflection and integration at the end of a session.

Role of Facilitators

CARL ROGERS'S GUIDELINES FOR FACILITATORS   Carl Rogers (1969) was a severe critic of traditional education and advocated learning facilitation rather than instruction. He suggested that the most important factor in facilitating learning is the relationship between the facilitator and the learner. The ideal facilitator is genuine, caring, trusting, respectful, empathically understanding, sensitive, and an excellent listener.

Rogers offers the next guidelines, suggesting that an ideal facilitator (adapted from Rogers, 1969, pp. 164–166):

- *Sets the mood or climate*. If he or she trusts in the group and individuals, this attitude will be communicated in many subtle ways.
- *Elicits and clarifies purpose*. He or she creates a learning climate if contradiction and conflict are welcome and learners feel free to be open about their purposes.
- *Relies on the learners to be motivated* by those purposes that have meaning for them.
- *Makes a wide range of learning resources* available to the learners.
- *Is a flexible learning resource* for the learners, to be used as a counselor, lecturer, or advisor as needed, limited only by the facilitator's comfort and ability to serve such purposes.
- *Responds to both the content and the emotion* of learning discussions.
- *Becomes a participant* of the learning group, expressing views as an individual rather than the leader disseminating knowledge.
- *Shares his or her feelings and thoughts*. The facilitator gives feedback and reacts to learners as individuals but does not judge or evaluate the learners.
- *Listens for the expression of strong feelings*, and tries to understand these feelings and communicate this understanding. The facilitator accepts and constructively addresses feelings that create tension or bonding.
- *Recognizes his or her own limitations*, including those that prevent him or her from following the listed guidelines. When feelings or attitudes arise that obstruct learning, the facilitator reflects on them and, when he or she recognizes them as coming from within himself or herself, "he [*sic*] will find the air cleared for a significant interchange. . . . Such

an interchange can go a long way toward resolving the very attitudes which he has been experiencing, and thus make it possible
for him to be more of a facilitator of learning" (p. 166).

ALLEN TOUGH'S IDEAL FACILITATOR   Tough (1971, 1982) investigated
adults' learning projects and developed a profile for the ideal learning project helper (i.e., one who can be considered a facilitator for learning,
such as a coach. According to Tough, the ideal facilitator shows these
characteristics:

- Is warm, loving, accepting, caring, approving, supportive, encour-
aging, and friendly
- Regards the learner as an equal
- Has confidence in the learner
- Does not want to take control away from the learner
- Dialogs with the learner, listening, accepting, understanding, respon-
ding, and helping
- May expect to gain as much as he or she gives
- Is probably an open and growing person, frequently a learner seek-
ing growth and new experience — spontaneous and authentic

Expertising

We mentioned earlier that expertise was an early topic for cognitive psychologists. Educational theorists Carl Bereiter and Marlene
Scardamalia (1993) pointed out that expertise was a process, not a thing
to be possessed. For that reason, one of us (Linda) has referred to the
process of developing and maintaining expertise as "expertising," the
subjective experience of which is "flow" (Page, 2005). Csikszentmihalyi
(1991) describes the result of every flow activity he studied:

> It provided a sense of discovery, a creative feeling of transporting the
> person into a new reality. It pushed the person to higher levels of per-
> formance, and led to previously undreamed-of states of consciousness. In
> short, it transformed the self by making it more complex. (p. 74)

When a person engages in this complexity-enhancing process over
time — in general, requiring some 10,000 hours of practice — expertise
in that field or endeavor is the result. Remember that flow occurs at

the point where there is challenge, but not so much that it overwhelms capability. The repetition of flow activity expands the limits of one's capability so that greater challenges may be taken on. And, to repeat, expertise is not a thing that is acquired and put in the bank. It must be an ongoing process—it must be continual expertising—for expertise to be maintained.

Furthermore, Bereiter and Scardamalia (1993) make it clear that expertising is not an isolated, individualistic process. They agree with Csikszentmihalyi (1996) that social contexts that are nonjudgmental, respectful, and encouraging are more likely to produce flow and expertise.

When coaches understand this, we can adopt learning principles to encourage expertising and the development of higher levels of performance and capability on the part of our clients. These principles also apply to the development of expertise in coaching.

Linking Learning Theory to Coaching

Adult education became a topic of academic and professional concern when it expanded beyond schools to encompass learning at all stages of life. The principles apply generally learners of all ages, except they take into account the greater prior experience of adults. Coaches have mainly applied these principles in one-on-one learning, but the increasing use of coaching for teams and organizations make learning principles even more relevant for coaches.

Learning principles could well provide an outline for coach training:

- Encourage flexibility and self-direction.
- Take prior experience of the learner into account.
- Orient to what is relevant to the learner.
- Focus on goals.
- Provide accurate and frequent feedback and reinforcement.

Recommendations for an effective learning facilitator also apply almost directly to coaches:

- Be empathetic and curious.
- Seek to understand subjective meaning through questions.

- Avoid advice, instruction, and taking the role of the expert.
- Create a safe environment in which the learner can explore options.
- Engage the client as an equal.
- Provide resources as needed by the client.
- Manage one's own needs and maintain awareness of one's own limitations.
- Expect to learn and develop along with the learner.

Expertising is one way to conceive of the necessity for balancing challenge and existing capacity in order to encourage ongoing development of clients.

Coaching institutions and the profession of coaching owe a debt of gratitude to educators for providing a pillar that helps to lift coaching above mechanistic assumptions about how people learn.

ACTIVATING THE MIND AS A COACHING PILLAR

In the brief review of behaviorism in chapter 7, we stressed its demise as the major influence on psychological theory and research. However, there is one very clear connection between behavioral ideas and modern neuroscience. One of the most-cited assertions of neuroplasticity is a phrase that is attributed to Donald Hebbs: "neurons that fire together wire together." That is, the more often neurons fire in association with one another, the more likely they are to fire in association with one another. This claim is, at base, rather like the stimulus-response theory of behaviorism. For that reason, some theories of brain activity are called "neo-associationist."

Studies comparing brain activity when leaders are engaged in various tasks are taking management and leadership theory into the realm of neuroscience. Psychometric measures that include brain activity are already emerging.

Developmental research into attachment has been a major influence in the recognition of the importance of social relationships to cognitive, emotional, mental health, and brain development. Thus, developmental psychology has been part of moving beyond individualistic limitations.

Cognitive psychology has begun to overlap with social psychology, and both have become more integrated with neuroscience as the social aspects of the human brain have been revealed.

Something must happen in the brain in order for learning to occur. There is evidence for the involvement of certain brain structures in learning: the hippocampus, the amygdala, the prefrontal cortex. Procedural learning appears to be stored in a different place in the brain from semantic learning. However, neuroscience has not yet provided a detailed and integrated description of what happens when learning occurs, much less exactly how or why. This is partly because, as Rose (2005) and Brothers (2001) point out, we are in the very early stages of the development of neuroscience.

The increasing ability of learners to deal with complexity as they engage in flow and develop expertise echoes discoveries in systems theory regarding how systems change. The connections a learner makes in perceiving patterns, learning skills, and creating meaning are made possible by neuronal connections. Given certain conditions, all of these connections increase in complexity as a human being engages with others and reflects on life's experiences. In chapter 9 we consider the Neuroscience Platform that deals with the connections and problem-solving activities we call thinking.

Neuroscience Platform — Cognition

The agents at Roberto's real estate agency were dissatisfied. One or another complained to him almost daily that they weren't getting the support they needed, that his portion of commissions was too high, that he simply wasn't a good manager. Who was behind this unrest, he wondered, and why did they do what they did? They certainly were not being loyal to the firm. He talked to each agent individually, identified the three ringleaders, and fired them. Instead of improving the situation, however, morale and sales deteriorated, other agents quit, and the agency was on the verge of bankruptcy. In desperation, Roberto took the suggestion of a colleague and set up an appointment with a coach.

After introducing coaching and listening to his concerns, the coach surprised Roberto by focusing not on the impending bankruptcy or the misbehavior of the agents but on that all-important question Roberto had asked himself when he became aware of the difficulties: "Who is behind this, and why did they do what they did?"

At the end of a series of sessions that explored this and other questions he typically asked himself, Roberto realized that by asking that question, he had assumed that a person or people were causing the problem. If the problem had to do with his business model or with events outside the agency, he would never identify the cause by asking that question. By asking that initial question, he had gone down a path of prejudging his troubles as being caused by the people who complained about them.

Second, once Roberto realized that he had prejudged the situation without really finding out what was going on, he came to look at the complaints through the eyes of the agents, recognizing that they were simply messengers rather than culprits.

Furthermore, until he began asking "What can I do to make this better?" his thinking was mired in past blame and fault-finding rather than on future solutions. He was limiting his ability to harness expectations and promote change. The solution began with his awareness of why he had behaved as he did.

At the most general level, what we do is move toward what we perceive as rewarding and away from danger. But this movement is mediated by our thinking. As Marilee Adams (2004), has found, our thinking is guided by the questions we ask *ourselves*. We are constantly trying to decide which is which, interpreting the meaning of what happens to us and what others do and what the effects are. Our minds are busy even when we do not want them to be, as when we are trying to fall asleep but that big meeting tomorrow keeps coming to mind. And when we do fall asleep, our brains still actively dream, even if "we" are not consciously aware. In the process of "flow," we can be thinking but also not consciously aware of it—more like being "lost" in thought. Most of our thoughts are taken up with social rehearsal or replay or anticipation or regret. And thinking cannot be separated from feeling. Because thinking is so central to all that we do, it is a natural subject of study, but that does not mean it is easy to study.

- Is thinking just having a conversa`tion with ourselves, inside our heads? If so, do babies who have not learned language think?
- Do some people think better than others?
- Can people who do not think so well learn how to think better?
- How does thinking relate to intelligence?
- Do people who know a lot think better?
- How can we make ourselves think some things and not think other things?
- If we get rid of emotions and only think logically, would that improve our intelligence?
- Why is so much of our thinking memories about what has already done and gone?

- How can we make sure we "remember" to return that phone call tomorrow? How can it be "memory" when it is in the future?
- What does attention have to do with thinking and memory?
- Who is it who is paying attention?

Psychologists and neuroscientists have tried to deal with confusion surrounding the common term "thinking" by calling what they study "cognition." As we described earlier, the "cognitive revolution" burst out of psychology's behavioral straitjacket and began to experiment with answers to questions such as the ones just listed. At first, the messy topics of emotions and context were excluded in an attempt to narrow and clarify the definition. But there is no way to totally split off "cold" cognition from "hot" emotions without destroying our ability to function as human beings. And, as psychiatrist Leslie Brothers (2001) points out so cogently, it may be that psychology's definition of "person" as being separate from the social surround is preventing neuroscience from developing a brain-based language because it is locked into the common equation that mind equals individual brain.

We deal with these topics in the next sections:

- Memory
- Awareness
- Mapping and predicting
- Dilemma model
- Practice guide for coaching with the brain in mind — Make decisions and solve problems

MEMORY

If we could not remember, we could not learn, and we would have to decide anew whether to approach or avoid every experience. Most of what we think of as thinking involves memory in some way. Even remembering to be aware requires a certain type of memory.

Types of Memory

Cognitive psychology divides memory topics into *short term* and *long term* (Eysenck & Keane, 2005). Short-term memory, including what we have referred to as working memory, is limited to what we can pay attention

247

to. Depending on how much attention we pay and for how long, items in short-term memory can be "stored" for the long term. This long-term storage is quite vast, although we cannot always access it—we know we know that person's name or what to call that new plant in the garden, but we just cannot remember.

We are also able to "remember" things without consciously knowing that we do. This is a capacity we have from before birth, as indicated by the research on babies' preference for music heard while they were in the womb (Levitin, 2006). This is called *implicit* memory. Throughout our lives, we can react to the present moment as if it were a past event but not know it is the past that we are "bringing into" the present via implicit memory. We remember implicitly without consciously recalling what it is we are remembering, or even being aware that it is a memory we are reacting to rather than what is happening to us in the immediate present. Psychotherapists are particularly interested in this type of memory, but it is important for coaches to understand it, too.

Explicit memory is what we commonly mean when we speak of remembering. The ability to make this kind of memory does not happen for human beings until we are around 2 years old, at about the same time that we learn to speak a language. Based on explicit memory, we know that we know something, even when we cannot remember what it is exactly.

Memory can also be divided into *declarative*, or knowing *what*, and *procedural*, or knowing *how*. Declarative memory includes the ability to remember episodes in our lives as well as general and semantic knowledge, such as the language we speak, which is not connected with a time or place. Procedural knowledge is body and movement memory—how to ride a bike, to swim, to tie a shoelace, to play an instrument. The fact that stroke or brain damage can leave us unable to recognize a shoelace or declare what it is but still be able to tie (procedurally) a bow when it is placed in our hands is evidence that these maps are stored in different parts of the brain.

Researchers have also recognized the difference between *retrospective* memory, or remembering things from the past, and *prospective* memory, or remembering to do something or think of something in the future. Setting an alarm to remind ourselves of a phone call we intend to make during a busy day is an example of an external aid to prospective memory.

However, from the perspective of the brain, the basis of all these types of memories is connections between neurons. Indeed, Eysenck and Keane (2005) point out that many of the devastating effects of brain damage likely have to do with decreased ability to integrate or make connections between different parts of the brain that are specialized for specific memory functions. For that reason, rather than focusing on the typical varieties of memory, we look at the general ability of the brain to make connections and then to form maps at different levels of resolution or generality.

Working Memory

The brain tries to automate everything possible. There is a functional reason for this that is not commonly understood: it would not be possible to consciously consider every bit of information that flows into our brains.

We have already pointed out that there is a difference between our working memory, or what we are aware of, and the billions of connections throughout our brain that can be drawn on for automatic reactions — the long-term memory store. David Rock (2009) suggests that working memory is like a stage, one that is quite small. Everything that we wish to pay attention to has to go on that stage. Once a character is "onstage," it must be lighted with attention or, like an actor with a bit part, it will exit the stage, and we will find ourselves attending to a new actor or scene. Working memory can accommodate just a few items at a time, but backstage, so to speak, outside our awareness, there is an almost unlimited warehouse for long-term storage.

Working memory is used for a number of things:

- *Understanding*. When we are trying to make sense of a new idea, it comes onto the stage of our working memory. Right now as you are reading this book, you are using your working memory to understand it. If you find yourself just skimming through or dozing off, you are not using much working memory. In order to understand what is on the stage populated by the characters or ideas in this book, you consciously attend to or metaphorically shine a light on what you are interested in understanding. You may be asking "Do these ideas make sense? Are they right for me? Do they match with what else I know? Can I do something with them? What are the connections between them?" Paying enough attention to ask questions like that, whether they are answered or not or whether the idea is simple or complex, takes quite a lot of effort. A flow of energy must be maintained in order to keep the light of attention shining. Our minds regulate the energy that must be put into attention in order for anything to be kept in mind, and this flow can be interrupted easily, meaning our attention will be distracted.

- *Decision making.* You wake up one day and wonder if you should make that sales call or catch up on paperwork. In order to make that decision, you have to put two "characters" on the stage — sales call and paperwork — and attend to each in order to compare and contrast them. Part of this is visualizing what might happen if you make the call versus complete the report that is due. Decision making doubles the flow of energy required to attend to the variables.

- *Memorizing.* If someone has just told you a phone number and you have to remember it, you rehearse it over and over, repeating it without stopping to think about anything else. If you are able to do that long enough, and over enough practice sessions, the number will become hardwired. That is, the neural connections will have been strengthened by use so that you will be able to recall the number at a later time. This function of working memory is central to coaching because coaching is about change. Every new activity that we do, every new idea that we think, even every old habit we want to stop doing must have its time in the spotlight of our working memory. Our ability to regulate the flow of energy, to pay attention when we want to and to ignore incoming stimuli that would distract us, is what enables us to establish whatever it is that we know.

- *Recalling.* Working memory is also needed to bring information out of long-term memory and onto your stage. You need to hold the information you are looking for in mind, to find it in memory. Recalling requires quite a lot of effort to do, especially for old memories.

- *Inhibiting.* Just as understanding an idea requires putting information onto your stage, sometimes we also need to keep information off the stage — to inhibit attention going to something. This also can require a lot of effort at times.

Limits of Working Memory

If working memory is so important to coaches, we need to understand several important characteristics:

- *Limited capacity*. The working memory stage is very small. It can fit only a few characters at any one time. Although George Miller helped launch the cognitive revolution with his 1956 article suggesting that we can hold around seven items in working memory, some researchers suggest that at about four items, we need to start utilizing chunking (grouping two actors as "the soldiers" or "the sisters") or other memory techniques in order to keep them in memory. The common belief is that phone numbers are seven digits because that is the most we can hold in short-term memory. Whether that is true or not, most of us need to write those seven numbers down or keep repeating them to avoid their slipping offstage.

- *Easily distracted*. Even when there are only one or two actors onstage, there are many comings and goings in this theater. It is tempting to turn the spotlight on the attractive person in the front row or the couple having an argument in the back row or the usher trying to toss someone out of the audience. Our attention shifts not only at that moment, but wherever we shine the spotlight becomes the new stage. We are a fickle audience. We have to put out immense energy to actually keep our focus on our intended stage.

  Because we are so easily distracted, the effort of focusing on one thing is similar to physical exertion. Harold Pashler (1997) reported that one's physical force is significantly decreased by engaging working memory. In other words, our capacity to lift a weight is decreased if, at the same moment, we are also trying to remember something. The effort of paying attention, in a sense, reduces the effort we can put into a physical task, such as running or lifting. This finding supports the emphasis in sports psychology on mental preparation for physical performance.

- *Subject to internal and external threats*. Not only can the stage of attention get crowded, think of what Daniel Goleman (1995) calls the "amygdala hijack." If a dangerous-looking character walks onstage, working memory can be overridden by threat responses from the limbic system.

251

- *Easily overwhelmed.* Neurons have a limited signaling capacity of some 2,000 signals per second. Although we each have perhaps 100 billion neurons, specific circuits have limitations. Those involved in working memory are vulnerable to being flooded by the intense signals of the error-detection response. Uncertainty, rejection, unfairness, or even just ambiguity can bring on the error response. The noise of error-detection signals drowns out whatever else we are trying to focus on. To use working memory most effectively, we need to have a quiet stage.

If something is important enough that we want to remember it long term, our best strategy is to automate it (i.e., practice until it becomes hardwired). The process of making a habit, behavior, or idea automatic begins the first time it is put into action, but complex activities require a good deal of practice. Fortunately, simple actions and concepts do not require more than a few repetitions. We learn the path to our room in a hotel quickly, just as we learn how to insert the card key so as to open the door to the room. We say this is fortunate because of the energy and effort that would be required to keep everything we do in working memory. The process involved in hardwiring, called long-term potentiation, generally is under way after doing an activity just three times.

As a result, most of us are not aware of what we are doing. That sounds like an insult, but it is actually an advantage because of the limitations of working memory. A good example has to do with driving a car. Most people who have driven on one side of the road all their lives find the prospect of driving on the other side when visiting a foreign country terrifying. They are surprised by how hard it is because they are no longer used to paying attention to their driving. On the other side of the road, they grip the wheel and pay constant attention for a day or two before new hardwiring begins. That experience illustrates having to become conscious of an activity that we have hardwired but also of the fact that hardwiring can be changed.

Whatever we do over and over in our lives has been hardwired: the way we speak to people, plan our week, work at our computer, and file our papers. Also, the way we think about ourselves, our attitudes, and our behaviors. Our very concept of who we are is formed by the same processes of connecting neurons and automating those connections through practice. Making any of those things conscious again in coaching will result in discomfort for the client, just as driving on the other side of road would do. The client must put greater effort to pay attention during this process.

Linking Memory to Coaching

There are three key ways to improve the capacity of working memory:

1. Visualizing
2. Chunking
3. Ordering

VISUALIZING   The brain has roots in a long evolutionary history, so we share commonalities with our ancestors. Those common parts include visual processing, as proto-humans thought and communicated visually for millions of years, before the capacity for language developed. The modern human brain has circuits in its visual cortex that are deeper and richer even than in our auditory cortex. About 1 million fibers carry visual data versus just 30,000 for hearing. We seem to be able to process complex information better using visual cues. To the brain, there is no significant difference between seeing a concept in real life and seeing it in the mind's eye. That is one reason for the effectiveness of visualization in sports psychology as well as for the extensive use and power of work with metaphors.

When we see a picture in our mind's eye, such as when we use a metaphor, we create a mental map quickly and with minimal effort. Visual mapping takes a fraction of a second and can be done even when we are distracted. For example, if we are asked to picture an elephant battling a mouse, the scene comes to mind quickly along with the complex concept it represents. Compare this to being asked to process this information: A very large character is in conflict with another character that is hundreds of times smaller. It takes much less effort to "get" the concept in the first instance than the second.

Another reason for the effectiveness of visuo-spatial references is an aspect of the brain's prediction function. Human beings are meaning making. When we connect an event with what happened before or will happen later, or with another event that is similar or dissimilar, or with people or themes that are related in some way, we are taking part in the self-creative, or autopoietic, nature of the human system. We continually make up stories or narratives and thus notice characters, places, and forces. All of the 3,000 to 7,000 different languages in the world have this in common: They enable people to name and describe the behavior of or what happens to people or objects, places or location, and forces or actions. Filmmakers and novel writers build every story around the framework of who does what to whom and the consequences, emotional journey, or lessons learned. Using visuals helps us tap into the power of what the brain does well naturally.

Earlier in this chapter, we used a visual that David Rock created to understand the concept of working memory: a stage. Having that picture makes it easier to grasp and hold complex relationships in mind than abstract language would allow. Holding a richer map in mind for a longer time enables more connections to be made. Another way of saying this is that when we "see" something, we understand it better. "I see what you are saying" is a common way to indicate that we understand, especially for those of us who have a preference for visual thinking. In coaching, we can create visuals through metaphor, analogy, story, or drawings, such as on a whiteboard or paper.

Using external (outside the brain) visuals such as a whiteboard to summarize a challenge also further frees the working memory from having to keep the whole image in mind while manipulating its parts. As organizer David Allen (2001) puts it, this allows us to have "minds like water."

CHUNKING Studies have shown that we learn complex routines by chunking them into smaller groups. Early studies in expertise (de Groot, 1965) revealed that experts such as chess masters store maps of chess moves and even whole games by "chunking," or categorizing, complex information that they access by category name. Chunking enables our working memory to learn, remember, or decide more effectively. Chunking is a useful way to improve our capacity to learn.

Chunking depends on the human mind's capacity for narrative. We group together by characteristics (all the men), by sequence (what came first, then next, then next), by relationship (all our cousins), by activity (the nurses), by position (the managers), or by any principle or theme our ingenuity can devise (everyone who thinks the animal that best represents them is a wolf).

When we chunk several items we want to remember into a single group, we then have to remember the group. The advantage of chunking is that remembering one item is easier than remembering 3 or 10 or 52. We are more likely to remember that single chunk, though, if it is meaningful to us. In chapter 15, we present the SCARF model developed by David Rock (2008). David has chunked five brain-calming principles of status, certainty, autonomy, relatedness, and fairness by combining the first letters into a meaningful word. This is just one technique that many students, marketers, and computer programmers use routinely.

ORDERING   Related to its incessant meaning-making or narrative function, our mind likes to fit information together. Key aspects are ordering, prioritizing, putting things first or last, and showing how things relate to each other. The brain circuitry that allows this is extensive: We hold rich maps of how people connect with each other, their relative status, and what our status is in relation to everyone we know. And that is just one example.

When working memory becomes overwhelmed because of too many choices or too much information at the same time, a common solution is to step back and create order. This might consist of making a list of all the possibilities related to the goal or topic at hand (externalizing the information visually) and then deciding just the next step. At the macro level, Wheatley (1992) suggests this is exactly how a complex organizational system manages change: by getting clear on goals, having good communication, and taking one step at a time. By putting concepts in order, we can see where to start rather than wondering what comes next and "what if . . . ?" We reduce anxiety and the sense of being overwhelmed that comes from the amygdala's response to uncertainty. As the amygdala is calmed, cognitive functions such as working memory may be energized.

Dynamic stability of a complex system requires the management of change toward positive ends. For positive change, we must clear up working memory, first, so we have attentional resources for what is important and, second, so we can focus on what is positive in order to recruit the power of expectation.

AWARENESS

Our brains connect past and present experiences into patterns from the moment we can be said to have a brain, even before we are consciously aware of making connections, and even while the very structure of the brain is being built. Steven Rose compares this complex process to "the remaking of the aeroplane in mid flight" (2005, p. 118). Why would we have the capacity to do this? That is, from an evolutionary perspective, what advantage does the automatic ability to create connections bestow on us?

Siegel (2007a) refers to the human brain as "an anticipation machine" (p. 173). Setting aside the use of the word "machine," this terminology implies an advantage to prediction. If we can use changes in input to predict what is going to happen, we can make adjustments before it happens. Mental maps enable us to add past experience to present perception so as to guide future behavior. As Hawkins (2004) says, "It is the ability to make predictions about the future that is the crux of intelligence" (p. 18). If prediction confers such advantages, no wonder the human brain is so complex, going well beyond the "sense-associate-act" sequence of simple nervous systems. Not only must it associate incoming sensory data and react to it in the here and now, it must connect that with stored remembrances from the past and with imagined scenarios for the future.

As we have discussed, some important maps, such as those that connect incoming sensations with danger, must be activated automatically. Conscious processing is too slow and too limited, so the amygdala is hardwired to stay on guard without our consciously telling it to.

We can induce the effects of hardwiring by practicing something over and over until it becomes automatic, in line with the oft-quoted statement of Donald Hebb that "neurons that fire together wire together." When two neurons fire simultaneously or in sequence, they associate, or form connections that make it more likely for one to fire when the other does. Practicing until neurons become automatically associated is the secret of mastering any complex skill, from speaking a language, to riding a bike, to masterful coaching.

We rely on practice-induced hardwiring to drive a car at the same time as carrying on a conversation. Practicing activities repeatedly enables us to fill in blanks, to anticipate what should be there even when it is missing or mistaken. For instance, we learn to read words in blocks rather than letter by letter. Therefore, popele raed snetenecs lkie tihs eevn wtih ltetres rerararnegd. Text messaging relies on this capacity. We approximate all the time in situations where information is missing or masked. This tells us that the message being sent has redundancies, or more than one way to get at the meaning, but it also reminds us of our top-down capacity to draw on previous information to *construct* reality, and not just to rely on what's actually happening in front of us.

Priming

Even in the short run, we can "prime" our perceptual system by what we pay conscious attention to. If you decide to have children, suddenly you begin to notice mothers with strollers everywhere. You have never "seen" them before. Where did they all come from? The changed output (noticing strollers) is information not about input (there are no more actual babies in the world) but about a change in your perceptual process triggered by your decision to have children. That mental act affects the very firing of neurons in response to visual stimuli.

The other side of this phenomenon is that we do not notice details that are unrelated to our intentions. Students participating in a study by Simons and Chabris (1999) were assigned to count the number of times people in a video passed a basketball back and forth. Fifty percent of the participants were so intent on their assigned task that they did not notice a gorilla-suited accomplice walking through the action, facing the camera, and pounding its chest. Of course, when shown the video clip a second time, after being asked about the gorilla, they noticed it immediately.

Coaches can remind clients to "set" their intentions before a meeting or presentation so they "mind" what they have decided ahead of time would be relevant. Our movement toward what we desire can be enhanced by recruiting our perceptual system to notice desire-related events or information. This recruitment happens when we ask questions that consciously remind ourselves of future intentions. *Where's Waldo?* is a series of children's puzzle books by Martin Handford, who draws specific characters (such as Waldo and a wizard) as tiny characters buried in incredibly complex scenarios. Knowing what Waldo looks like (he wears a red striped hat and glasses, and carries a walking stick) and knowing that the object of the game is to find where he is "hiding," it is possible to locate him on the page. Children, perhaps because of their less-hardwired expectations, are very good at this game. But even children need to know what they are looking for in a complex world in order to find it reliably.

One of the experiments indicating that neurons fire in anticipation of a stimulus involved monkeys, whose visual systems are very similar to those of humans. Edmond Rolls and his colleagues (Rolls & Deco, 2002) mapped the neurons that became active when monkeys saw a red triangle. For monkeys who had learned to expect a red triangle, he found that those same neurons were activated even before the triangle was presented. As Hawkins puts it, when there is some degree of expectation, the "neurons involved in sensing become active in advance of actually receiving the sensory input" (Hawkins & Blakeslee, 2004, p. 81). The effects of expectation are so strong that we are likely to perceive what we expect even before it has shown up.

Linking Awareness to Coaching

Think of what this means in coaching. If neurons involved in sensing become active in advance of receiving sensory input, looking for what is wrong means we literally see more of what is wrong. This applies to coaches as well as clients. If we coach people about what they are doing wrong, we will see those mistakes, and so will they. Our clients' threat response may be triggered by our judgmental attitude, and the social nature of our minds and brains will lock us in a mutual downward negative vortex. Coach someone expecting to appreciate their strengths, and you will see many more of those and be able to point them out to clients, who will see them as well. Depending on how coaches manage expectations, either a negative downward vortex or a positive upward spiral is possible. Thus, how we mind can affect how we brain, or what our sensory apparatus is capable of picking up.

Our social relationships are also involved in this process. A leader in organizational thinking, Ori Brafman, and his brother, psychologist Rom Brafman (Brafman & Brafman, 2008), have documented how a mere suggestion can bias our perception. Before being introduced to someone, we may have overheard the remark, "Oh, yes. He is very charming—*too* charming, if you know what I mean." When we meet this person, we may perceive his smile as being false. But what if the overheard remark was about some other person entirely? Because of our unconscious capacity to influence not just what clients look and listen for but what they actually see and hear, our own focus on their strengths and potential can have a powerful effect on what they perceive.

Christopher Peterson (2006) based a "three good things" exercise on similar principles developed by Martin Seligman, founder of Positive Psychology. Before going to bed each night for a week, participants were assigned to notice and write down three things that went well during the day. He found that "counting one's blessings increases happiness and decreases symptoms of depression" (p. 39), and that this effect lasted for six months of follow-up for those who continued the exercise. We do not know exactly why this happened, but it is likely that the participants' intention to look for blessings meant they saw more of them. These in turn "primed" or triggered their expectations so that they perceived other positive events more readily during the day and perhaps were more likely to wake up happy the next morning. Peterson reports that several married couples incorporated the exercise into a nightly routine. Presumably, sharing blessings with one's partner makes it more likely that our positive expectations will be triggered by the person we sleep and wake up with.

Coaches can use the power of awareness to help clients perceive and move toward their intentions. Repetition of this movement can result in hardwiring, or the shift of conscious intention to automatic processing, that enables us to act on information without requiring the limited resources of attention.

MAPPING AND PREDICTING

The human brain makes patterns of connections in our ongoing quest for meaning. We have spoken of these patterns as mental maps. Our ability to create these maps is related to our ability to predict what will happen in the future.

Jeff Hawkins, inventor of the PalmPilot, has been studying the functioning of the neocortex, the outer layer of our more recently evolved brains, in an attempt to build better interfaces between people and machines. In his research, he has taken the concept of maps to another level. These ideas were first released in his book *On Intelligence* (Hawkins & Blakeslee, 2004). Hawkins thinks of maps formed in the neocortex as being the basis of our intelligence, and lays out a theory for the principles involved in storing them.

Hawkins believes that our intelligence is a function of prediction. Eysenck and Keane (2005) describe a series of experiments like those Rolls and colleagues (2002) did with monkeys. These indicate that, even at the level of neurons, when we have come to expect something, like a red light, the visual receptors typically affected by the flash of light will fire *in advance* of the light itself turning on. In effect, this means that we map out how we expect everything in life to occur. We are able to process huge amounts of data coming into our brains each second because we are only comparing the data to our predictions and ignoring that which matches what we expect, not interpreting all the data at once. Studies of reading, perception, and cognition provide considerable research support for this idea. Mimicking this principle enables digital video cameras to save storage space by recording only what changes from one scene to the next.

For human beings, when our predictions are confirmed over and over, that sequence of events becomes automatic so that we do not consciously go through the process of thinking, "I just heard someone yell 'fore' and I'm on a golf course. That means a ball might be headed my way. That ball might hit me, and that would hurt. Perhaps I should duck." Instead, we duck immediately, without taking the time to think about what it *means*. Speed is one good reason for some predictions becoming hardwired so that sensory signals indicating danger trigger our taking protective action immediately, without having to go through the slower process of consciously asking what the signal might mean.

Thus, patterns of connections enable neurons to work together to predict and act seamlessly. This is the mark of an integrated brain. Much of our automatic intelligence is based on processes of prediction, many of them automatic or hardwired.

Error Detection

A key part of our circuitry involves noticing when data do *not* fit with predicted patterns. We discussed error detection with regard to stress in chapter 5. When an error is detected, whether in our visual, auditory, or any other circuit, an "error" signal is given off. Then, according to Hawkins and Blakeslee (2004), "When the sensory input does arrive, it is compared with what was expected" (p. 81). If we are expecting a red light but the light flashes white, the comparison with the expected red flash is enough to set off the error detection system, and we take notice. In many instances, the mismatch is picked up by a part of the prefrontal cortex called the orbitofrontal cortex (OFC), just behind the eyes. The OFC is sometimes called the error detector because it lights up if we do not trust someone, if we see something not quite right, or if we sense some ambiguity. When this occurs, our amgydala is also aroused.

Groups of interconnected neurons are constantly gathering information from the environment. They check the incoming information against information that is expected. In that sense, neurons are like prediction machines, constantly looking out for us and asking, "Is this what I was expecting?" Any time a neuronal group "notices" there is a difference between what is expected and what is actually occurring, those neurons suddenly light up like a Christmas tree. That is, they become energized or excited. Jeffrey Schwartz describes this in detail in his book, *The Mind and the Brain* (Schwartz & Begley, 2002).

At the moment that an "error" is detected, energy is routed to those neuronal groups. For example, imagine sitting quietly looking out a window. Suddenly a quarter of the window goes really dark. Your attention is drawn to the dark patch very quickly, as part of a first reaction called an orientation response. You lean forward for a closer look. Your muscles tighten and your stomach turns. When you realize it is just an awning being rolled down, you relax, but before you knew what that unexpected change was about, you were on intense alert.

Things in our environment that are unexpected or different—anything that is not what is normally expected—gets immediate attention. This is true for sound, smell, taste, touch, visual data, and ideas.

This is one reason to avoid giving advice in coaching. If the advice is unfamiliar to the client, the resulting uncertainty can set off an error-detection response. If the idea is familiar, the client make take the advice as a challenge to his or her status. Not taking this into consideration can mean the client rejects the idea before appraising it, thus putting another barrier in the way of change.

The existence of error-detection circuits explains several phenomena:

- Why we are so problem-focused: It energizes us.
- Why the media always seems to focus on bad news: It gets our attention.
- Why a road accident makes people stop and stare: Unexpected danger demands attention.
- Why people can easily enumerate all the things they do wrong but struggle to list their strengths: We notice difference more easily than confirmation.

Our filters, values, and beliefs, all patterns or hypotheses for how best to function in the world, are examples of maps. These become a sort of operating manual for our mental processes. We are often not conscious of these maps because they were learned implicitly or practiced so often that their connections are hardwired into the brain. In many cases, it is to our advantage that we follow these maps automatically.

However, we can also create hypotheses, make connections, and form maps that are wrong. Or they may have been useful guides at one point in our lives (say, in childhood or in stressful circumstances) but no longer apply. Thank goodness in this case that hardwiring is not necessarily permanent. Coaching is a way of rewiring what has become automatic. During coaching conversations, we test or challenge a client's hypotheses. We separate the concrete "facts" from the "interpretations" that are self-created. These conversations can help bring a client's map to consciousness. Reappraising or reframing may help make that map fit current circumstances more appropriately. Similarly, reprioritizing a set of maps, by asking about how consistent they are with previous commitments or value statements, is a common way of recruiting the motivating effects of cognitive dissonance to assist change.

Connections Are Pleasurable

There is no way to avoid change. Marvin Minsky (1986) claims that the brain is mostly engaged in changing itself, adjusting its internal functioning to meet changing demands. The brain can be thought of as a connection machine, constantly making connections to reflect conclusions about how everything "out there" fits together. If you look under a microscope at the brain of a stillborn child, you would see lots of neurons but very few connections, like a forest that is not very dense. In children of three or four, there are many more connections; in adult brains, there is such a thicket that you can hardly see through it. We spend our whole lives connecting neurons.

Just a little over 10 years ago, the claim would have been that that is all we do: Adults connect only those neurons that we are born with, because the adult brain does not produce new ones. But this conventional wisdom, accepted for years in neuroscience, has been overturned. Science writer Sharon Begley (2007) tells the story of neurogenesis pioneer Elizabeth Gould's breakthrough research that found new neurons in the hippocampus of adult rats and primates. Following up on this, neuroscientists Fred Gage and colleagues confirmed the appearance of new neurons in the hippocampus of human adults (Eriksson et al., 1998). This discovery strengthened the claim for adult neuroplasticity.

However, it is true that most activity in the brain involves creating connections between existing neurons and pruning these connections. We are born with twice as many neurons as we have by age 10, when we settle down with roughly 100 hundred billion. We say "roughly" because there is no accurate way of counting neurons as yet. Estimates vary from 30 billion to 100 billion in an adult brain.

What is most relevant to coaching is the process of making new connections. There is some indication that the brain "likes" making connections between parts that have not previously been connected. By way of analogy, think of a real estate developer looking at two parallel highways. Linking the two with a new highway opens up a large new area for development. The brain seems to operate in this way, opening up new territories by connecting existing sets of maps (which are themselves connections of neurons) in new ways.

Humor is an example. When we hear a funny joke, the energy behind our laughter comes from making an unexpected connection between maps in the brain. If the joke required connecting to a map that we did not have (as when people from a different background do not "get it"), we would not laugh. If the joke was too obvious or one we have heard before, we do not laugh because we already made the connection in the past. Jokes are funny because they connect existing maps in new and unexpected ways.

Likewise with music. Daniel Levitin (2006) makes the point that we delight in music that connects familiar sounds with rhythms, melodies, or harmonies that are just different enough to surprise us but not so different as to shock us. Musicians "play" between these boundaries.

The energy that arises any time our brain sees things in a different way or connects existing maps along new pathways is a very positive experience. The most popular television series in 2006 worldwide was *CSI: Crime Scene Investigation*. The show is structured around information that at first does not make sense. Familiar characters gather bits of data that do not fit together. False leads heighten the tension. Finally, in the last few minutes, all is resolved and the mystery is solved. This buildup of energy because of a lack of connection and the ultimate release when connections are revealed is a universal approach to storytelling.

Similar feelings accompany solving a puzzle. Arriving at the solution oneself can produce a sense of accomplishment and increased status, but even being told the answer is accompanied by a good feeling. Of course, as the research on happiness shows, the positive rush of energy from a new connection like this is short, a little like eating chocolate. Perhaps that is why some people consider themselves addicted to crossword puzzles and others will spend days or weeks putting together a jigsaw puzzle. Finding a word or a place for each piece gives a short burst of positive feelings.

These bursts of pleasure may be considered the subjective experience of increasing complexity. In coaching, a connection is often referred to as an insight—a moment of clarity when everything makes sense. A coaching dialogue often consists of multiple insights, which help the client to raise self-awareness, create choices, and engage in actions to achieve their desired outcomes. Coaches help clients improve their maps of the world, and when a set of maps—a giant puzzle about life—suddenly falls into place, it can feel very rewarding. A model for this, David Rock's "Four Faces of Insight" is presented later in the chapter in Figure 9.1.

Disconnections Irritate

Making new connections is a positive experience, especially when the connection is unexpected and opens up new territory. The other side of this is that maps that do not fit irritate us. That is, disconnections irritate.

Any leftover or unremembered piece of data seems to keep coming up in our thoughts until we resolve the mystery. Having unresolved loops like this is uncomfortable enough to keep us watching that TV show even when we know we should go to bed. This may also be an explanation for the compelling nature of unanswered questions, even questions we are not aware of asking (Adams, 2004).

When we recognize someone in the street but just cannot remember her name, we often find ourselves puzzling over and over until the name "comes to us." Once we get the answer, we feel a rush of relief and think something like "Thank goodness I don't have to think about that anymore." The relief occurs because, without our necessarily being conscious of it, a part of our brain has been using energy in sorting through name maps in order to make the connection with the face we have seen.

This energy drain can occur with anything that matters to us and that does not fit together. In his book on organizing, David Allen (2001) suggests that we are drained by having to keep unresolved "loops" in our head, including "remembering" to do things in the future. He recommends a reliable system for recording these dangling connections and returning to them only at the appropriate time so that our mind is free to "flow like water." This concept is an essential component of a brain-based approach to coaching.

Linking Mapping to Coaching

Disconnections or mismatches of maps are often what bring people to coaching.

Example: "If I'm Honest with Him, I'll Lose My Job"

Lois has a high-priority map that could be labeled "integrity and honesty." As a result, she values honesty in every situation and feels upset when she does not tell the truth. However, she also has a survival map, and that includes warnings about how not to get fired.

She brought this dilemma to coaching: "I know I should tell my boss that his habit of only looking for things to criticize really affects morale in the office. But I'm afraid if I'm honest with him, I'll lose my job."

Lois had been going over one map in her mind ("I should tell him") and then the other ("I'd better keep quiet or I'll lose my job"), and then back

(Continued)

to the first. It is as if these two "parts" of herself had been locked in an argument with each other. Without some way to resolve the impasse, Lois would continue to draw on energy to no avail. She has managed thus far because her boss often is oblivious to what is going on in the office.

The coach suggested the empty chair technique (which we present in chapter 10). Lois realized that she herself was focusing only on what her boss was doing wrong. She came up with a plan to point out every time that he even hinted at an employee's positive performance, and this resulted in a changed atmosphere in the office. Her boss even became more engaged in the office camaraderie. Lois had made a connection between what she wanted in the office and how she was operating. Coaching provides the opportunity to make new connections more quickly than may be achieved without it.

In using techniques such as the empty chair, it is important to remember that a key element of coaching is inviting people to work toward their positive vision for the future. This leverages their motivation, rather than concluding that addressing the least-feared or smaller weakness (such as the boss's being disengaged) is a way to move forward. Thus, coaching promotes solutions that have been proven effective but may not be a client's automatic first approach. Combine this lack of familiarity with a possible threat (such as Lois's fear of being fired), and it is no wonder that clients resist change.

It is also important to remember that context, especially the relationship within which an invitation to make connections occurs, has a great deal to do with whether a person approaches the experience with curiosity and exploration or whether he or she avoids it. When we feel safe, we humans are explorers, approaching new discoveries with delight. "The fear or alarm response . . . kills curiosity and inhibits exploration and learning. If people are anxious, uncomfortable, or fearful, they do not learn" (Perry, 2006, p. 26). That is, they do not make new connections and create new maps. Knowing how to create the conditions for learning is a key skill for coaches.

The way an individual makes sense of the world is through creating maps. These maps are the key to understanding how an individual learns, makes decisions, and lives day-to-day life. We are continually evolving and creating new maps or making new connections. Coaching is an enabler of these connections. Coaching conversations can help focus a client constructively, challenge existing maps that are not serving the client, and also expedite new connections and reduce disconnections.

DILEMMA MODEL

Many times people "know" what they have to do but face obstacles in doing it. In the examples earlier and throughout this book, we have outlined a number of techniques to help clients focus on successes in the past and reappraise obstacles so they gather the energy to make these changes. But what about the instance where a person just cannot think of what to do?

Example: Nothing Seems to Fall into Place

Melanie cannot decide on her career direction. As an administrator in a small but growing company, she has had to do a bit of everything. Now she has the opportunity to focus on finance or operations or marketing. She likes some parts of each of those potential jobs but not others. She scours the assessments she has completed over the years. She goes over and over the newly minted job descriptions, but nothing seems to fall into place as the best fit. On her next coaching call, she complains of being tired but unable to sleep well. Overall, she is feeling frustrated at not being able to figure out this dilemma.

Here are some other examples of dilemmas:

- You want to exercise more but do not think you have enough time to do that and get through all your e-mails.
- You want to write but do not think you are a good enough writer.
- You need to improve sales in your territory but have no idea how.
- You do not get on with an employee you need to work closely with.

Think of these as puzzles the brain has tried and so far failed to solve. In his book *Quiet Leadership*, Rock (2006) reveals a model for just these circumstances.

With dilemmas, a part of us wants to achieve something but we perceive that something is in the way. Our brains and minds are doing what they do—processing information, working out what to do next to achieve our goals—then suddenly we hit an impasse. Everything comes to a standstill. This is a situation where consciously and logically working at the same dilemma leads to nothing but frustration. As is so often the case, we try harder at the very techniques that are not working—going over the goal and the obstacle again and again. Frustration or feeling "stuck" is the emotional summary of this mental impasse. What is needed is an insight. This is what Rock and his colleagues have investigated.

After poring over research on insight by others and by his colleagues, Rock himself faced a dilemma: How can all these data be turned into something useful to coaches and to anyone who wants to understand and encourage insight? Rock puzzled and puzzled over this question. Then, while looking out the window of a plane and thinking about nothing in particular, the answer came to him in a flash: Our faces tell the story! "In an instant I pictured how people's faces changed considerably when they had an insight. I felt strongly that if leaders could recognize which 'face' people had on at any time, it might make them more effective at improving thinking" (Rock, 2006, p. 104).

Four Faces of Insight

Figure 9.1 presents Rock's process for engaging our out-of-consciousness mental resources.

Face 1: Awareness of Dilemma. When we are aware of a dilemma, our physical state shows in a facial expression of concern. This is the

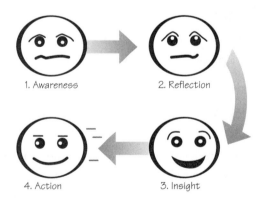

Figure 9.1 Four Faces of Insight
First published in *Quiet Leadership*, ©David Rock, 2006.

outward expression of a frustrated or puzzled or "stuck" state of mind. Try this yourself: Think very hard about something you have not figured out yet. Then look in a mirror. Your brow may be furrowed, your mouth crimped, the muscles around your eyes tight. Your whole body may be tense, your mind may be churning with options, your inner dialogue may be like a shouting match. You are trying and trying to figure it out.

Example: Having Trouble Sleeping

Melanie from the last example is keeping herself so focused on the problem of this job versus that job that she is having trouble sleeping. But all this energy is not moving her toward a solution. The coach begins by acknowledging her dilemma and confirming her request to be coached through it. For leaders who are not formally engaged as coaches, this step requires asking for permission to talk about the issue.

Face 2: Reflection. This face looks quite different. It is more relaxed and does not have that intense, staring concentration. Neurolinguistic programming practitioners have noted the signs of inner processing. Have people ever turned their eyes toward you but you know they are not really looking at you? Instead, they are staring out at space or, more precisely, staring *into* space, as if they are examining some processes going on inside their own heads. In brain terms, this face indicates that a person has, to continue our stage metaphor, dimmed the lights on the stage of attention to the outside world. Doing this allows our unconscious, like the writers backstage, to come up with a next act that may not have been remotely contemplated before. Very often this entails a shift in perspective—an entirely new setting or story line or even a new play.

Example: "How Will You Know . . ."

For Melanie, the coach's question, "How will you know when you have the ideal job?" sent her immediately into reflection. The coach was wise enough to allow the silence that Melanie needed for inner reflection. Coaches must be particularly aware of this shift when they coach by telephone and cannot see facial expressions. Fortunately, a state of mind is conveyed along many information channels, so vocal signals of a lowered tone, slower rate of speech, and perhaps a deep breath also indicate Face 2 processing.

269

Face 3: Illumination. This face often depicts what is referred to as the "aha!" moment. From somewhere among all the patterns our minds have created in our brain circuitry, a new connection is made, one that does not appear in our interoffice memos or timelines or project management software. We experience this as coming from nowhere, but of course it has simply been folded away in the wardrobe room or put somewhere backstage that the spotlight of our working memory has not had access to. Our nearly unlimited unconscious storage facility has yielded exactly the answer we have been looking for, but only when, in a sense, we stopped looking or listening so hard and instead allowed ourselves to see and hear more softly.

Example: "I Got It!"

Melanie was silent, but her mind was clearly active. Suddenly she exclaimed, "Of course. I got it! I don't want to work there at all. Here's my chance to start my own business!" Her face brightened into a smile and she began talking nonstop. She moved into a state of excitement and even joy, as if she had been plugged into an electric current. In fact, something similar to that had happened in her brain as she released energy from making new connections.

Face 4: Motivation. This face follows immediately upon an "aha!" People can barely sit still. Their eyes are darting around as if searching for the next thing to do. This is the moment for action or commitment to action and setting up accountability checks. It is important to encourage action at this point rather than slowing it down and reconsidering, which risks a return to a dilemma state. The worst thing a coach can do when someone is in the motivation state is to try to halt his or her performance.

Example: What Is the First Step?

Melanie's coach simply asked, "OK, what is the first step toward this new goal?" The two examined the steps, got the goal clear, and set up a check-in for the following appointment. Melanie hung up from the call and made an appointment with her soon-to-be former boss.

Linking Dilemma Model to Coaching

When we create a new connection, we experience a positive charge of energy. When we cannot find a connection that resolves a dilemma, we feel challenged, our energy is drained, and we keep going over and over it like a loop on an old-fashioned tape recorder. If you pay attention to your stream of thoughts, you may find that you spend much of your mental energy on the same challenges, without making progress, going over the same routes. This is tiring, frustrating—and ideal territory for coaching. In *Quiet Leadership* (2006), Rock incorporates the Four Faces of Insight into six steps to transform performance at work.

PRACTICE GUIDE FOR COACHING WITH THE BRAIN IN MIND—MAKE DECISIONS AND SOLVE PROBLEMS

The many facets of what we call "thinking" are what make us human. We are able to connect present results with past events and remember that pattern so as to predict the future. This is what enables us to move toward reward and away from danger in the elaborate ways human beings do. To a large extent, why we do what we do depends on our ability to make connections, remember them, form maps, and even become aware of those maps so we can change them.

Mostly, we do what we have done before. We may at one point have made a conscious decision to turn here or there or respond this way or that. This decision created the beginning of a map in our brains which, with repetition, has become hardwired. That is, we repeat the pattern so automatically that we are often unaware of doing it, much less of deciding to. Our ability to operate in this way has tremendous advantages. It means that we do not have to burden our working memory, our limited thinking resources, with deciding anew on every action we are taking. We can walk and talk at the same time.

This hardwiring function is a great advantage—until, for whatever reason, we want to do something different. What if our hardwired responses, the ones we practiced so much that we keep doing them no matter what, keep us doing them no matter what? What if it starts to matter a good deal that we move in new directions, respond differently because of changing circumstances, or explore possibilities we never even imagined? It is at this clash of old patterns with new demands that leaders are challenged and coaches are typically called on.

Coaches already have proven knowledge, skills, and mind-set from the bedrock and pillars that anchor the history of the field. How do we add capacity based on knowledge of the brain to support leaders in meeting these challenges?

Considering the question "Why do we do what we do?" and our thinking processes has deepened our understanding of how to use our powers of prediction, make new connections, and become aware of hardwiring we want to work around. To the guides already presented, we add these:

- Communicate in short, specific sentences that maximize limited working memory.
- Move among thinking levels so as to be able to simplify, chunk, and shift perspective with ease.
- Facilitate my own and others' insights by
  - Creating and inviting a quiet mind.
  - Focusing on connections rather than details.
  - Allowing insights to emerge without interruption.
  - Noticing and attending to insights when they emerge.
  - Encouraging the flow to action.

For many years in cognitive studies, thinking was separated from feeling or emotions. Neuroscience has clearly shown that such a separation is useless at best. A systemic integration of thinking and feeling is particularly important if our goals have anything to do with improving our emotional state. The question that guides part IV is "How can we feel better?"

How Can We Feel Better?

In the search for a mutual body/mind that is emerging from the systemic paradigm shift, we have looked at bodily clues that can indicate when changes have pushed us outside the limits of dynamic stability and the formula that brings us back into that healthful state. In part III we compared explanations for human behavior that are based on mechanistic assumptions with those arising from a systemic worldview. We recognized the limits of conscious mental processing and became aware of how to listen to the quieter connections that flow from the back of the brain when we set up a context for insight. In this part we turn to a topic that has been seen, in turns, as the enemy of civilized behavior, an indicator of mental illness, a missing element in understanding cognition, the key to motivation, an indicator of happiness, or the secret of social success: feelings, emotions, or "affect," as they tend to be called in research.

In the ideology that justified Western Europe's exploration and "discovery" of so-called primitive peoples and their genocide or enslavement to support its expansion, "savages" (and women) were thought to be ruled by their emotions. Objective, rational thought was the mark of men who thereby had the right, even the duty, to make others their subjects. Emotional outbursts ought to be controllable by rational, scientific argument. Cases where that control failed were surely indications of mental illness, as with women who persisted in claiming they had been abused by "gentlemen" who by definition could not be guilty of such wanton behavior. Psychotherapy, literally "tending the soul," arose in the 19th and 20th centuries to treat these and other emotional disorders. However, the mechanistic paradigm limited the conception of these disorders, and of feelings in general, in a number of ways:

- Emotional disturbances, and emotions themselves, were seen as determined by heredity, environment, or intrapersonal failures.
- The role of interpersonal relationships was minimized or conceived of as consisting only of objectively measurable stimuli.
- The fleeting nature of emotions made them untrustworthy as indicators of happiness, so the goal of psychotherapy had more to do with reducing symptoms of illness than promoting some value-laden (and therefore unscientific) measure of health and wellness.
- Feelings and thoughts were separated, making it possible to imagine that thinking was a higher-order process than emotions and should control them.

In pursuing the question "How can we feel better?" we trace the changes in these conceptions and the emergence of the systemic paradigm.

CHAPTER 10

Bedrock — Psychotherapy

Ishi's treatment by anthropologists from 1911 to 1916 was at least kindly. Not so for the treatment of soldiers traumatized by their World War I experiences. Medical doctors practiced what can only be described as torture in order to force "shell-shocked" men back to fight at the front. Alfred Adler was drafted to serve in the Austrian army as a physician during the war, just as he was on the verge of establishing a new approach to treating mental illness after he split from the Freudian circle in 1911. Adler's new approach took into account people's uniqueness, creativity, and social connections. But the war and his military service put an end to professional conferences, speeches, writing, and organizing a new therapeutic endeavor.

Always an excellent and humane observer, what did Adler make of the terrors and tragedy of the war? He wrote precious little about it, but it is clear from his subsequent behavior that something had changed for him. After the war, as if on a mission, Adler dedicated himself to activities that he hoped would lead to a different future for humankind than was indicated by its war-torn past: setting up child guidance clinics in Viennese schools to help children and their parents live cooperatively; mentoring teacher educators from around the world in his techniques; extending psychotherapy to families and groups; speaking in public on the principles of his commonsense approach to mental health; writing books in what today would be called the self-help genre, such as *What Life Could Mean to You* (Adler & Brett, 1998); and lecturing in university classes of physicians, social workers, and teachers. He continued providing psychotherapy to patients and supervising psychotherapists, but psychotherapy for him had taken a different turn, one that had much in common with the field of coaching that would emerge some seven decades later.

Psychotherapy is an application of philosophy, health practices, and psychology to treating mental illness. Many people assume that psychotherapy and psychology are the same, or that psychotherapy came into existence as an applied subfield of psychology. But worldwide, most psychotherapists are not part of the psychology profession but rather psychiatrists or other medical doctors, social workers, clinical counselors, psychiatric nurses, occupational therapists or, simply, psychotherapists (Orlinsky & Rönnestadt, 2005). Psychotherapy, literally "tending the soul," has its own history that is at least as old as that of scientific psychology.

The two fields do, however, have strong and ongoing connections. Both encroached on what had been the church's exclusive dominion — psychology to study the soul and psychotherapy to treat the sick soul. Many definitions of psychotherapy include "treatment by psychological means." Psychology's emphasis on the individual divorced from social context was mirrored in psychotherapy's location of mental illness within an individual. Psychotherapy also inherited Western medicine's tendency to define health as absence of disease. As a result, it bears the stigma of being sought only when one is identified as "sick." These two limitations provided opportunities for coaching to step in with a more systemic alternative.

- Why do we sometimes act crazy?
- Why do some of us lose touch with reality to such an extent that we cannot function?
- Why is it that insanity in one context is tolerated or even honored in another?
- Are some of us destined by our genes or upbringing to go insane?
- Is mental illness a result of chemical imbalance that can really be treated only with drugs?
- Does psychotherapy work?
- How do we know if it does or does not work?
- Where do we draw the line between mental health and mental illness?

- Is it possible to stop thinking of ourselves as victims of mental illness and instead create conditions that allow us to reach our full potential?

Many of these concerns lie largely outside the professional interest of coaches, whose ethical guidelines prevent us from treating mental illness. What is most relevant in our discussion of psychotherapy is what has not received much attention: healthy functioning, antecedents to happiness, and conditions for success and fulfillment. It is this space that coaching has filled, aided by other fields, such as positive psychology.

HISTORICAL INTERLUDE

Major Figures in Early Psychotherapy

Sigmund Freud

Although psychotherapy practice with individuals has been traced back to as early as 1775 (Ellenberger, 1970), most people assume it started with Austrian physician Sigmund Freud (1856–1939). Freud developed an approach he called psychoanalysis. To be blunt, Freud provides few models for coaches to draw on. However, he is such a seminal figure that a brief discussion of his ideas can be helpful, specifically for comparison with later approaches.

The genesis of Freud's psychoanalytic approach came during the late 1800s when he sought a scientific treatment for what were called neuroses and hysteria. After investigating various approaches, some of which met with considerable opposition, he began to meet with colleagues in 1902 to discuss the then-revolutionary idea that what patients said might indicate the source of their problems. He came to believe that neurosis stemmed from culturally unacceptable, thus repressed and unconscious, desires and fantasies of a sexual nature. Later he theorized that aggression could be explained by these drives also.

Freud concluded that the reasons people use to explain their behavior are not at all the "real" reasons. Rather, people's personalities are made up of three conflicting aspects, and their behavior indicates which of these predominates at any moment:

1. The unconscious id, insisting on seeking pleasure, and damn the consequences

(Continued)

---

2. The largely unconscious superego, which represents an internalization of social norms and which battles to contain the id's wild impulses
3. The conscious ego, which negotiates between the two conflicting forces and ingeniously invents defenses that more or less successfully justify resulting behavior in the real world

Despite Freud's emphasis on listening to what people say, he conformed to a mechanistic paradigm in ignoring their subjective talk as a mere mask for his "objective" conclusions about their unconscious reality. He also assumed that people are "driven" by libidinal forces, much as a steam engine is driven by the pressure of steam. To mix metaphors, these forces can become "impacted" as a result of repression, which can result in more or less serious mental illness. He also approached psychological treatment as a largely individual matter. These ideas were enormously influential in early-20th-century acceptance of the dynamic power of the unconscious. Freud's generally dark and pessimistic view of human nature seemed to fit with experiences of the time. However, most of the specifics of Freud's theory have been superseded or expanded by new psychotherapies and advances in cognitive psychology and neuroscience.

To simplify greatly, we might say that the assumption "We are our demons" summarizes Freud's theory. Through enough "talk therapy," patients become acquainted with these internal demons and gain insight about how to live with them. As a treatment strategy, psychoanalysts offer themselves as a "blank screen," with as little of their actual lives as possible intruding so that patients can project their unconscious drives and conflicts without interference from the therapist's personality. Psychoanalysts listen and listen, then offer interpretations or conclusions they have drawn from observing the patterns offered up in the patient's "free association." The assumption is that the interpretations are truths that the patient denies at the peril of being labeled "resistant." Breaking down this resistance is an intense process, generally requiring three to five sessions a week over three to seven years minimum. Patients who can afford the treatment may be in therapy throughout their adult lives.

Freud can be credited with the widespread acceptance of seeking treatment to improve individual mental health. One hundred years ago, there were few resources for treating people with mental illness beyond institutions for severe cases. Now there are psychiatrists, psychotherapists, clinical psychologists, social workers, and counselors across every city in the Western world. Freud's concept of the unconscious being a driver of our behavior has also contributed to the practice of increasing self-awareness through reflection, which has proven to have merits of its own. Even today, Freud's voluminous writing is read, often with a sense of reverence, by students in almost every field of human science.

However, Freud has also engendered great controversy, with critics claiming that his denial of the reality of sexual abuse has caused tremendous suffering (Masson, 1984); his attitude toward women and sexuality has supported discrimination (Keller, 1986); blaming the patient for resistance adds an unconscionable burden on someone who is already ill (Page, 1998); his requirement of therapist neutrality denies the power inherent in the relationship (Miller & Stiver, 1998); his emphasis on conflict and catharsis ignores the importance of connection (Surrey, Stiver, Miller, Kaplan, & Jordan, 1991); and his intolerance of ideas that were different from his own held back the development of psychotherapy (Breger, 2000). Because of these and many other claims, Nobel Prize–winning doctor Sir Peter Medawar described psychoanalysis in 1972 as "one of the strangest and saddest of all landmarks in the history of 20th century thought" (p. 68).

Alfred Adler

From a coach's perspective, Alfred Adler (1870–1937) is an entirely different matter. In 1902 Freud invited Adler (Hoffman, 1994) to join the Wednesday-night discussions that saw the birth of psychoanalysis. At that point, Adler's ideas about psychotherapy had already begun to develop, and he contributed concepts such as inferiority complex, defense mechanisms, and aggression drive to psychoanalytic theory. However, his independent views resulted in his being expelled from the Psychoanalytic Society in 1911. An oversimplified but memorable way to capture the differences between the two men is that Freud believed women envied men's penises (a biologically determined drive) whereas Adler believed women resented men's power (a socially constructed goal). As mentioned, Adler's development of his own approach to psychodynamic psychotherapy was interrupted by World War I, when he was drafted to serve as a military doctor in the Austrian army.

(Continued)

Hoffman's (1994) excellent biography of Adler does not describe his wartime experiences in detail, but the results are clear.

It was as if Adler had somehow uncovered in the rubble of World War I a crystal ball revealing the theoretical underpinnings of what, almost a century later, would become coaching — underpinnings that today are being confirmed by neuroscience research. Although many of these ideas are not associated with Adler, and his contribution generally is minimized in psychology and psychotherapy outside the Adlerian tradition itself, Adler was uncannily prescient in making the assumptions that human beings are:

- *Socially embedded*. There is no such thing as an isolated human being. In fact, the moment a person's status or belonging in a group is threatened or construed as being threatened, the potential for conflict arises.
- *Creative meaning makers*. Understanding people's psychology requires understanding their phenomenology, or the subjective meaning they give to events and behavior.
- *Dialectically constructing and reconstructing themselves within the constraints of heredity and environment*. "Both are giving only the frame and the influences which are answered by the individual in regard to his styled creative power" (Ansbacher & Ansbacher, 1956, p. xxiv).
- *Goal-oriented*. To understand people's behavior, it is much more important to know their intentions, values, and longer-term purposes than what drives them from the past. In fact, people's stories of their past reveal their goals in the present and future rather than a factual report of what happened.
- Integrated, unique, whole persons. Creativity, meaning making, goals, values, emotions, thought, physicality — all are linked systemically to yield the person we are. For individuals, the tasks of work, friendship, and love (some Adlerians also include self and spirituality) are unavoidable and interconnected.

Adler disagreed with Freud's idea of imposing a tripartite personality structure — id, ego, superego — on all people. He promoted discovering and treating each individual's unique structure. He used a German word, *Individuum*, referring to a person's "indivisible" nature, to name his approach. However, this word is translated in English as "individual," with an emphasis on individualism, or separation of a single person from the group. It is ironic that one of the first psychotherapies to insist on the importance of social connection and to treat groups, families, and organizational systems ended up being called individual psychology.

Reading Adler's assumptions today may create a "ho-hum" response, as they are widely accepted and increasingly supported by psychological and neuroscientific research. However, they are a very early example of the shift to a systemic paradigm. Adler was very much a theoretical pioneer in the early 20th century. His contributions are seldom mentioned in psychological or coaching literature for many reasons:

❑ Adler focused on changing the world rather than on writing scholarly literature.
❑ His acceptance in teaching, parenting, and social work led many academic psychologists and psychiatrists to treat his theory as unworthy of their attention.
❑ The hostility he and his students faced from Freudian psychoanalysis was daunting, especially in North America.

Adler's ideas are consistent with a number of coaching approaches:

❑ Appreciative inquiry (Bergquist, 2003; Cooperrider & Whitney, 2005)
❑ Co-active coaching (Whitworth, Kimsey-House, & Sandahl, 1998)
❑ Developmental coaching (Cook-Greuter, 1999; Laske, 2006)
❑ Inner game (Gallwey, 2001; Whitmore, 1996)
❑ Intentionality and social psychology (Bandura, 1986; Lewin, 1975, 1999)
❑ "Learner-judger" model (Adams, 2004; Goldberg, 1998)
❑ Phenomenology and existentialism (Frankl, 1984; Sartre, 1993)
❑ Positive psychology (Csikszentmihalyi, 1990; Seligman, 2002)
❑ Reflective practitioner and action research (Argyris, 1993; Argyris & Schön, 1974, 1978; Schön, 1983)
❑ Social constructivism (Berger & Luckmann, 1966; Piaget, 1928; Vaihinger, 1911, 1925; Vygotsky, 1978)
❑ Systems theory and application (Bateson, 2002; Mead, 2001; Senge, 1990; von Bertalanffy, 1968)

In what is perhaps his most important contribution, Adler sought to identify mental health as more than just lack of disease. He proposed

(Continued)

the concept of "social interest" as a measure of what we would today call "wellness" in its broadest sense. People, he said, are born into a paradox: On one hand, we are alone at the center of a self-created universe. On the other hand, our very survival depends on nurturance by those around us. Social interest is a way of resolving this paradox by identifying our own best interests as irrevocably bound up with the interests of others. Social interest is characterized by a sense of belonging to the whole human species, and indeed to the universe, as well as by the motivation to contribute our unique capacities to the betterment of humanity and the world.

For all these reasons, it is reasonable to consider Adler as a grandfather of coaching. He is also considered a precursor to the self-help and humanistic movements discussed in this chapter.

Carl Jung

Carl Jung (1875–1961) was from Switzerland and was 19 years younger than Freud and 5 years younger than Adler. Both of the younger men were closely involved with psychoanalysis after the turn of the 20th century (Jung became chairman of the International Psychoanalytical Association in 1910), and both developed independent interpretations that resulted in their separating from Freudian circles around 1912. However, Jung's emphasis on spirituality and archetypes, his idea that humans share a "Collective Unconscious" in addition to the personal unconscious of Freud's theory, and the principle of synchronicity influenced countercultural movements of the 1960s, and Jung is therefore generally better recognized than Adler.

Jung was the only surviving child of a Swiss Reform minister and his wife, who suffered from bouts of depression during her son's childhood. An isolated and introspective child, Jung explored his own personality and reactions to family and social stresses. After becoming fascinated with the newly emerging psychoanalytic movement toward the end of his medical studies, Jung was greatly influenced by his association with Freud and counted him as a mentor throughout his life. Jung's variation on psychoanalysis, which he called Analytical Therapy, is widely practiced throughout the world. But he also read, wrote, and investigated topics outside psychotherapy, such as mythology, Eastern and Western philosophy and spirituality, sociology and anthropology, literature, and the arts.

His theory of personality types (Jung, 1923), starting with the dichotomy between introversion and extraversion, formed the basis for a personality assessment tool that is widely used in both psychotherapy and coaching: the Myers-Briggs Type Indicator MBTI®. Developed during World War II by Catherine Cook Briggs and her daughter, Isabel Briggs Myers, to help women decide how they could best help in the war movement, the assessment (Myers et al., 1998) covers people's attitudes, information-gathering functions, decision-making patterns, and lifestyle preferences measured according to four dichotomies:

1. Extraversion (E) versus Introversion (I)
2. Sensation (S) versus iNtuition (N)
3. Thinking (T) versus Feeling (F)
4. Judging (J) versus Perceiving (P)

People's personalities may be characterized by any of the 16 resulting combinations.

Aside from the assessment itself, which is used extensively in organizational consulting, a basic coaching principle is that none of the dichotomies represents an objective right or wrong, good or bad. And no one is completely described or determined by their type. As with all typologies, the assessment is one of many sources of information. It may be useful in indicating what job or personal contexts may feel most "at home" to a person, and why he or she finds some activities more problematic than others.

Jung's emphasis on spirituality provided a connection with both the wellness and the humanistic movements of the later 20th century.

The major figures associated with the early popularization of psychotherapy—Sigmund Freud, Alfred Adler, and Carl Jung— set the stage for a myriad of varieties, or "schools," of psychotherapy. Each school had its version of what it considered to be the right theory or technique. At the most general level, the battle was between psychodynamic approaches that paid attention almost exclusively to an individual's internal motivation and behaviorist approaches that insisted on the primacy of external reinforcement techniques. During the last part of the 20th century, three trends combined to create a new context for psychotherapy that is much more supportive of a systemic worldview. We discuss these trends and the influence of psychotherapy on coaching under these headings:

- Humanistic movement
- Trauma and its social implications
- Research revealing transtheoretic common factors
- Linking psychotherapy techniques to coaching
- Resource Section: Mental Health Issues — How *not* to do psychotherapy
- Psychotherapy as bedrock for coaching

HUMANISTIC MOVEMENT

Humanistic psychology, often called humanism, or the "person-centered approach," developed in the 1950s as an alternative to psychoanalysis and behaviorism. Humanistic psychologists believe that individuals are controlled by their own values and choices and not by the environment, as behaviorists think, or by unconscious drives, as psychoanalysts believe. The goal of humanistic psychology is to help people function effectively and fulfill their own unique potential. To simplify, the person-centered approach says, "We are our human needs."

The humanistic approach focuses on:

- Individuals and their needs, including personal choice, free will, and creativity
- Conscious experience, drawn out of the concept of phenomenology (the study of immediate experience)
- Human nature in its entirety

Humanistic psychology draws on the philosophical concept of humanism and was the first movement to popularize Adler's focus on mental health rather than on mental illness. The field laid the foundations for the human potential and personal development movements, the adult education field, and much of the thinking in the counseling field.

Abraham Maslow

One of the founding theorists behind humanistic psychology was American psychologist Abraham Maslow (1908–1970). Maslow was originally a behaviorist who became dissatisfied with the field, partly as a result of his association with Alfred Adler. He developed the theory of self-actualization (Maslow, 1943, 1971) based on the idea that each of us has an innate desire to achieve our potential through using our unique abilities.

Although the high level of generality of Maslow's self-actualizing model makes it difficult to test in research, its intuitive "rightness" has helped it stand the test of time over several decades. A powerful idea that has still not been superseded in psychology, it is a model that most coaches would subscribe to, whether they are aware of its source or not.

Out of Maslow's work on self-actualization came his well-known Hierarchy of Needs. The hierarchy is represented in many sources as a pyramid with multiple levels. The bottom level is physiological, representing needs for survival. The second level is safety and security needs. After these come the social needs for love and belonging, followed by ego needs of self-esteem. Finally, the apex of the pyramid is self-actualization.

In Maslow's theory, each need must be met before the next need above can be dealt with. Exceptions have been cited, such as heroes giving up their lives to come to the aid of strangers. Scholars argue about whether the needs are independent rather than arranged in a hierarchy. Nevertheless, the idea of taking care of lower needs first makes intuitive sense. Coaches may find it useful to refer to the hierarchy in exploring health practices. As a basic example, if we are hungry and have nothing to eat, it is hard to focus on how our career may help us to feel better about ourselves. Clients may not be able to move toward increased self-esteem if their "lower" needs have not been met.

Maslow's work has had an influence on management theory, especially in the realm of how to motivate others. Reasoning from his hierarchy, workers may have difficulty developing a cooperative work environment if they do not feel that they are safe within it. Employees who are motivated by satisfaction at work rather than by financial gain may in fact assume a certain basic level of income. In this case, their search for work satisfaction would be difficult to maintain if they were worried about feeding themselves and their families.

In parent education and education in general, self-esteem that comes from making one's own choices is assumed to provide a basis for a "higher" self-actualization motive. Many forms of therapy also make this assumption and guide clients to understand their own and others' needs.

Maslow also described in more detail what a psychologically healthy person might look like, an exciting development in a field that focused so much on illness. According to Maslow (1968), self-actualized people:

- Are efficient and accurate in perceiving reality.
- Are accepting of themselves, of other people, and of nature.
- Are spontaneous in thought and emotion, rather than artificial.
- Are problem-centered (rather than blaming people for problems).
- Are concerned with the eternal philosophical questions of human-kind.
- Are independent and autonomous.
- Have a continued "freshness of appreciation" of ordinary events.
- Often experience a sense of oneness with nature.
- Identify with all of humanity and are democratic and respectful of others.
- Form very deep ties, but only with a few people.
- Appreciate for its own sake the process of doing things.
- Have a philosophical, thoughtful, nonhostile sense of humor.
- Have a childlike and fresh creativity and inventiveness.
- Maintain an inner detachment from the culture in which they live.
- May appear temperamental or ruthless, as they are strong and independent people guided by their own inner visions.

Carl Rogers

The other key figure from the field of humanistic psychology is Carl R. Rogers (1902–1987), an American pioneer in psychotherapy theory and research, who challenged the basic assumption that the therapist is the expert. Rogerian psychotherapy was widely embraced for its human-istic approach. It is also referred to as "client-centered" or "person-centered" psychotherapy. This is a nondirective approach to ther-apy, where "directive" means any therapist behavior that deliberately attempts to alter the client in some way. Directive behaviors include giving advice, offering treatments, teaching, persuading, diagnosing, and making interpretations. Despite the success of Rogers's ideas, many of the clinical therapies practiced in the United States are still directive by nature. Coaching, however, has embraced the non-directive ideal, and Rogers was cited extensively by coaches who were asked to acknowledge those who influenced them (Brock, 2008).

TRAUMA AND ITS SOCIAL IMPLICATIONS

The women's liberation movement that began in the late 1960s was accompanied by criticism of the tendency of psychology and psychotherapy to ignore the experience of women and to generalize about mental health and treatment from studies of men alone. One important phenomenon that was explored was the effect of violence against women (Brownmiller, 1975).

At the same time that the women's movement was revealing the extent and psychological consequences of rape and domestic violence involving women, veterans returning from the Vietnam War were exhibiting extensive physical and psychological symptoms. Theorists (van der Kolk, McFarlane, & Weisaeth, 1996) began to see a pattern of trauma and resulting disabilities across present and past war experiences, violence against women, and abuse of children. Research evidence accumulated, resulting in the addition of a new diagnosis to the *Diagnostic and Statistical Manual* (American Psychiatric Association, 2000): post-traumatic stress disorder, or PTSD. The significance of this diagnosis is that for the first time, the cause (or etiology) of a mental disorder was recognized to be a social event, albeit one outside what is considered "normal," rather than some internal conflict or deficiency on the part of the victim. The out-of-proportion rage of the war veteran, the passivity of the rape victim, or the tendency of people who were abused as children to "go somewhere else in their minds" was shown to be an understandable reaction to traumatic stress. This was a significant step in recognizing the importance of context in mental illness. If context is recognized as being important in causing illness, surely it must be taken into account in creating wellness. This emphasis on context is an important influence in the shift to a systemic perspective.

RESEARCH REVEALING TRANSTHEORETIC COMMON FACTORS

Psychotherapy in the 20th century was a contentious field. As mentioned, Freud excluded Alfred Adler from the psychoanalytic inner circle, and Carl Jung went his separate way. Behaviorism in psychology spawned behavior modification, which ridiculed psychodynamic therapies as being "subjective" and unscientific.

The behaviorist approach informed many techniques (see Erwin, 1978; Rimm & Masters 1974), including behavior therapy, aversion therapy, and electroshock therapy. For decades, a substantial part of clinical psychology drew from behaviorist principles. It was not until the introduction of cognitive and humanist approaches in the 1950s and 1960s that a shift occurred (see Bechtel, Abrahamsen, & Graham, 1998, especially pp. 15–17). However, behaviorist principles still hold sway in many fields, including school psychology, psychiatry in institutions, and some domains of psychological research. Cognitive therapy has been melded with behaviorist techniques to produce cognitive-behavior therapy, and the resulting treatment has received a good deal of support from research based on manuals that prescribe how the therapist should treat the patient (see Nathan & Gorman, 1998).

Psychotherapy was considered part of medical practice to such an extent in the United States that psychiatrists (medical doctors) in the 1950s took psychologists Albert Ellis and Harold Mosak to court for practicing medicine without a license. (They were exonerated, opening the door for psychologists to practice psychotherapy.) Each of the hundreds of schools or approaches to psychotherapy claimed that it had the best or correct or only approach. After all, their patients got better, didn't they?

A dash of very cold water was thrown on psychotherapy in 1952 when Hans Eysenck published an article claiming that psychotherapeutic treatment was no better than doing nothing at all. That is, according to Eysenck, allowing patients to recover on their own, with no psychotherapy whatsoever, yielded about the same outcome as those who had received psychotherapy. Eysenck (1953) directed his criticism particularly toward psychoanalysis. Eysenck called for better ways of measuring outcome, but it was easy to conclude that psychotherapy was an expensive and quite unnecessary procedure. This conclusion, and the fact that it was backed up by research, galvanized the formerly competing schools so that they began to cooperate in examining their work more systematically.

Interest in psychotherapy research began to build around the same time as the cognitive revolution in psychology proper, when processes inside the "black box" of the mind became legitimate subjects for scientific study. Over the next few decades, computer technology made it possible to do research on ever more complex interactions, such as those that characterize psychotherapy. The Society for Psychotherapy Research (see Internet links) brought together psychotherapists from a wide range of therapeutic approaches and professional backgrounds to share their findings. After many years and thousands of studies, many of them very carefully designed and methodologically sophisticated, some results can be stated with confidence. And those results open the door to more systemic, holistic, socially embedded, and positive approaches that have stimulated the emergence of coaching.

The first question that psychotherapy researchers answered, in response to Eysenck's devastating critique, was "Does psychotherapy work better than no treatment at all?" The general answer, as Norcross (2002) summarizes, is yes. Nathan and Gorman (1998) describe more specifically that certain therapeutic techniques work better with some patients than with others and that some techniques work better with some mental disorders than others.

The second question was "What is it about psychotherapy that works, that accounts for the improvements shown in outcome research?" The results of this line of research may have direct relevance to coaching. Hubble, Duncan, and Miller (1999) brought together a number of studies of psychotherapy and counseling applications to find common factors among those that were successful. Their research astonished adherents of competing schools: The techniques and theories that took up most of the attention in psychotherapy training accounted for only about 15% of the variance or likelihood of successful outcome. Whatever the theoretical orientation of the therapist, the strongest predictor of success had to do with characteristics of the patient—about 40% of variance ("variance" meaning how much a factor contributes to making a difference).

One lesson that coaches may draw from this research is the importance of learning about the client from the client's subjective perspective, rather than applying preconceived notions or assumptions to the coaching engagement.

Coaches learn to differentiate their practice from psychotherapy and counseling, as suggested by David Orlinsky's (2007) differentiation in the introduction to this book. We do not yet have the research that clearly shows all the differences and similarities between coaching and psychotherapy. At the same time, there clearly are commonalities: Two people (in individual coaching and in therapy) relate to one another with the intention that one will benefit from the interaction. Thus, one candidate for similarity is the relationship between the patient or client on one hand and the therapist or coach on the other. The research compiled by Hubble et al. (1999) showed that the relationship was the largest factor — about 30% of variance — over which the therapist has some influence. Learning theorists (Johnson, 2006) recognize the importance of a caring teacher or mentor in creating the conditions for a student to learn, and anecdotal and experiential evidence in coaching concurs.

The remaining 15% of the outcome has to do with a factor that had been dismissed as "interference" or "irrelevant" in medical research: the placebo effect, or client expectations. We discussed this factor at length as part of the formula for dynamic stability in chapter 6. The fact that psychotherapy research shows it to be a substantial contributor to getting better supports our claim that it is an important factor in coaching.

Many research methods and strategies have been developed or borrowed from fields other than psychology — for example, qualitative approaches of sociology and anthropology — to deal with the subjective and relational reality of psychotherapy. Thus, psychotherapy research supported the overturn of the focus on "objectivity" and factors internal to the individual that derived from the logical positivist worldview. This has resulted in an impetus for coaches putting themselves in the shoes of the client, or the subjectivity that is characteristic of coaching.

LINKING PSYCHOTHERAPY TECHNIQUES TO COACHING

We have chosen to focus on six approaches from psychotherapy and counseling that are directly relevant to coaching:

1. Person-centered therapy
2. Gestalt and expressive therapies

3. Cognitive and cognitive-behavioral therapies
4. Neurolinguistic programming
5. Solution-focused therapy
6. Metaphor and narrative therapy

These approaches yield techniques that may be useful both in coaching and in psychotherapy and counseling. Because ethical standards do not allow coaches, in their role as coaches, to practice psychotherapy, it is important to be able to discern when a client should be referred to a psychotherapist or counselor. Therefore, after discussing these approaches, we provide information written by certified mental health professionals to help coaches differentiate their practice from that of psychotherapy.

Person-Centered Therapy

Carl Rogers (1951) developed a nondirective method in which the therapist was supposed to listen with acceptance and without judgment. He believed that the client or person seeking therapy (he preferred not to call them patients) was responsible for improving his or her own life and was likely to have the best answers for how to do this. This is a key principle of much of the coaching field now as well. If Adler can be referred to as a grandfather of coaching, Rogers is often considered its father (Brock, 2008).

Roger's theory of a healthy person involved:

- An openness to all experience
- An ability to live in the moment
- The ability to follow one's own instincts
- Freedom in thought and action
- Creativity

Here are the basic tenets of person-centered techniques:

- *Unconditional positive regard.* The therapist holds on to a belief in people's potential and their ability to find their own answers, despite their behavior at any one time.
- *Genuineness or congruence.* The therapist's role is to encourage and support and to do this on an equal level with the client.

- *An accurate empathic understanding by helper.* The therapist is there to provide empathy and understanding, not direction, allowing clients to heal themselves. Therapists check their understanding of what a patient says with a brief restatement for the client to verify or correct. The therapist trusts that the open acceptance of the client's statements will foster the client's natural process of actualization.

Rogers also worked with the idea of a "self-concept," which consists of the "ideal self," the "self-image," and "self-esteem." His concept of self-esteem was picked up by the human potential movement and propagated in schools and in parent education.

The person-centered approach was one of the most popular within psychology in the 20th century and contributed a great deal to the systemic paradigm shift. It brought subjectivity back into psychotherapy. It also laid the foundations for the study of happiness, cognitive (not just biological) motivation, and peak performance, fields especially important to coaching.

There is a great deal of similarity between coaching and humanistic approaches such as that of Rogers. The statement, presented as an article of faith, by pioneer coaches Whitworth, Kimsey-House, and Sandahl (1998) is that clients are "creative, resourceful, and whole" (p. 3). As with coaching, the primary intent of humanistic approaches is to comprehend the client's internal frame of reference, focus on the client's perception of self and the world, and draw out the client's own wisdom and resources. A coach practices unconditional positive regard toward the client at all times.

Coaches are taught to reflect back and accept the client's statements rather than imposing some supposedly objective "truth" or interpretation. Listening skills are based on the extensive elaboration of Rogerian techniques by Allen Ivey and colleagues (Evans et al., 2004) resulting in a textbook that is widely used in counseling and psychotherapy courses. Good listening skills provide the backbone for an approach that conveys empathy to the client.

Finally, a coach must behave in a way that is congruent with his or her values and let the client be fully aware of the coach's authentic self, rather than hiding behind a veil of objectivity. While these skills are demanding, they constitute core competencies for coaches.

To take another perspective, despite the positive influence of believing that individuals may have their own answers, especially if they are encouraged by unconditional positive regard, there is a drawback. When a coach relies entirely on empathy, he or she may end up reinforcing the client's inability to change. Therefore, coaches take responsibility for believing in a person's greater potential, even when that person does not see it, and even when reminding a person of his or her potential may seem directive.

Gestalt and Expressive Therapies

Fritz Perls (1893–1970), a German-born psychiatrist, and Laura Posner Perls (1905–1990) combined the humanistic approach with Gestalt psychology to create and develop Gestalt therapy after the couple immigrated to the United States. The German word "Gestalt" roughly translates to "whole" or "form." Gestalt psychologists claim to consider behavior holistically. "The whole is greater than the sum of its parts" is a phrase that comes out of experiments in the Gestalt tradition. In applying the concept to therapy, Gestalt therapists notice the client's postures, gestures, and tone of voice rather than just the content of words. Many other forms of therapy emphasize the whole sensory experience of clients: art, music, dance, and psychodrama, to name a few.

The theory behind such applications maintains that in order to interpret what we receive through our senses, we automatically organize the information. For example, when we see one dot, we perceive it as such, but when we see five dots together, we "see" them as a "row of dots." Without this tendency to group our perceptions, that same row would be seen as "dot, dot, dot, dot, dot," taking longer to process and reducing our interpretive ability. Gestalt theory claims that grouping is based on the four principles of similarity, proximity, continuity, and closure. More recent neuroscience findings show that our interpretations indeed cannot be separated from our sensations.

One of the key researchers in Gestalt psychology (as opposed to its application in Gestalt therapy) was Wolfgang Köhler (1887–1967). He developed insight theory, often called the "aha!" phenomenon. Insight theory claims that we learn by immediate and sudden recognition and that individuals often use insight when solving a problem or determining their response to stimuli. Clearly, this idea is directly counter to the behaviorist idea that learning is based on stimulus-reward, stimulus-reward accumulating over time.

Köhler based his ideas about insight on his observations of chimpanzees. Food was placed out of the chimps' reach while objects such as sticks were placed close by. Köhler observed that some of the chimps learned more quickly than others and that though they used trial and error to reach the food, their attempts did not build step by step, as you would expect if reinforcement were the mechanism. Nor were their attempts random. Köhler theorized that the chimps used insight to solve the problem (Blosser, 1973). Today, neuroscience has allowed us to understand the process of insight much more thoroughly so that coaches can help clients set up conditions to make insight more likely, as illustrated by Rock's (2006) "Four Faces of Insight" model presented in chapter 9.

The many expressive therapies share the humanistic assumption that we are whole beings and that our subjective experiences can be discerned by what we do physically and what we feel emotionally. Changing behavior and thinking patterns may be useful techniques, but not to the exclusion of changing feelings, including both sensations and emotions.

One very influential technique that has proven useful to coaches is the "empty chair" (Greenberg, 2002). The technique is particularly effective when a client is stuck, either in an internal or external conflict or not knowing which of two options to choose.

Example: "Why Don't You Just Do Things the Way I Tell You to Do Them?"

Sanjay thought he had solved an ongoing problem with getting financial reports on time when he hired a bright young bookkeeper, Maxine. However, after several weeks, he told his coach that he felt things were worse than before he hired her. After listening carefully to Sanjay's complaints, the coach thought that he could benefit from seeing things from Maxine's perspective. Of course, the coach could suggest that Sanjay have a conversation with the bookkeeper herself, but he thought an empty chair exercise might make that conversation more productive.

Coach: Let's say that Maxine is sitting here in this empty chair. What would you say to her?

294

Sanjay: *Why don't you just do things the way I tell you to do them? Why do you keep coming and asking me about every little detail? You don't need to understand everything. You don't need to question everything we do here. Why don't you just do it?*

The coach listens for the point where Sanjay seems to run out of steam and starts to repeat himself.

Coach: Now stand up and move over to the empty chair and when you sit in it, become Maxine having just heard all that you said. What's your reaction as Maxine?

It is crucially important that the client actually physically move to the formerly empty chair. Remember that this technique is based on an assumption of holism and necessitates shifting sensations and perceptions.

Sanjay as Maxine: *I'm doing the best that I can. I'm trying as hard as I can. It's just that nothing seems to make sense the way that my former job did.*

Coach: What about your relationship with Sanjay, your boss? Talk to him in this empty chair.

Sanjay as Maxine talking to Sanjay: (*taking a moment to think*) *It seems that every time you come into my office, you're looking for something wrong. I get so nervous that I start to make mistakes and then I'm questioning everything I do.* (*long pause*)

Coach: Would you like to take the Sanjay chair again?

Sanjay, back in the chair as himself: *I can see that I'm pushing you because I'm so anxious to clear up this mess with the financials. I guess that doesn't help you focus on what you need to do.*

Coach: How might this understanding help you approach Maxine next time you go into her office?

As presented, the exercise is done in person, but it could be just as effective over the phone as long as the client actually moves from chair to chair. The Sanjay example is condensed; it actually went on for nearly 45 minutes, but it is representative of the kind of change that can take place as a result of utilizing an empty chair in this way.

Role playing, where the coach becomes an actor in whatever drama is engaging the client, and psychodrama, where a whole scenario is played out with other people, are related expressive techniques that may be used in individual or team coaching. To avoid having the session turn into therapy, the coach must keep the focus on practical, work-related issues rather than straying into inner emotional conflicts that must be referred to psychotherapists.

Gestalt therapy contributed to a major strand in the history of coaching. Stimulated partly by the group work of Kurt Lewin (1947), Fritz Perls led seminars based on his approach to psychotherapy at the Esalen Institute in Big Sur, California, beginning in the early 1960s. The T-group movement had started in 1946 in Bridgeport, Connecticut, when Lewin had been invited to help a group deal with ethnic tension after World War II. T-groups represented an attempt to understand the social dynamics that contributed to problems in organizations. At that point, the "T" in T-group stood for training. After Lewin's untimely death, colleagues formed the National Training Laboratory and used the technique in organizational consulting. Perls applied T-group techniques in his seminars. Meeting in groups where members confront each other as a way of developing self-awareness soon became popular in West Coast counterculture. Werner Erhard combined group confrontation with Zen philosophy in the first Erhard Seminars Training, or EST, in 1971 in San Francisco, California. Later, EST became Landmark Education, which offers training worldwide and was cited by a large number of coaches interviewed by Vikki Brock (2008) as a major influence in the history of coaching.

Cognitive and Cognitive-Behavioral Therapies

As we discussed in chapter 9, cognitivism became the dominant approach in psychology in the second half of the 20th century, replacing behaviorism as the popular paradigm for understanding human behavior.

Cognitive therapy is an application of scientific psychology that focuses on teaching patients how to retrain their thinking patterns. It uses awareness, logic, testing, and practice to alter distorted attitudes and perceptions that lead to problematic behavior. Automatic, habitual thoughts form the basic data around which treatment is built. A client's thoughts are presumed to be the cause of emotions. Therefore, cognitive therapists help the client recognize distorted thinking and replace it with more realistic ideas that then yield more desirable feelings and behavior. The focus is on the present and future rather than uncovering past "causes" for difficulties.

Major features of cognitive therapy include (Schulyer, 1971):

- An active, structured dialogue
- Focus on the here and now
- Goal-directed, problem-solving collaboration
- Limited time frame
- Assumption that thinking drives emotions which drive behavior
- Use of homework assignments
- Avoidance of interpreting unconscious factors

Studies done in the 1970s showed that behavior therapy was more effective when it was extended with cognitive elements. Thus, cognitive-behavior therapy (CBT) was born. CBT has been shown to be as effective as drug treatment for depression, panic attacks, obsessive-compulsive disorder, and other problems of excessive anxiety.

RATIONAL EMOTIVE BEHAVIOR THERAPY Albert Ellis (1913–2007) is a psychologist who developed rational emotive therapy (RET), one form of cognitive therapy (Ellis, 1974) that had many connections with Adler's individual psychology (Ellis, 1957). As behavioral outcomes of thinking and emotions became more recognized in cognitive psychology during the 1990s, Ellis added "behavior" to the name of his approach: rational emotive behavior therapy (REBT) (Ellis, 2003). REBT and CBT share a good deal of common ground.

Ellis's REBT is a practical, action-oriented approach to coping with problems and enhancing personal growth. REBT focuses on the present: on currently held attitudes, painful emotions, and maladaptive behaviors that can sabotage a fuller experience of life. REBT therapists seek to help people uncover their individual beliefs (attitudes, expectations, and personal rules) that frequently lead to emotional distress.

REBT assumes that humans are prone to adopting irrational beliefs and behaviors which get in the way of their goals and purposes. Often these irrational attitudes or extreme philosophies take the form of dogmatic "musts," "shoulds," or "oughts"; they contrast with rational and flexible desires, wishes, preferences, and wants.

The presence of extreme philosophies can make all the difference between healthy negative emotions (such as sadness or remorse or concern) and unhealthy negative emotions (such as depression or guilt or anxiety). For example, one person's philosophy after experiencing a loss might take the form: "It is unfortunate that this loss has occurred, although there is no actual reason why it should not have occurred. It is sad that it has happened, but it is not awful, and I can continue to function." Another's might take the form: "This absolutely should not have happened, and it is horrific that it did. These circumstances are now intolerable, and I cannot continue to function." The first person's response is accompanied by sadness, while the second person may be well on his or her way to depression.

Most important of all, REBT maintains that individuals have it within their power to change their beliefs and philosophies profoundly and thereby to radically alter their state of psychological health. To accomplish this, REBT employs a technique that can be valuable in coaching when clients maintain that they have no control over their emotional reactions or the behavior that results. The ABC framework (Ellis, 1974) clarifies the relationship between activating events (A); our beliefs about them (B); and the cognitive, emotional, or behavioral consequences of our beliefs (C).

Example: "This Shouldn't Be Happening to Me!"

Drago lost his temper and stomped out of a management meeting after being told that his new project had been canceled by the client. For a month after the incident, he fumed and complained, and his vice president finally suggested that he see the company's internal coach.

"I gave my lifeblood to this project," he told his coach. "I was persuaded to leave my old position just to take this on. No one could do it better than me, I was told. Now the client gets bought out, and where does that leave me? Sure, they pay a penalty to our company for breaking the contract, but I'm still left without the project that was going to make my career! You can't blame me for getting mad. I couldn't help it. I'm still mad. And that's making everything worse. I can't think or concentrate on my other work and my boss is getting after me."

"Let's look at the ABC of this," suggested the coach. "You're saying that A, the activating event, was when the client canceled the project. And the consequence, or C, is that you got angry."

On a flip chart, the coach writes the letter A (project canceled) and the letter C (anger) with an arrow from A to C (see Figure 10.1a).

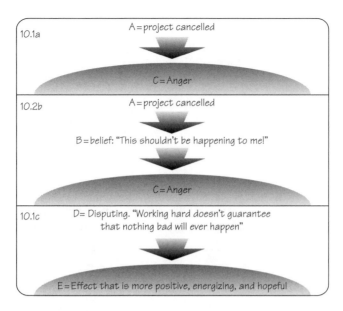

Figure 10.1 Example of Ellis's ABC Model

"Right. That made me really angry."

"But what's between the cancellation and your anger?"

"What? Nothing. It just makes me mad, that's all. I can't help it."

"One thing I know about you, Drago, is that you think fast. I believe that you thought through Step B so quickly you weren't even aware of it. What do you believe about Step A, the cancellation, that would lead to the consequence of so much anger? What are you telling yourself about A?"

The coach erases the arrow and inserts the letter B, labeling it "Belief," as in Figure 10.1b.

Drago is silent for a while. "I guess...I've just been working so hard. I don't deserve this. This shouldn't be happening to me!"

The coach writes this sentence next to the B on the flip chart.

"What comes to mind when you look at this?" asked the coach.

Drago smiles. "You know, if one of my people came to me with this, I'd tell them they had been working hard and that they didn't deserve such a thing. And that they had a right to be upset. And that I wish nothing bad would ever happen to them. But . . . I guess working hard doesn't guarantee that nothing bad will ever happen."

"You've just gone through D and E. You do think quickly," said the coach. "D is disputing, or taking a commonsense look at your belief. You tried

(Continued)

299

working on C, or your feelings, but nothing changed. Then when you became aware of the belief connecting A with C, you could see that you were making the unreasonable demand that things *ought* to work out the way you wanted. After D, or disputing and making the belief more realistic, you were able to shift to E, an effect that appears to be more positive. You certainly look more relaxed." (See Figure 10.1c.)

"That's right. I feel hopeful again. I think I'm ready to get back to work."

Changing how we think about a perception (or how we filter it through our beliefs or the questions we ask unconsciously) can change how we feel about it. In effect, this ABC model, which is similar to other forms of cognitive or cognitive-behavioral therapy, illustrates that mental activities or predispositions can mediate between experiences and emotional responses.

In working with the ABC framework, REBT employs three primary insights:

1. While external events are influential, psychological disturbance is largely a matter of personal choice in the sense that individuals consciously or unconsciously select either rational beliefs or irrational beliefs at (B) when negative events occur at (A).

2. Past history and present life conditions strongly affect a person, but they do not, in and of themselves, *disturb* the person; rather, it is the individual's responses that disturb him or her, and it is again a matter of individual choice whether to maintain the philosophies at (B) which result in disturbance.

3. Modifying the philosophies at (B) requires persistence and hard work, but it can be done. Ellis himself was a very colorful figure who did not hesitate to use strong language and humor in disputing people's irrational beliefs. He accused people of "muster-bating" or "should-ing on themselves" when they demanded that events turn out according to their assumptions. He assigned people whose fear of judgment by others was paralyzing exercises to get them used to looking ridiculous, such as by taking a banana on a walk at the end of a dog leash. His techniques were directive but often quite effective.

The main purpose of REBT is to help clients replace absolutist philosophies, ones that are full of musts and shoulds, with more flexible ones.

Part of this includes learning to accept that all human beings (including oneself) are fallible. Achieving one's goals is connected with learning to increase one's tolerance for frustration. REBT does not deny the importance of empathy, unconditional positive regard, and authenticity on the part of the practitioner. However, REBT views these conditions as neither necessary nor sufficient for therapeutic change to occur.

COGNITIVE THERAPY   In medical school in the 1940s, Aaron T. Beck (born 1921) turned his attention from psychiatry to neurology because of the lack of research showing the effectiveness of psychotherapy available at the time. He joined the Psychiatry Department of the University of Pennsylvania in 1954, and, influenced by the cognitive revolution in psychological theory, he developed a clinical approach that he named cognitive therapy. Developed a few years after Ellis's REBT, Beck's approach has been enormously influential, partly because of the extensive ongoing research that Beck and his students have conducted beginning in 1959.

According to Beck (1976), cognitive therapy seeks to:

- Identify cognitions (thoughts) relevant to the presenting problem.
- Recognize connections among cognitions, affects (emotions) and behaviors.
- Examine evidence for and against key beliefs revealed by the cognitions.
- Encourage the client to test beliefs in real situations (homework).
- Help the client choose those beliefs that are supported by evidence.
- Teach the client to carry out the cognitive process independently.

The central insight of cognitive therapy as formulated over three decades ago is that thoughts mediate between stimuli, such as external events, and emotions. A stimulus elicits a thought—which might be an evaluative judgment of some kind—which in turn gives rise to an emotion. In other words, it is not the stimulus itself that elicits an emotional response directly but our evaluation of or thought about that stimulus. This is similar to Ellis's ABC Model described in Figure 10.1, with the stimulus being A, the thought B, and the emotion C.

Two ancillary assumptions underpin the approach of the cognitive therapist:

1. Clients are capable of becoming aware of their own thoughts and of changing them.
2. Sometimes the thoughts elicited by stimuli distort or otherwise fail to reflect reality accurately.

Example: "That Made Me Feel So Hopeless"

Her career coach wondered why Elise didn't apply for a job that seemed to be what she was looking for.

"What's that about, Elise?"

After some thought, Elise replied, "I just don't have the heart to try again after I missed out on the last job. It was such a perfect match, but then I didn't get it. That made me feel so hopeless that I don't even want to try again."

"So let me understand. When you didn't get the last job you applied for, you lost hope. But what did you tell yourself about not getting the job?"

"Maybe they're right and I just can't do this kind of work. Maybe I should just give up and look for something entirely different."

"So, you didn't get the job [stimulus], you figured that's because you couldn't do it [thought], and you ended up feeling hopeless [emotion]."

"Yes, that sounds right."

"Let's look more closely at your thoughts about not being able to do the job. What are the requirements for it?" Elise and her coach went over the requirements for the type of position she was applying for and compared them with her training and experience. This step was similar to Ellis's D, or disputation, in which the client is asked to supply evidence. It was clear from the evidence that Elise did indeed have the qualifications required—that her thoughts did not match reality.

"So why do you think even a qualified person like you might not have been hired?" asked the coach [generating an alternate explanation].

"Well, I did make the short list, so I wasn't entirely out of the running. And I was told that we were an incredible group of candidates. When I think of it like that, it was probably just the luck of the draw. Maybe I shouldn't worry about the one that got away and just try again."

COGNITIVE-BEHAVIORAL THERAPY   As with REBT, the word "behavior" is commonly added to cognitive therapy. Often cognitive therapists assign homework or ask clients to test the reality of their beliefs in action. The idea is that people can behave their way into thinking differently and then think their way into feeling differently—which then in turn motivates them to behave differently.

Donald Meichenbaum, born in 1940 in New York City, developed a version of CBT that he calls cognitive-behavior modification (1977). He has shown the value of observing patterns of thoughts to reveal core beliefs that, when changed, can produce more lasting effects. His work is supported by neuroscience evidence that determined mental activity can actually affect brain structure and thus make changes more reliable (Schwartz & Begley, 2002).

A coach can use many of the principles of CBT in coaching by helping a client learn how to improve the quality of his or her thinking.

Example: Changing Habits Is a Snap

Oleana's experience is an illustration of combining behavioral with cognitive techniques. Oleana revealed to her coach that she was continually putting herself down. "I'm always telling myself 'That was stupid' or 'You're such an idiot.'"

After spending some time in a session exploring how this kind of self-talk drained energy and created negative feelings, and making sure that Oleana wanted to make a change, the coach gave her this assignment: "Put a rubber band around your wrist and snap it every time you call yourself 'stupid' or 'idiot' or any other insult. Combine that with a journal in which you record all the good things you accomplish each day."

Two weeks later, Oleana reported that she had only needed a handful of snaps to remind her how unpleasant her negative self-talk was. As she caught herself more often and focused on accomplishments rather than self-insults, she found herself more able to enjoy her work and being with her family.

In summary, cognitive therapy shares common ground with coaching. They are both designed to be short-term, goal-oriented interventions, often with homework assignments. Both fields tend to work with intelligent, logical people and attempt through language to reframe people's perceptions of themselves or refocus their thinking in a new way. They both assume that people create, or construct, their lives within the constraints of heredity and environment rather than being determined by either. Cognitive therapy tends to be more directive than most coaching approaches.

NeuroLinguistic Programming

Speculation about artificial intelligence (AI) contributed to the cognitive revolution that occurred in the late 1950s in psychology. The field of computer science was in its early years and drew on mathematics, engineering, communications and information theory, and cybernetics. Cybernetics is the study of self-directed systems (Wiener, 1948). A very well-known concept that was introduced by cybernetics is "feedback" — a necessary function of any system that must adjust its behavior in order to reach its goal. Norbert Wiener (1894–1964), an American theoretical and applied mathematician and founder of cybernetics, applied his discoveries to human beings and to society in his book *The Human Use of Human Beings* (1950). AI and cybernetics captured the imagination of scholars, practitioners, writers, and the public, and it seemed reasonable to compare human thinking processes to a computer: A computer has hardware, and we have a brain; a computer operates using software, and we operate using our minds; a computer is programmed by a specific language, and we also have a language. Surely how we use language and our other channels of communication indicates the inner architecture of our minds and brains.

This is the logic behind neuro-linguistic programming (NLP) founded in the early 1960s by Americans John Grinder and Richard Bandler. As Robert Dilts (1983) puts it:

> The basic premise of NLP is that there is a redundancy between the *observable macroscopic patterns of human behavior* (for example, linguistic and paralinguistic phenomena, eye movements, hand and body position, and other types of performance distinctions) and *patterns of the underlying neural activity governing this behavior*. (p. 3, emphases in original)

The power of close observation and deducing underlying mental patterns was modeled by Milton Erickson (1901–1980), an influential American psychiatrist and hypnotherapist who inspired Grinder and Bandler as well as many other psychotherapists.

Although we now know that the computer analogy does not match human brain processing in many ways (Hawkins & Blakeslee, 2004), the comparison of computers to brains spurred the development of a number of NLP techniques for practitioners to:

- Expand their sensory awareness so as to observe recurrent patterns of behavior in clients.
- Notice the responses their own behavior elicits in themselves and others.
- Determine what these patterns indicate about clients' internal representations and neural connections.
- Observe how these representations and connections affect clients' sensory experience and internal mental maps.
- Promote clients' abilities to learn, communicate, make choices, and motivate themselves (adapted from Dilts, 1983, p. 6).

One of the best-known applications of this process has to do with recognizing another person's representational system. If a coach asks a client a question and the client pauses momentarily as if searching "inside" for the answer, NLP suggests that a person's typical inner processing will be one of three types:

1. *Visual.* The client flicks his eyes up and to the right, breaking visual connection with the coach momentarily. Then the client returns his gaze to the coach and increases his speech tempo while giving the answer, using words connected with vision: "The way I see it, my boss is really in the dark. I don't think she has a glimmer as to how to move forward."

2. *Auditory.* The client leans her head slightly down, puts a hand over her mouth, and says "Hhmmm" and then "returns" with an answer that is laced with auditory cues: "That sounds impossible. Nothing about it resonates with me."

3. *Kinesthetic.* The client looks down and to the left, perhaps even closing his eyes. "I feel so uncomfortable even discussing this. Just thinking about it gets me hot under the collar."

The coach who is able to match the client's processing style is more likely to communicate empathy, not just by what is said but by being in line with, in tune with, or in step with how the client processes information.

A related NLP technique is modeling. How does a person master any skill or ability? The topic of expertise has generated a good deal of interest in cognitive psychology and education. NLP teaches that a learner can observe the sensory signals of an expert—how he or she stands, moves, and speaks — and ask questions that reveal what is going on in the expert's mind at the moment that expertise is demonstrated. Then the learner "models" or takes on these physical attributes, attitudes, and thinking patterns in approaching whatever is the target for mastery.

Example: Modeling Expert Psychotherapists

One of us (Linda) modeled expert psychotherapists as part of her NLP master-level certification in 1991. She identified a half dozen people she considered to be expert psychotherapists. In this case, it would have been disruptive for her to observe them at work, but she did closely watch, listen, and get a feel for (notice the three representational systems: visual, auditory, and kinesthetic) how they described their work. She decided she was particularly interested in the time just before they opened the door to welcome a new client. What was going through their minds at that very moment?

Although these experts were psychotherapists and not coaches, what she found is likely to have relevance for the coaching process. Every one of the master psychotherapists said that at the moment just before greeting a new client, they were in a state of mind that combined curiosity, anticipation, and openness:

- "I have no idea what could be on the other side of that door," said one. "It is as if a whole new world was about to open up before me."
- "I imagine the door as about to open on a vast pantry. It's stocked with an enormous number of wonderful items, some of which I may be familiar with, but mostly surprises and new discoveries."
- "I do my best to approach that moment empty of preconceptions or judgments. I want to be free to take in what is there, not what I think should be."

Several years later in her coaching studies, Linda was struck with the similarity of attitudes between expert psychotherapists and what was expected of coaches.

With its emphasis on attending to multisensory aspects of communication and its speculation about underlying neural patterns, NLP can be seen as a precursor both to coaching and to modern neuroscience.

Solution-focused Therapy

Solution-focused therapy (also referred to as solution-focused brief therapy [SFBT]) is a short-term goal-focused therapeutic approach that helps clients change by identifying and constructing solutions, thus putting it on the creative or constructive side of the deterministic-constructive polarity. A solution-focused therapist is likely to:

- Focus on the client's present and future, not the past.
- Help clients identify solutions that will remove the barriers to having the life they want.
- Encourage clients to identify and do more of what is already working.
- Keep the therapy course brief (as few as three to six sessions) since the sessions do not include discussing the past.

Solution-focused therapists operate on the premise that the future is created and negotiated. The future is not a slave to past events in a person's life. In spite of past events, even ones that were traumatic, a person can negotiate and implement many useful steps that are likely to lead to a more satisfying life. Solution-focused therapists also operate on the assumption that clients have all the resources, skills, and knowledge to make their lives better, if they decide that they want things to be better.

The deepest roots for solution-focused therapy are found in the works of Gregory Bateson (1904–1980). Bateson was a British-born anthropologist who moved to the United States and worked in diverse fields: evolutionary biology, psychiatry, genetics, ethnology, cybernetics, and communication theory. He was influenced by the works of Milton Erickson, the hypnotherapist from whom neuro-linguistic programming took its inspiration, and in fact introduced NLP founders Richard Bandler and John Grinder to Erickson. Bateson never put forward a theory of psychotherapy, but his work on communication theory and language had great implications for solution-focused therapy.

In a Batesonian approach, the therapist's job is to facilitate change by gathering information about clients' purposes and the context in which they operate and then by offering new descriptions and providing safe ways for them to achieve their goals.

Solution-focused therapy gained popularity in the late 1970s and 1980s in North America, as interest in trauma therapy was being stimulated by the women's movement and the return of veterans from Vietnam. The demand for psychotherapy was increasing at the same time that the development of health maintenance organizations (HMOs) added to the growing reluctance of insurance companies to cover more than 20 to 25 psychotherapy sessions in a calendar year—and often many fewer. Abandoning the idea of a complete personality overhaul that had been characteristic of long-term therapy, practitioners sought ways to manage dysfunctional symptoms in the short run.

The term "Solution-Focused Brief Therapy" was first coined in 1982 through the work of the Brief Family Therapy Center in Milwaukee, Wisconsin, founded by Insoo Kim Berg (1994) and Steve de Shazer. The model they developed is used around the world in numerous settings with a variety of clients and problems: drug and alcohol abuse, domestic violence, school problems, chronic mental illness, case management, child protection investigations, corrections, criminal justice, prison populations, social services, and residential treatment programs. It has a wide appeal because of its simple, practical, and respectful approach to working with people.

Developed from an inductive process and often described as coming from a different paradigm, SFBT differs from problem-solving approaches in its philosophy and techniques. The "problem-solving" paradigm that is common to many psychotherapy treatment models can be described as a medical model that focuses on treatment of disease and removal of symptoms rather than on wellness. Contrasted with this, SFBT can be described as a solution-building approach (Berg, 1994; DeJong & Berg, 1998; de Shazer, 1985). The differences between these two models have implications for clinical practice in psychotherapy, and the emphasis on solutions rather than problems brings SFBT closer to coaching.

Coach training generally emphasizes that coaching is not focused on problems. But that does not mean clients do not bring problems to coaching or that problems are not often the motivation for clients to seek coaching. The difference is in how problems are dealt with. Solution-focused therapy identifies goals and focuses on the resources a person shows in achieving them. The concentration is on health and on coping abilities, and the emphasis is on connecting with the person, not the problem. Coaching shares this approach.

Solution-focused therapy uses language as its primary tool, based on the assumption that language shapes and molds the perception of reality and that some conversations are more useful than others. The conversation models used by Berg (1994) and de Shazer (1985) are widely used and can apply to coaching:

- *Presession change.* Ask your client if anything is better since making the appointment. Clients may not even realize they have taken a step forward already.
- *Problem talk.* If an alcoholic complains about losing his or her job, the solution-focused therapist talks about the job loss issue, not alcohol, although that may come up later if the client wishes. "The problem is the problem, not the person."
- *Exceptions to the problem.* Help clients to see times in their past when they overcame their problems. Identifying these solutions can defuse the power of the problem over clients. For example, "Tell me about the time that you have resisted the urge…"
- *Coping questions.* Example: "You have been through a lot the last couple of months. How in the world have you coped with so much, while going to school (or holding down your job, taking care of the children, getting up in the morning, etc.)?"
- *Miracle question.* Example: "Imagine that tonight while you are sleeping something like a miracle occurs. The miracle is that whatever problem brought you here has been resolved. Because you were sleeping, you won't know the miracle occurred. What is the first thing that tells you that this miracle has happened? What is different?"
- *Setting goals.* Whatever detailed goal or outcome the client chooses must be supported by actions.
- *Scaling questions.* Ask the client to express her or his feelings about the problem on a scale of 1 to 10. Example: "On a scale of 1 to 10, where 1 stands for how badly you felt when you first decided to come and talk to me today and 10 stands for how you will feel when you don't need to come to see me anymore, where would you say you are at right now?"
- *At the next session.* "How did you manage to get all the way up to 2? That's 100% improvement from the day you called. How did you do it? What would it take you to move up 1 point higher? When you move up 1 point higher, what would your best friend (or mother, boyfriend, etc.) notice that will tell him or her that you are doing a little bit better?"

309

Solution-focused therapy is a close match to coaching. Many coaches have been trained to use this approach. Some coaching schools even refer to their method as solution-focused coaching.

Solution-focused therapy and coaching both:

- Focus on building upon the client's own strengths and competencies.
- Believe the client has most of the answers already.
- Recognize that all clients have the potential for growth and self-discovery.
- Require the therapist and coach to be supportive, directive, and challenging.
- Use the client's definition of the problem or dilemma as the agenda for problem solving.
- Focus on clear, attainable goals.
- Focus on the present and the future rather than lengthy discussions of the past.
- Recognize the importance of the client's responsibility for any change.
- Rely on the importance of conversation and language used with their clients.

Metaphor and Narrative Therapies

The theme of constructivism, or creativity, has been mentioned a number of times in this book. Its influence can be seen in Adlerian, NLP, and solution-focused psychotherapies. The idea that people construct, or create, what is real to them, and that they do this socially, has received a boost from recent neuroscience discoveries that the brain is more malleable in adulthood than previously thought, that mental activity can result in structural changes to the brain, and that connection with others is a major impetus for brain development.

Trends in psychotherapy that make particular use of the principles of constructivism are metaphor and narrative therapies.

Milton Erickson's use of metaphor was influential in the family therapy work of Jay Haley (1971) and Virginia Satir (1983, 1988), and metaphor is a key component of Salvador Minuchin's (1974) work with

310

families. There are many ways in which the family therapies and family counseling approaches may be useful to coaches, and we recommend that coaches pursue those of interest, always remembering that coaching is not therapy.

Metaphors connect our ability to picture images with our verbal communication. They are also a bridge, to use a metaphor, that carries meaning from the metaphoric image to whatever it is referring to. That is, if Matilda says, "John is a real anchor to this work group," she is not, of course, suggesting that John is literally made of a heavy metal that sinks to the bottom of the bay and hooks to rocks. (By the way, we will leave the question of metaphor versus analogy to our English major colleagues. In this context, saying "John is *like* an anchor" will engage the same metaphoric process.)

In the example, Matilda is expecting her listeners to take the meaning that surrounds the concept of an anchor and apply that to the person, John, *as if* he has those qualities. Constructivism suggests that when a therapist finds a metaphor that can shift the meaning a person or family gives to some troubling element, the reality of that element can shift. Metaphors are often used in reframing an event—for example, from "doors closing" to "other doors opening."

However, a good deal of therapeutic metaphor is therapist-generated. That is, the therapist observes the individual's or family's behavior, imagines a metaphor that might be useful, and then presents it to the client or clients. Richard Kopp (1995) developed a different metaphor technique that is much more coachlike. He recommends utilizing client-generated metaphors that are more appropriate for a coaching intervention because they do not risk imposing the coach's meaning on the client's process. Although Kopp called his book and approach metaphor therapy, he and others have applied it in a coaching context, so it might just as well be called metaphor coaching.

METAPHOR COACHING   The process of engaging a client's own metaphor to effect change involves several steps that must be preceded by a conversation locating the client in or in relation to whatever issue is being explored. (The seven steps in the example are adapted from Kopp, 1995; Kopp, 2007, p. 34; and Page, 2007.)

Example: Alice Holds on Tight to the Reins

Alice was a recent external hire in a financial services firm and has been working with her coach to develop her ability to have coachlike conversations with her new direct reports. Her efforts have been largely successful except with Allan, who is many years her senior and has been at the firm for decades. She began by focusing on Allan: "He's so arrogant. He pretends to listen to me but then acts like I don't exist." The coach asks her to describe her experience with Allan, to talk about what seems to be most problematic with him.

Step 1. *Noticing metaphors.* Here is Alice's description of the issue with Allan: "I try to have conversations with him, but I keep getting tripped up [notice metaphor] by how angry I am. I don't want to throw that into the mix [metaphor] right at the start of the conversation, so I hold back [metaphor] and just keep the talk light [metaphor] and really on the surface [metaphor]."

Step 2. *Focusing on the metaphor.* Coach asks: "When you say that you 'hold back,' what image or picture comes into your mind?" [Note: In order to be effective, Kopp insists that this question be asked in exactly this way. Replace 'that you hold back' with any metaphor that you have noticed being accompanied by an increase in physical or emotional energy. The image does not have to be visual, although it often is. It can be sounds or physical sensations.]

Alice responds: "It's like I'm holding tight to the reins of these powerful black stallions, to keep them from stamping on everything in front of them." [Note: Clients usually pause before answering and appear to be searching "inside." They may close their eyes or defocus and break their connecting gaze with the coach. They are entering what Kopp calls the "metaphoric domain" where they can examine the image that gave rise to the metaphor without reference to the situation that they were describing. If they come out of that inner state and deal with the external the situation, in this case saying something like "I guess Allan gets me really angry," guide clients back to considering the image itself, to staying in the metaphoric domain: "Let's talk about that image of the horses."]

Step 3. *Exploring the metaphor as a sensory image.* Coach suggests: "Describe the scene." And asks: "What else is going on?" And: "What led up to this—what was happening just before?" [Note: The effectiveness of this technique depends on fully exploring the image as the client conceives of it. Coaches will soon discover that they are likely to interpret metaphors differently from their clients. A principle of coaching is that the client's interpretation guides the discussion. But more important, working with the client's interpretation is more efficient because there is no need to sell him or her on its relevance.]

Alice: "It's a country road, a bit muddy. I'm riding these two black stallions like in a rodeo—one foot on each one's back. They're trotting along nicely but all of a sudden they start to gallop ahead. I'm trying to stop them so they don't trample anyone."

Step 4. *Exploring feelings associated with the metaphor image.* Very important: Coach asks: "What's your experience of holding tight to the reins?" Or "What are you feeling as you hold tight to the reins?" [Note: Replace "holding tight to the reins" with whatever image you are exploring in your work with the client. It is crucial that the client put her- or himself into the image and feel its emotional effects. Again, different people are likely to feel differently about "holding their horses," and it is important for the coach not to assume that the client is experiencing what the coach or anyone else might feel.]

Alice: "I'm holding on with everything I've got. My teeth are clenched and every muscle is tight. I'm afraid if I let go, I'll lose my balance and there will be a disaster. So I just hold on."

Step 5. *Changing the metaphor image.* Coach asks: "If you could change the image in any way, how would you change it?" [Note: It is the client who suggests the change, or even whether there should be a change, not the coach. Once again, it is critical that this step be conducted in the metaphoric domain. That is, if Alice says, "Well, I could just fire Allan," that requires stepping out of the metaphoric image and talking about the problematic situation. Instead, the coach guides Alice back to the image.]

Coach: "But just talking about those powerful horses, how would you change that image?"

Alice: "What I'd really like to do is pull hard on the left rein and guide the horses through this gate into a field that's all fenced in." [Note: To make this technique effective, the client needs to explore this new image in as much detail as the original image was explored—see Steps 3 and 4.]

Coach: "What's the scene? . . . What happens next? . . . What's that experience like for you?"

Alice: "The horses gallop around inside the fence—but they go over there where I can get off safely. Then they settle down and start to graze.

(Continued)

313

I start to breathe again and feel my neck and arms and whole body relax. They're still there, but I don't have to deal with them right now."

Step 6. *Creating connections with original image.* Coach asks: "What connections do you see between your original image of holding back the stallions and the situation with Allan?" [Note: Both the coach and the client will be tempted to make leaps into providing solutions for the situation. In order to be most effective, continue with this step-by-step approach and explore the original connection first.]

Alice: "I'm on my way in my new job, pushing hard to get where I want, and Allan seems to just get in the way. Just seeing him there makes me frustrated and angry."

Step 7. *Applying the changed image to the present situation.* Coach asks: "How might the way you changed the image apply to your current situation?"

Alice: "You know, I don't think my anger has very much to do with Allan at all. Certainly he doesn't deserve that level of anger from me—he's just walking down the road. I haven't bothered finding out where he is going. Maybe I should put my hard-driving attitude to pasture until I at least get to know him better." [Note: Coaches are trained to get a commitment for action from clients once they have an insight such as this. However, in our experience, metaphor work is so powerful that clients do not need reinforcement. The two of you may find yourselves referring to "stallions" on and off throughout the rest of coaching together. Asking "What might be different when you next see Allan?" is a way of checking on the effects of the metaphor work.]

Psychotherapists who read this case will likely wonder if there is therapeutic work to be done with Alice. We discuss guidelines for referral more generally in the Resource Section on mental health issues. In Alice's case, it would be worth finding out four things about her anger:

1. Is it *persistent*? "Has your anger been an ongoing problem over time?" Does Alice keep returning with the same issue, despite having dealt with it over and over in coaching?

2. Is her presentation *incongruent*? When Alice is exploring her anger, not as a quick remark but really seeming to recall it, is her body language consistent with the content? That is, does she look angry or at least serious? If a client is relating sadness, is she smiling and laughing?

3. Does her anger *extend* across time and different contexts? The coach might ask, "Do you find yourself holding the reins like this

often, in many other situations? . . . Has this been going for a good part of your life?"

4. How *strong* is her anger? "What would happen if you lost hold of the reins? You said 'disaster.' What do you mean by that?"

Alice should be referred to a psychotherapist if:

- She keeps returning with the same issue, despite having dealt with it over and over in coaching.
- She seems quite disconnected from her anger, as if it is happening to someone else.
- Her anger is a problem in many times, places, and types of situations.
- She or the coach is worried that Alice or someone else might be harmed as a result of her anger.

In this case, Alice responded, "No, I'm quite surprised, actually. Being angry like this is not something I'm used to. And by a 'disaster' I mean that I might raise my voice when it's not really justified. Then I might lose some of the respect I've worked so hard to gain in the office." In subsequent sessions, she moved on to other issues. The coach mentioned that Alice might find it useful at some point to explore with a psychotherapist the reasons why Allan triggered this response but otherwise simply carried on with coaching for this and other workplace issues.

NARRATIVE COACHING   Narrative and metaphoric approaches share constructivist and other assumptions of the systemic paradigm (Drake, Brennan, & Gotz, 2008). The idea that stories create meaning in our lives is not new. Adler (Ansbacher & Ansbacher, 1964) hypothesized that the stories we tell about our childhood experiences actually reveal more about our present-day values and future goals than about what really happened "back then." The discoveries of neuroscience have provided support for narrative techniques.

Storytelling has been particularly effective in trauma therapy, with patients being invited to incorporate their traumatic memories into a narrative as a way of gaining some control over their effects. Telling one's story as part of a supportive healing group is particularly effective.

Narrative therapy was developed by Australian Michael White and his New Zealand colleague David Epston (1990). Its connection to coaching is obvious because of its emphasis on collaboration, on externalizing problems faced by a client ("The person is not the problem, the problem is the problem."), on the potential for a person to reshape her or his identity, on discovering unique exceptions that may serve in this reshaping, and on the social nature of the process (White, 2007).

References to creativity in coaching would not be complete without mentioning the work of Thomas Leonard (1955–2003), a very creative force and a major influence in the development of coaching (Brock, 2008). Leonard founded Coach University, a coach training school; Coachville, a network of coaching courses and resources; and a number of enterprises such as TeleClass.com, a virtual learning center delivered over telephone bridge lines. He was co-founder of the International Coach Federation in 1994. Until his untimely death in 2003, Leonard was a tireless author (e.g., Leonard, 1998) and promoter of coaching and coach training.

Resource Section: Mental Health Issues—How Not to Do Psychotherapy

Whatever techniques we borrow from psychotherapy, we must remember that coaches must not present ourselves as applying these techniques to treat mental illness. When coaching strays into this territory, we are ethically obliged to refer clients to a qualified mental health therapist or counselor. But how do coaches know when that boundary has been or may be crossed? To answer that question, we include this discussion on how coaches can identify boundaries and uphold the ethical commitment to practice within the limits of their training and profession.

One of us (Linda) is a trained psychotherapist who is certified as a Licensed Clinical Professional Counselor in the state of Illinois. She approached her coach training with a preconception that she already knew most of what she would be exposed to. She was surprised to find that there are many skills, a breadth of interdisciplinary knowledge, and a mind-set that focuses on solutions, opportunities, and strengths that goes beyond what is typical in psychotherapy. Thus, she realized the importance of the principles and applications that are presented in this book.

As a coach, Linda found that she had to avoid responding to clients according to her previous training as a psychotherapist. Despite her Adlerian background, which espouses most of the assumptions of coaching, she particularly needed to catch herself before offering advice or interpretations. She decided in the early days of her coaching practice to differentiate coaching clients from psychotherapy clients and not to engage in psychotherapy with clients who had contracted for coaching. She refers such clients to other psychotherapists.

Coaches who are not trained as psychotherapists face a different problem. The question will inevitably arise, as it did in the case of Alice's metaphor of wild horses: How do I distinguish between problems and issues that fall legitimately under my field of competence as a coach and those problems and issues that call for the services of someone trained especially to diagnose and treat mental disorders? What do I do if I discover and come to feel that the person I am working with has issues that are beyond my area of expertise?"

As in all coaching situations, the answer is to become proactive in acquiring basic information about the limits of the coaching engagement and some of the approaches for helping both coach and client make an appropriate, well-considered decision. The resources in this section provide ways to begin this task.

The best instrument for understanding the client's state of mental health is a thorough and comprehensive entry interview. Although it can be quite brief, an interview should include:

- Questions about overall health and any significant physical problems. Sometimes what looks to a layperson like mental illness, such as depression, may in fact be the signs of physical illness. A medical checkup is a wise recommendation if there is any question in the coach's mind—or even if there is not.
- Questions about life status, concerns, any history of emotional problems or relationship problems. The focus in coaching will not be on the past, but eliciting a very brief discussion of past psychological treatment may prevent future errors of judgment.
- Questions to determine whether clients are coming to coaching as another way of seeking relief from problems that typically are treated psychotherapeutically. Or is the goal more coaching

(Continued)

related: to find ways to self-activate potential and overcome a normal range of self-imposed barriers or beliefs that are holding clients back from more fulfilling experiences of achievement and accomplishment?

Coaches cannot be expected to know what they do not know. Psychotherapists receive extensive training in recognizing and diagnosing serious mental disorders. Coaches do not need to know all the decision-making processes that go into diagnosis. They can, however, be sensitive to the four indications that we discussed in the case of Alice and the black stallions: At any time before or during coaching, coaches should refer clients to psychotherapists when issues fit the PIES model:

P—persistent, having been around a long time or not responding to attempts to change. "How long has this been going on?"

I—incongruent, not matching their nonverbal communication, as when clients smile and laugh when describing a very sad situation. "I hear that this is a very sad situation, but I don't see sad in how you are acting. Am I missing something?"

E—extensive, affecting their ability to function in many areas of their lives. "Where else does this show up in your life?"

S—strong, having an effect that is out of the ordinary, especially if the coach or client begins to worry that someone might get hurt. "Are you thinking someone might get hurt? . . . Is someone's well-being at stake?"

Linda developed the acronym PIES to provide coaches with a simple way to remember these guidelines. The types of questions suggested may help in gathering more information.

More generally, a coach may feel, after working with a client who originally presented as within the coach's range of competence, that the client is failing to thrive or move forward despite approaches that usually meet with success. An ongoing pattern like this may be a sign that the client has failed to reveal or may be unaware of other issues. Establishing a trial period with all clients of three to six sessions followed by revisiting the original intake material may help to identify situations like this.

Coaches should feel free to explore mental health resources on the Internet, especially since clients are likely to have done so. Both should remember that diagnosis of disorders is a complex task that requires hundreds of hours of training and supervised practice. It is good to be informed but not to assume that information alone, especially unverified information published on the World Wide Web, is equivalent to expertise in applying that information.

That said, sometimes clients present with a diagnosis provided by a mental health professional. A client may seek coaching for a career or other issue in addition to what is being discussed with the therapist, and the client may ask that the coach and therapist coordinate their work. In such cases, coaches need to be able to discuss diagnoses intelligently with their professional colleagues. To help with this, Internet sites such as 4therapy Network (www.4therapy.com/consumer) and Internet Mental Health (www.mentalhealth.com) give overviews with ample links for exploring mental health themes. The American Psychiatric Association sponsors a site that discusses mental health symptoms and issues: www.healthyminds.org.

Once coaches suspect that the issues may surpass their boundaries, to whom they refer clients depends on local laws governing psychotherapy. Coaches should familiarize themselves with the laws that apply in their own jurisdiction and encourage clients who live elsewhere to utilize resources there.

Having a network of several mental health practitioners will enable coaches to share observations and concerns about a particular client where the client has granted permission for both professionals to discuss the case. As we mentioned, some clients need and want both psychotherapy and coaching, and some clients who require psychotherapy at one point may later return for coaching. Making clear and unambiguous arrangements with referral practitioners helps those practitioners feel comfortable referring a person back when he or she is ready for coaching.

Finally, every coach must have a signed and dated agreement with each client that includes a straightforward disclaimer and clear statement of what coaching is and is not so there will be no confusion in the client's mind. This sample disclaimer should be revised

(Continued)

319

to meet the coach's description of her or his method and any local requirements:

Sample disclaimer:

I understand that [coach or coach's firm] makes no claim to diagnose or treat mental illness. Coaching is an educational and collaborative method in which I optimize my potential by raising awareness, identifying choices, and taking selected actions. In engaging [coach or coach's firm], I acknowledge having received and understood this disclaimer.

[Client signature and date]

This section was written in collaboration with Frank Mosca, Ph.D., a certified mental health professional.

Psychotherapy as Bedrock for Coaching

Like ontology, medicine, and psychology, psychotherapy has participated in the shift from a mechanistic to a systemic paradigm that has also contributed to the emergence of coaching.

In reaction to psychoanalysis, which posited that unconscious forces determine human behavior, and behaviorism, which relied on stimulus-response determinism, the third wave of humanistic therapies insisted that human beings have the wherewithal to construct their own reality and that what is important in this self-determination is the subjective meaning they give to their lives.

The expressive therapies reminded practitioners that they were dealing with whole people — physical, mental, and emotional — and cognitive therapies took advantage of the cognitive revolution in psychology to focus on the maladaptive thoughts underlying mental health problems. As computer use became more widespread, neuro-linguistic programming took advantage of the computer metaphor to introduce short-term techniques for programming desired changes in people's behavior and helped practitioners focus on underlying neural patterns. Solution-focused techniques emphasized people's strengths and what they could

320

accomplish in the future, and metaphor/narrative approaches relied on the social nature of the construction and reconstruction of reality.

In many ways, Adler's suggestions that people are socially embedded, goal seeking, creative, and holistic are being confirmed today despite having been largely rejected or ignored during his lifetime. These trends are changing the face of psychotherapy and being embodied in the profession of coaching. Beginning as out-of-mainstream-science, these trends became stronger as they were taken up by positive psychology, research on emotional intelligence, and other approaches that accentuate the positive. We explore these in chapter 11.

Pillar—Accentuate the Positive

Daniel Siegel (1999) tells a poignant story of a man who had trouble relating to his wife and daughter. Although he was a reliable and caring husband and father, he wondered if there was not something more. When Siegel asked how he was feeling, he was not quite sure. As hard and as often as he thought about it, he did not seem to be able to access his emotional side. Then he and his daughter went SCUBA diving on a vacation. There, deep in the ocean, they could communicate only using gestures. The man felt something stirring in his consciousness. He had not been able to trigger an emotional response by thinking or talking about it, but through physical gestures, he had a moment of delight in the underwater world around him. He also felt a connection with his daughter. This was the beginning of the uncovering of his emotional life.

What does it mean to be mentally healthy?

As we have pointed out, much of modern medicine and psychotherapy has assumed that mental health meant the absence of symptoms. Although ridding ourselves of disease must surely be a part of health practices, it is our contention that coaching has arisen as people realized that there must be more to being healthy than just not being ill. A new subdiscipline, positive psychology, is dedicated to studying just this topic. Both coaching and positive psychology are founded on the belief that people want more from life than an end to suffering. They want to lead meaningful, fulfilling lives. Presumably this quest can be traced back to the beginning of humanity itself.

We have said that Adler emerged from his experience as a military doctor in World War I with a mission to promote positive human characteristics that could make war no longer possible. He had concluded that when people feel connected to their family and community, and eventually to all life in the universe, they develop a capacity for contributing to others that he called "social interest." Social interest was, for him, the measure of human health and well-being. The reception his ideas received illustrates the nature of science of his time. Although Adler taught many psychotherapists, started schools and institutes, wrote some of the first self-help books, and lectured extensively to lay audiences in Europe and the United States, his ideas were ridiculed by scientific psychology as being too value-laden. His early contributions to the positive side of psychology were largely forgotten by mainstream academics. Like coaching itself, the quest for positive health has become widely appreciated as part of social science only during the last few decades.

- What makes people truly, authentically happy?
- Does seeking pleasure lead to a fulfilling life?
- What part do traditional virtues like honesty, generosity, and gratitude play in our lives?
- Why is it desirable to cultivate "good character" in our children and ourselves?
- How do positive emotions affect our psychological well-being? Our physical well-being?
- Are there values or virtues that are more or less common in all cultures?
- What is the best way to live?
- How can we develop resilience?
- How can we influence others to be happier and more productive?

Traditional psychology and psychotherapy cannot answer questions such as these. For much of its history, psychology has conformed to a mechanistic paradigm that sought to understand the human condition objectively, in a value-free manner. Much of psychotherapy is concerned with diagnosing and treating mental illness rather than understanding and promoting mental health. In contrast, positive psychology focuses on increasing well-being, valuing virtues, and seeking to understand what makes people truly happy. Drawing on groundbreaking research, positive psychology has shifted the social science focus from attempting to describe behavior objectively, outside any system of values, to unabashedly defining and valuing a better life. Positive psychology invites psychosocial change agents to shift from pathology, victimology, and mental illness to a focus on happiness and fulfillment, human performance, positive emotions, and strengths. Little wonder that Vikki Brock's (2008) research on the theoretical genealogy of coaching lists positive psychology as a major contributor.

HISTORICAL INTERLUDE

Personal Beginnings of Positive Psychology

As described in previous historical overviews, health and disease were inseparable concerns of classical philosophy and medicine. As Western science and medicine took on the physical body side of the mind/body divide, concerns about happiness remained in the "soul," or nonmaterial domain of religion and spirituality. Psychotherapy and psychology ventured into this domain during the mid-19th century only by virtue of treating illness or by "objectively" exploring behavior from a materialistic stance.

Nearly a century later, Martin E. P. Seligman took up a mission of his own, as he describes in his book Authentic Happiness (2002). As a graduate student, Seligman conducted an experiment that helped to loosen the hold of behaviorism on experimental psychology. He discovered that dogs that were shocked with electricity and had no chance to escape often gave up trying to escape even when they could. Stimulus/response theory could not completely explain this finding, which Seligman named "learned helplessness." As a professor in the psychology department at the University of Pennsylvania, he went on to study the cognitive beliefs underlying optimism and pessimism and published Learned Optimism in 1968, a runaway best seller. Since then, he has published more than 20 books and 170 articles on motivation and personality.

(Continued)

During 20 years of clinical research, Seligman became more and more interested in how to apply the principles he was discovering. He outlined techniques that help people rise above depression and pessimism to build optimism and create happiness. He presented his readers with a self-test for optimism and then went on to give a map of how to change pessimism into optimism.

In 1998 he became president of the American Psychological Association (APA). As he thought about what he might accomplish in this position, he recalled an experience with his five-year-old daughter. As they raked weeds in the garden, Seligman criticized the girl for throwing the leaves and dancing under them rather than focusing on the task at hand. His daughter stalked off, only to return in a few minutes to remind her father that the previous year, on her fifth birthday, she had decided to change her habit of whining. "That was the hardest thing I've ever done," she said to her father that day. "And if I can stop whining, you can stop being such a grouch" (Seligman, 2002, p. 28). Despite his previous knowledge, fame, years of scientific research, and eminent position, Seligman realized that it was his daughter who had issued the challenge of his lifetime.

As a result, Seligman decided to take psychology in a new direction. He chose to focus on positive psychology as a theme for his term in office as APA president. He insisted that mental health should be more than the absence of mental illness.

So that interest in positive psychology would not disappear after his term of office ended, Seligman brought together a team of experts from related areas to build a solid research base for the new field. These people included Mihaly Csikszentmihalyi, who wrote Flow (1991); Edward Diener, a psychologist who had been studying happiness set points for years (1984); Barbara Frederickson, a social psychologist at the University of Michigan (2001); and Chris Peterson, who helped to systematize and gather research related to positive character traits (Peterson & Seligman, 2004).

The team set about to gather all the psychological studies on happiness, how it is gained, and what it means. However, they were able to find precious little in the way of past research on the general topic in psychological literature. The team then realized they had to go outside Western psychology to investigate beliefs and teaching about mental health and happiness beyond definitions of mental disease and illness. They examined philosophical traditions, spiritual texts, and research from around the world to gather ideas about characteristics of truly healthy human beings.

When Seligman wrote Authentic Happiness (2002) to describe his experiences and that of the positive psychology team in establishing this new field, it became another best seller. The field has now been widely accepted by the academic community. Science based on logical positivism had eschewed the promotion of values by scientists because values were assumed to bias scientific research and interfere with objectivity. But the new findings of positive psychology connected values with the search for wellness, and this contributed to the breakdown of prohibition against values-oriented science. In January 2005, Time magazine ran a feature/cover story entitled "The New Science of Happiness," which explained the research to lay people and confirmed its usefulness and acceptance.

Positive psychology is a science with extensive relevance for the coaching profession. It can be considered a major pillar in raising coaching above the disease orientation that held sway in the helping professions during most of the 20th century. Although dozens of specific techniques are presented in the positive psychology literature (see, e.g., Peterson, 2006), research shows that the positive mind-set is what is most effective. It is important for coaches to acquaint themselves with the concepts that the field has developed. In this chapter, we review main approaches of positive psychology and related inquiries:

- Learned optimism
- Science of happiness: Pleasure, engagement, and meaning
- Resilience
- Emotional intelligence
- Accentuate the positive as a pillar for coaching

LEARNED OPTIMISM

Learned Optimism is the title of Seligman's 1968 book. It is also a set of ideas that are just as relevant today as they were then. The ideas of learned optimism are some of the most insightful and useful models for any type of coaching.

Seligman started his research, ironically enough, by identifying and studying the concept of "learned pessimism," specifically in animal experiments. This was a more cognitive approach to the phenomenon he had earlier identified as "learned helplessness." He noticed that animals would stop attempting an activity, such as pressing a lever, after a widely varying number of failures. Some would stop after one press; others would go on for another 10. He became curious about whether this type of difference would hold true for people, and he identified that indeed it did: Individuals would give up on particular activities after widely varying numbers of failed attempts. He came to believe that some people persevered longer than others because of differences in "explanatory style."

An explanatory style is our individual way of explaining what happens to us. An optimistic explanatory style means we do not see defeat as permanent, as applying in all circumstances, or as affecting our basic worth. A pessimistic explanatory style is characterized by the opposite — misfortune is forever, applies across the board, and is our own fault. (You will recognize these as examples of "maladaptive thoughts" from cognitive therapy.)

In summary, a pessimistic style explains setbacks or failures as:

- Permanent
- Pervasive
- Personal

An optimistic style, in contrast, explains positive events in this way. An optimistic style explains negative events as:

- Temporary
- Local
- External

A pessimistic style, in contrast, explains positive events in this way.

Example: Jim—"I've Never Been Able to Hold onto Clients and I Never Will"

Jim is a broker with a pessimistic explanatory style. He lost an account and told his coach, "That's it. I'll never make my target. I bet every account will turn out this way. I've never been able to hold onto clients, and I never will." [Note the permanent, pervasive, and personal elements of this explanation.]

At the next session, he was pleased to tell his coach that he had won a new account, but then he "discounted" this win by saying, "But it's only one account. Can't count on a next time. It's just blind luck anyway." The coach recognized these remarks as examples of Jim's pessimistic explanatory style. Over time, the two were able to use a combination of techniques, some of which are outlined in the text that follows, to help Jim recognize his pessimistic self-talk and substitute more positive explanations.

In order to identify clients' style at the beginning of coaching, coaches can use the Seligman Attributional Style Questionnaire (SASQ), which yields a continuum from optimism to extreme pessimism based on 48 statements. More details can be found in *Learned Optimism* (1990) or at the University of Pennsylvania's Positive Psychology Center (see Internet links), which provides several questionnaires based on this work.

Practices based on learned optimism have a lot in common with basic approaches and competencies of cognitive therapies and of coaching. In coaching, we ask clients to look underneath the surface content of what they say to reveal their assumptions and filters, separating facts from interpretations of events. Doing this helps develop self-awareness that enables thinking patterns to change.

Seligman (1990) suggests that developing a more optimistic way of explaining events (defeats are temporary, only apply to this situation, and are not our fault) will stop us from dragging down our success in work, relationships, health, and every other part of life.

Does Optimism Really Make a Difference?

Our earlier references to the role of the observer in quantum mechanics and to the importance of expectations make the answer to this question not at all surprising. In over 500 studies around the world, the SASQ has been shown to predict mood, motivation, and performance. Research has shown that optimistic people are more likely to be determined, decisive, and persistent. They believe that they will achieve success frequently and that their failures will be short-lived. Their optimism inspires them to achieve success. They live longer, on average by 8 years, and have less illness. Yes, the difference is significant.

Individuals who are pessimistic may suffer from feelings of hopelessness and depression and be more prone to poor physical health and even death. Seligman (2002) cited a study completed by the Mayo Clinic in which "optimists had 19 percent greater longevity, in terms of their life span, compared to that of pessimists" (p. 10).

In an interview with Seligman, one of us (David) asked how people start shifting from pessimism to optimism. Seligman replied:

> I think the way most people start is to find out the costs of being a pessimist. As a pessimist, it's always wet weather in the soul. They don't do as well at work, and they get colds that will last all winter. They find themselves failing in crucial situations and their relationships go sour very easily. So when people have those kinds of hurts, if they can find that there is something useful in positive psychology, that's where they start.

In their book *How Full Is Your Bucket?* authors Tom Rath and Donald Clifton (2004) cited recent studies showing that negative emotions can be harmful to health. They also suggested that negativity might shorten life. However, they pointed out that positivity must be grounded in reality. Happy marriages are founded on positive interactions, according to a ratio that cannot stray by much. Five positive interactions for every one negative interaction is the magic ratio for marriage, and three positive interactions for every one negative interaction is the ratio for a happy work environment.

This brings us to an important point. Optimism should not be confused with simplistically "being positive" no matter what is going on. Seligman (2002) and others (Peterson, 2006) present evidence that the effects of optimism do not come from an unjustified positivity but from thinking negatively less often. Learned optimism is about building greater resilience and improving our performance by changing the way we interpret events, not by pasting on a happy face in every situation.

Linking Learned Optimism to Coaching

The effective coach is someone who can realistically appraise a situation and yet maintain aspects of the optimistic approach. Seligman (1990) suggests a balance between the two, even a need for a pessimistic perspective when the stakes are high. For instance, he suggests that airline passengers do not want an overly optimistic pilot.

To summarize, learned optimism suggests retaining faith that we will prevail in the end, regardless of the difficulties, but being ready to deal realistically with those difficulties. Jim Collins (2001) refers to this as the "Stockdale paradox" after an American prisoner in the Vietnam War who survived with just such a sense of balanced optimism.

In coaching, we want to help clients focus on what they can control. Our interpretation of events is one thing we can control. Having a good understanding of learned optimism can help a coach ask questions that reveal how clients' interpretations reduce their effectiveness. According to Seligman (1990), optimism can be learned. Coaching can help.

SCIENCE OF HAPPINESS: PLEASURE, ENGAGEMENT, AND MEANING

What do we mean by "happiness"? That was one of the first questions addressed by the new field of positive psychology. Is happiness a temporary state of mind? Or can we describe some people as generally happy (or grumpy, as Seligman's daughter accused him of being)? What is the relationship of happiness to things or activities we take pleasure in? How is it related to the things we desire? How does it relate to work or to the people around us? How does it relate to values and purpose? What do our strengths have to do with happiness? Where does "flow" come in?

Positive psychology has explored these questions and identified three distinct kinds of happiness: the pleasant life, the good life, and the meaningful life. This theoretical framework is one of the central ideas in the field.

The Pleasant Life—and Its Limits

The pleasant life is all about everyday pleasures. This type of happiness is also called hedonic happiness. This is the happiness that comes from buying a new outfit, eating a good meal, or celebrating with friends.

A good deal of scientific research has focused on this type of happiness, with some surprising findings. Edward Diener, a psychologist at the University of Illinois, proposed that people have a "happiness set-point" (Diener, 1984). He cited data showing that lottery winners are no happier one year after their good luck than they were before. Scientists call this "the hedonic treadmill." We adapt to any improvement in our circumstances and then start from that point to seek more pleasure, so our happiness is short-lived.

The majority of us have a steady level of joy in life, whatever our life circumstances may be. As Diener's research on lottery winners shows, the more "stuff" we demand from life, the unhappier we become if do not get it. Richard Layard (2003) summarized research across different countries, income levels, and age groups to support this claim.

People are bad at predicting what will make them happy. Princeton psychologist Daniel Kahneman won the Nobel Prize in Economics in 2002 for his work in this area. He found that people focus on the peak of an experience and on the end, ignoring what happens in the middle. Thus, if something starts and ends well, we tend to react well to it. Laura Rowley (2005) has provided a brief but informative overview of Kahneman's findings.

The things that do make us happy are not the things we expect. Peterson (2006) surveyed a number of studies that correlated different elements with happiness and life satisfaction. He found that the correlation of such admired qualities as physical attractiveness, income, intelligence, education, and social class with happiness and life satisfaction was negligible. Psychological attributes such as percent of time experiencing positive feelings, gratitude, optimism, self-esteem, and frequency of sexual intercourse, however, showed relatively large effects, along with being employed—with the caution that none of these measures is strong enough on its own to determine happiness. Perhaps even more telling is the international research (Diener & Diener, 1996) that showed most people are above the midpoint of the happiness scale most of the time.

Thus, when coaches work to help clients reframe their pessimistic explanations, we can have confidence that we are not likely starting at a low point of happiness—just one that can be higher more often.

The Good Life—Engagement and Flow

The good life is often referred to as eudaemonia, a concept initially addressed by thinkers such as Thomas Jefferson and Aristotle in considering the "pursuit of happiness." It is believed that in eudaemonia, time stops and self-consciousness is blocked. An individual experiencing this state is in what Csikszentmihalyi calls "flow" (1991). To achieve this state, people need to know what they are good at (their "signature strengths"—to be discussed), then organize their life around those strengths, and honor and use them more.

The "good life" is a life of engagement, of being immersed in activities we enjoy, including family life, hobbies, and work activities. The good life means we are engaged in activities that stretch and challenge us. This theory is reiterated by Richard Layard (2005), who explains that psychology, neuroscience, sociology, and applied economics have shown the causes and consequences of happiness. He believes that setting goals is necessary to our feeling happy, and he supports this belief by observing how children test themselves by seeing how fast they can run or high they can climb.

FLOW   Flow is the gratifying state that we enter when we feel completely engaged in what we are doing. The characteristics of flow have been described as follows:

- The task is challenging and requires skill.
- We concentrate.
- There are clear goals.
- We get immediate feedback.
- We are deeply and (seemingly) effortlessly involved.
- We have a sense of control.
- Our sense of self vanishes.
- Time stops.

The best-known researcher in this field is Mihaly Csikszentmihalyi (1991), an American-trained psychologist from Hungary. His life's work has been to study what makes people truly happy. Drawing on years of systematic research, he developed the concept of "flow" as a metaphorical description of the mental state associated with feelings of optimal satisfaction and fulfillment. His analysis of the internal and external conditions giving rise to flow show that it is almost always linked to circumstances of high challenge, when personal skills are used to the utmost.

Long before Csikszentmihalyi's research, however, the concept of "being at one" was part of the practice of Eastern spiritual traditions, such as Buddhism and Taoism. In sports, we hear athletes speak of "being in the zone" when they are in a state of peak performance. They report this state as being highly gratifying. Csikszentmihalyi was the first researcher to study these phenomena in a scientific way.

To conduct research on the conditions of flow, Csikszentmihalyi pioneered the experience sampling method (ESM) as a means of measuring the amount of flow people were experiencing. People are given a pager that goes off at random times all day. When the signal sounds, they write down what they are doing, where they are, and whom they are with, then rate the contents of their consciousness numerically: how happy they are, how much they are concentrating, how high their self-esteem is, and so on.

In a study of 824 American teens, Csikszentmihalyi (1996) divided free time into active versus passive components. Games and hobbies are active and produce flow 39% of the time. They produce the negative emotion of apathy 17% of the time. Watching television and listening to music, in contrast, are passive and produce flow only 14% of the time while they produce apathy 37% of the time. He found that the typical mood state for American teens watching television is mild depression.

Flow can come in any activity, from reading to writing, singing, painting, or even doing a spreadsheet or building a house. In order to live the good life, we need to know what our strengths are and spend time in the experience of flow using these strengths.

SIGNATURE STRENGTHS   The study of human strengths is a key component of positive psychology. Seligman (2002) says that, in order to increase happiness, we must not only remove unhappiness but also understand what actually increases our sense of well-being. Having fewer negative emotions is important, but it does not guarantee having more positive ones. Research is showing that a sense of well-being and fulfillment comes from an understanding and daily exercise of our personal strengths.

The Values in Action (VIA) Strengths Inventory (University of Pennsylvania AuthenticHappiness- see Internet links) was the first major scientific project undertaken from the perspective of positive psychology. According to this groundbreaking work (Peterson & Seligman, 2004), there are 6 ubiquitous virtues (found in traditional teachings around the world) into which a series of 24 strengths can be categorized:

1. Wisdom and knowledge
2. Courage
3. Humanity
4. Justice
5. Temperance
6. Transcendence

Clients may complete the inventory online and then receive a printout that shows their top five strengths. This system provides critical tools for any coach to understand the primary resources their clients bring and to provide a framework to focus clients on utilizing those strengths to their best advantage. *The Journal of Positive Psychology* (see Internet links) contains several relevant articles to illustrate research in this arena (e.g., see Peterson, Park, & Seligman, 2006). Studies now show that people tend to have the greatest engagement in life when they are able to constructively use their signature strengths.

LINKING "THE GOOD LIFE" TO COACHING   Flow is a state that many clients desire in their work and personal life. Coaches who understand the characteristics of flow can ask their clients whether they are experiencing flow in the activity in which they are engaged. In order to increase the opportunity for a state of flow, Seligman (2002) suggested a recipe that coaches can integrate into their work with clients:

- Identify your signature strengths.
- Choose work or activities that let you use your strengths every day.
- Recraft your current work to use your signature strengths more and more often.
- If you are the employer, choose employees whose signature strengths mesh with the work they will do.
- If you are a manager, allow employees to recraft the work within the bounds of business goals.

This approach makes work more fun, transforms the job or the career into a calling, increases flow, builds loyalty, and is decidedly more profitable for the business. Infusing work with gratification makes for a long stride on the road to the good life.

Marcus Buckingham has written a series of books (Buckingham, 2007; Buckingham & Clifton, 2001; Buckingham & Coffman, 1999) that take a more business-oriented perspective in reinforcing the notion of utilizing strengths. He highlights the importance of searching for specific strengths that refocus people on core goals and purposes so that they can stop wasting energy on relations and job activities that they simply have no interest in pursuing. Buckingham has been with the Gallup organization for 17 years, and its Web site (www.gallup.com) is a rich resource, although access to its test or evaluative instruments is on a subscription basis.

Example: Marilyn—"I Have No Idea What's Going on with Them"

Marilyn is the chief executive officer of a small professional services company. She found that her professional and administrative team members were often in conflict. "He treated me like I'm a complete moron," or "Why can't she just do what I asked her to do rather than questioning everything?" or "I have no idea what's going on with them." Because the professionals were on the road working virtually, it was very difficult to schedule enough face-to-face team-building exercises to develop better relationships and more understanding of one another. Marilyn realized that an assessment instrument might provide a shortcut to better understanding but feared that the personality measures she was familiar with often identified weaknesses that the employees would hesitate to share. Her coach suggested the VIA Strengths Inventory. Marilyn found that its emphasis on positive resources meant that employees both completed the assessment and were willing to reveal the results to the rest of the team. After a meeting where people talked about the strengths that the team as a whole exhibited, working relationships showed a marked improvement.

Two specific exercises are used in positive psychology to help people expand the awareness and use of their strengths:

1. *Use your strengths in new ways.* Identify your signature strengths and create ways to use them in new parts of your life.
2. *Strengths date.* This is fun for couples. Identify the strengths of both partners and work out an activity that would use both people's strengths. Coaches may also suggest a similar exercise for work groups.

Coaching is by nature focused on solutions, and therefore it is strengths-based. Coaches should understand and work with the concept of strengths, using some of the tools just mentioned or widely available elsewhere. The concept of growing our strengths ties in directly with the findings from neuroscience about the brain. Focusing our attention on our weaknesses magnifies them. Attending instead to our strengths increases our capacity to use them.

In summary, the science of flow provides useful knowledge and tools for coaches. Coaches should know the conditions that bring about and inhibit flow and help their clients achieve more flow in life. After all, coaching is about improving performance, and our performance is best when we are in the zone.

The Meaningful Life — Beyond Ourselves

The meaningful life is about using our natural strengths in the service of something larger than we are. This is the route to obtaining abundant and authentic gratification. In fact, according to Seligman (2002) and the positive psychology researchers, the larger the project or mission that we attach ourselves to, the more meaning we can harness.

This discovery of modern positive psychology reminds us of lessons from ancient traditions and spiritual and religious practices as well as from psychotherapists such as Alfred Adler (1956), Abraham Maslow (1968), and Viktor Frankl (1984).

LINKING "THE MEANINGFUL LIFE" TO COACHING Richard Boyatzis (Boyatzis, Smith & Blaise, 2006) asserted that compassion — the act of focusing our attention on the needs of others — reverses the damaging effects of stress. Compassion not only reduces stress, it helps to heal its effects. The ability to focus on others is thus an important part of developing a meaningful life. The next exercises have been developed by positive psychology researchers to expand our capacity to connect with others.

- *Three blessings.* At the end of each day, identify three things you are grateful for and why.
- *Gratitude visit.* Think of someone you are truly grateful to. Write a letter to the person identifying how and why, then visit to read the letter aloud.

- *Gratitude journal.* Sonja Lyubomirsky and her colleagues (2006) found that conscientiously counting one's blessings by writing them in a journal once each week for six weeks significantly increased subjects' overall satisfaction with life. A control group that did not keep journals showed no such gain.

Seligman (2002) believes that pursuing all three types of happiness, resulting in lives of pleasure, engagement, and meaning, is what it takes to lead an authentically happy life. He and his colleagues discovered that, just as we can train to play the violin, we can train ourselves to be happy. Clients can use the exercises just listed in coaching to do just that.

RESILIENCE

How do people deal with happenings that are clearly not positive? Resilience is the process of adapting well in the face of adversity, trauma, tragedy, threats, or even significant sources of stress, such as family and relationship problems, serious health problems, or workplace and financial stressors. It means bouncing back from difficult experiences.

In a *Psychology Today* article, Paul Stoltz remembered a plane trip at age 12 with his father. The plane had been delayed and the two sat watching a stream of people marching through the airport, none of them seeming to have any life or energy.

"Dad," Stoltz asked, "why are these people so dead?"

"I guess it's because life is hard," his father answered.

"So am I going to end up like that, too?" . . .

"Some people seem to be able to escape." (Wellner & Adox, 2000, p. 3)

Stoltz says this exchange planted the seeds for his research on strategies for dealing with adversity. He found that resilience is not a trait that people either have or do not have. Everyone is born with some resilience. Certain people learn to apply it day after day. They prefer to be problem solvers rather than victims. Relevant to coaching, resilience involves behaviors, thoughts, and actions that can be learned and developed.

Stoltz published the results of his research in *Adversity Quotient: Turning Obstacles Into Opportunities* (1997). He used the acronym CORE to represent how deal with adversity:

C: Control—recognize your own power in a situation.

O: Ownership—what part of the problem do you take responsibility for solving?

R: Reach—do not catastrophize or let the problem leak into other parts of your life.

E: Endurance—do not let adversity get you down for long.

Resilience involves a complex set of traits, but a primary factor is having caring and supportive relationships within and outside the family. These relationships create love and trust, provide role models, and offer encouragement and reassurance to help build a person's resilience. Neuroscience research shows that relationships based on attuned interactions actually affect brain structure, increasing the connections in the brain that yield emotional control, the ability to concentrate, and a good deal of what is called emotional intelligence (Goleman, 1995, 2006; Siegel & Hartzell, 2003).

Many of the available models regarding resilience pertain to children and youth. However, interest in adult resilience models and measures has been increasing since the study by Salvatore Maddi and Deborah Kobasa (1984) on the hardiness of executives facing the stress of AT&T restructuring in the 1980s. This trend has also increased with the discovery that the adult brain is more adaptable than previously thought.

Linking Resilience to Coaching

Coaches may find helpful several instruments to assess adult resilience, including one short test (consisting of just eight questions) developed by Karen Reivich and Andrew Shatte (2002).

Coaches may easily recognize signs of resilience, since many of the factors that characterize resilience also contribute to an effective coaching engagement:

- The capacity to make realistic plans and take steps to carry them out
- A positive view of oneself and confidence in one's strengths and abilities

- Skills in communication and problem solving
- The capacity to manage strong feelings and impulses

At times, clients who are typically quite resilient seem not to be able to access their normal resources. If we think of resilience as a sort of seawall that protects us from waves of stress, very strong tsunamis may overwhelm even the most resilient of us. In these cases, the coach may help with these in-the-moment suggestions:

- When anxiety strikes, your breathing may become shallow and quick. You can control the anxiety by controlling your breathing. Inhale slowly through your nose, breathing deeply from your belly, not your chest.
- Stress will make your body tight and stiff. You can counter the effects of stress on body and brain if you relax your muscles.
- Try positive imagery. Create an image that is relaxing, such as visualizing yourself on a secluded beach.

Longer-term resilience is a trait that can be learned and developed. If a coaching client identifies a goal of building resilience, the 10 strategies listed on the APA Help Center (www.apahelpcenter.org) may be useful. In addition to these, some people write about their deepest thoughts and feelings related to trauma or other stressful events in their lives, thus activating the storytelling power of narrative therapy. Meditation and spiritual practices can help build connections and restore hope.

Coaches may provide tips for building resilience if their clients show an interest in this topic. Clients may need to build resilience in order to access coaching and other resources that will allow them to cope with changes in their lives. Ethical considerations require coaches to refer clients to mental health therapists when severe or ongoing stress affects their basic life functions.

EMOTIONAL INTELLIGENCE

Research on emotional intelligence has developed in parallel with positive psychology, and there are many connections between the fields. Emotional intelligence involves the ability to perceive, assess, and positively influence one's own and other people's emotions and intentions.

Some early psychological researchers recognized the importance of emotional intelligence versus intellectual or cognitive intelligence. We introduced David Wechsler, the author of two of the most-utilized intelligence tests, the Wechsler Adult Intelligence Scale and the Wechsler Intelligence Scale for Children, in chapter 7. Psychometrics text writers Kaplan & Saccuzzo (2005) suggested that, although he is commonly thought to have focused solely on cognition as the definitive aspect of intelligence, Wechsler thought factors such as emotion and motivation were necessary for a person to act intelligently.

Robert Thorndike (1910–1990) wrote about social intelligence in the 1930s. However, the concept did not become popular until Howard Gardner (1983, 1993) introduce "multiple intelligences." Gardner theorized that intrapersonal and interpersonal intelligences are as important as the type of intelligence measured by IQ tests.

In 1990 Johan D. Mayer, David Caruso, and Peter Salovey introduced the term "emotional intelligence" (EI) to the psychology world (see Mayer et al. 2000), describing it as "a form of social intelligence that involves the ability to monitor one's own and others' feelings and emotions, to discriminate among them, and to use this information to guide one's thinking and action." Mayer and colleagues (2001) led many research programs to develop valid measures of EI and explore its significance. They conceived of a four-branch model of EI, which includes the capacity to:

1. Accurately perceive emotions
2. Use emotions to facilitate thinking
3. Understand emotional meanings
4. Manage emotions

In 1995 Daniel Goleman popularized the term in his best-selling book, *Emotional Intelligence* (1995). Goleman divided emotional intelligence into five competencies:

1. Identify and name one's emotional states and to understand the link between emotions, thought, and action.
2. Manage one's emotional states—control emotions or shift undesirable emotional states to more adequate ones.
3. Enter into emotional states associated with a drive to achieve and be successful.

4. Read, be sensitive to, and influence other people's emotions.
5. Enter and sustain satisfactory interpersonal relationships.

Goleman felt that these competencies happened in stages beginning with number 1 and only then moving to number 2, and so on. More recently he has modified this model to include only 4 domains and 19 categories (Goleman, Boyatzis & McKee, 2002):

1. *Self-awareness.* Emotional self-awareness, accurate self-assessment, self-confidence
2. *Self-management.* Emotional self-control, transparency, adaptability, achievement orientation, initiative, optimism, conscientiousness
3. *Social Awareness.* Empathy, organizational awareness, service orientation
4. *Relationship Management.* Inspirational leadership, influence, developing others, change catalyst, conflict management, building bonds, teamwork and collaboration

Goleman (1995) believes that EI competencies are not innate talents but learned abilities. Thus, clients may overcome gaps they identify in any of these categories. This finding is important for coaches to remember.

Linking Emotional Intelligence to Coaching

Clients benefit when coaches integrate EI into their coaching practice. Assessing and teaching EI helps improve relationships, and research shows that social factors are more important to clients' long-term success than are technical ones. Empathy, self-awareness, self-regulation, and the ability to read the emotions of others are foundational skills for clients who wish to make positive changes in their personal or work lives. Goleman's books should be on every coach's shelf as a resource to be shared with clients.

Several instruments are available for measuring emotional intelligence:

- *BarOn Emotional Quotient-Inventory* (BarOn EQ-i®). This self-report instrument assesses personal qualities that enable some people to exhibit better emotional well-being than others (High Performing Systems Inc., see Internet links).
- *Mayer-Salovey-Caruso Emotional Intelligence Test* (MSCEIT). In this test of ability, the test taker performs a series of tasks that are designed to

assess his or her ability to perceive, identify, understand, and work with emotion (Multi-Health Systems Inc., see Internet links).

- *Emotional & Social Competency Inventory* (ECI)/*Emotional Competency Inventory*. In these two 360-degree instruments, people evaluate individuals within an organization or the organization as a whole. These audits can provide an organizational profile for any size department within the company. The Emotional Competency Inventory works with the 19 competencies just described (Hay Group®, 2008).

Does emotional intelligence matter in the workplace? The Consortium for Research on Emotional Intelligence in the Workplace keeps track of the latest EI research in diverse fields such as management, leadership, psychology, sociology, and neuroscience. Research gathered by Cherniss (1999) shows that EI supports good working relationships and positive behaviors.

ACCENTUATE THE POSITIVE AS A PILLAR FOR COACHING

Coaching and positive psychology are linked in many ways. Many positive psychologists consider themselves to be coaches in some form, and many coaches are studying positive psychology. In addition to the University of Pennsylvania's programs (see Internet links), Harvard Medical School and McLean Hospital are sponsoring a Coaching and Positive Psychology Initiative (www.harvardcoaching.org - see Internet links). Robert Biswas-Diener and Ben Dean (2007) have published a book that builds on several years of Dean's use of positive psychology training for coaches (www.mentorcoach.com - see Internet links).

Positive psychology suggests a model of the good coach as a happy and optimistic person. To listen for another person's potential takes optimism. Positive psychology rejects the value-free requirement of logical positivism and unabashedly aims to help people make positive changes in their life. Coaching embraces the same mission. Positive psychologists help their clients lead a life that is happier, more engaged, and more deeply meaningful, just as coaches do.

Coaches assume that their clients are whole and healthy human beings who can discover many of their own answers. We encourage clients to rediscover the passion in their work and lives. Being able to apply the concept of levels of happiness and helping clients raise those levels if they wish to do so is a large part of unleashing a client's potential. Positive psychology has shown many ways to do this.

The goal for us as coaches is also to lead a life that is happier, more engaged, and more deeply meaningful. By internalizing these principles in our own lives, we become an inspiring model for those with whom we work, helping to "infect" them with a cheerful outlook that enhances all of us.

As positive psychology and the many applications of emotional intelligence were emerging, developmental psychologists and child psychiatrists were studying attachment and its effects on adult pathology as well as positive relationships throughout life. Observations arising from these studies have stimulated questions among neuroscientists, such as "What are the neurological correlates of positive emotions and emotional intelligence? Are we stuck with brains that produce either happiness or unhappiness because of our past attachment experiences?"

The response that we are not "stuck" in this way is supported by the discovery that adults who were insecurely attached in childhood can actually "earn" or develop secure attachment and many of the qualities identified by positive psychology as necessary to authentic happiness. The pillar of positive psychology rose above the assumption that human values, such as what is considered positive rather than negative, were mere objects of study. This new subdiscipline sees values as guides to what makes life worth living, which has helped to break the hold of the disease model on psychotherapy. It also stimulated neuroscience to provide evidence regarding how it is possible to change one's values to yield more positive results.

CHAPTER 12

Neuroscience Platform— Emotions

"Rapunzel, Rapunzel, throw down your hair." In the fairy tale, Rapunzel's long hair allows the handsome prince to climb up to the tower and rescue her from her imprisonment. The assumption is that they were both overwhelmed by their attraction for one another. But what would have happened to the pair's feelings after the rescue and return to safety had been accomplished? The passion of Romeo and Juliet, despite the opposition of their parents, is immortalized in drama, dance, and music, but what if the two teenagers had lived and the families had reconciled? Would the passion of the lovers have remained as strong? Emotion researchers have wondered about the passions that are aroused when they are forbidden or dangerous. In a series of experiments, they have discovered that physiological arousal, even when it has nothing to do with love or attraction—but rather with danger or rebellion—can be interpreted by our minds as overwhelming passion. If we meet an attractive person on a suspension bridge or while rappelling down a cliff, we are likely to find him or her more attractive than if we had met on solid, safe ground. In other words, emotions are not just another category of human experiences like cognition or physiology or relationships. Emotions affect and perhaps even encompass them all.

"Feeling" is a term that applies both to sensations and to emotions. At one time, sensations were treated as mere signals that convey information to the brain for processing. We have shown that our capacity to

345

sense our internal and external environment is saturated with "higher-level" processes such as expectations and fear reactions.

In general, positive emotions draw us forward, toward what we perceive as rewarding, and negative emotions repel us. Almost by definition, then, human beings ask, "How can I feel better?"

In responding to that question, Albert Ellis disputed people's tendencies to link situations directly with their emotions, as in "That remark *made* me so angry!" We have seen that both psychotherapy and coaching ask people to become aware of the often-unconscious beliefs or questions that mediate the situation-emotion link. But thinking is only a part of the equation.

Here we suggest that emotions indicate an integration of brain/body, mind, and social information sources. They serve as "great summarizers" of our current state or frame of mind. Thus, they are "strange attractors," or points around which bodily states, memories, perceptions, and actions form the unique patterns that make us who we are. Over time and repeated often enough, these become our personalities, our ongoing subjective sense of self.

Emotions can help us become conscious of how we are creating meaning in our lives from moment to moment. In indicating our current state of mind, they enable us to identify limits to our ability to see possibilities. Marilee Adams (2004; Goldberg 1998) calls one such state that of the "Judger" and suggests that it is a response to implicit questions such as "Whose fault is it?" In contrast, the state of the "Learner" opens possibilities and is triggered by questions such as "What happened?" or "What do I want?" This awareness leads to more choices for us and more opportunities to help clients become aware, explore their choices, and engage in satisfying actions.

- What are emotions and what do they do for us?
- Why have emotions anyway?
- How do they relate to our physical sensations, to our memories, and to our actions?
- What information does emotion convey?
- What is the relationship between integration and emotion?
- Do emotions represent our "true selves," or are they charlatans that mislead us and reduce our capacity to reason?
- Why are emotions so easily triggered by other people?

- How can we have more positive and fewer negative emotions?
- How can we use attention consciously to reduce the effects of threat?
- Do the claims of spiritual practices have any basis in scientifically measurable facts?
- Can mindfulness practices actually improve our minding, braining, and relating?

Feeling as sensation and feeling as emotion are related, but they have been studied by different fields and researchers. The study of sensation is more likely to be found in physiology, anatomy, and psychophysiology. Emotions were largely ignored, except as measurable and conditioned behavior, during the behaviorist era of psychology. Even after the cognitive revolution in the late 1950s, it took several decades for cognitive scientists to focus on emotions rather than primarily on cognition (Mahoney, 1991). Goleman gathered convincing evidence of the importance of emotions in his 1995 book, *Emotional Intelligence*, which has had a significant impact on coaching.

The word "emotion" is closely related to "motivation." Both are derived from the Latin *movere*, "to move," with the "e-" in emotion a variant of the Latin *ex*, or "out." Emotions are an evolutionary adaptation that motivates organisms to respond to environmental changes. The first practical thing we should remember is that the strength of an emotion is not related to the truth of our interpretation of it. That is, we can feel very strongly that someone intentionally meant to insult us without that being true. Likewise, we can remain sanguine about, say, a customer complaint that should motivate us to act, and act quickly. In other words, emotions convey information, but it may take some reflection and experience to know if that information is about an input (environmental change) or the processes that generate and regulate emotional responses. Without that awareness, how we move may make a situation worse rather than better. Coaching is one opportunity for such reflection.

Despite the recent interest in emotions and the general agreement about their importance, experts in the field disagree about exactly what emotions are. Psychologists use the term "affect" to describe patients' emotional states. "Feelings" are subjective experiences of emotions. "Mood" refers to emotions in the medium term, while "disposition" is a more long-term description. Robert Plutchik (2007) and Richard Lazarus (1991) developed taxonomies of emotions. Paul Ekman (2003) studied emotional expression cross-culturally and developed training materials that can help coaches and others recognize even fleeting emotions in facial expressions.

Are emotions physiological responses similar to what we observe in other mammals (Panksepp, 1998)? Are they the result of our recognizing a change in our bodily state, as William James (1950) proposed? (We see a bear, start running away, and then realize we must be afraid because we are running.) Or do we run because we are afraid (Cannon, 1927)? Such formulations do not take into account the complexity of our emotional responses. Daniel Siegel (2007a, b) has proposed that this confusion can be overcome by thinking "integration" every time we hear the word "emotion." Siegel defines integration as the linking of differentiated elements, in this case the whole system of brain, mind, and relationships. That is why we call emotions the "great summarizers." Following Siegel's suggestion enables us to see emotion as an integration of all of these:

- Mental maps that include memories, interpretations, physiological reactions, and behavioral tendencies linked as a "state of mind"
- Our amygdala's continual scanning for threats and the results of finding them
- Status and the importance of connections with others in our social field

In this chapter, we discuss emotions as indications of integration under these headings:

- State of mind
- Scanning for threats
- Status and belonging
- Emotion regulation
- Practice guide for coaching with the brain in mind — Keep cool under pressure

STATE OF MIND

Some emotional experiences can be very fleeting. The delight of making a funny remark or supplying a little-known fact in a conversation

348

can disappear quickly. And, fortunately, this is also true for most minor slights. Adaptation is an aspect of all human senses. Repetition of the same stimulus over time results in less and less response, or a reduction in the transmission of information. After a while, noxious smells become more bearable or even disappear. Perhaps not so fortunately, the 20th bite of chocolate mousse does not taste so sweet as the first.

Less fleeting is what is commonly called a "mood," or what we are calling a "state of mind." Emotions that are not fleeting indicate a pattern of interrelated physical and mental elements. This terminology suggests that different aspects of our mental processes trigger each other, or are linked and thus integrated.

Example: "Ma, I'm Coming Already!"

Jonathan decides to spend two days in his childhood home with his parents and younger sister who is home for the holidays from university. As vice president for sales and marketing at an athletic equipment company, he had just made a presentation to a conference on the East Coast regarding a successful training program he had implemented. His family would join him from their home on the West Coast as soon as the children were out of school.

Going up the stairs to the room that was his for the first 18 years of his life, Jonathan had a feeling that was both familiar and strange. Was it the smells from the kitchen? Or the wood grain of the banister? His room had become a guest room, with a double bed in it, but there were still signs of his presence—the bulletin board, the thumb tack holes on the back of the door where his Fleetwood Mac poster had been. He gazed out the window as fleeting images flashed through his mind—seasons passing, sneaking out to a late game, the neighbor's new car. But the car was not new anymore. In fact, the neighbor had moved. A sensation like a warm but prickly blanket covered him, and his body seemed to contract and slump. His sister's voice on the phone in her room next door was irritating. Would she ever get off the phone? After all, he had people he wanted to talk with, too. He shook his head, remembering that he had a mobile phone now.

He changed from his business suit into a sweatshirt and comfortable pants. Just as he was headed downstairs, his mother called out, "Now, don't dawdle, you two. We don't want supper to get cold waiting for you."

Jonathan couldn't keep the irritation out of his voice. "Ma, I'm coming already!" He hadn't spoken like that to his mother since he was 18.

What would turn a 33-year-old successful corporate up-and-coming father of three into an 18-year-old chafing under his mother's attention? The answer helps us know how to manage our emotional states as well as to use our brain, mind, and relationships to construct a self that we can more often be proud of.

If we think of emotions as integration, we can recognize the value of the information an emotion provides: Jonathan's irritation is a summary, like a headline in a story made up of mental maps triggered by sensations (smells, the texture of the banister, the scene outside his window, sounds of the house) that he is only partly aware of. All this in turn triggers pathways of neurons that affect his physiology (he feels smaller), his interpretations (his sister is always on the phone), and what he is likely to do (yell back at his mother). That irritated feeling represents a state of mind that could be labeled "always being hassled by my parents." This state is very different from "I'm a successful manager." He was "in" this confident state of mind at the conference but slipped into the irritation state of an 18-year-old when that state was triggered by his returning to his childhood home. This must have felt strange indeed for Jonathan, although we all make similar shifts daily.

We may be more used to shifting states that accompany our roles as parent, commuter, worker, and friend, so we do not notice those changes. It is the unusual shift, such as Jonathan's being at home without his wife and children for the first time in 15 years, or a shift signaled by extreme emotions, that catches our attention.

Example: "He Refused a Sale"

The outdoor pub owner became incensed when a delayed bus passenger pulled up a chair and plugged in her laptop without buying a drink. When she apologized and offered to buy something, he refused and insisted that she leave. The pub owner's state of anger was so extreme that he refused a sale. This may be a one-time reaction at the end of a long, hard day, or it may be a common pattern for this pub owner. In any case, it indicates a state of mind that might be summarized as incensed anger.

Linking State of Mind to Coaching

Based on the understanding that attention changes the brain, the more often an incident occurs that can be interpreted as "How dare that passenger take advantage of me?" and the more it is interpreted that way, the more mental maps are formed of being cheated and the more one's physiology of threat is activated, the more likely this state of mind will characterize a person's ongoing subjective experience. The pub owner may even be described by others as an angry person.

And, as we mentioned previously, our brains are structured for social participation, so a state like this in one person can easily trigger a similar or complementary state in another. The shorthand way of saying this is emotions are contagious. The bus passenger feels unjustly accused — after all, she tried to apologize. She offered to buy a drink. She leaves the pub promising never to go there again and to complain to her friends so they will not frequent the place either. "That will show him!" she thinks, expressing a vengeful state of mind in response to the pub owner's incensed anger.

The term "toxic work environment" applies to settings where inter-actions such as these are the norm. Coaches often work with leaders who wonder how to change these situations. The first step is simple but not easy to accomplish: We must start by becoming conscious of our present state of mind. Only then can we consciously shift it, using the many techniques described throughout this book.

The reason such situations are called "toxic" is that they metaphori-cally poison productivity and creativity. People trigger and share states of mind that inhibit their potential. Quite literally, stress that comes from a perception of danger, especially the insecurity of social relation-ships, reduces the brain's ability to see the big picture, reflect on one's own state of mind, and see things from another point of view.

Scanning for Threats

The amygdala is an almond-shaped organ buried in the middle of the brain, between the body-regulating "lower" part (the wrist and heel of our brain-in-hand) and the "higher-level" cortex, including our oft-mentioned prefrontal cortex (represented by the first and second digits of the fingers in the brain-in-hand). For a review of the brain-in-hand model, see the Introduction. Sensory signals are routed through the amygdala, like a rapid wiretap, on their way to the conscious parts of our brains. Although the amygdala is commonly thought of as the emotional

351

center of the brain, when it is stimulated, it does not generate happy emotions, so much as anxiety and fear.

The amygdala scans everything and everyone we come into contact with to identify potential threats, even without being told consciously to do so. In small groups characteristic of human prehistory, scarcity of resources made everyone dependent on everyone else, and the dangers were physical and immediate, such as hungry predators. In such circumstances, the survival value of an always-active amygdala is obvious. However, in a complex organization, dangers are more likely to be ambiguous (a coworker who is both admiring and jealous), psychological (deadlines), and remote (merger and acquisition decisions made in the boardroom). When the amygdala does its job in these circumstances, the resulting anxiety and fear may become a burden, especially in an organization trying to create a common culture and sense of shared values and vision.

Goleman (1995) terms this state of inappropriate arousal an "amygdala hijack." That is because, in its aroused state, the amygdala has several effects that are important for coaches to be aware of:

- *Generalizing*. Amygdala arousal can activate mental maps that are only tangentially related to the situation at hand. A new hire's voice reminds us of our always-critical aunt. The weather on the day of an important meeting is suspiciously like it was that time we got bad news. Memories that we encoded implicitly, out of awareness, are not accompanied by a sense of remembering when we recall them. We are not aware of "recalling" anything, just of the present sense of dread. Thus, the immediate situation can be colored by negative associations without our being aware of where they come from.

- *Reducing metabolism in the prefrontal cortex*. To the extent that they are localized in the brain, the processes of reasoning and decision making are centered in the prefrontal cortex, the portion of the brain behind the eyes and forehead. Amygdala arousal reduces the flow of energy to this portion of the brain; thus it becomes more difficult to problem-solve and think "rationally" when the amygdala is aroused. In a sort of teeter-totter effect, as amygdala arousal increases, planning and decision-making parts of the prefrontal cortex decrease.

- *Erring on the side of pessimism.* Because the output of the amygdala is fear and anxiety, even ambiguous input can end up feeling like doom. A neutral change may trigger the negative response of one person's amygdala, and others are then more likely to be triggered by that response. The chief executive takes a month off to work on a personal project, and the office gossip concludes that the company is going under.
- *Not distinguishing psychological from physical threats.* Researchers at the University of California at Los Angeles (Eisenberger, et al., 2003) showed that we register psychological pain, such as insults or rejection, in the same part of the brain as physical pain. Words may not leave the same scars as sticks and stones, but they can hurt in the very same way.

In essence, says neuroscientist Bruce Perry (2006), "fear destroys the capacity to learn" (p. 23).

Even under the best of circumstances, what we can be conscious of, or keep in mind, is limited in time as well as in number of items. The average time people can hold an idea in mind, in good conditions, is about 10 seconds. This goes also for holding an idea not in mind, or trying not to think about something. Stress or anxiety creates an alert signal that keeps demanding our attention, making it hard to hold other ideas in mind.

Thus, even when we try to defend against an insistent amygdala alarm, it tends to take over. Compared to positive feelings, negative amygdala-related responses are triggered more easily, come on faster, are more intense, and last longer. Think of having even a mild argument with someone, then going back to your desk. Is it easy to get back to the project you are working on, or do you somehow keep mulling over the argument, like an echo reverberating in your mind?

When we perceive a threat, the amygdala signals a stress response that includes the release of cortisol. This hormone is part of the sympathetic nervous system's flight-or-fight response. However, long-term unrelieved stress inhibits cognitive and immune system functioning. Fear, concern about status, and anxiety can impair working memory, thus reducing our capacity to process and store information. Increased levels of cortisol result in long-term damage to the hippocampus, the part of the brain central to memory and learning. This has been observed, for example, in people diagnosed with posttraumatic stress disorder (see Perry, 2006).

But sometimes the danger is real. Sometimes, as Malcolm Gladwell reveals in *Blink!* (2005), we had better pay attention to that out-of-awareness inkling that something is wrong. Sometimes our working memory is too limited to put together all the clues that justify the amygdala alarm, even when the clues are actually there. Sometimes there is a fire even if we do not consciously smell the smoke.

From the perspective of the mind, changes in the output of the sensory/perception system can inform us about the input, about what it is that we are observing or sensing. The brake lights on the car in front of us go on, and without thinking (remember that the amygdala works fast), we slam on our brakes. Or we just have a feeling that something is not quite right, and sure enough, that great deal turns sour. Thank goodness, the amygdala is on constant guard duty and is doing its job in these circumstances.

But, like oversensitive smoke alarms, the amygdala can mistake benign signals for dangerous ones. And the information can be about the sensory/perception system itself, not about the input. This is the case where implicit memories that we do not know we are remembering trigger the amygdala in the absence of input from our senses that truly indicates danger. One extreme example described by a psychotherapy colleague of Linda's was that of a patient who fainted periodically, seemingly for no medical reason. During therapy, she discovered that a certain shade of red, one that might appear, for instance, on someone's clothes, triggered the fainting spells. Fainting can be seen as a reaction of the autonomic nervous system to the perception of extreme danger. Where neither fighting nor fleeing is possible, playing dead may be the only option. In nature, this is illustrated by the hog-nosed snake, which goes limp and lifeless in the face of threat. In therapy, the patient was able to connect her fainting with having witnessed a very bloody accident as a young child in a situation where she could not fight or run away.

Linking Scanning for Threats to Coaching

Because coaches do not provide psychotherapy, we would refer cases such as just described to a qualified professional who does. But coaches often face a similar puzzle with clients: Does the client's reaction of fear and anxiety indicate:

- Real and present danger from outside or inside the self (i.e., information about input)?
- A real and present neutral or positive event that the client has mistakenly interpreted as danger (i.e., information about input that has been mistakenly interpreted in the minding process)?
- The triggering of a past implicit memory that feels real and present but is not (i.e., information about the mental process itself)?

The question is "How do we know the difference?" In order to even ask that question, we need to help our clients become aware that their perceptions may have other interpretations.

First of all, we must understand that the input we think is purely from our senses in fact arrives already saturated with amygdala and "top-down" (i.e., highly interpreted) processing. By the time we become conscious of our reaction, we have already climbed several rungs on a ladder of inference (Argyris, 1990) from lower rungs of specific, concrete data to higher rungs of richly elaborated interpretations. These interpretations may indicate a state of mind that is not resourceful or open to alternate possibilities.

For instance, "The bouncer kicked me out" requires several interpretations beyond "the bouncer said, 'You can't come in without a jacket.'" "She was boiling mad" is more abstract or on a higher level of interpretation than "Her face got very red, she clenched her fist, took a step toward me, and started speaking really loudly." "Kicked me out" and "boiling mad" are easier to connect with general state of mind reactions such as "How dare he?" and "I'll get back at her." The first step in avoiding reactions that make the situation worse is awareness. And awareness is aided by getting as close as possible to the raw sensory data: what was said, what was done, what was actually seen or heard. Marilee Adams (2004) suggests that a question such as "What happened?" is likely to stimulate a learning state of mind, one that is open to alternatives. Coaches are trained to ask questions that elicit information stripped of its top-down implications in order to set the stage for creative responses rather than mindless reactions.

The next step is to generate options for interpretations other than the ones that the client automatically arrived at. Because amygdala arousal can reduce processing power in the prefrontal cortex, clients benefit from "borrowing" the less-aroused brain of the coach to aid in generating these options. This is an example of sharing the flow of information and energy.

Next, coach and client discuss ways to test the options. This process is similar to the cognitive-behavioral technique of identifying cognitive distortions and then testing them against reality. This process engages all three inseparable elements of health as presented in Figure 1.3 on page 26: becoming more aware of the workings of one's own mind; neural integration of past and present; and connecting with others to enhance both mindfulness and neural integration.

STATUS AND BELONGING

One of the most powerful triggers for a shift in resourcefulness has to do with status. Why do we feel excited or even special when we see a famous person in a coffee shop? It is unlikely that the television or movie star came there because of us. Why do we line up for hours for an autograph or to shake hands with someone we have seen on TV? Somehow, our association with a higher-status person increases our own status. And status is of great importance to the brain.

Reduced status when we are dependent on others could be accompanied by terrible consequences. At the extreme, if our status is reduced to the point that we are unacceptable to the group and we no longer belong, our very survival is brought into question. Around the world, one of the most terrible consequences of breaking societal norms is being expelled or treated as if one does not exist. In many societies, this is a punishment worse than being executed, and often results in death. Threats such as this provide a ready trigger for an amygdala highjack. Thus, response to reduced status is highly visceral, releasing a flood of cortisol that inhibits thoughtful processing.

Richard Boyatzis and his colleagues (2006) found that of the three types of stress—having too much to do, dealing with ambiguity, and being seen/observed by others—it is being seen by others that contributes most to stress. When, for example, stressed research participants were being evaluated by others and therefore risked a reduction in status, their cortisol levels remained high for 50% longer, taking an hour or more to return to normal.

In a study published in *Science* in 2003 (Eisenberger, *et al.*), researchers used functional magnetic resonance imaging (fMRI) to scan the brains of participants as they played a computer game called cyberball. In cyberball, participants think they are playing an onscreen version of catch with two other people who are using computers linked to their own. For a while, the two other people throw the ball regularly to the participant's onscreen character, but after a while they stop and begin to throw the ball only to each other.

In reality, the other people do not exist and the "game" is simply an automatic computer program, but the participant does not know this and feels the sting of social rejection. Using fMRI, researchers found that this experience of social rejection activated an area of the brain that also lights up in response to physical pain: the anterior cingulate cortex. Thus, the experience of social rejection shows up in the same part of the brain as when we experience physical pain.

This research also helps us understand why people go to such lengths to avoid being wrong in an argument. To be wrong means our status is reduced, while the other's is increased. Good mediators know how to affirm aspects of both sides in an argument in order to keep participants' mental processes from being hijacked by status threats. It is a technique of judges and arbitrators to berate the party who wins as a way of reducing the sting of defeat, and loss of status, of the party who will be disappointed in the results. At least the losing party has the comfort of seeing the winner being excoriated.

The concept of status can also be used in coaching to bring an unconscious process of assigning status to the conscious level with clients. As coaching conversations often deal with clients' relationships, it may be useful for them to think about the status that goes with roles or interactions. The status that clients assign to others will impact the way they deal with them, whether they are conscious of this or not. Awareness of this dimension gives clients the ability to reappraise (if relevant) and/or to act more purposefully.

Another important consideration in this context is the relationship between coach and client, particularly in an organizational context where clients might have been assigned to a coaching relationship rather than seeking it themselves. In these instances, it is important for the coach to consider the impact that being required to seek coaching may have on clients' perceived status and whether clients see the coach as threatening in some way. Even in situations where clients eagerly seek coaching, the challenge of new learning may trigger status, stress, or fear responses.

Linking Status and Belonging to Coaching

In coaching, we are called on to provide feedback to clients. Consider what could happen from the perspective of the brain when we say the word "feedback": If the client has an unconscious expectation that equates feedback to criticism, he or she may perceive this as a threat. Not looking good in the eyes of someone important is threatening to our status, as we have described. The limbic system goes into overdrive and the brain pumps out cortisol, resulting in reduced functioning of the prefrontal cortex. The amygdala starts to generalize, or make connections between things it would not normally connect. The coaching connections we hope to make are overridden by fear and anxiety.

It is important that the coach handles feedback appropriately to ensure that it is received constructively. The coach's relationship, empathy, and intuition with the client are all important. This is also why "priming" a client by starting from an appreciative perspective, asking permission to go down the feedback path, and using strengths-based language are important techniques.

EMOTION REGULATION

Being able to manage one's emotions is highly valued in business and is a mark of a healthy prefrontal cortex. But what does it mean in practice?

As mentioned, "affective" is the term used in psychology and neuroscience to refer to what is more commonly called "emotions." The new field that combines social psychology, cognitive psychology, and neuroscience (social cognitive neuroscience) is also referred to as social-cognitive-affective neuroscience. The journal in which much of current research in this integrative field appears is called *Social Cognitive and Affective Neuroscience*.

James Gross and colleagues from Stanford University have pursued research about how people control or attempt to control affect, a field called emotion regulation (Gross, 1998; Gross et al., 2006). Let us say we overhear a coworker say something upsetting about a project we have been working hard on: "It's going nowhere fast. What a waste of time and money!" Before even getting upset, we can dismiss the coworker as being inept or uninformed. Or we can remind ourselves of the positive review that our boss just gave us. We can also think of how pleased we will be, and perhaps how chastened the coworker will be, when in the future the project turns out to be a glorious success. These strategies fall in the general category of what Gross calls "antecedent-focused strategies," which include naming and reappraisal or reframing techniques.

Reappraisal or Reframing

Reappraisal is another name for reframing or recontextualizing an issue. In a common experiment, participants are asked to look at a photo of a group outside a church. They see people crying and feel sad. But if they are asked to reappraise the event as a wedding, their emotions shift. As a result of reappraisal, the participants changed their state of mind.

We can also accomplish this consciously, as research by Kevin Ochsner and James Gross (Ochsner et al., 2001) has shown. The part of our brain responsible for reappraisal is the right and left ventral lateral sections of the prefrontal cortex, which are just above our temples. When we reframe, we activate these sections of the prefrontal cortex. As the prefrontal cortex gets activated, the amygdala gets deactivated.

Ochsner and his colleagues examined what happens when people reappraise the emotional impact of a scene (Ochsner et al., 2001). Years of social psychology research had shown that if, when looking at a disturbing or unseemly picture, people can step back and reevaluate what they are looking at, they can minimize its emotional impact. The researchers used fMRI to decipher some of the neural pathways associated with this phenomenon. They showed study participants an unpleasant photo and asked them either to be aware of their feelings or to attempt to reappraise what they were seeing. The reappraisal group were allowed to recognize that the photo was disquieting but were instructed to think about it as a scene from a movie.

Ochsner and colleagues found that when people reappraised the scene in this way, areas in the brain's frontal cortex that are involved in cognitive control became active but those involved in emotion became less active.

The opposite occurred when people were asked simply to become aware of their feelings. These findings suggest that cognitive reappraisal may lessen the emotional impact of an experience by turning off the brain's emotion response centers. It also tells researchers that if they want to understand the psychology of reappraisal, recognizing the interaction of cognitive and emotional processes will be important (Ochsner et al., 2001).

In referring to emotional reactions, Daniel Goleman (1995) coined the terms "high road" and "low road." Low-road functions are those that occur automatically and quickly. Hearing a noise in the night and suddenly feeling your heart jump is a low-road function. Realizing that it is just the cat is a reappraisal characteristic of a high-road function. While realizing that the noise was not a threat halts the further release of stress hormones adrenaline and cortisol, it takes time for their effects to dampen down. We might try to appoint the high road as the boss, but we need some careful listening and coaching if we are to win the cooperation of the low road.

Reappraisal, or reframing (as it is called in psychotherapy), is referred to many times in this book and is a core concept in most approaches to coaching. When clients reappraise events, they are more likely to remember their content. When clients repress events, the negative emotion is what they remember. Reappraisal dampens the amygdala. Every moment involves some kind of reappraisal or naming of what has taken place. Making this process a conscious practice is one way to manage change. However, not all reappraisal is useful to clients. We have learned from positive psychology that a pessimistic explanatory style involves reappraising positive events as temporary, local, and an anomaly. The role of coaching is to help clients make optimistic reappraisals so they can build their resources and move toward greater fulfillment.

The reappraisal process is a matter of becoming aware of often-unconscious interpretations, bringing relevant filters (values, beliefs, culture) to consciousness, and introducing changes in our maps that enable us to maintain dynamic stability. In this way we see direct links to ontology, psychology, neuroLinguisitic programming, and systems theory.

Reappraisal can be seen as a core muscle to be developed in coaching. When we pull apart the difference between an event and our interpretations of it, we are setting the stage for reappraisal. When an issue upsets us and a coach asks us to reflect on the event, we are taking that first step toward reappraisal. Reappraisal is what allows people who have had serious accidents, such as loss of a limb or worse, return to their previous state of happiness after about a year has passed.

Think of framing as a metaphor. One metaphoric image might be a picture frame that indicates what the artist thinks is important to look at. Moving the frame to include another scene or painting would direct our attention to new information. This is an example of reframing context.

Another metaphor could be the frame of a house, the joists and studs and struts that determine the basic shape of the building. Changing the frame could change the very type of building, making it a retail store rather than a home. This is an example of reframing meaning. Both of these images apply to the concept of reframing that is a technique in psychotherapy, as well as to research on reappraisal being conducted by neuroscientists.

Example: From Delivery to Design

Mark is chief executive of a consulting firm that had seen its market share slip in the face of stiff competition. Mark asked his executive coach to facilitate a series of team meetings to analyze the situation. As a result, it became clear that the firm could not distinguish itself from its competition by its delivery of consulting services. Rather, its professional staff had a unique capacity to design service packages that the firm could sell to other consultants. This was a context reframe, from delivery to design. The designer-consultants were freed to do what they do best and the marketing department was given a new context in which to sell the firm's design capacity.

Example: "Could His Ability to Focus Be Useful to You?"

Arnette complained to her coach about an employee that she described as wearing "blinders." "He has no interest in what other people in the office are doing. He only pays attention to what he thinks is important," Arnette said.

"In what ways could his ability to focus be useful to you?" asked the coach. This reframe of the meaning of her employee's behavior helped Arnette reassign his duties to take advantage of what she now was able to see as a strength.

Reframing is a skill that can be practiced by coaches and learned by clients. One exercise to strengthen that skill is illustrated by the "On one hand. . . . On the other hand. . . ." sequence from the musical *Fiddler on the Roof*. Think of any event:

- *It is snowing hard today.* On one hand, that means I will miss the income from canceled appointments. On the other hand, I will be able to spend some very special time with my children who are staying home from school. On the other hand. . . .
- *I have a big presentation to do.* On one hand, I am anxious. On the other hand, my anxiety means that this is important enough to me to put a lot of energy into it. On the other hand. . . .
- *My new boss always has a scowl on his face.* On one hand, he may be upset with me. On the other hand, he may be feeling overwhelmed with all the new demands and wondering if the staff, including me, will support him. On the other hand. . . .

The argument on either "hand" must be plausible. The crucial question is which side the client will choose to act on. A frame that interprets the new boss as needing support has a very different emotional tone and resulting actions from the frame that assumes he is being critical. To assume that this choice is a meaningless one ignores that fact that practicing a particular frame over and over establishes it as a constituent of a familiar state of mind, even as part of who we are. As clients learn how better to reframe, they also learn that they can make a difference in how their brains work.

Reframing is what results when people train themselves to ask different questions that put them on a path to "Learner" rather than "Judger" (Adams, 2004).

In a paper published in 2004, Jeffrey Schwartz, Henry Stapp, and Mario Beauregard claimed that the use of reframing presupposes that mental processes can have an effect on brain activity. If practitioners believe emotional states are mere epiphenomena, or reflections caused by underlying neurobiological realities, it is unlikely that they will encourage clients to develop their own abilities to reframe. Yet evidence of the efficacy of both types of reframing accumulates. "There are now numerous reports on the effects of self-directed regulation of emotional response, via cognitive reframing and attentional re-contextualization mechanisms, on cerebral function" (p. 3). That is, reframing changes the brain.

In addition to "antecedent-focused" techniques of reappraisal or reframing, the other general set of strategies discussed by Gross (2006) are "response-focused" and are applied once the emotion has taken hold and we are already feeling angry or humiliated and physiologically aroused. What can change our emotional response once it has been activated and we are in a state of mind we do not want or at least do not want others to know about? Researchers have shown that what most people think works well and what actually works well are two very different things.

Suppression

In one experiment, described by Kevin Ochsner at the NeuroLeadership Summit in New York (see Internet links), subjects were asked to guess how well different strategies would reduce the effects of an upsetting incident. Would talking with someone else about how they felt be effective? No, most people said. What about controlling their emotions so others would not know what they were feeling? Yes, that should work, many subjects answered.

After being shown upsetting videos, subjects were assigned to work with partners and divided into two groups. One member of each pair in group 1 was told to talk about how she or he felt after watching the video. In the other group, one member of each pair was instructed to suppress his or her emotions, not letting the other know what they were. That is, both partners in one group talked about emotions while one partner in the other group suppressed them.

Both groups were tested as to how well their strategies reduced physiological arousal. Results were exactly the opposite of what the subjects thought they would be: Talking about emotions reduced blood pressure and other measures of arousal whereas suppression had no such effect. And these results were not limited to just one experiment or one point in time. Gross (2006) summarized: "Over the longer term, individuals who make more frequent use of suppression show worse functioning in emotional, interpersonal, and well-being domains" (p. 8). Although they may feel heroic or tell themselves they are doing what is expected, suppressors are actually negatively affecting their health and relationships by attempting to control the expression of emotion.

Naming

When we have already entered a state of emotional arousal, we often talk to others about our experience, and that seems to help clear the mind. Telling our troubles to a Guatemalan worry doll, then placing it beneath our pillow will, according to legend, erase those worries by morning. Similar practices spanning many cultures affirm the idea that putting problems into words can blunt the emotional impact of those problems. Centuries of thinkers—from Dutch philosopher Baruch Spinoza (1632–1677), to William James, to every psychologist who practices talk therapy—have recognized this peculiar power of language. But is there evidence to back up these claims?

Going back to the cyberball research showing that social rejection results in activation of the pain-registering anterior cingulate cortex, the researchers also found that people who had relatively less activity in that area had more activity in the ventral lateral prefrontal cortices. These people also reported feeling relatively less distress as a result of participating in the game. These areas of the prefrontal cortex are associated with verbalizing thoughts and producing language. In general, higher prefrontal cortex activity is associated with lowered limbic activity. According to the researchers, this finding suggests that putting feelings into words may activate a part of the prefrontal cortex that suppresses the area of the brain that produces emotional distress.

In another study, Lieberman and his colleagues (2007) tested this language hypothesis more directly. They asked 30 participants to view pictures of angry, scared, or happy-looking faces. Half of the time the participants tried to match the target face to another picture of a face with a similar expression. The other half of the time they tried to match the face to a word that correctly labeled its emotion. Using fMRI, the researchers found that when the participants labeled the emotions using words, they showed less activity in the amygdala—the area of the brain associated with emotional distress. At the same time, they showed more activity in the ventral lateral prefrontal cortices—the same language-related areas that showed up in the cyberball study.

The links between perceived threat and reduced cognition have a deep relevance to coaching. We often make poor judgments about situations when our senses are impaired by fear. The coaching process can bring this often-unconscious process to the conscious mind, where it can be named and normalized. Calming the amygdala by naming the threat literally allows for more activity in the problem-solving portion of the brain. Simply asking the clients about their feelings before and after talking through a status threat can give them a firsthand understanding of this process.

Linking Emotion Regulation to Coaching

How do coaches help clients moderate responses so they do not interfere with coaching? Johnson (2006) asks a similar question about mentoring: "[H]ow can we assist learners in self-modulating the fears that originate in the limbic system? The key is in the space created by the mentor-learner relationship, spaces where the learner feels uniquely seen by the mentor, valued, and safe" (p. 66). In this quote, "learner" can be replaced by "client" and "mentor" by "coach." The importance of the coach-client relationship is recognized in coach training. Being uniquely seen and valued by the coach and feeling safe with her or him are prerequisites for coaching clients.

On one hand, going over and over the details of an incident we feel bad about only strengthens the neural pathways that connect the perception of the situation with our emotional response. One of us, David, illustrates this in workshops by asking participants to practice coaching with clients about the situational details of an issue with questions such as "Tell me more." He then asks participants to compare that experience with asking them to pay attention to their client's *attention*. Over and over, participants find that paying attention to attention produces more impact. This, however, does not mean colluding with a client who is *trying not* to attend to her or his emotional distress. Naming that emotion and engaging cognitive reappraisal can reduce the impact of negative emotions without triggering unhealthy effects of suppression.

Practice Guide for Coaching with the Brain in Mind — Keep Cool under Pressure

We began part IV by discussing the mechanistic bedrock of psychotherapy. As constructivist approaches and positive psychology went beyond that bedrock, psychotherapy has come along as well. Discoveries that psychotherapeutic techniques such as reframing can result in structural changes to the adult brain (Schwartz & Begley, 2002) have created great excitement in the psychotherapeutic community. Professional conferences feature brain-related themes; the theme for the 2008 Society for Psychotherapy Research Conference was "Neurobiological and Sociocultural Contexts of Psychotherapy and Psychotherapy Research." And books such as Louis Cozolino's *Neuroscience of Psychotherapy* (2002) and Norman Doidge's *Brain that Changes Itself* (2007) abound. In a sense, this should not come as a surprise. If psychotherapy is at all effective, how could it not produce long-term changes in our thinking processes? This is one similarity between psychotherapy and coaching.

A trend that lifts coaching above its problem-oriented bedrock is represented by positive psychology and other fields of research and application including resilience and emotional intelligence. Asking what makes people truly healthy and happy necessitates thinking about values and other unseen but important variables introduced by a systemic approach.

Emotions have been defined in many ways. They have been promoted as guides to happiness and avoided as barriers to rational action. We have proposed that they be seen as great summarizers, or an integration of brain, mind, and social factors that indicate one's current state of mind. Knowing oneself in this way, as we have repeated in this book, opens the door to consciously choosing methods for changing one's state of mind. Taking this conscious step over and over strengthens brain connections so that a desired state of mind becomes familiar and even automatic. It may even start to feel like one's real self.

Coaches can add these competencies to their ability to help clients potentiate, or become ever more like the self they wish to be:

Keeping the brain in mind means that coaches are able to:

- Shift attention to solutions rather than problems.
- Explain what is happening in the brain when, for example, it becomes difficult to maintain the "big picture" when experiencing stress.
- Reappraise, label, and name intense negative emotions and help others learn to do the same.
- Recognize without taking personally the automatic danger response when one's own or another's status is threatened.

In the short run, these methods enable coaches and leaders to maintain a cool head, or at least recover more quickly, in the face of threats and upheaval. What may be more important is the discovery that the brain cannot become a human brain without social input—that our brains are made for participation, as Leslie Brothers (2001) makes clear. That is, when we are able to regulate our emotions, we serve as an influence on the participating brains around us. Thus, in order to fully understand the mind that is emerging in this era, we must look more closely at the third leg on the stool of mental health: attuned relationships.

If we must take social interaction into account in understanding how people change, then the shift from a paradigm that assumes top-down mechanisms for directing groups of people to one that allows for more equal participation fits with the move toward both neuroscience and coaching. It is in the heart of "command-and-control" culture—modern organizations—that just such a shift is occurring. We turn now to an examination of management and organizational theory to explore that shift.

How Can We Get Along?

If we have the eyes to see, we quickly realize that nothing we eat, touch, wear, use, or travel in could exist without the coordinated input from millions of other people. But none of this happens on its own. People must *organize* to make these miracles happen. Part V is about our changing understanding of how we get along with one another in order to produce the lives we lead. And about how we could get along better to produce a life that we imagine is possible.

The scientific approach to managing groups of people at the turn of the 19th-to-20th century fit well with classical mechanics: analyze the elements of a job, divide it into small units, then assign workers to perform each unit over and over in order to maximize efficiency. In this assembly-line process, someone had to keep the big picture in mind and make sure that all the elements came together as a complete product in the end. Rather like a general on a battlefield, those in command had to control the overall production. The support of the populace for the military during World Wars I and II probably contributed to the acceptance of this command-and-control bedrock.

But as early as the 1940's, veins of democracy began to appear more widely and deeply in North American bedrock. Social psychologist Kurt Lewin compared the effects of democratic, authoritarian, and laissez-faire leadership (Lewin, 1947). Alfred Adler's student, psychiatrist Rudolf Dreikurs, taught democratic childrearing in the tenements of Chicago (Dreikurs & Soltz, 1964). Global spiritual traditions were being newly explored in philosophy. Cognitivism was redefining what could be called legitimate scientific inquiry in psychology. Humanism and constructivism were being promoted in psychotherapy. Unrest was brewing that would erupt in the anti-racist and anti-war movements in the late 1950's and 1960's.

To a great extent, the new ideas were simply modern expressions of old questions about human nature: Are people basically savages who need to be controlled and made to do what is right? Or are their basic good natures distorted by authoritarian demands, and they need to be free to express their potential? During the last half of the 20th century, command-and-control orthodoxy began to give way to trends that coalesced into what we call "coaching." What were considered heresies by management at mid-20th century are now coaching orthodoxy.

In part V, we touch on some important contributions to a shift from hierarchical management to participatory leadership. One of these contributions comes from research in social, cognitive, and affective neuroscience that indicates the extent to which our species is systemically interconnected.

CHAPTER 13

Bedrock — Management

The story is told in many forms in many cultures. In some versions, it represents the difference between heaven and hell. In others, it is a warning about greed and thinking only of oneself. It can also be seen as indicating the necessity for people to work together:

A traveler arrives in a strange land and, being hungry, follows the smell of something cooking. She is surprised to pass people on the path who seem to be on starvation's door. Emaciated and miserable, they reach out to her with withered hands and arms, but she has nothing to give them. She enters a great hall and there in the middle of the room is a huge cauldron full of delicious-looking stew, where the wonderful smells are coming from. But the only utensils available are spoons with handles too long for anyone to put the stew in their mouths. Although there is food aplenty, no one can eat. Seeing this misery, the traveler runs from the hall, determined to leave this land. But in the very next village, the same smell attracts her again. She is even hungrier now, so she risks taking the path to a hall that looks identical to the one she had just left. But there is no sign of starvation here. Cherry-cheeked people are strolling to and from the entrance. When the traveler enters the hall, she sees the same cauldron with the same delicious-looking stew and the same long-handled spoons. But there the similarity ends. In this hall, every person dips in a spoon and feeds the stew to a neighbor. The traveler takes her place feeding and being fed. Everyone has a part to play. No one goes hungry.

Considering those accomplishments of ancient civilizations that could have been achieved only by planning, coordinating, and allocating resources among groups of people (think Stonehenge, pyramids, Great Wall, or even hunting large beasts), management must have been practiced for a very long time. In this chapter, we show how current changes in organizations have led management theory to question assumptions of individualism and hierarchy; at the same time, the theory is only just beginning to provide systematic evidence to evaluate its approaches. Thus, although management theory may be seen as a prototypical application of the mechanistic paradigm, current organizational issues such as globalization and rapid change have forced it to pioneer some systemic-like approaches.

- How do managers separate what really works from what is supposed to work?
- If what really works is not generally approved of or is immoral or illegal, what is to be done?
- How do managers handle the need to appear trustworthy even when they must betray people's trust in order to carry out their responsibilities to the organization?
- How can short-term profit demands be balanced with long-term investment (human, resource, and infrastructure) demands?
- How can the self-interest of workers be reconciled with the self-interest of the organization?
- If these interests cannot be reconciled, how can the resulting conflict be dealt with?
- What works best for what purpose: command and control or flattened hierarchy?
- How can we predict what we cannot control and control what we cannot predict?
- What motivates good work?
- What are the characteristics of a healthy organization?

These questions and many others are dealt with every day by managers in both for-profit and not-for-profit organizations, not to mention political appointees and bureaucrats in government and governmental agencies.

HISTORICAL INTERLUDE

Technological advances some 10,000 years ago spurred the development of agriculture and the accumulation of its products. Surpluses needed management and tempted raids, and armies were organized both to expand territory and to guard against its loss. All of this required techniques of management, although those techniques usually were passed on informally according to inherited class or caste positions and not consciously taught or codified. One exception was *The Art of War* (1983) written by Chinese general Sun Tzu some 2,700 years ago, around the time of Confucius. Although widely studied in military circles over the ensuing centuries, the treatise is actually more a philosophical approach to conflict that, when successfully applied, actually avoids physical battles. Thus, it has extensive political and business applications.

The principle of using people's self-interest to gain advantage is often traced to the Italian Niccolò Machiavelli (1469–1527), whose guide to the acquisition and maintenance of power, *The Prince,* was published in 1531 after his death (Constantine, 2007). The adjective "Machiavellian" is used to represent an extreme of ruthless power seeking, but this view ignores the author's more subtle recognition that there are times when immoral actions may lead to common good whereas following common ideals of morality may lead to terrible consequences. Modern business management under capitalism faces many of the issues that Machiavelli dealt with in the early days of the Renaissance.

Management studies were elevated to an academic discipline in the early 20th century. It was in 1921 that the Harvard Business School began the first master's in business administration degree, although the Wharton School of the University of Pennsylvania had been teaching business courses since 1881 and Dartmouth College's Tuck School of Business had offered graduate-level training since 1900.

Thus, at the time when science was becoming the *sine qua non* of psychology, a similar trend was happening for management, especially in North America. Engineer Henry R. Towne (1884–1924) wrote an article called "Engineer as Economist" in 1886 and promoted the idea of bringing scientific principles from engineering into the organizational management arena.

(Continued)

In 1911 Frederick Taylor published a book that promoted four principles for designing processes for the workplace:

1. Processes should be based on the development of a true science.
2. The selection of workers should be guided by this science.
3. The education and development of workers should be guided by this science.
4. The science should be used to promote intimate and friendly cooperation between management and workers. (Taylor, 1964)

The application of the first three of these principles became known as scientific management. "Taylorism" has often been blamed for the hierarchical, command-and-control atmosphere in many companies that modern coaching methods seek to moderate. However, the fourth principle indicates that Taylor's stated intentions were to create conditions that were more fair to workers than, for example, arbitrary setting of quotas at the whim of management.

There is some controversy as to whether Taylor put his intentions into action or simply hid command-and-control intentions within more cooperative language (Stewart, 2006). "Scientific" in Taylor's terms, as with psychology in general, hid an underlying value assumption: The purpose of all the time measurement, efficiency studies, and standardization of tools and jobs was to increase production, to the benefit of management and owners. In practice, "intimate and friendly cooperation" has been promoted only when increased production was the outcome, but this fact is seldom publicly acknowledged in management circles.

Management consultant and philosopher Matthew Stewart (2006) targets Taylor in his scathing criticism of management theory: "Taylorism, like much of management theory to come, is at its core a collection of quasi-religious dicta on the virtue of being good at what you do, ensconced in a protective bubble of parables (otherwise known as case studies)" (p. 3).

Scientific management was presumed to be value-free because of its use of quantitative measurement. However, as Stewart points out, Taylor did not publish the results of his measurements so that others could replicate or disprove them. His claims of scientific legitimacy substituted for actual scientific method. Nonetheless, Taylor's success—as measured by influence rather than scientific legitimacy—is evidenced by the fact that

Japanese businessman Yoichi Ueno introduced Taylorism to Japan in 1912. The "Japanese management style" evolved into "quality assurance," which was brought back to North America in the 1970s by Ueno's son, Ichiro Ueno.

Aside from any unacknowledged value position, is it true that productivity is a matter of analyzing time and motions and creating efficient conditions, processes, and consequences? Elton Mayo was part of a team of researchers that attempted to show a relationship between worker morale and productivity. From 1927 to 1932, they took behaviorist assumptions out of the laboratory and did a series of experiments, called the Hawthorne Studies, at Western Electric's Plant in Chicago, Illinois.

Researchers installed improved lighting in a small test room and brought in a randomly selected group of workers to do their jobs under observation. As expected, productivity improved. Surely, the researchers assumed, this was because of the improved lighting. Thus, they expected that productivity would not improve for the other group of workers, also randomly selected, who were working under less than optimal lighting conditions. But no, productivity improved for this control group, too. What was going on?

Eventually, the researchers concluded that the cohesion created when the small groups of workers were separated out and treated as special was what accounted for the productivity increases — not objective factors such as lighting or number of breaks or comfortable seating.

Bolstered by these results, Mayo published a book in 1933 that pointed to the relationship between boss and worker as the key to business success. He promoted the "nondirective interview" as a means for providing an opportunity for employees to "talk through" any workplace issues they might have. Thus, the human relations school of management was born just at a time when economic hardship created a move to bring humanity into the previously "scientized" North American industrial world. The nondirective interview has more than a passing similarity to coaching, which shows that its roots in management theory go back to the early part of the 20th century. Grant (2003) found the first reference to coaching, as defined in this book, in an article by C. B. Gorby published in 1937.

(Continued)

Discoveries in occupational mental health further supported trends toward relationships more in line with Mayo's studies. In 1919 Elmer E. Southard (1876–1920), a psychiatrist and professor at Harvard University, interviewed 4,000 workers who had been fired from their jobs. He concluded that 60% lost their jobs because of "social incompetence" rather than difficulties with the work itself. This observation was taken up many years later in research summarized by Daniel Goleman in *Emotional Intelligence* (1996). Many coaches rely on Goleman's work, and on the development of emotional intelligence assessments, to guide their coaching in the workplace.

Management theory has to do with how to organize the work that people do. Although the focus of much of management education is on financial and physical resource measurement and control, ultimately organizations are about people. As one textbook (Johns & Saks, 2005) puts it, "Organizations are social inventions for accomplishing common goals through group effort" (p. 6). Therefore, our survey of management and organizational theory and their relationship to coaching includes industrial/organizational psychology and social psychology.

In chapter 12, we discussed the importance of research in establishing a scientific base for psychotherapy. Because it is an applied field, psychotherapy research has had to be concerned not only about doing good science but also about whether its techniques actually can be put into practice in the real world. Management theory faces similar challenges and opportunities in overcoming its come-and-go fad reputation. The statistical method of meta-analysis can help managers develop a systems perspective and a way of thinking about complex change that characterizes *leadership* rather than just management.

We discuss these topics in this chapter:

- Management theory
- Industrial/organizational psychology
- Social psychology
- Meta-analysis
- Management as bedrock for coaching

Management Theory

A master's degree in business administration—an MBA—typically indicates education for management. The standard curriculum focuses on financial and physical resource management and control, relating back to the principles of scientific management from the beginning of the 20th century:

Concern with actually making products or providing services is closest to Taylor's scientific management approach. Organizations want to measure and improve the amount that can be produced, its scheduling, the reduction of inventory, product or service quality, and efficiency of operations. This reflects what Douglas McGregor (1960) renamed Theory X, meaning a pessimistic assumption about human nature that resulted in the need for top-down control, punishment, and rewards. But subsequent organizational theorists, such as Elton Mayo, proposed adding to Taylor's "hard data" time-and-motion studies the "softer" side of human motivation, which McGregor dubbed Theory Y, or the assumption that people are self-motivated and willing to take responsibility for improving productivity. MBA students learn techniques that reflect both "hard" and "soft" approaches. The material presented next draws on Steven Silbiger's *The Ten Day MBA* (1999), a summary of the curriculum of major business schools in the United States.

"Hard" Side of Management

ACCOUNTING   Organizations communicate within and without in the language of hard numbers. Accounting is the function that gathers, organizes, evaluates, stores, and compares numbers that measure what it owns, what it owes, how its operations perform, and where it will obtain the cash to keep operating. Financial statements are the outcome of the accounting function, and management uses them to get a snapshot of what it and its owners have accumulated versus what it owes (balance sheet), of what it has earned and spent over a specified period (income statement), and when it receives money versus when it has had to spend it (statement of cash flows).

QUANTITATIVE ANALYSIS   Organizations need to measure whether one option is likely to be more profitable than another (decision tree analysis), how much cash is needed and will be generated by current operations and future investments (cash flow analysis), what the current value is of different future investments (net present value analysis), and how variables relate to one another (regression analysis). MBA students learn the basics of probability theory and statistics in order to apply these techniques to questions of how the organization should invest its resources in order to optimize its success.

FINANCE   How should an organization be structured, given the purposes of its founders or owners? (profit? charity? service? public shares?) How should it invest, given various goals, risk, and tax considerations? These are questions answered by people trained in finance. The numbers provided by accountants and quantitative analysts are the basis for a financial manager's recommendations concerning business investment decisions.

ECONOMICS   Although economics shares a numbers focus with the hard topics listed above, predicting details of global boom-and-bust cycles (macroeconomics) is a far cry from the certainty of careful accounting. On a smaller scale, microeconomics helps organizations decide whether to act when output, time, and money are limited (opportunity cost), whether to add capacity (marginal revenue and cost), at what point customer demand is satiated (marginal utility), whether reducing or increasing price will affect sales (price elasticity), and the effects of different competitive market structures.

"Soft" Side of Management

MARKETING   At a fundraising dinner, Linda sat next to a marketing executive at a major U.S. bank. When asked how she saw her job, the executive did not skip a beat: "Marketing is about everything our business does," she said. "Absolutely everything has to do with marketing." Although successful marketing has a great deal to do with numbers, like the hard topics just listed, we include it in the "soft" section here because it draws on high-level strategy and creativity as well as on understanding of human motivation and relationships. Marketing depends on developing a plan using a circular process: Analysis of consumer and context, of competitors and one's own organization, of how the product will be delivered, of the mix of advertising and public relations methods, and of the economic situation. This analysis is performed and then reperformed until all the elements fit together and support one another.

ETHICS   This topic is a much more recent addition to business education curriculum. It is not so much a matter of teaching what is "right," although managers need to know the measures that have been and are being legislated to curb unethical business practices. Ethics education has more to do with raising awareness of the dilemmas that face organizations of all kinds. For example, in Canada, boards of directors are charged with the duty to further the interests of the corporation. Shareholders commonly assumed that this means furthering their interests; however, what if a proposed merger will dilute shareholder equity in the short run? Shareholders who need to sell shares immediately would not see the merger as being in their best interests. Arguments about whether organizations have a responsibility to stakeholders beyond immediate owners, employees, and customers have arisen as environmental concerns mount. Students in business ethics classes learn to perform a stakeholder analysis, listing the harms and benefits, rights and responsibilities of anyone potentially affected by a particular action. But after all these considerations, weighing the different interests becomes a matter of soft judgment.

STRATEGY   Strategy is comprised of all the knowledge and skills, hard as well as soft, that are required to develop strategic plans for organizations. The Seven S Model of McKenzie Consulting (Peters & Waterman, 1982) prescribes a way for examining an organization as a whole so as to determine whether it could use a complete overhaul (reengineering) or minor adjustments. The Seven Ss include:

1. *Structure*. Is the company organized along customer or geographic or product lines?
2. *Systems*. What are the procedures, both formal and informal, for carrying out the functions of the organization?

3. *Style.* Closely related to *culture*, is the organization slow-moving and conservative or quick-to-act and innovative?

4. *Staff.* How are employees hired, trained, retained, appreciated, motivated, appraised? Many a change initiative has failed because the *people* on whom it depends were not motivated to cooperate. This often-forgotten element is where business coaching can bring the greatest benefit.

5. *Skills.* There are basic skills, such as whether an employee speaks the language of customers, knows how to enter figures into the bookkeeping system, or can repair the machines in the factory. Added to these are the soft skills of relationship management and teamwork that are also the special targets of coaching.

6. *Superordinate goals/values.* It is invaluable for an organization to have an executive who can define, communicate, and hold steady to goals that reflect its values. This is another area where executive coaches can be helpful. Carefully defined goals enable an organization to plot a course and know when it has arrived. Values serve as a template for decision making every step of the way.

7. *Strategy.* In responding to or anticipating changes, especially external ones, an organization has a number of options. It can:

   • Redefine its product line or the business it is in.

   • Decide how to expand, either by increasing its share in old markets or penetrating new ones with either product diversification or new products altogether.

   • Take a new look at the competition's similar products, at new entrants, at supplier or buyer changes, or at the intensity of rivalry (Porter, 1980).

   • Enhance its competitiveness by differentiation, by having the lowest price or highest productivity, or by focusing on a particular niche.

   • Ward off the dangers of business cycles by balancing its portfolio with businesses or product lines that cancel one another's vulnerability.

ORGANIZATIONAL BEHAVIOR   Whatever numbers are generated by hard data analysis, the consequences must be communicated and decisions made and executed in the real world of people and their relationships.

Industrial/organizational psychology and social psychology are two sub-disciplines of psychology that have contributed greatly to the bedrock of coaching that is management theory. We examine these subdisciplines later in this chapter.

Linking Management to Coaching

Organizational coaches are often called on when solutions to problems based on hard analysis are undermined because soft considerations, such as ethical dilemmas, style, human relationship skills, individual and group diversity, and values, have been ignored. In these cases, coaches may believe that it is their coaching skills that count and they do not need to have knowledge of the particular issues or general business in which they are asked to coach. They are, after all, not hired as consultants who are assumed to have specific business expertise. However, successful executive and organizational coaches often say that their familiarity with a specific industry may get them the job, even though *as coaches* they do not give advice or apply their knowledge as a consultant would. Certainly a familiarity with the language and ways of thinking of managers will smooth communication.

INDUSTRIAL/ORGANIZATIONAL PSYCHOLOGY

This subdiscipline of psychology studies human behavior in the workplace and applies psychological findings to understanding and improving relationships in industry, business, and organizations in general. Many human resources employees, trainers, career and outplacement counselors, and independent organizational consultants have been trained as industrial/organizational (I/O) psychologists. Therefore, trends in psychology and in related fields such as psychotherapy and counseling have influenced organizational theory and practice.

For example, after World War II, interest in egalitarianism and democracy aided the emergence of "third wave" humanistic psychotherapy, as discussed in chapter 10, which also influenced management theory and eventually coaching. Much of this influence was expressed in the popular self-help movement and in trends such as quality circles. Stewart (2006) does not see these trends as entirely benign:

> Each new fad calls attention to one virtue or another—first it's efficiency, then quality, next it's customer satisfaction, then supplier satisfaction, then self-satisfaction, and finally, at some point, it's efficiency all over again. If it's reminiscent of the kind of toothless wisdom offered in self-help literature, that's because management theory is mostly a subgenre of self-help. (p. 3)

In response to this criticism, it should be pointed out that management theory has also depended on I/O psychologists for assessments that are used extensively in hiring, placing, and developing personnel. The process of analyzing a position, devising a job description, and helping to match potential employees is an important part of I/O training. Several widely used career, personality, emotional intelligence, ability, and performance measures, among others, were devised in order to help organizations manage human resources.

I/O psychology has also not been immune from other critics who took aim at unexamined assumptions in psychology following the liberation movements of the 1960s. As Prilleltensky (1994) stated, this belief was common in most of 20th-century psychology: "Inequality, power, discrimination, and the like are the result not of injustice but of lack of scientific progress" (p. 141). However, power itself is a topic of research in I/O psychology, although it is seldom accompanied by the type of self-examination that Prilleltensky promoted. Different types of power have been identified:

- Coercive, based on fear
- Reward, based on the expectation of receiving praise, recognition, or income
- Referent, derived from being well respected, whatever one's formal position
- Legitimate, indicating the formal status one holds in an organizational hierarchy
- Expert, coming from one's own skill, knowledge, or experience

Leadership theory is a related field that has gained importance in I/O and management circles in the late 20th and early 21st centuries and shows promise of overcoming the hierarchical assumptions. When every member of an organization—or, indeed, anyone in any walk of life—is encouraged to exhibit qualities of leadership, this can be seen as the development of referent power, unrelated to a formal position, and fits with a participatory rather than a command-and-control mentality.

Linking I/O Psychology to Coaching

I/O psychology may be seen as overlapping extensively with organizational development and management theory. Nascent I/O activities at the beginning of the 20th century relied on the predominant scientific worldview that prescribed value-free objectivity and behavioral measurement. Research within the field, as well as social trends outside it, shifted the emphasis to taking into account the subjective, nonobservable motivations of both workers and managers. Links to coaching are extensive:

- Sometimes what cannot be observed (e.g., group cohesion) is more important than what can be observed (e.g., quality of lighting).
- Desires, goals, solutions, or even the root of a problem may be seen very differently according to one's perspective.
- Eliciting and respecting different perspectives may be the most important step in improving performance.
- When individuals in an organization achieve goal congruence, performance and productivity improve.
- The primacy of productivity or profit remains a largely unexamined assumption of I/O psychology and the management theory it supports, as is true also for organizational coaching.
- Worldwide gaps in wealth distribution and ecological crises present an opportunity for both I/O psychologists and coaches to think carefully about the distribution of power and the purpose of our activities.

SOCIAL PSYCHOLOGY

We have claimed that North American emphasis on individualism was a limitation that showed itself in psychology, the "'master' science of human affairs," as Prilleltensky (1994, p. 28) called it. It would seem reasonable for social psychology to have been an exception to this limitation. However, with a few notable exceptions, this subdiscipline of psychology did not take the "social" part of its name seriously until late in the 20th century. A 1999 article on early social psychology in the prestigious *APA Monitor Online* stated:

> Psychologists . . . continued to emphasize the individual in society rather than the structure of society itself, which was largely left to sociologists. This approach fit well with American individualism and the increasingly behaviorist definition and interpretation of psychological phenomenon [*sic*].

HISTORICAL INTERLUDE

In Europe, sociologists theorized about the influence of society on suicide (Emile Durkheim, 1858–1917), the behavior of crowds in contrast to that of the individual (Gustave LeBon, 1841–1931), and the existence of a herd instinct (Wilfred Trotter, 1872–1939). William McDougall (almost two decades before his "Battle of Behaviorism" with behaviorist James Watson) published a book entitled *Social Psychology* in 1908, but the book and the field did not garner much interest until one of its applications proved enormously useful in the lead-up to World War I.

When the United States entered the war in 1918, the government faced a difficult problem. Woodrow Wilson had been reelected president on a peace platform. How could public opinion be shifted from supporting a peace candidate to supporting his leading the nation into war? Edward Bernays (1891–1995), a nephew of Sigmund Freud, was influenced both by his uncle's theories about people's uncivilized unconscious core and by European theorists such as LeBon who proposed that groups have enormous impact on attitudes and actions of their members.

As an employee of the U.S. War Ministry, Bernays and his colleagues crafted a program of "Four-Minute Men." In cities and towns all over the United States, men who held positions of influence in their communities were recruited and trained to give short (four-minute) speeches about the reasons for fighting the war in Europe. They then were directed

---

to "spontaneously" stand up in the audience at theaters, at social engage-
ments, at local business meetings—wherever people gathered—to promote
the government's war agenda. Even young boys, presumably seen as future
business and community leaders, were trained as "Junior Four-Minute
Men" to do their part in exhorting their schoolmates, and presumably their
parents, to support the war.

The success of this effort to apply psychological principles to everyday
life propelled Bernays into a career in public relations, where he established
many of the principles still practiced today. It also set the stage for widespread acceptance of the new subdiscipline of social psychology.

In 1924 Floyd Allport (1890–1978) published *Social Psychology*, a book
with the same name as McDougall's previous publication. It was Allport's
book that sent social psychologists, as distinct from sociologists, into the
laboratory to experiment with how individuals were affected by social situations. Research exploded in the late 1920s, further supported in the 1930s
by Gardner Murphy's *Experimental Social Psychology* and Carl Murchison's
Handbook of Social Psychology textbooks. In the years since, university students
in the millions have participated as "subjects" in thousands of experiments as
varied as human imagination itself. However varied, most such experiments
shared the assumptions of objectivity, skepticism about good intentions and
the necessity to keep the nature of the experiment from subjects in order
to prevent expectations from affecting results, as well as the focus on the
individual.

However, as evidence accumulated, its subject matter influenced the
field of social psychology to participate in the shift to a less individualistic approach. Many of the topics investigated by social psychologists
have relevance to coaching, which is, after all, a social relationship with
the goal of promoting change.

Influence and Persuasion

How social situations change people's behavior and beliefs has long been
a topic in social psychology. For example, social psychologist and marketing professor Robert Cialdini was interested in influence and persuasion.

He was dissatisfied with social psychology experiments because their results were difficult to apply outside the laboratory. So he studied successful salespeople and engaged in sales training and sales programs himself to see firsthand what worked.

The "evidence" Cialdini collected was not the same as that of his colleagues who conducted more traditional laboratory experiments: He assumed that if salespeople were making a living, they must be doing something effective. He set about to describe what that was and identified six principles that he called "weapons of persuasion" (Cialdini, 1984, 2007). Not only have these "weapons been verified time and again as the explanations for why persuasion works, but Cialdini's research methods brought hands-on, participatory research more into the mainstream of scientific inquiry. Here are the weapons Cialdini described:

- *Reciprocation*. Anthropologists consider reciprocity to be a universal social norm. Free samples trigger this "should." If you do something nice for me, I should return the favor.
- *Commitment and consistency*. According to Leon Festinger's (1957) theory of cognitive dissonance, people are reluctant to behave in ways that are inconsistent with their public commitments. This principle is applied to management when employees are asked to agree in writing to a development plan after a performance review.
- *Social proof*. If we see other people, many other people, doing something, we are more likely to do it. Stores that have midnight sales count on crowds to influence increased sales.
- *Authority*. If someone we recognize as being in a position of authority tells us to do something, we are more likely to do it. An actor in a lab coat will sell more aspirin than a physician in a sweatsuit.
- *Liking*. People we like are more likely to be able to persuade us. Cialdini cites Tupperware parties as examples of this principle.
- *Scarcity*. When we perceive that something is scarce, we are more likely to purchase it so as not to lose the opportunity. Limiting quantities and times for sales trigger this response.

Other Topics Relevant to Coaching

Many of the next topics overlap with cognitive psychology and have increasing relevance to neuroscience.

SELF-FULFILLING PROPHECY There may be no more important social psychology concept for coaches than the idea that our expectations evoke behavior in others that end up confirming our expectations. Most of us are familiar with the "Pygmalion" experiments that showed students getting better grades when their teachers were told they were high-potential learners (Rosenthal, 1991). However, as Rosenthal makes clear, expectations alone cannot magically turn reality on its head. Expectations seem to have the greatest effect on low achievers who may not have experienced the encouragement and attention that accompany belief in their potential.

ATTITUDES From measuring an individual's attitudes on people, events, behavior, and even attitudes themselves, the extent of social influence became obvious, emphasizing the importance of social context. People tend to believe what people who are important to them believe. Even when the others in a group are strangers, the tendency to conform to a unanimous opinion by others is very strong (Asch, 1955).

GROUP PROCESSES Kurt Lewin (1975) compared the output of groups of boys who were led by authoritarian, laissez-faire, or democratic leaders. The authoritarian group accomplished more than the laissez-faire group, but only when they were being supervised. Not surprisingly the laissez-faire group accomplished little, but, contrary to the expectation that boys resent any guidance at all, their group had lower morale than the democratic group, which accomplished more even when they were unsupervised.

In the Robber's Cave Experiment, Muzafer Sherif and colleagues (1961) manipulated relationships between groups of boys at a summer camp to produce competition and conflict and then cooperation.

These experiments illustrated the importance of social context and stimulated hundreds of subsequent studies on the conditions that result in conflict or cooperation within and between groups.

SELF-INTEREST AND ALTRUISM In contrast to the typical social psychological view that helping behavior is always an expression of self-interest,

Dan Batson (1991) designed ingenious experiments to show that, when people feel empathy, they may be motivated to act in the interest of another person without regard to their own benefit.

SOCIAL LEARNING   Studies of the role of social interaction in learning helped to displace Freudian psychoanalytic theory (Dollard & Miller, 1950) and behaviorist assumptions (Bandura, 1977). Observational studies of social interaction (Goffman, 1959) and sociolinguistics (Labov, 1966) provided multidisciplinary evidence for contextual and systems thinking.

SELF-PERCEPTION   As social context has come more into focus over the last half of the 20th century, the role that our relationships play in our self-identity, self-esteem, and self-image has become an important topic, bridging social psychology, psychopathology and developmental psychology (attachment studies), and neuroscience, particularly Siegel's "interpersonal neurobiology" (1999). This integration has culminated in the 21st-century development of the field of social neuroscience.

SOCIAL COGNITION   This new field has morphed into social cognitive neuroscience, representing an integration of social and cognitive psychology with brain research. Leon Festinger's (1957) proposal of cognitive dissonance is an early attempt to explain people's resistance to new information that conflicts with existing beliefs or attitudes or knowledge. Controversial experiments such as Stanley Milgram's (1974) research on obedience in the 1960s and Philip Zimbardo's (2007) prison experiment at Stanford in 1971 changed both people's ideas about the strength of social influence and ethical limits in research.

In 1986 Bandura published *Social Foundations of Thought and Action* in which he proposed that people are proactive, self-reflective, and self-organizing rather than driven by inner impulses or shaped by external environmental forces. His views accelerated the integration of social psychology, cognitive psychology, and neuroscience with adult learning, thus contributing to the shift from a mechanistic to a systemic worldview.

Kurt Lewin's (1947, 1999) work with groups was one base for sensitivity and human relations training, the T-group movement of the 1960s, and eventually some of the applications that led to coaching.

Social Psychologist as Myth Buster

The most important contribution of social psychology to coaching may be its skeptical attitude. Social psychologists might be considered the "myth busters" of psychology. Some of the common beliefs that social psychologists have challenged include:

- *The validity of hindsight.* After we discover what happened, people have the tendency to believe they "knew it all along" or that others should have been able to predict it. Actually sorting through causes and predicting results ahead of time is much more difficult to do.
- *Modesty.* People are more likely to attribute their success to others when they describe their accomplishments publicly rather than in private, thus bringing into question the truth of their modesty.
- *Taking credit.* Most of us are likely to overestimate our contributions to socially desirable outcomes—that is, we all have the tendency see ourselves as above average.
- *The value of positive thinking.* Both anecdotal and experimental evidence indicates that believing in ourselves and our ability to accomplish what we want to do can help us avoid resignation and persist toward our goals. However, the hidden danger is that when failure or disappointment comes, we have only ourselves to blame.
- *Attribution.* Although there are some cultural differences, we place responsibility for behavior on people's internal personality or disposition more often than is warranted. We tend to underestimate the influence of the situation or circumstances. Attribution is also related to whether we tend to assume that we can control events in our lives (internal control) or whether we believe others do (external control).
- *How we draw conclusions.* Our preconceptions often guide how we perceive and interpret information. We ignore information about what is most common, are more swayed by memorable events than by facts, are fooled by the illusion of correlation (if B happens after A happens, then A must cause B), and believe that chance events are somehow under our control (see Nisbett & Ross, 1989).

Linking Social Psychology to Coaching

Social psychologists have promoted more careful thought about these and other topics because of their attitude of questioning everything accepted as "common sense." It may be difficult for coaches to adopt this attitude, as they are exhorted to believe in their clients' potential even when the clients do not. But in order to help clients reach that potential, coaches need to be conscious of when to ask probing, difficult questions and when to display no doubts.

In summary, early social psychologists were concerned mainly with the effects of social groups and society on the individual, in keeping with the individualism of the mechanistic worldview.

- Techniques of public relations and propaganda were developed during this era. More recent research on influence updates these approaches.
- Shifts toward contextual, interactive, dialectic assumptions accompanied the proliferation of social psychological research into a variety of topics, such as attitude, learning, obedience, and self-perception.
- The integration of developmental and cognitive psychology with social psychology combined with neuroscience to stimulate a new field of research in the 21st century: social cognitive and affective neuroscience.
- Social psychology's skeptical attitude has yielded many discoveries that broaden our understanding of ourselves. Coaches may find the attitude contrary to that which often is promoted in coaching, but it may be useful as one of a coach's tools when an honest, rigorous assessment is demanded.
- Studies comparing brain activity when leaders are engaged in various tasks are also taking management and leadership theory into the neuroscience realm.

META-ANALYSIS

Parts of this section might just as easily fit into the Psychometrics section of chapter 7 or the Research section of chapter 10. We have included it here partly because of the emphasis on metrics in management theory, but also to indicate the importance of a "meta-" approach to organizational change.

A key aspect of systems theory and its linkage to coaching is the concept of working with clients to help them see the patterns in the systems in which they are living. This requires taking a "meta-view," *meta* being based on a Greek word for "across" or "over." By taking a meta-view of the various systems, a client increases awareness and knowledge of patterns, and gains the ability to choose how to influence and/or change those patterns in the future.

Clarity of Distance

In his book *Quiet Leadership* (2006), David Rock coined the term "the clarity of distance" to mean the ability we have to see situations more clearly when we are not close to them. David describes our tendency to get too close to the details, or be preoccupied with an agenda, or have an emotional connection to an issue, that results in blocking out information. This often leads to the inability to see important high-level elements of a situation—in other words, to take a meta-perspective.

In the coaching relationship, the coach plays the role of agenda-free observer who can offer clarity of distance to clients by feeding back to them what the coach is seeing.

The systemic perspective questions the positivistic assumption that an observer actually can be separate from whatever event is being observed. However, this does not mean that we should give up on achieving a useful perspective on what is going on, one that takes advantage of clarity of distance. Rather than rejecting all observations as flawed, scientific inquiry in a systemic paradigm requires, first, that observations be gathered from as many different perspectives as possible. This is the kernel of 360-degree assessments. An observer who is at some distance from the event can provide unique feedback.

An additional requirement for usefulness is transparency—that any agendas or interests or emotional connections be acknowledged.

Meta-analysis

Meta-analysis is a statistical approach to achieving a meta-view. Meta-analysts translate results from different studies to a common metric and attempt to draw general conclusions. The first meta-analysis was performed by the eminent statistician Karl Pearson (1857–1936) in 1904. Meta-analysis is used in statistics, epidemiology, and evidence-based medicine.

The scientific method involves a series of individual experiments or groups of experiments that produce results reported in the scientific literature. One experiment, either successful or not, is not considered conclusive. Only when the conclusions have been verified repeatedly, perhaps with variations that test alternative explanations, are they generally accepted as valid. Over time, research studies accumulate on a particular topic, for example, the effects on heart attacks of taking aspirin. Some studies show the effects of higher doses, some of lower doses, some with people who have already had heart attacks, some with younger people, some with older, and so forth. Some show no effect at all. How does one get a picture of what all this means so that doctors know what to recommend to their patients? Systematic summarizing of highly variant data is exactly what meta-analysis was designed to do. Meta-analytic researchers take great care to find all the relevant studies, assess each study for the quality of its design and execution, and combine the findings from individual studies in an unbiased manner. In this way, they aim to present a balanced and impartial summary of the existing research evidence.

Overview Effect

The "overview effect" is a term coined by book author Frank White in 1998 in his book of the same name. It is the examination of the impact on human society of actually being able to see the whole planet Earth from space. According to White, this global visualization has had a macro-impact on culture, economics, politics, and social fabric in general over the past half century. Although it may not be readily recognized or acknowledged in day-to-day human activity, the overview effect of the space age is real even at the micro-scale of music, publications, communications, and mental comprehension. This effect is compounded by increasing availability of information and images through the Internet.

White (1998) suggested that every step beyond a known realm provides an overview of that realm and yields deeper insight into how it fits into the greater picture. Children leave the womb, their schools, their families, their hometowns, and often their countries and continents. Each of these moves permits an overview that includes the past, more limited, perspective. Each new perspective permits greater understanding and the chance to alter actions based on these new experiences and insights, perhaps even to become a transforming element in the new context.

Our ability to see a paradigm relies on our moving beyond it to a new paradigm. We cannot see the shape of a cloud when we are flying through it. As we get farther away, its outline becomes more visible. From the perspective of the new, systemic worldview, we can see the shape of the mechanistic paradigm more easily than we could when it was more predominant, when we were more "in" it.

Based on interviews with and writings by 29 astronauts and cosmonauts, White (1998) shows how experiences such as circling Earth every 90 minutes and viewing it from the moon have profoundly affected space travelers' perceptions of themselves, their world, and the future. One astronaut stated, "I guess it's a bit like being a savage from the rain forest, suddenly stuck into Notre Dame." After six space walks, the astronaut described the experience of viewing the planet from outside the shuttle. "You're in the environment, as opposed to looking at [it] through a window, which is like watching it on TV," he says. "It's not like looking at the fish—you're swimming with the fish."

Linking Meta-View to Coaching

We are not proposing that coaches become meta-analytic researchers, although it is our hope that coaching research soon will be producing enough data to justify and even require such statistical methods. Our point here is that coaches can learn from the concept of meta-analysis the ability to shift levels of generality in order to perceive patterns when they are coaching.

How taking a meta-view relates to coaching is illustrated by looking at a client's view of his or her "ideal self." We have discussed the concept of "strange attractors" in chaos theory or points in a person's life that seem to be anchors for patterns. One's "ideal self" is one of these anchors.

Example: From "Overempowering"
to "Building Collaboration"

Ken works in human resources for a multinational food products company. He came to coaching because a recent performance review revealed his difficulty with delegating. He describes his problem as "overempowering" his direct reports. He assigns them duties and is surprised when they do not accomplish what they are directed to do. This conceptualization locates the "problem" as a weakness inside Ken. The only pattern he is aware of is what is not working for him.

Coaching helped Ken take a more systemic and strengths-oriented perspective. He investigated both his internal values, as represented by his "ideal self"—a leader who invites people to do their best—and external factors. He discovered that his internal pattern of trusting people to motivate themselves coincided with the company's desire to build collaborative teams.

When the "problem" of overempowering was recast in this meta-view or systemic framework, Ken began to ask how he could effectively empower his team rather than how to fix his flawed self. That is, he began to appreciate and operate from his "ideal self" image in support of the company's ideals. He realized that he could not answer this question in isolation and began to inquire and listen to his supervisees. Not only did this provide him with information for building a team (information about supervisee patterns), the activity itself was also team building. The resulting improved relationships enabled Ken to discuss more fully the requirements for completing a task and made it more likely that the supervisees would come to him when they were not sure of what they were doing.

This is an example of how the coaching process can assist clients to take a much broader perspective, including all of the internal and external patterns that are present in the system. By completing an informal meta-analysis in this way, the client has a new perspective and a much more reliable foundation on which to make future decisions.

To the extent that coaches self-manage their own agendas, they can contribute an overview that provides clarity of distance. This enhances the client's ability to take a meta-view. As the coaching conversation unfolds, the coach can see patterns that are revealed across different areas of a client's life. With clarity of distance, the coach can make connections that the client is too close to see. In this way, coaching assists clients to create meaning and draw overarching conclusions, thus completing their informal meta-analysis.

MANAGEMENT AS BEDROCK FOR COACHING

As the long-handled spoon story at the beginning of this chapter illustrates, people have to work together in order to survive. How to organize that work is the question. We have seen in this chapter that management theory, beginning as it did with a very "hard" analysis of time-and-motion studies, has evolved toward a more contextual and systemic view. The early human relations strand in management theory has received greater attention during the past few decades as the importance of the human side of organizations has become more recognized. Both coaching and management theory have been criticized for lacking systematic self-examination and the willingness to hold themselves accountable through rigorous evaluative research. We look forward to the day when meta-analyses will generate evidence regarding which organizational coaching and development procedures work and how.

As we shall see in chapter 14, research and applications regarding positive organizations, psychological capital, and human capital in general complement individual coaching in transforming hierarchical authority into participatory leadership. This is why coaching, with its genesis in contextual and community aspects of systemic thinking, will undoubtedly continue to serve as a means to promote positive change in organizations.

CHAPTER 14

Pillar — Leadership

A folktale called "Stone Soup" has been told in many versions in Europe and North America, including ones by the Brothers Grimm, by storytellers from Scandinavia, Eastern Europe, France, Portugal, and England, and by children's authors and even cartoon characters such as Donald Duck.

A hungry traveler arrives in an impoverished village and knocks on the door of one ramshackle house.

"I have nothing to feed you," says the old woman who answers the door. "See?" She motions toward the pot sitting empty in the front yard.

"No problem," says the traveler in a much happier tone than would seem to fit the circumstances. "I have a special stone here." He pulls a rock about the size of his palm from his pocket. "With this stone, we can make enough soup to feed ourselves and the whole village!"

Despite worrying that the traveler was a bit daft, the woman decided she had nothing to lose in humoring him. They put the stone carefully into the big pot, put the pot on the fire, and started filling it with water. A neighbor came out to investigate.

"What are you doing?"

"We are making the most wonderful soup you have ever tasted," said the traveler. "You're welcome to have some."

"But it's just a stone and water."

"Oh, it won't be ready until we put in some seasoning."

The neighbor thought for a moment. "I've got some salt and pepper in my picnic basket," and went to retrieve them. While he was gone, the neighbor on the other side brought over a chicken carcass that she was going to throw out because she had nothing to put with it to make soup.

"Might as well put it in with the stone," she said as she tossed it into the pot. People passing by remembered a sprig of dried basil or a lone onion or some wilted cabbage leaves or a few grains or beans they had at home, none of which was enough for a meal on its own. But added to the soup pot, they began to look like quite a feast. The delicious smell attracted more villagers and more small contributions.

The villagers were happily enjoying their meal when Aloo, a mechanic who knew nothing about cooking, exclaimed, "There's a big stone in my soup!"

"That's the special stone that the traveler brought to start the soup," explained the old woman. "It's easy—even you could do it, Aloo."

"Well, then," said Aloo, patting his full belly, "I think I will. Everyone's welcome to come to my house tomorrow for stone soup."

Like the long-handled spoon story, this tale advocates collaboration. But it also illustrates the concept of leadership. Management theory can be criticized for lacking scientific methodology, but it can claim the virtue of having to apply its theories in the real world. Thus, because of its dependence on groups of people working together, it could not get away with extreme assumptions of individualism. Charts and financial statements and analysis of data have been shown over and over to miss the human element. Furthermore, evidence has accumulated that command-and-control hierarchies are less productive than organizations that invite engagement and participation. But taking advantage of this fact requires leadership rather than authoritarian rule.

Almost daily, modern organizations also face unpredictable changes that yield only to systemic thinking. As coaches, we often work with leaders who want to influence the interactions of a complex system, whether in the workplace, family, or social circles. Our focus here is on the shift from management to leadership in complex organizations, but these principles and suggestions can be applied to influencing complex systems in general.

It is easy to get lost in the details of a situation and not step back and take a meta-perspective in order to grasp underlying dynamics and patterns. Peter Senge (1990) says, "The real leverage in most management situations lies in understanding dynamic complexity, not detail complexity. . . . Starting with detail complexity rather than taking a systems approach often ends up with 'fighting complexity with complexity'" (p. 72). Managers need to look at the whole system over time and see the underlying relationships in order to gain insight that enables them to lead, not just to manage. So managers have had to go beyond organizing the resources and systems that exist. They have had to become leaders.

- What are the differences between managing and leading?
- If leaders are not supposed to tell people what to do, how can they be effective?
- At what level in an organization do managers become leaders?
- Are people leaders if others do not follow them?
- What is the ideal relationship between leaders and followers?
- Can everyone be a leader?
- What is the relationship between systems thinking and leadership?

The shift to leadership did not happen overnight but rather was the result of a series of attempts to overcome hierarchical, command-and-control structures that today still are entrenched holdovers of Taylorism. Art Kleiner (2008) compares these assaults on assumed managerial truths to what religions call "heresies." These once-heretical ideas are now the orthodoxy of organizational coaching. As a result, organizations are now taking a lead in applying approaches from fields that are first cousins to systems theory: field theory and social network theory. Systemic thinking in organizations, even though the organization in this case is the family, was given a boost by the development of family systems therapy. In addition, management theory has discovered the effectiveness of going beyond disease or problem orientation to take a strengths-oriented approach, as promoted by appreciative inquiry and the human capital movement. These topics are covered as aspects of the pillar of leadership:

- Organizational heresies
- Social network theory
- Family systems therapy
- Appreciative inquiry

- Human capital movement
- Leadership as a coaching pillar

ORGANIZATIONAL HERESIES

In his very readable second edition of *The Age of Heretics* (2008), Art Kleiner champions a series of corporate reformers—heretics—as being "the closest thing we have . . . to a true conscience of large organizations" (p. 13). These heretics recognized that, "like monks, the managers of corporations in the 1950s and 1960s began to systematically, and unconsciously, cut themselves off from any sense of responsibility for the rest of the world, even as their influence over it grew broader" (p. 9).

But though they protested the lack of social values, the heretics described by Kleiner did not abandon the corporate environment. Kleiner (2008) defined a heretic in this way: "someone who sees a truth that contradicts the conventional wisdom of the institution to which he or she belongs and remains loyal to both entities—the institution and the new truth" (p. 4).

From a coach's point of view, the ideas that were rejected by corporate orthodoxy during the last half of the 20th century are now largely embraced as the foundation for executive and organizational coaching. Here is a list of the heresies presented by Kleiner:

- Business is always personal. (p. 1)
- People are basically trustworthy; you cannot understand a system until you try to change it; people can rise to fill their highest potential; and small groups hold the key to beneficial change. (p. 19)
- Self-managing teams, in a well-designed operation, with oversight and awareness from the bottom up, are far more productive than any other known form of management. And they exalt the human spirit. (p. 48)
- A company can move itself forward only by moving its community forward. (p. 85)
- Awareness must be cultivated, because the future cannot be predicted or planned in a mechanistic manner. (p. 121)
- A mechanistic way of thinking cannot sustain itself. (p. 155)
- To change an organization, you must know—and change—yourself. (p. 186)

- Corporations might play a role in shifting the world to a more ecologically responsible, humanist age. (p. 226)
- The purpose of a corporation is to change the world. (p. 269)

Kleiner describes the challenges, struggles, battles faced by corporate leaders—not necessarily those with the highest positions, or even any positions, within corporations, but leaders nonetheless—who sought to use the wisdom of everyday life to help big business make a positive difference in the world. He calls this wisdom the "vernacular spirit:"

> [C]orporations can't realize any of this unfulfilled potential with the prevailing management culture—the culture of the numbers. That is why the restoration of vernacular spirit inside corporations is so essential—and probably inevitable. . . . If companies exist to build wealth, they can do so only by building a more effective, more intelligent community than anyone else has built. (2008, p. 319)

Linking Heresies to Coaching

Leading an institution simply to recategorize its current resources, replicate its existing systems, and advance toward where it already is does not qualify as leadership. What may now be considered heresy could be the very path that fulfills an organization's potential. Coaches promote the development of leaders by encouraging them to stretch all the way from a meta-perspective of highest values to the concrete necessity of accountability without losing their humanity in between. Using a model that integrates well with coaching and a systemic worldview, leadership theorists Jeannine Sandstrom and Lee Smith (2008) describe five roles for Legacy Leadership® (see Internet links):

1. Holder of Vision and Values™ (about direction and commitment)
2. Creator of Collaboration and Innovation™ (about the environment of working relationships)
3. Influencer of Inspiration and Leadership™ (about connecting with individuals, the heart of relationships)
4. Advocator of Differences and Community™ (about distinction and inclusion)
5. Calibrator of Responsibility and Accountability™ (about execution and performance) (www.coachworks.com)

Since the most efficient complex systems are self-organizing, Clippinger (1999) argues, they are not controlled in the traditional sense. Due to nonlinearity, their performance is also difficult to plan or predict. The leader's dilemma is this: "Because complex systems adapt from the bottom up, there is no way of planning for change, and the goals and policies of organizations are emergent and indeterminate" (p. 6).

Under such circumstances, the goal of leadership becomes not controlling from above but rather influencing self-organization from below. Control is not imposed but emerges if leaders create the right conditions and incentives, as with Best Practice 3: Influencer of Inspiration and Leadership™ in Sandstrom and Smith's (2008) list. Leaders also need to allow for uncertainty and natural selection (i.e., the feedback of consequences, or accountability).

The Biology of Business is a collection of papers edited by Clippinger (1999) that provides numerous case studies of self-organizing businesses. It serves as a resource for both organizational coaches and leaders who are looking for approaches and examples for managing complexity.

Field Theory

Perhaps the most important heretical contribution to management and organizational theory was Kurt Lewin's field theory—the proposition that human behavior is the function of both the person and the environment. Expressed in symbolic terms, the formula is $B = f(P, E)$. This means that one's behavior is related to (or a function of) both one's personal characteristics and the social environment in which one finds oneself. This is a step beyond the tendency to ignore context.

HISTORICAL INTERLUDE

Kurt Lewin (1890–1947) represents a major exception to the individualistic approach of North American social psychology. Considered by many to be the most charismatic psychologist of his generation, Lewin's influence was wide ranging, from modeling rigorous experimental methods, to promoting democratic ideals, to exposing the world, to the significance of entire disciplines: group dynamics and action research.

Born in Germany, Lewin brought a more context-sensitive European approach to the United States in 1932 as a visiting professor at Stanford University. His influence in America was immediate, through his writing and teaching. He went from Stanford to Cornell, to the University of Iowa, and then to the Massachusetts Institute of Technology, where he established and directed the Research Center for Group Dynamics.

Lewin's belief that social-psychological phenomena can be studied experimentally was an important impetus for scientific research. He carefully tested human behavior in a controlled setting. His research also showed that events must be studied in relation to one another and that both the individual and the group are important. His research helped to better explain leadership atmospheres and group dynamics. The group dynamics movements of the 1960s that had such an influence on coaching can be traced to Lewin's contributions.

Field theory may seem obvious now, but most early psychologists were locked into either psychoanalysis or strict behaviorism. Lewin (1975) thought of motives as goal-directed forces. He believed that we all occupy a "life space" that is made up of both internal and external factors, including other people and even imagined ideas. His dynamic conception of social, cognitive, and affective factors foreshadows current concepts. Lewin tested his novel theories and in doing so laid the foundation for modern research in human relations. We could not understand leadership without his groundbreaking work. He introduced an understanding of context into a psychology that assumed the predominance of the individual person.

The principal characteristics of field theory as Lewin (1975) described it may be summarized in this way:

- Behavior is a function of the field that exists at the time the behavior occurs.
- Analysis begins with the situation as a whole from which the component parts are differentiated.
- The concrete person in a concrete situation can be represented mathematically.

403

- The theory emphasizes underlying forces (needs) as determiners of behavior and expresses a preference for psychological as opposed to physical or physiological descriptions of the field.
- A field consists of everything that is going on in the situation, all being mutually interdependent. This is much like the definition of a system that we discuss in chapter 2.

Lewin applied field theory through a "force field analysis" that provides a framework for looking at the factors ("forces") that influence any given situation. The analysis identifies at forces that are either driving movement toward a goal (helping forces) or blocking movement toward a goal (hindering forces). It is a significant contribution to the fields of organizational development, process management, and change management within management theory. Force field analysis is a useful technique for looking at all the forces for and against a decision. In effect, it is a specialized method of weighing pros and cons. By carrying out the analysis, you can plan to strengthen the forces supporting a decision and reduce the impact of opposition to it.

There are three steps in carrying out a force field analysis:

1. List all forces for change in one column and all forces against change in another column.
2. Assign a score to each force, from 1 (weak) to 5 (strong).
3. Draw a diagram showing the forces for and against change. The forces should be drawn proportional to their score.

Example: "I Have to Improve Delegation"

Simpson was told in his performance review that he had to improve his delegation skills. He was a well-liked manager but, perhaps because he valued being well liked, he avoided holding his direct reports accountable. Simpson and his coach came up with a plan to ask his staff for a timeline whenever they were assigned a task. This was not something he had been doing. At the next coaching session, Simpson reported that he had not asked for one timeline since the previous meeting.

The coach suggested examining the situation using a force field analysis, illustrated in Figure 14.1. On a blank sheet of paper, Simpson wrote his planned change down the center: "Get timeline commitment when delegating." On the left, he listed the forces for change and rated the strength of each from 1 to 5. He gave the assignment from his performance review, "I have to improve delegation," a rating of 4 with "Will make follow-up easier" a 3 and "May reduce number of meetings" a 2.

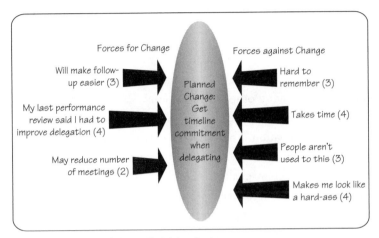

Figure 14.1   Example of Force Field Analysis

When Simpson listed the forces against change, it was obvious why he had not acted on his plan the week before. With "Hard to remember" and "People aren't used to this" both rated as 3s, and "Takes time" and "Makes me look like a hard-ass" as 4s, it was clear that the forces against change were stronger than the forces for change.

"Clearly," said the coach, "this is not a change you're willing to make right now. What would be the consequence of your deciding not to change?"

When asked in this way, Simpson realized that he was not willing to risk his job in order to avoid making the change. So he and the coach took each force for change and talked about how to strengthen it. For example, after realizing that the bonus that would come with a more positive performance review could buy him the new boat he wanted, he raised "I have to improve delegation" to a 5.

Then he worked on ways to reduce the forces against change, for example, by meeting with his staff to explain his plan so they would understand what he was doing and why. He found they appreciated the possibility of reducing the number of meetings. With these adjustments, the forces shifted toward change, and Simpson was able to proceed toward his goal with confidence.

This technique is an effective way to work with the client to "see" the system and determine how to influence it—by strengthening the forces for change, reducing the forces against change, or deciding on a different action that has more likelihood of succeeding. This is a very simple example, but the procedure can help clients assess the forces of both simple and complex change at many different levels: individual, organizational, or industry-wide.

Action Research

In addition to his many other contributions, Lewin helped develop action research (1999). Action research combines empirical methods, social action, and controlled evaluation. That is, people plan to act, act, and then consider the results of their action in a spiral that uses this information to inform the next planning-action-evaluation cycle. This cycle, where results of past actions feed into consideration of what to do next, has been shown to be an element in the development of expertise (Bereiter & Scardamalia, 1993). Lewin's work is further developed in the action-reflection cycle (Boyatzis & McKee, 2005b) presented in chapter 5.

Lewin conducted many action research field studies to understand social problems. His concept of field theory developed from this approach, with its assertion that human interactions are driven by both the people involved and their environment. Lewin focused particularly on the interactions among races and the influences that affect intergroup and intragroup relations. Ultimately, he wanted to identify the factors that could make diverse communities function without prejudice and discrimination. He also investigated reasons for unproductiveness of groups.

Linking Field Theory to Coaching

- *Insight inventory.* Some coaches ask participants to describe how they are in two important environments: their work and their personal worlds. Comparing the two profiles helps clients determine how different environments affect their behavior and better understand why that is the case.
- *Decision making.* Sometimes a coaching client will be faced with a complex decision involving change. The force field analysis is

a valuable tool that the coach can present to the client to facilitate decision making.

- *Understanding client behavior.* Field theory's most important contribution to coaching is the assertion that clients cannot understand their behavior without taking into account the environmental factors that contribute to that behavior. Just as important, if clients plan to attempt behavioral changes, they should examine the likely effect on their environment in advance. In organizational coaching, a 360-assessment gives the coach and client more accurate knowledge about the client's environment.

- *Action research.* If, indeed, as Lewin claimed, you cannot understand a system until you try to change it, then the best way to increase an executive client's understanding of his or her organization may be to encourage them to "just do it." If people are conscious observers of the consequences of introducing change, they will learn the concrete lessons of systemic thinking.

SOCIAL NETWORK THEORIES

The intuition that the success or failure of societies and organizations often depends on the patterning of their internal structure is probably as old as humankind. This is implied, for example, by the emphasis put on descent lists in the Bible. Anthropologists have developed techniques for recording relatedness among members of tribal communities, and sociologists and urban ethnographers have mapped social connections within gangs and neighborhoods.

Beginning in the 1930s, a systematic approach to theory and research on social relationship patterns emerged, as detailed in Linton Freeman's history of social network analysis (2004). A social network theory is a set of ideas about individuals represented within systems of social connections. Individuals are thought of as "nodes" or "actors" in a system, connected to others. Patterns of connection form a "social space," and social network analysis maps and analyzes this social space.

In 1934 Jacob Levy Moreno (1889–1974) introduced the ideas and tools of an early social network theory called "sociometry" (Moreno, 1960). Moreno was born in Romania, grew up and became a psychiatrist in Vienna, and immigrated to New York in 1925. He brought with him a dedication to working with people in their actual social settings rather than in a private office removed from their day-to-day lives. The word "sociometry" comes from the Latin *socius*," meaning "social," and the Latin *metrum*, meaning "measure." As these roots imply, sociometry is a way of measuring the degree of relatedness among actors. A sociogram is a graph of these measures.

Measurement of relatedness can be useful not only in the assessment of behavior within groups, but also for interventions to bring about positive change and for determining the extent of change. For a work group, sociometry can be a powerful tool for reducing conflict and improving communication because it allows the group to see itself objectively and to analyze its own dynamics. It is also a powerful tool for assessing dynamics and development in groups devoted to therapy or training — or team coaching.

Moreno coined the term "sociometry" and conducted the first long-range sociometric study from 1932 to 1938 at the New York State Training School for Girls in Hudson, New York. As part of this study, Moreno used sociometric techniques to assign girls to various residential cottages. He found that assignments on the basis of sociometry substantially reduced the number of runaways from the facility.

In related developments, Alex Bavelas worked with Kurt Lewin at the University of Iowa and later at MIT. Although the work of Lewin's Research Center in Group Dynamics was called field theory rather than social network theory, there are important connections between the two.

After Lewin's death in 1947, Bavelas formed the Group Networks Laboratory and conducted a study of communication networks and how their structures affected the ability of groups to solve problems. He assigned one group to use communication that was essentially a circular chain where each person could communicate only with his or her immediate neighbors. This group was forced to use a democratic process to solve the problems.

Another group used a starlike model where one individual could communicate with everyone but the others could communicate only with each other through that central person. This modeled the classic authoritarian process. When Bavelas asked the groups to perform simple tasks, the authoritarian group was much faster at coming up with the answers to the problems given. Yet when the task was more complex and had more subtle issues to resolve, the democratic group was consistently able to solve the tasks more rapidly, with better outcomes. The members of this group maintained higher morale. This research linked Lewin's work on leadership with communications and network models.

The analysis of social networks emerged as a key technique in modern sociology, anthropology, social psychology, and organizational development. Research in a number of academic fields has demonstrated that social networks operate on many levels, from families to countries. They play a critical role in determining the way problems are solved, organizations are run, and individuals succeed in achieving their goals. In social network theory, people are referred to as "actors."

Discrete mathematics works with things that vary in discrete clumps rather than in a continuous flow. The relationship between one logical statement and another, for example, is not the same as the relation between the size of a leaf at one point in time and its size at another. There is no smooth, continuous process such that the first logical statement "grows" smoothly into the next. Each is distinct and stands on its own. Modern mathematical methods for manipulating things like logical statements, sets of objects, and bits of information are important in computer programming. Patterns of people interacting in groups can be identified using discrete mathematics.

Freeman (2004) reports that it was not until the 1970s, when modern discrete mathematics experienced rapid growth and powerful computers became readily available, that the study of social networks became an interdisciplinary specialty. Since then it has found important applications in the study of organizational behavior, interorganizational relations, the spread of contagious diseases, mental health, social support, the diffusion of information, and animal social organization. Today social network analysis has become an international effort with its own professional organizations, textbooks, journals, research centers, training centers, and computer programs designed specifically to facilitate the analysis of structural data. Its success is related to the more general acceptance of the systemic worldview.

From the outset, the network approach to the study of behavior has involved two commitments:

1. It is guided by formal theory, organized in mathematical terms.
2. It is grounded in the systematic analysis of empirical data.

The power of social network theory stems from its difference from traditional sociological studies, which assume that it is the attributes of individual actors—whether they are outgoing or inhibited, attractive or unattractive, charismatic or unnoticeable —that matter.

Social network theory produces an alternate view, one that is fully appreciative of context. The assumption is that the attributes of individuals are less important than their relationships and ties with other actors within the network. This approach is useful for explaining many organizational phenomena, although it leaves less room for individual agency or the ability of individuals to influence their success.

The "small world" phenomenon is the hypothesis that the chain of social acquaintances required to connect one person chosen arbitrarily to another person chosen arbitrarily anywhere in the world is generally short. The concept gave rise to the famous phrase "six degrees of separation" after a 1967 small world experiment by psychologist Stanley Milgram, which found that two random U.S. citizens were connected by an average of six acquaintances. Current Internet experiments continue to explore this phenomenon. So far, these experiments confirm that about five to seven degrees of separation are sufficient for connecting any two people.

Linking Social Network Theories to Coaching

Coaches must be aware of their clients' social networks. We are living in an increasingly connected world where actions of seemingly unrelated people can affect the lives of others drastically. Clients will have many networks that affect their behavior, including work, family, friends, sports teams, social clubs, and so forth. In order to spark insights about these effects, clients should be asked about all these networks. Coaches also should be aware of their own social networks in order to be more self-aware and to tap into resources that may be useful to clients.

Organizational coaching also provides an opportunity to utilize formal social network theory, which may require the services of experts in the field. In general, network analysis focuses on the relationships *between* people instead of on characteristics *of* people. These relationships may be comprised of the feelings people have for each other, the sharing of information, or more tangible exchanges such as goods and money. By mapping these relationships, social network analysis helps to uncover the informal communication patterns present in an organization, which may then be compared to the formal communication structures. These patterns can be used to explain several organizational phenomena. For instance, the place employees have in the communication network influences their exposure to and control over information. Since the patterns of relationships bring employees into contact with the attitudes and behaviors of other organizational members, these relationships also may help to explain why employees develop certain attitudes toward organizational events or job-related matters (theories that deal with these matters are called contagion theories).

FAMILY SYSTEMS THERAPIES

This section relates to topics that are dealt with elsewhere in this book. We include the section here because, after all, a family is a type of organization, and many of the dilemmas facing parents are similar to those facing management. Describing this field may give a different perspective in applying the somewhat complicated concepts of systems theory. Family systems therapies also represents a practical bridge from mechanistic individualism to a systemic contextual approach.

As participants in the systemic paradigm shift during the last part of the 20th century, many psychotherapists began to take a systems perspective. They recognized that traditional individualistic psychotherapy often ignores the fact that one individual may be expressing the difficulties that the whole family is experiencing. The "identified patient" can be a case of mistaken or at least misplaced identity. Several psychotherapists recognized that looking at the family members and their relationships as a system with nonlinear dynamic characteristics makes it more likely to influence change.

Another motivation grew out of more negative experiences. Often intense psychotherapy with one member of a family or a couple would appear to be successful in that the treated person would improve. However, the family or marriage would disintegrate. How, asked some therapists, can we count such an outcome as an unmitigated success? Yes, there are times when an individual would be better off divorcing his or her family or partner, as in instances of abuse. But what about the times when one partner's development in therapy simply leaves the other behind? Doesn't systems theory tell us that all the elements in a system affect one another? Should there not be at least an attempt to treat the system as a whole?

Family systems therapy is a response to these concerns. To emphasize their rejection of the idea that people can be treated as isolated units apart from their closest social relationships, many family therapists do not call themselves psychotherapists. This approach echoes the refusal of Alfred Adler to treat individuals separate from their social context. Modern systems theory has further elaborated that stance and has developed highly effective methods for treating family and relationship problems. Family therapists consider the family to be a system of interacting members. As such, the problems in the family are seen to arise out of the interactions in the system rather than being ascribed exclusively to the faults or problems of individual members and their internal dynamics.

Some of the key developers of family therapy include:

- Nathan Ackerman, a psychoanalytic therapist
- Walter Kempler, a Gestalt therapist
- Salvadore Minuchin, who defines himself as a structuralist
- James Framo, who deals with object relations
- Jay Haley and Cloé Madanes, specializing in communications
- Murray Bowen, developer of the systems theory of the family

Murray Bowen's theories are closely aligned to coaching (Kerr & Bowen, 1988). Beginning in the 1950s, Bowen developed family systems theory based on eight concepts:

1. Differentiation of self
2. Nuclear family emotional system
3. Triangles
4. Family projection process
5. Multigenerational transmission process
6. Emotional cutoff
7. Sibling position
8. Societal emotional process

Linking Family Systems Theories to Coaching

We focus here on the concept of triangles since many business coaches confront this issue in their coaching practice. A triangle is a three-person relationship system. In psychology, a triangle is considered the smallest stable relationship because the system can continue even if, over time, every one of its members is replaced. Yet a triangle can contain a good deal of tension, as coalitions shift power among the relationships. Shifting the tension can stabilize the system without resolving underlying issues.

Often a triangle involves one in conflict and two in harmony. A triangular relationship like this creates anxiety for the "odd man out," a position that is difficult for most individuals to tolerate. This creates a dynamic push for change, although the temptation is to change who takes the "out" position rather than to recognize the underlying issues that affect all three members of the triangle.

Example: "They Take Turns Wearing the Dunce Cap"

Edna manages a three-person production team in a data management company. She begins a telephone coaching session with a big sigh. "What's that about?" asks her coach. "They're at it again. Over the last month, I swear it's been like a kindergarten classroom. They used to work so well together, but now Mick is feeling like a victim because Zoreen and Jane agreed on vacation schedules without consulting him."

"Didn't you say last time that Zoreen and Mick were ganging up on Jane, saying she was taking the easy assignments and making them look bad?"

"Oh, yes. And next week, Jane will feel sorry for Mick and the two of them will find something about Zoreen to complain about. It's like they take turns wearing the dunce cap."

"It sounds like there's a lot of tension that gets traded back and forth. If you step back and look at the team as a unit, what might be an underlying source of worry or concern for them?"

"Oh, looking at it from that perspective, I just realized something! There's another work group that got disbanded because we shifted to a new technology. That has nothing to do with the Mick, Zoreen, and Jane group, but I'm not sure they know that. Maybe they're feeling like the axe is about to fall on them."

Edna worked with her coach on planning a meeting with the group as a whole in order to invite them to share their concerns. She discovered a sense of uncertainty that they had been barely conscious of. She was able to assure them that their positions were secure, and they went back to their previous cooperative working patterns.

413

In effect, the apparent issues of triangulation serve as a sideshow that keeps group members, managers (and, in the case of a family, parents) busy so that they end up ignoring the issues whose solution would actually make a difference.

Business coaches often are caught up in a triangle with a client and the client's employer, who is also the coach's sponsor. Being aware of the situation allows a coach to reduce the tension as the coaching process unfolds. Business coaches must be clear at the beginning of the coaching relationship that they must report progress to the sponsor but that client and coach will agree on the content of these progress reports. If the coach ignores the potential for triangulation, client and coach soon face tension with the employer.

Many external coaches insist on making it clear to the organizational sponsor that the purpose of coaching must be to serve the interests of the client who is receiving coaching, on the basis that ultimately this will serve the needs of the organization that has hired the coach. For example, if as a result of coaching the client decides to leave the organization, it is assumed that the organization is better discovering this lack of fit sooner rather than later.

Systems such as families sometimes relate in ways that can be toxic to the individuals involved in the system. Coaches often deal with clients who have been caught up in a system and continue to repeat patterns derived from the behavior of others in the system. A coach, like a family systems therapist, can point out the interaction patterns that the client may not have noticed. By increasing the client's awareness of the larger patterns, the coach helps the client recognize options that may lead to a more satisfying state.

Appreciative Inquiry

It may seem that businesses and organizations would be the last place to look for shifts from hierarchical to systems thinking and from deficit to strengths orientation. Yet, the idea of a command-and-control center that makes all the decisions while workers just take orders has been questioned not only as ineffective but even in some circumstances as dangerous. In important research in organizations that cannot afford to make mistakes — nuclear plants and aircraft carriers, for instance — Karl Weick and Kathy Sutcliffe (2001) found that distributing power throughout the organization actually made disaster less likely.

Appreciative inquiry, as developed by David Cooperrider of Weatherhead School of Management at Case Western Reserve University (see Srivastva, Cooperrider et al., 1990), is the approach that replaces deficit judgment with an openness to the positive. This approach has the advantages of helping an organization orient to the future, encouraging the people in it to be open to learning and creating new possibilities, and aiding understanding and cooperation among diverse individuals. Many of the virtues of appreciative inquiry are similar to those of positive psychology. In a sense, it is management theory's parallel to the development of positive psychology.

Just as with positive psychology, however, it is all too easy to skim the surface of appreciative inquiry and decide it just means making nice all the time. Gervase Bushe (2007) compared its effectiveness in different contexts and concluded, "A focus on the positive is useful for appreciative inquiry, but it is not the purpose. The purpose is to generate a new and better future" (p. 36). Bushe found that just being positive was not as effective in transforming an organization as attending to "generativity" at each stage: generative questions, generative conversations, and generative actions. For instance, in six of the seven cases he studied that ended up being transformational, actions were assigned nonhierarchically, in response to individual and group styles and circumstances. In nearly all of the 13 incremental, rather than transformational, cases, actions were assigned centrally and according to a preset top-down plan.

In an interview with Suzan Guest (2007), Bushe explains further: "'[G]enerativity' occurs when a new way of looking at things emerges that offers people new ways to act that they hadn't considered before. Embedded in that is also the motivation to act in more positive ways" (p. 24).

Linking Appreciative Inquiry to Coaching

Many coach training organizations refer to Cooperrider's appreciative approach, and most teach a form of coaching that has many similarities to it. Sara Orem, Jackie Binkert, and Ann Clancy wrote *Appreciative Coaching* (2007) in order to make the connections even more clear. They describe Cooperrider's four-dimensional framework from a coach's perspective, starting with a preliminary defining fifth element that is similar to traditional goal setting but is more like brainstorming:

1. *Define*. Coach and client explore topics that are most important for the client's future, without judgment on the part of the coach. The client chooses the topic for the remaining Ds.

2. *Discover*. Regarding the selected topic, the client is asked to identify energizing and life-enhancing forces plus whatever might be the foundation of those forces. Bushe's emphasis on generative questions is crucial here.

3. *Dream*. The coach guides an exploration of client longing for a "new and better future." According to Bushe (2007), it is important for the client to become aware of his or her emotional attachment to these dreams. The coach is invited to listen with openness and acceptance even when this exploration elicits negative emotions about undesirable events in the past. Often that clears the way for consideration of new possibilities.

4. *Design*. In a series of "generative conversations" with the coach, the client constructs scenarios based on the dreams and begins to identify those that capture his or her passion and commitment.

5. *Destiny*. Here is where Bushe's generative actions come into play. Simply assigning homework, as is typical in behavioral-oriented therapies, does not leverage the energy that can come from a client's deciding what will be most effective on his or her own terms.

Coaches who work in organizational settings use these stages with teams, encouraging everyone to take part in offering options, scenarios, and actions and in appreciating one another's contributions (Bergquist, 2003).

Both Bergquist (2007b) and Bushe (2007) stress the importance of traditional skills and techniques in organizational coaching. Bergquist insists that structural changes must accompany the process and attitude focus of appreciative inquiry. Bushe suggests that traditional consulting techniques may be necessary in order for organizations to get the most out of an appreciative approach. That these two authors feel it necessary to remind their colleagues of the importance of traditional management approaches is an indication of a growing acceptance of appreciative principles in organizational circles.

Human Capital Movement

Developments in organizational theory can be seen as systemic pillars that raise coaching above its mechanistic precursors. Several such developments contribute to the human capital movement.

Interest in how to create positive organizations parallels the research and practice of positive psychology discussed in chapter 11. *Positive Organizational Scholarship* (Cameron, Dutton, & Quinn, 2003) and articles such as "Positive Organizational Scholarship: An Idea Whose Time Has Truly Come" (Wright, 2003) document these trends. According to Chris Peterson (2006), such organizations are characterized by these virtues:

- *Purpose.* A shared vision of the moral goals of the organization, which are reinforced by remembrances and celebrations
- *Safety.* Protection against threat, danger, and exploitation
- *Fairness.* Equitable rules governing reward and punishment and the means for consistently enforcing them
- *Humanity.* Mutual care and concern
- *Dignity.* The treatment of all people in the organization as individuals regardless of their position (p. 298)

Referring to what McKinsey & Company have called a war for talent in today's organizations, Fred Luthans and his colleagues (Luthans, Youssef, & Avolio, 2007) have investigated those employee characteristics that research has shown to be significantly related to performance at work. These are not long-term characteristics of personality but states that are amenable to development. Here are the four psychological capacities that meet these criteria:

1. *Self-efficacy.* Drawing on Albert Bandura's social cognitive theory, this concept has to do with a person's confidence that she or he can gather and apply the resources to meet goals in a specific situation.
2. *Hope.* This concept has to do with being motivated to apply one's willpower and a sense of success in finding a way to reach goals.
3. *Optimism.* In chapter 11, we reviewed the research by Martin Seligman on learned optimism, or the tendency to explain positive events as pervasive, permanent, and personal. For Luthans and

colleagues, optimism includes the ability to adapt this explanatory style to the realistic demands of the workplace.

4. *Resiliency.* The ability to bounce back from setbacks is another quality included in the repertoire of psychological capital.

Linking Human Capital Development to Coaching

In a special issue of *The International Journal of Coaching in Organizations* devoted to organizational coaching and human capital development, Brenda Smith (2007) makes a business case for coaching people to transcend the "Working Strategy" that focuses on driving shareholder value by increasing revenue or cutting costs. As Bill Bergquist describes in an article in the same issue, traditional accounting techniques consider investments in machinery and buildings to be assets, whereas investments in the human beings who do the work, through payroll and benefits, are treated as expenses. Although the shift to a new "Winning Strategy" is difficult and messy, Smith argues that a focus on soft skills and talent is crucial:

> "Talent" as a construct presupposes a way of integrating people as a key component of business strategy — not as an expense but as an investment in an intrinsic asset. According to Bruce Sommerfeld, CTO of Dallas-based Capital Analytics, L. P., human capital represents the differential between the book value (hard assets) and the market value (share price) of a company — intangible assets. In 2006, more than 80% of the S&P 500 came from intangibles: good will, intellectual property, branding, structures, processes, etc. This elevates the importance of the quality and quantity of effort people contribute to profit. The implications are huge. The profit motive hasn't changed, but the means for getting there has. (Smith, 2007, p. 10)

In arguing that coaching can help to bring about such a shift, Smith and others locate both organizational theory and coaching firmly in the new systemic paradigm.

LEADERSHIP AS A COACHING PILLAR

"Leader" is another name for the organizational "heretics" described by Art Kleiner (2007). Rather than preserving what *is*, which is characteristic

418

of management, leaders have a vision of what could be, and they include others in defining and putting that vision into action. They understand that an organization is a dynamic system that cannot be held still. Like someone walking, an organization must maintain stability while it is adjusting to internal and external change. This is dynamic stability, the mark of a sustainable system. By developing specialized functions, redesigning existing structures, and increasing the communication among all these, it becomes an ever more complex system that can maintain greater stability despite even more intense challenges. Depending on what those challenges turn out to be, any person or any team might become the leader that the organization needs at that moment. The shift from manager to leader involves not just an orientation to the future but also the recognition of the importance of every person seeing himself or herself as a leader. How this can be accomplished is being investigated by a new field established by David Rock called "NeuroLeadership."

CHAPTER 15

Neuroscience Platform— NeuroLeadership

You and your fellow students volunteered for this experiment, but you had not met before. All the volunteers watched this video, and it was really gross—car accidents and maimed bodies. Then you went into a small conference room and you thought you were supposed to talk about the impact of the video. But your partner acted like it had not had any affect at all. He kept trying to make small talk, and he seemed to have no reaction when you said you had felt like throwing up. His behavior added to your discomfort about the video. When the experimenters measured your blood pressure, it was way higher than normal.

In experiments such as this by James Gross and others (2006), the negative effects of trying to suppress emotions applied not only to the suppressors, the subjects who had been instructed to try to hide their reactions, but also to their partners who had no idea about the instructions. This is just one of many research studies showing that our emotions have an effect on others in our environment—even without their being aware of it. The human brain is superbly designed to share information and energy with others. In an organization, negative emotions can be poisonous; leaders depend on positive ones to facilitate collaboration.

Once we address the topic of management and leadership in organizations, we are engaged in conversations about relationships. A conversation involves sharing energy and information. Certain types of conversations require a mutual resonance of the mechanism that provides for the flow of energy and information (our brains) and the process that regulates that flow (our minds). Over time, such conversations result in attuned relationships that further stimulate brain integration and the capacity of the mind to reflect on itself. Daniel Siegel (2007b) has concluded that health and wellness involve the three irreducible elements of an integrated brain, a reflective mind, and attuned relationships. We have suggested that a human being who is continually potentiating is characterized by these three elements. We are a physical species, a conscious and self-conscious species, and a social species.

We have looked at the ways the brain is hardwired to prepare us for challenges to our survival, and we have noted that human beings cannot survive without relating to other people. As Leslie Brothers (2001) has pointed out, "The human individual doesn't really exist as a person until he or she takes up and participates in forms of social life" (p. 90). Ignoring this fact leads to what she calls "neuroism," a trend that, at its worst, takes the cultural and psychological assumption of individualism as an article of faith and identifies a single human mind with a single human brain, thus ignoring the social connections necessary for both to exist. We have pointed out the extent to which this assumption is reflected in bedrock psychology, even social psychology. Brothers claims that the ability of neuroscience to develop a truly scientific theory is limited by its adoption of such psychological language and underlying concepts of the supreme individual.

The trend in organizations from management to leadership, combined with Brothers's warnings about neuroism, is a call to move beyond the mechanistic paradigm that gave rise to psychological individualism. There is much work for neuroscientists to do in overcoming that cultural background. We hope to support our neuroscience colleagues in responding to Brothers's call by recognizing the irreducible importance of social relationships to brain and mind functioning.

- Why are relationships so important to us?
- What constitutes a good relationship?
- How do relationships relate to our survival, development, and well-being?

- Why are we so sensitive to put-downs?
- How is it possible for us to mirror in our own minds what we see others experiencing?
- What are the benefits of developing a theory of mind, a sense that others have desires, intentions, and feelings that are as real to them as ours are to us?
- How can coaching enhance our relationships?
- Does our social environment determine who we are and what we do?
- If we construct our reality socially, then how can we construct it better?

We accept that, in every way that matters, our brain functions and mental processes cannot be teased apart from the social fabric in which we live. We have discussed the necessity of an attachment relationship for the human infant, and we have indicated that relationships such as coaching can have positive effects on adult mind and brain functions and even brain structure. We now examine in more detail our social relating processes under these headings:

- Collaborative, contingent conversations
- Our social brains
- Theory of mind
- Repairing relationships — *Sange*
- Resolving conflict — Stop and Grow
- Calming threats — SCARF
- Practice guide for coaching with the brain in mind: Get along with others

COLLABORATIVE, CONTINGENT CONVERSATIONS

An important input for the process of relating to others is a particular type of conversation that Daniel Siegel (1999) has called "collaborative, contingent conversations." They are, first of all, collaborative in that both parties make contributions to the ongoing interaction. There is no one with a gavel to call on the next person to speak. Second, there is no agenda or script that must be followed. What each person says is dependent on and responsive to what the other person just said, and vice versa.

Even when a topic or subject matter is at the center of the conversation, it appears to be by moment-to-moment agreement. Either participant may change the subject.

We should mention here that, while "conversation" is often taken to mean just verbal interaction, and often just its semantic content, we mean to include every channel of communication (Page-Hollander, 1973): linguistic, paralinguistic (verbalizations and vocal qualities that are part of speech but not part of language per se—like "uh" and "yeah"), visual, kinesthetic, and even smell and perhaps taste. We mean collaborative and contingent in every way, recognizing that our minds and bodies are in constant nonverbal conversations, stimulating many associations of which we are unaware.

A parent exchanging gestures with a preverbal infant provides a template for these conversations. Infant and parent are present in the moment, gazing at each other, their attention taken up fully by the other. The infant coos a sound, and the parent coos back. The infant smiles at the parent's response and the parent smiles in return. The infant coos again. If the parent responds too loudly, the infant looks startled. The parent becomes quieter and calmer. The infant calms also and coos a slightly different sound. The parent responds with a similar sound and adds something new. And on and on.

To nonparenting adults, this may seem like a meaningless game. However, in the absence of "conversations" like this, including similar physical give and receive that evolve into sharing experiences and stories as the child's language ability develops, children fail to thrive. Development of neural connections in the prefrontal cortex, the part of our brains that enables us to control emotions and relate to other people, depends on our experiencing contingent, collaborative conversations and the ongoing relationships in which such conversations occur.

Conversations like this play a unique part in the development of our brains, our minds, and our relationships, for three reasons:

1. They are literally associated with the growth of the infant brain, especially the prefrontal cortex that we have already suggested plays such an important role in the integration of social and mental functions across time and areas of the brain. More recent research

shows that the prefrontal cortex in adults is similarly nurtured by the collaborative, contingent conversations we have. Such conversations seem to play a part in the "earning" of secure attachment by adults who missed out on it as children. In short, collaborative, contingent conversations grow our brains. The similarity of such conversations to the ideal of a coaching interaction is obvious to anyone who has experienced coaching.

2. These conversations are examples of and enable attuned relating processes that, we are suggesting are irreducible requirements for mental health. As educator Sandra Johnson (2006) puts it, "literally looking into the eyes of the affectively attuned other is another significant form of social interaction that can assist in promoting development" (p. 67).

3. Because of their stimulation of the prefrontal cortex, collaborative, contingent conversations strengthen mental capacities that are mediated by that part of the brain. The capacities that are particularly relevant to social sharing are attuned communication, empathy, and intuition, including the ability to know that others have thoughts and desires as we do. In looking at this list, we are reminded of Alfred Adler's attempts to define mental health, rather than mental illness, as "social interest" or going beyond empathy to "having an interest in the interest of others."

Linking Collaborative, Contingent Conversations to Coaching

Are coaching conversations collaborative and contingent? A survey of competencies promoted by coaching associations such as the International Coach Federation and the European Coaching and Mentoring Association would suggest that they are meant to be. Coaches are trained to be "present" in coaching sessions, putting their full attention on the client and the interaction. They are not to operate themselves as expert advice-givers or as judgmental authorities. Coaches are taught to elicit the client's agenda rather than imposing one of their own. Certainly the ideal for coaching conversations is very similar to collaborative, contingent conversations.

As far as we know, no research exists that compares the qualities of *actual* collaborative, contingent parenting conversations with *actual* coaching conversations. Nor is there proof that, even if they are similar, the same benefits would accrue for the coaching client's brain and mental processes. We do know that other adult interactions can have positive effects, such as those between a therapist and client (Norcross, 2002) or between spouses, one with a secure attachment history and the other without. Therefore, it is a good guess that coaching interactions likewise have a beneficial effect on the brain.

In fact, it may be that collaboration and contingency are part of what account for the positive outcome of coaching. Psychotherapy research has shown that relationship factors account for about 30% of the variance in positive outcome for clients. This is a strong argument for being present, for engaging in collaborative interaction, and for avoiding judgment or control that may trigger a status threat for clients.

Our Social Brains

In *Friday's Footprint*, UCLA psychiatrist Leslie Brothers (Brothers, 1997) illustrates her claim that the human brain is built for social interaction. Brothers views the amygdala as the social, not the emotional, center, with social issues such as status and belonging being the ones we feel strongest about.

A new scientific field has emerged that is dedicated to these ideas, called social cognitive neuroscience (SCN). The field is new, with its first two academic journals launched in March (*Social Cognitive and Affective Neuroscience*) and June (*Social Neuroscience*) of 2006. *American Psychologist* announced the arrival of the new field in an article written by Ochsner and Lieberman and published in 2001. Most neuroscience up to the turn of the 21st century exhibited the individualistic orientation of the mechanistic paradigm, focusing on the functioning of a solo brain. SCN subscribes to the contextual orientation of the systemic paradigm by studying the interrelatedness of brains and minds in the social field.

Social neuroscience also considers the human experience at multiple levels, from the molecular to the functional, to the psychological, to the observable, to the social world and wider society. SCN brings together social and cognitive psychology with brain science methodology in the hope of deciphering the neural processes underlying complex behaviors that have puzzled human sciences for years—topics such as stereotyping, influence, attitudes, and self-control—and how these in turn influence brain function and structure. Many of these topics were studied in the past by different fields in parallel, without using language that indicated how similar the underlying phenomena may be. SCN shares with interpersonal neurobiology (Siegel, 1999, 2007a, b) the goal of sharing results and developing a common language so researchers from different fields can talk with one another (Lieberman, 2007).

According to Matt Lieberman, one of the key contributors to SCN, for three-quarters of the time that we are not concentrating on work or something outside ourselves, we are thinking about our social relationships. Our brain has been formed over time by its environment, and our environment is predominantly a social one. So the environment that we live in is more social than physical.

Given that much of coaching focuses on improving a person's ability to interact with and influence others, it makes sense that coaching could benefit from the findings of SCN.

One such finding is that emotions are contagious. The strongest emotion in a team can ripple out and elicit the same emotion in others, without anyone consciously knowing this is happening. Thus, our state of mind can be influenced by interaction with others. In an organizational context, the leader's frame of mind can have a powerful effect on others. Coaching can assist leaders to be aware of this and thus enable leaders to make choices about the mood they want to invite within the organization. Future research can be expected to help us understand how some people's emotions are more contagious than others'.

The rich history of attachment research combined with neuroscience and other fields such as anthropology, psychiatry, and linguistics, yields the recommendation that we relate to people from whom we "catch" emotions that are beneficial to us. We consider these attuned relationships to be one of the three irreducible elements of health and well-being. The others are an integrated brain and self-reflective mind.

Attuned relationships occur when two people engage in what we have described as collaborative, contingent conversations. Adult educators concur, drawing on SCN for evidence that "the brain actually needs to seek out an affectively attuned other if it is to learn. Affective attunement alleviates fear, which has been recognized by many in the field of adult learning and development as an impediment to learning" (Johnson, 2006, p. 66).

The feeling we get when we connect intensely with another human being in this way is the opposite of the stress response that happens when we feel threatened. When we interconnect our emotions, goals, and thoughts with those of others, we bring about a release of oxytocin, a highly pleasurable chemical. This occurs when two people are dancing together, playing music together, or having mutually gratifying sex as well as having quality conversations. It seems the brain is built to reward quality connections and interconnectivity.

Another way of asserting the importance of connectivity is to say that there is no such thing as an individual brain divorced from connections with others. We have discussed the prescient notions of Alfred Adler, who refused to work with clients as if they were isolated human beings. The dehumanizing effects of total isolation are only partially countered by our amazing ability to carry our relationships with us, in our imagination, and to carry on conversations in our minds "as if" another person is present.

The connection between a coach and a client is often termed "rapport." We become aware of rapport most often when it is absent. The field of psychotherapy went through a phase of blaming the client for any lack of rapport, labeling such clients "resistant." Coaches can fall into this trap by not realizing that rapport is a function of the relationship between coach and client, not a characteristic of one or the other individual.

It is true that sometimes a client may not want to be involved in coaching, or the coach may not want to work with this particular client or in this particular context. This does not have to destroy rapport, as long as the two collaborate in recognizing what is actually going on in the present rather than what someone or something says should be going on. The two can then collaborate in deciding what to do about the situation, perhaps by ending or delaying coaching.

Often we are not aware of what it is that has disturbed rapport. We may feel uncomfortable or irritated or anxious with a client. This may be the result of a mismatch of unconscious behavior and expectations, often resulting from culturally influenced implicit mental models. We are not used to people sitting so close or so far; speaking so loud or so soft;

or gazing at us so intently or not looking at us when we speak to them. Communication between people of different cultures and subcultures can trigger discomfort that makes connection difficult. Exploring these areas with clients can not only establish the rapport that makes coaching effective, it may also model ways for them to consciously create more fulfilling relationships at work or in their personal lives.

We have indicated that our beliefs, values, and culture create the filters through which we see the world. Social neuroscience shows that how we understand, empathize, and socialize with others is also filtered by our mental processes. Clients' mental models will guide how they navigate their social landscape, whether in an organizational or a personal context. Therefore, it is useful for both coaches and clients to become mindful not only of our own beliefs and values but also how we interpret the beliefs and values of others in our environment — including one another in a coaching relationship. The ability to do this overlaps with Daniel Goleman's concept of social intelligence (2006) and is part of the output of relating that we identify as intuition.

Linking Social Brain Concepts to Coaching

There is a claim in some coaching circles that all clients have all the solutions they need and the coach is simply there to help uncover those resources. But how could that be? For an individual to have every solution would mean that each of us must have experienced every possible contingency. Sometimes we face entirely new situations that we have not developed the mental "muscles" to deal with. As anthropologist Robert Redfield (1953) showed, even prehistoric societies faced changes beyond their imagining. How much more is that true today, with the rate of change increasing exponentially?

No human being can have had all possible experiences, no matter how much change or how many moves. But having social brains enables us to draw on the experiences of others. We mentioned social psychologist Lev Vygotsky in chapter 7 in the section on developmental psychology. He believed that the most important measure of intelligence was not what people can do on their own, but what they can do with just a little help from their friends. He called this the "zone of proximal development" (Vygotsky, 1978). For example, when a child is frightened at first hearing a dog's bark, she can "borrow" her father's calm attitude and over time learn to calm herself.

In coaching, we connect with clients in order to help them expand their "zone of proximal development." When we enter collaborative, contingent conversations, we are opening our experiences to our clients so they may draw on those resources. It is the coach's responsibility to recognize less-than-optimal resourcefulness, not to correct it but to invite the client to ask whether more is possible. An invitation like this may be all it takes for the client to shift into a more resourceful state. But in some cases, clients may need to "borrow" from the coach's experience as scaffolding in order to build their own (Johnson, 2006).

Example: A Performance Review that Encouraged Development

Colleen was pleased with her promotion to head the service department at an electronics chain. The fact that she was provided with a coach meant that the company thought of her as "high potential." However, when it came to conducting performance reviews with her staff, all she could think of was her own devastating experience with her overly critical former boss. She did not want anyone else to go through that, but she had never experienced a performance review that encouraged development. Her coach suggested they role-play a review using a coaching mind-set.

The crucial element in role-playing is that the learner takes on all the relevant roles, so Colleen started by describing the employee whom the coach would play. The coach played that role, and Colleen delivered a review to her coach as employee.

The two talked about how they each experienced the interaction and then switched roles.

The coach used the information that Colleen had provided when she role-played speaking to her employee. But now, in role-playing Colleen, the coach focused on how the same facts could be delivered in a way that encouraged and advanced the employee's goals. After this run-through, Colleen tried again, but this time she used as much of the coach's approach as she felt comfortable with.

This practice session helped Colleen conduct reviews with her coach's demeanor and words consciously in mind. It was not long before it became automatic for her to access an encouraging approach in conducting performance reviews.

There is a link here to neuroplasticity, or the brain's ability to grow. In simple terms, the coaching process stimulates new connections and likely even the production of new neurons. Having more neurons to use and flexing this mental muscle more regularly means that change becomes easier for clients. This is what we mean by "self-directed neuroplasticity."

THEORY OF MIND

Philosophers, especially since the time of Descartes, and 20th-century scientists, especially more recent cognitive psychologists, have puzzled over the human capacity for developing a "theory of mind"—that is, the ability to grasp that others have beliefs, desires, and intentions that are different from our own. It is often implied or assumed (but not stated explicitly) that this does not merely signify conceptual understanding that "other people have minds and think" but also the recognition that these thoughts and states and emotions are real and genuine for these people, just as ours are for ourselves.

This concept is not just about a cognitive theory, for it is closely related to empathy. "Empathy" means experientially recognizing and understanding the states of mind, including beliefs, desires, and particularly emotions of others without injecting our own. This is commonly characterized as the ability to put oneself into another's shoes. In describing empathy, Alfred Adler used the phrase "See with the eyes of another, hear with the ears of another, feel with the heart of another." But how people might do that was a matter of speculation: Was it taught by experience or learned by modeling, or did we just appear to empathize when actually we are pursuing our selfish ends?

The discovery of mirror neurons (Gallese, Fadiga, Fogassi, & Rizzolatti, 1996; Rizzolatti, Fadiga, Gallese, & Fogassi, 1996) as discussed in chapter 3, opened up an entirely new possibility. Might the firing of neurons when observing the intentional actions of others account for our capacity for empathy and our ability to develop a theory of mind? It does appear that we grasp the experience of others through direct experience of ourselves, through sensing, not thinking. When someone is feeling sad, we know so partly because we also feel sad.

It makes sense, then, that we develop a theory of mind because we understand another's mind almost as if we were in it—or as if they were in ours. We have already noted how very different each person's brain is. If that is the case, then we need some special advantage to be able to navigate the social world intelligently and overcome the vast differences between us. If we are to anticipate what others will do, which we have defined as the hallmark of intelligence, we literally need to know how, despite all its differences, that other mind thinks.

Thus, theory of mind generally covers two separate concepts:

1. Understanding that others also have minds, with different and separate beliefs, desires, mental states, and intentions
2. Being able to form operational hypotheses (theories), or mental models, with some degree of accuracy, as to what those beliefs, desires, mental states, and intentions are

A theory of mind appears to be an innate potential ability in most humans (and, some argue, in certain other species), but it requires social and other experience over many years to bring to adult fruition. It is probably a continuum, in the sense that different people may develop more or less effective theories of mind, varying from very complete and accurate ones through to minimally functional.

Studies of young children show that they develop a theory of mind between the ages of four and six years. Before they have this, children have difficulty playing hide and seek effectively: They do not realize that others cannot see them when their own eyes are closed but they are in full view.

Many of Shakespeare's plays involve characters misunderstanding others' intentions. In *King Lear*, for example, we need to hold in our own mind as the audience the various intentions of the players. The tragedy that unfolds emanates from the misreading of these intentions. In everyday life, big brains are needed to find our way through a complex social world. Even in a current "romantic comedy" series on television, dramatic tension typically arises when characters mistake the intentions of others or fail to communicate what others need to know in order to understand their intentions.

With each person we meet, we wonder: friend or foe, threat or resource, trustworthy or not? It is efficient and perhaps even safer to have a way of anticipating or predicting these qualities before the consequences are played out. It is believed that much of the high-level capacity of our brains, such as working memory, evolved to manage social complexities such as these.

In the animal kingdom, it has been found that the bigger the brain, the bigger the social group. Based on brain size, humans might be better off in groups of about 150, which is the size of a typical English village or a hunter-gatherer group; it is how we lived throughout most of human history. It is also the size of many departments in corporations.

The brain has strong memory circuits for relationships between people. We remember people more easily than things and things more easily than concepts. Think of the number of people you could summon to mind in an hour and how well you could describe your relationship to each of them. Our memories of our interconnections are vast. For example, memory experts remember several decks of playing cards in random order by creating a story of how characters represented by the cards relate to each other.

One aspect of our ability to have a theory of mind is that people know they are important to us when we show that we think of them even when they are not present. Beginning a coaching session by asking about the important presentation a client gave after the last session lets him or her know that the coach carries not just the client's identity but a sense of what is important to that client. Rapport in coaching and other relationships is greatly dependent on exercising the amazing capacity for theory of mind.

Linking Theory of Mind to Coaching

As a beginning coach, one of us (Linda) attended a demonstration of a master coach working with a woman who was trying to decide between two jobs. At one point in the demonstration, seemingly out of nowhere, the coach asked, "I'm feeling some kind of discomfort in my stomach." The client was amazed—she had been bothered all day by a stomachache, and recognizing that feeling opened up the solution she had been looking for.

How could the coach have known about the stomachache? How does intuition happen? We do not know for sure, but a good possibility would be mirror neurons. Most coaches could give many such experiences, and paying attention to our own seemingly inexplicable sensations or seemingly unrelated thoughts or fleeting emotions makes them more likely. As coaches, our most important tool is our own mind, and much of the power of our mind comes from the ability to put ourselves in our clients' shoes—to see with their eyes, hear with their ears, and feel with their hearts.

This capacity always comes with the warning that we never assume that what we are perceiving or feeling is necessarily relevant to the client. Even when it may be, to impose that assumption is likely to trigger a status threat. Asking respectfully acknowledges the client's personal space and establishes a collaborative interaction so that even a mistake can contribute to understanding or creating more choices.

REPAIRING RELATIONSHIPS–*SANGE*

Despite our best intentions, any training we may have had as coaches, and our capacity for theory of mind, sometimes we do or say something that results in a client feeling threatened or annoyed in some way. We try to explain, but that just makes things worse. How do we recover and help our client feel safe enough to continue learning? We have discussed our hardwired sensitivity to status threats. Sometimes when a client perceives that status has been threatened, he or she reacts with anger in an attempt to subdue another or gain the upper hand. Even when we do not intend to threaten someone else's sense of belonging, our brains are unique; we can intend one thing only to have the impact be exactly the opposite. Therefore, even the most attuned relationships occasionally are ruptured.

In a culture of competition, "put-downs" are a way to gain advantage. Rudolf Dreikurs, psychiatrist and student of Alfred Adler, identified one cost of this pattern of interaction. He called it "the ironclad logic of social living" (Dreikurs, 1971, p. ix). The moment a person feels unfairly treated, she or he begins plotting how to "get back," as inexorably as water runs downhill. Most of us do not need to look beyond our own relationships and organizations to see examples of this. "Employee engagement" and "flat organizations" are seen as ways to combat the productivity-damaging effects of command-and-control organizational cultures.

On a more personal level, Malcolm Gladwell (2005) refers to several studies that show how inadvertent insults can result in costly consequences. For example, patients are likely to forgive medical errors by doctors who treat them respectfully but are more likely to sue those who do not. Psychotherapists have recognized the importance of repairing relationship ruptures in order to maintain a therapeutic alliance. Learning theorists insist on the importance of a caring relationship if a person is to engage in learning (Johnson, 2006). Although we do not yet have similar empirical research on the role of the relationship in coaching, it is a safe assumption that damage to the coaching relationship affects the outcome of coaching.

Given that we all occasionally step on others' toes, how can we take responsibility for our part in a rupture without putting ourselves down or triggering another round of conflict and perhaps a permanent rupture? There is perhaps no more useful relationship skill than knowing how to apologize in order to restore a working relationship.

In Japanese Buddhism, this is called *sange*, pronounced SAHN-gay. *Sange* refers to becoming aware of effects we have created and making amends that restore harmony with others and develop our own wisdom. This ancient practice is supported by what we now know about the brain.

PREPARATION FOR *SANGE*   Do this before saying anything to the person to whom you will apologize. Apologies most often go awry because we couple them with a defense of our own position or a reason why what we did should be excused or an explanation of why we did it. This does not help. In effect, we are adding "and you *should* forgive me" to our apology. Saying "should" to someone is always likely to arouse a status threat reaction. To add this insult to the perception of having already been injured only perpetuates the rupture.

Sometimes we are not sure we should be the ones apologizing. It is better not to apologize at all than to do it grudgingly. Remember how sensitive we are to other people's intentions. The other person's mirror neurons pick up on motor signals well before conscious processing. In such a sensitive situation, we cannot expect our lack of sincerity to go unregistered, even if it is not consciously noticed.

To shift a state of "It's not my fault," we invite you to have this conversation with yourself: "However small the part I played in this rupture, I played some part in it or it wouldn't be bothering me. Among all the chain of choices I made leading up to this rupture, what could I have done differently? What choice or choices can I genuinely regret making or not making?" This internal conversation triggers a state of awareness and choice.

Example: "All You Ever Do Is Whine!"

In an interdepartmental meeting regarding information technology strategies, human resources director Frank allowed his frustration from a previous meeting to spill over. When Selma from accounting pointed out that his new idea would mean extra work for her, Frank responded, "All you ever do is whine!" Selma clenched her jaw and Frank saw a red flush spread underneath her collar. For the next three days, Selma was "too busy" to return calls or e-mails regarding the project Frank was supposed to complete by the end of the week. Frank realized he needed to apologize in order to repair the rupture in their working relationship.

Frank began by realizing that he had not dealt well with his frustration at the time of the meeting preceding his outburst to Selma. His statement "All you ever do..." was simply not true. If that was all Selma ever did, they would not have been able to work together in the past. Frank realized he had, quite simply, misspoken, and that warranted an apology. He made an appointment with Selma, making sure they both had the time and privacy to talk. He then followed the first principles of sange.

Steps in Sange

- *S—simplicity.* Keep it simple. Say, "I apologize for making that remark." Or "I am very sorry for forgetting your vacation request." No excuses. No explanations. Focus first on apologizing for what you are responsible for doing or not doing. Avoid the temptation to elaborate on how bad or guilty you feel. This can be seen as a demand for pity and for making *you* feel better. As much as possible, think about how the other person feels. If it can be said simply, you may want to recognize something like, "You didn't deserve that."

  Then stop and allow the other person to respond however she or he chooses. You cannot control the other's response, and to expect that the other person is ready to accept your apology only sets you up for an escalation of conflict. If the other person's status threat response is still active, she or he may react negatively. By understanding this, you may be able simply to let the reaction be what it is rather than allowing your own status to be threatened.

Example: "You Deserve Better"

After closing the door to Selma's office, Frank said, "I want to apologize for the remark I made at the meeting. You deserve better."

Selma replied, "You're right. I do deserve better. I've worked damn hard to support your projects. You know that."

- *A—acknowledgment*. After noting your responsibility for a choice that contributed to the rupture, put yourself in the position of the other person and acknowledge how he or she might have felt. "That must have felt so embarrassing for you." "I'm guessing that you felt quite alone."

  Once again, stop and allow the other to respond. You may have been quite wrong in your assessment, but that is not the point. Rather, by making room for the other person's feelings, you have acknowledged that his or her reaction is legitimate, and that is a big step toward calming a status threat reaction.

Example: "You Must Have Felt Really Hurt"

Frank: "You must have felt really hurt by that."
Selma: "Yes, I was."

- *N—needs of the situation*. What happens next is contingent upon the needs of the situation, in particular what the relationship needs in order to reach mutual goals. Determining this requires making a shift from "me versus you" to "we." One way to do this is to say what you want from an ideal relationship in this context: "I really want us to work well together." "I hope we can make this team really perform."

Usually lower-order competitive and vengeful goals, such as "You made me look bad and I'll get you for it," generate conflict and relationship ruptures. If you and the other person are in a common situation, in a system, then at some level your welfare is interdependent. What are goals at that level?

Example: "That's What I Want"

Frank: "We can really kick ass when we work together. That's what I want."
Selma: "Yes, that's what I want too. I just couldn't believe that you seemed to forget that."

- *G—gratitude.* Both appreciative inquiry and positive psychology have emphasized the benefits of being in a grateful state of mind. This moves us toward people rather than against them and assures us of belonging, thus opening up our creativity. What is it about the other person that you are truly, genuinely, sincerely grateful for? However difficult this situation has been, it could end up being a very important learning experience for you. What have you learned and how grateful are you for that?

  Again, once you have stated what you are grateful for, leave some room for the other to respond—without expecting any-thing in particular about that response. Again, activate your hub or impartial observer simply to allow that response rather than being captured by any potential threat or resentment. Sometimes you may be surprised at the other person's willingness to take responsibility.

Example: "You Hold Me to High Standards"

Frank: "The truth is, you don't whine. You hold me to high standards, and thank goodness. That's one of your greatest strengths. It's part of what I appreciate most about you."
Selma: "That's important to me. I can see how sometimes I go overboard with it and it sounds like I'm only complaining."

438

- *E—exploration.* Only when both of you have shifted to an appreciative perspective can you explore what you could do differently next time—what *you* can do, not what the other person should do. If you are still angry or in a one-up-one-down position, whatever you say will come across as a status threat. But from a collaborative stance, you can ask how to make amends.

Example: "I'm Going to Do My Best"

Frank: "I can tell you that next time I get frustrated, I'm going to do my best to just admit it rather than lashing out."

Selma: "And I'll work on saying something positive before I point out problems."

Frank: "Is there anything I can do to make this up to you?"

Selma: "Sure. How's about an extra week's vacation?" They laugh. "If that's not on the table, let's just have a cup of coffee and we'll call it even."

Not only do seemingly small interactions such as this restore working relationships, they also contribute to the increasing complexity, and thus the maturity and viability, of the relationship and the organizational system of which it is a part. Both Frank and Selma end up with greater confidence in themselves and each other, a greater sense of fulfillment because of the quality of their social relationships, and better productivity because they engage the synergy of collaboration. Interactions such as this are the building blocks of a collaborative organizational culture. They also build the parts of our brains that depend on collaborative, contingent social input—attuned relating.

Sange is a five-step technique that may help clients when they want to repair a relationship:

1. **S**— Simple apology.
2. **A**— Acknowledgment of the other's feelings.
3. **N**— Focus on *needs* of the situation.
4. **G**— Gratitude for other's strengths.
5. **E**— Exploration of how to prevent future ruptures.

Presenting this as a prescription is nowhere near as effective as asking clients to identify what it is about an apology they have received that works or does not work for them. However, the *sange* outline may help clients put words to what they have discovered, making it less likely that they will forget.

RESOLVING CONFLICT—STOP AND GROW

A similar caveat applies to techniques for conflict resolution. When a client and another person, or two or more clients in a team, are locked in a power struggle, it is helpful for coaches to be familiar with the principles that underlie how to resolve the struggle without either party feeling defeated.

Many times power struggles feel like the clash of an immovable object and an irresistible force. One person wants one thing and the other wants exactly the opposite. Each acts as if his or her very life depends on winning, or at least not losing, the struggle. If one wins, the other loses, and vice versa. This can paralyze a project or a department or even a whole company. Coaches or leaders may be called on to resolve the impasse.

It is often obvious to observers that the two protagonists are locked into a narrow view of the situation. But remember that fear and status threats can shut down our brain's capacity to see a bigger picture or consider other points of view. The question is how to calm the amygdala response so as to allow a meta-view to emerge. Often this can be accomplished by encouraging either or both protagonists to ask different questions.

Linda has worked with eminent psychologist Richard Kopp and Adler faculty member Jeanie Nishimura to develop a staged series of questions they call the Stop and Grow Model shown in Figure 15.1.

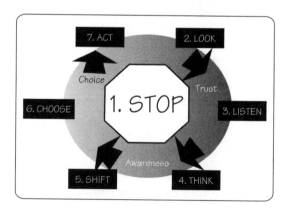

Figure 15.1   How to Stop and Grow
©2006, Adler International Learning Inc. *Reproduced with permission*

The questions are ones that a coach can use to help a client resolve a power struggle, whether the other person is present or not.

Using an analogy to a stop sign, here are seven types of questions to ask, followed by comments:

1. *Stop.* What am I feeling? Do I want to keep this up? If I keep doing what I've been doing, will anything change? Will the other person change if I do it harder? Has it worked so far? Has it worked in the past?

   Remember that naming an emotion calms the amygdala. Talking about it changes the feeling. Trying to suppress it maintains arousal and interferes with prefrontal processing such as seeing the big picture, regulating one's emotions, or empathy. Watch for a change in energy that indicates a reduction in arousal. At that point, the client may be ready to ask himself or herself a different set of questions. Asking for permission to introduce these may further calm the amygdala by reassuring the client of her or his autonomy in the matter.

2. *Look.* What actually happened when I got into this struggle? If I were a video camera, what would I have recorded? What specifically did I see, say, and do? What did the other person say and do? How did I respond? How did the other person respond?

   The point of these questions is to go down the Ladder of Inference to the concrete, specific details of what was said and done. When clients step back and imagine themselves to be a camera, they take on the perspective of an observer. This is another technique for calming an aroused limbic system. Stripping the conflict to the bare events sets the stage for building new meaning.

3. *Listen.* If I run the video in slow motion before my mind's eye, what was I telling myself at each point? What was I believing about what happened? What could the other person have been believing in order to say or do what happened? What questions must I have been asking to do that? What questions must the other person have been asking to do that?

   Albert Ellis insisted that A, or action, was connected with C, or consequence, only by going through B, or belief. But we are mostly unaware of B, and jump straight from what someone does to how we will react without recognizing the belief that connects them.

Rather than disputing the belief, as Ellis taught therapists to do, coaches rely on the ability of the clients to reappraise their belief once they are aware of it. These questions also activate the client's theory of mind so that they are more likely to be able to take the perspective of the other person.

4. *Think.* What are the feeling/belief patterns that this interaction represents? Am I thinking that the other person should see things the way I do? Is that related to any annoyance I feel? Ought he to do as I say without question? Is that connected with my anger? Does she not see that I am right and she is wrong? Could that be why I am feeling so indignant? Is he pushing me beyond my comfort level? Does that explain my resentment? What goal is indicated by this feeling/belief pattern? Do these (or any other feeling/belief patterns identified) show up anyplace else in my life?

This series of questions encourages self-reflection. It takes the focus off the other person—after all, it is futile to try to make someone else change. We can only change ourselves. If the client sees patterns across other areas of his or her life, making those connections may release a feeling of reward that will go a long way toward shifting his or her state of mind.

5. *Shift.* Quite aside from my feelings or goals or the other person's feelings or goals, what are the needs of the situation? What would be best for the organization? For the relationship? What unrecognized potential is there here? If I could do something to make all our dreams come true, what would it be? What are my values? What are the organization's values?

These are meta-perspective questions. They require the client to step up to higher and higher levels of generality. This activates the prefrontal cortex, which coordinates planning, emotion regulation, and morality.

6. *Choose.* What options can I commit myself to without regret or resentment? Which ones can I do without demanding that the other person change? Which is most likely to meet the needs of the situation? Which best reflects my values?

Remember that it is difficult under the best of circumstances for anyone to hold more than three options in mind at one time. Two is optimal. The above questions are designed to eliminate options until a very few are left. Having gone through these steps, it is likely that the client's brain has been calmed enough to free up working memory required for making a decision between two choices.

7. Act. What will make it most likely that I will put the chosen option into action? How can I hold myself accountable? What supports will help? What barriers might stand in the way? What have I learned?

Often, going through this process will result in a feeling of insight accompanied by energy that can be used for action. Coaches are trained to establish accountability so that thought exercises end up with changes in the real world.

The conclusion of this process is the beginning of the next cycle. At the point where we catch ourselves repeating unwanted behavior or not liking the consequences of new actions, we stop, beginning at step 1. Originally developed as part of a parent coaching curriculum, this model and others that represent cyclical processes have applications throughout our personal and organizational lives.

Calming Threats—The SCARF Model

At the 2008 NeuroLeadership Summits in Sydney, Australia, and New York, David Rock presented a model that utilizes the growing understanding of motivations underlying an approach versus an avoidance response (Rock, 2008). We have examined the effects on the brain of threats that arouse the limbic system, reducing the ability of the prefrontal cortex to plan and create. In organizations, this arousal and resulting avoidance behavior can be a major challenge to leaders who wish to promote collaboration and creativity. David's SCARF model provides an easy-to-remember guide that coaches can use to help leaders overcome this challenge. The term "SCARF" stands for:

- Status
- Certainty
- Autonomy
- Relatedness
- Fairness

Status. "The perception of a potential or real reduction in status can generate a strong threat response" (Rock, 2008, p. 46). And it is easy to arouse this response. Merely offering advice or telling someone how to do something better when they have not asked for help can imply a lower status. On the other hand, leaders, who understand how to reward employees with a status boost can reap the benefits of a more engaged workforce. Because we use the same brain circuits to evaluate ourselves as we do to evaluate others, even out-performing ourselves can elevate our sense of status.

Certainty. Uncertainty creates an error response, a mismatch between what we expect and what we are getting, that reduces our ability to attend to our goals. Many times, leaders withhold negative information for fear that it will create panic. In fact, even bad news can be preferable to not knowing. And even finding out when we will find out can be calming, as in being told "We will find out the answer and report back in 48 hours." Setting objectives at the beginning of conversations or meetings not only helps to organize discussion, it lends a sense of certainty. Leaders and their coaches would do well to keep the creation of certainty in mind, even in situations of uncertainty.

Autonomy. We have given examples of the beneficial effects of choice on brain and body. Autonomy has to do with the perception of control or choice over the environment, especially over potential stressors. Being given a choice feels good. However, working with others on a team requires that each member's autonomy is reduced. Leadership that allows the team to create its own ground rules for achieving organizational goals can help balance autonomy with group needs.

Relatedness. Alfred Adler posited the sense of belonging as a major motivator and contributor to mental health, and research by Baumeister and Leary (1995) supports this view. Whether one is "in" or "out" of the group is a judgment made very quickly by automatic brain processes, and meeting a stranger generates a rapid threat response. Moving from "out" to "in" is accompanied by a comforting release of the hormone oxytocin for both parties, and that further increases trust and the likelihood of collaboration. David points out that creating a feeling of connectedness among people who must work together but seldom or never meet, as in a globally scattered workforce, is a particularly challenging problem. Using technology, such as telephone bridge lines or videoconferencing to promote informal social interaction, is not a waste of time when the benefits of trust and collaboration are taken into account. Coaches who understand the dynamics of relatedness can help leaders meet this challenge.

Fairness. We have learned from anthropology that reciprocity is a universal value among human beings. From the perspective of the brain, we have a built-in unfairness detector, as parents will attest every time their children protest, "That's not fair!" The hierarchical model of management prescribes secrecy and a "do as you're told" mentality. But modern leadership practices recognize that transparency and open communication decrease employee dissatisfaction and sense of being treated unfairly. Of course, having clear ground rules and procedures and applying them consistently is crucial for an atmosphere of mutual respect. Asking teams to make their own decisions, such as for workload assignments, further enhances a sense of fairness.

Example: Maple Leaf Foods and Sunrise Propane

Management of the threat response becomes most crucial during a business crisis. When there is an actual threat, even leading to death, how can the SCARF model help to set things right?

Two Canadian corporations went through tragedies in the summer of 2008. An outbreak of the food-borne bacterium *Listeria monocytogenes* that resulted in several deaths was traced to a Maple Leaf Foods plant on August 23. Maple Leaf produces and sells processed meat products. One day later, a previous recall of some products was expanded, and the plant was shut down. Immediately, chief executive officer (CEO) Michael McCain appeared on television to speak openly about what was happening and to issue an apology; other leaders gave interviews in various media; the company took out informational ads; and a Web site was set up to answer questions from the public. Despite what was clearly a tragedy and could have been a disaster that spelled the end of the business, stock prices for Maple Leaf Foods dipped in September but by December were back at pre-August levels.

(Continued)

Sunrise Propane, a plant that stores and distributes propane, exploded on August 10, forcing 12,000 neighbors from their homes, destroying or damaging businesses and residences, and leaving a firefighter and employee dead. Sunrise's response was very different from that of Maple Leaf. The company remained tight-lipped, issuing terse statements only after conclusions could be reached, such as whether the employee had indeed been working during the explosion. Communications came from "the company" or a "spokesperson" rather than from a recognizable head of the corporation. Information was released grudgingly. In December 2008, a judge made a rare ruling directing the release of all government, regulatory, and company reports regarding the explosion to lawyers representing clients in a class-action suit. The company's stock is not publicly traded, so is difficult to track, but one can surmise that, today, much more negative reactions surround Sunrise Propane than Maple Leaf Foods.

What accounts for the contrasting results for these two companies? The tragedies of a *Listeria* outbreak and an explosion are guaranteed to produce a withdrawal response. Maple Leaf handled this with a SCARF-wise strategy; Sunrise Propane did the opposite. Maple Leaf CEO McCain made himself vulnerable by facing television cameras and reporters immediately rather than arranging for a scripted appearance. Dressed in an open-collared shirt that deemphasized *status*, rather than in a suit and tie, he appeared and behaved like any person who was facing a tragic situation. Sunrise Propane, by its silence, emphasized its distance from and higher status than the public or its victims.

Regarding *certainty*, Maple Leaf gave regular reports as to recall, plant closure, and the detailed inspection of every part of the plant that eventually identified one machine as harboring the bacterium. Sunrise left its employees, victims, and the public wondering.

Although CEO McCain took the lead in making appearances, Maple Leaf allowed *autonomy* to its other executives and leaders, encouraging them to represent the company's commitment to openness. Sunrise put out official announcements and directed inquiries to its designated spokesperson.

McCain demonstrated a sense of *relatedness* to those customers who had fallen ill or died. In his initial television appearance, he became emotional and allowed his grief to show. This demonstrated a human connection and allowed for others to feel the same. At least one blue-collar worker responded, "I trust that man." No such opportunity for connection occurred for Sunrise.

Fairness was demonstrated by McCain's apology and the company's willingness to negotiate a settlement with victims without being forced into it by the courts. Sunrise Propane is engaged in a class-action lawsuit.

Coaches can recommend the acronym SCARF to remind leaders to initiate brain-wise responses in day-to-day interactions. Aside from immediately freeing employees from a productivity-limiting withdrawal response, the organization will be practicing what may very well make the difference between survival and demise in the case of a crisis.

SCARF, *sange*, Stop-and-Grow, and other techniques presented in this chapter are merely the beginning of applying knowledge of the brain to NeuroLeadership. As research, conferences, and publications proliferate, coaches and leaders will gain even more ways to potentiate organizations and individuals in them.

PRACTICE GUIDE FOR COACHING WITH THE BRAIN IN MIND — GET ALONG WITH OTHERS

Fears for our safety and security stimulate an amygdala response. Modern research has confirmed that Alfred Adler was correct in positing a human need to belong (Baumeister & Leary, 1995), and we have described the brain's sensitivity to status threats. Uncertainty and change result in limbic system arousal, as does being boxed in with no choices. Being around people we do not trust or even people we do not know well adds to the stress response. Researchers at the Social Cognitive Neuroscience Lab at UCLA (Tabibnia, Satpute, & Lieberman, 2008) have found that the reward circuitry in people's brains is stimulated by being treated fairly whereas unfairness triggers avoidance and stress. Is it any wonder that organizations are often minefields for stress explosions?

We know that stress reduces our cognitive processing capacity — that being under pressure means we are much less likely to be able to take in information. And our capacity for empathy and seeing things from another's point of view is reduced when we are under stress. How, then, can an executive or organizational coach make it more likely that coaching will have an effect rather than being ignored or not even heard?

When coaches keep the brain in mind, they have the capacity to:

- Engage in collaborative, contingent conversations that lead to attuned relationships and repair damaged ones.
- Examine "mistakes" or conflict so as to know better which intuition or internal voice to listen to and which to ignore in the future.
- Reduce the danger response and increase the reward response by enhancing:
  - Status.
  - Certainty.
  - Autonomy.
  - Relatedness through trust.
  - Fairness.

Conclusion: What Are We Doing Here?

Ishi, the last "wild Indian" and last member of his tribe, faced enormous challenges when he left his northeastern California wilderness homeland and moved to San Francisco in 1911. He had to think and relate to others very differently, and neuroscience tells us that these adjustments were surely reflected in the very structures of his brain. The challenges to our minds, relationships, and brains are no less for us today than those Ishi faced. For the first time ever, we have seen our home planet from space or the moon. Not only are we facing possible extinction from natural disasters, as happened to the dinosaurs, but we are aware of these threats. Added to that are threats we humans have created or exacerbated, such as annihilation by nuclear weapons, climate change, or pandemics. Overcoming these threats will take all the creativity our young species can muster. Yet dangers such as these activate our limbic system, including the ever-on-guard amygdala, thus reducing brain functions that support creative thinking, problem solving, and big-picture planning.

Thus, we come to recognize the depth of what it means to be a social species. Now, as in the past, our survival depends on our ability to work together—to link our different skills and experiences into a complex system that consciously and deliberately moves toward a fuller expression of the highest values of humanity. This is the call to potentiate our species.

POTENTIATING

In this book, we have presented evidence for the deep historical and theoretical roots of coaching. We are also demonstrating how to deepen those roots through an understanding of neuroscience. We have defined the ever-increasing complexity resulting from a system's dynamic stability as "potentiating."

Here on this earth, we are making the choice of whether to answer a call that will determine the future of our species. In a certain sense, we are all Ishi. No one else really understands us or experiences the world exactly as each of us does. We are each reaching out from our unique selves, hoping to banish the fear of being the only one. This is not new, as the existentialists tell us. But now, with our never-before-available instant global communications and other ways to connect, we have a once-in-a-species opportunity to create an attuned social life that enables self-aware minds and integrated brains. Coaching has played its part in bringing about this opportunity, and it has a part to play in whether we take up the opportunity before us.

The genius of life is that, in moving away from threats and toward rewards, it fills all available niches for survival. The amazing variety of life on our planet as well as the diversity of human cultures attests to this dynamic. For the most part, this flowering happens without self-conscious direction. Most of human history has been the result of people reacting to forces that they could understand only dimly at best. Until recently, that dim understanding resulted from assuming that people were governed only by mechanical laws. However, as we continued to motivate ourselves toward survival by asking questions about ourselves and the world, we have discovered a truth: We are subjects in the creation of reality, not just objects. This conclusion is supported by a series of transformations from a mechanistic to a systemic worldview, as revealed in this book. A coach who is aware of these transformations and their implications is better prepared to help clients potentiate and evolve the new brains required to meet today's challenges.

WHAT ARE THE QUESTIONS?

Coaching has emerged as a response to age-old questions that were not adequately answered given the assumptions of the dominant Western

European and North American paradigm for the last three to four centuries: Newtonian mechanics. Coaching inherits the discoveries made by science during this era, conceived of as a theoretical bedrock, but has risen above that bedrock on pillars that have accompanied a shift to a new, systemic paradigm. The challenge for the future, not just for coaching but for the human species, lies in utilizing the science that embodies this new paradigm, brain science, as a platform for discovering how to think, relate, and therefore structure our brains so as to become the best species possible, or to potentiate.

WHO ARE WE?

The very possibility of asking "Who am I?" as a person and "Who are we?" as a group depends on being able to think of "me" or "us" as separate from the "I" or "we" who ask. Out of philosophical inquiry into this question, called "ontology," emerged an approach that is anchored in Newtonian assumptions. As with individual elements interacting according to these assumptions, inquiry began and ended with the individual person, who was assumed to be "supreme." However, social sciences in the late 19th and early 20th centuries, such as anthropology and sociology, and New Age philosophies began to shake this assumption. Thus, out of the bedrock of *individualism*, coaching has inherited a trend toward recognizing *relatedness*.

The trend toward recognizing our social embeddedness has been accelerated by globalization, systems theory, and quantum physics. Travel, communications, and commerce that have put people around the world in touch with one another has accelerated the exchange between Western and non-Western worldviews. Our recognition of our ties with one another and with our environment has encouraged our understanding of how systems work. And quantum physics has broken down the assumption of an objective observer, at least at the quantum level at which the brain operates. The very questions that people ask make a difference as to the responses that nature gives. So the pillar of social embeddedness lifts the human species from *observers* of how mechanistic laws play out in the world to *participants* in the creation of reality.

Neuroscience provides a scientifically validated platform for insisting that mindfulness—"awareness of the present, non-judgment and

451

acceptance"(Tang & Posner, 2008, p. 33)—is important to a person's reaching toward his or her potential. We call this process "potentiating," and we believe it is synonymous with goals of coaching. The ability to pay attention in the present to one's own thought processes not only helps coaches be present with others but also aids their brain development, conceived of as a complex, nonlinear, dynamic system.

As a result of this understanding and of their own mindfulness practices, coaches who put the principles of neuroscience into action come to *know themselves* better, and thus are able to:

1. Experience others directly through the senses, in the moment, rather than through narrative circuitry (stories coaches tell themselves *about* clients).
2. Develop and engage their own "Impartial Spectator," or self-observer, so as to reflect on and come to know themselves better.
3. Support clients in becoming more self-aware and self-appreciative.

How Can We Be Healthy?

Historically, medical practices included body-mind health promotion as well as prevention and treatment of disease. As Western medicine developed within the mechanistic paradigm, it focused on the physical body and left mental health and health promotion mainly to ancillary professionals and to public and governmental agencies. Nonetheless, the discoveries of physiology and research on stress have many applications to health in general and thus serve as bedrock for coaching. "Alternative" health practices, bolstered by globalization and New Age philosophy, became more mainstream during the 20th century. Along with research showing the connections between physical and mental health, they brought into question *dualism*, or separation of mind and body. The ancient concept of *holism* has been reintroduced to medical practice.

In health as in most human endeavors under the mechanistic paradigm, change was something that happened *to* people. But in some fields, such as athletics, the drive to perform better and better resulted in attempting to consciously make those changes. Solving the puzzle of how to help people change their physical and mental health habits also contributed to conscious studies of change and what prevents and accelerates it. These constitute a pillar that is important for coaches to understand as they encourage clients to see themselves not as *passive* victims of change but as *active* initiators, designers, and maintainers of changes they wish to make.

Only within the last decade or so has neuroscience provided support rather than discouragement for adults who wish to make profound changes. For at least 50 years, the received wisdom in brain science was that people structured their brains in childhood, and all they could expect as adults was some tinkering but not much else. Recent discoveries showing that adults, even elderly ones, can produce new brain cells as a result of experience (such as exercise) has exploded the myth of adult brain immutability. Thus, the concept of neuroplasticity has excited medical, learning, health, business, and many other communities, and has provided coaching with scientific evidence of the possibility of potentiation at any age. Potentiation requires the dynamic stability of the human system, and Jeffrey Schwartz and David Rock have developed a formula that brings together the elements for dynamic stability:

$$DS = (exptn - exprnce) \times AD^+ \times VP$$

Coaches are just beginning to understand the elements of change from the perspective of the brain. As they continue to do so, they will learn better how to *leverage change*, including being able to:

4. Recognize and balance the needs of physical brain/body, mind, and relationships.
5. Pay attention to attention (their own and others'), including metaphors, energy levels, signs of being stuck, and unconscious signals.
6. Support clients in catching themselves when they are about to repeat an unwanted pattern, veto that, choose a more beneficial path, and learn from the experience.

WHY DO WE DO WHAT WE DO?

During the 20th century in North America, people who wanted to understand human behavior typically looked to psychology, which became what one historian described as "the 'master' science of human affairs" (Prilleltensky, 1994, p. 28). However, psychologists were seeking to fit into a definition of scientists as objective seekers of value-free truth. Behaviorist research fit this paradigm, as did aspects of developmental and evolutionary psychology and psychometrics, but the relegation of the mind to a "black box" of no interest to science came under pressure by midcentury. Nonetheless, careful behaviorist and psychometric research has provided a bedrock for many coaching techniques, even as the trend has been from limiting research to *objective* observations to including the *subjective* experience of people.

The year 1956 is considered to be when the "cognitive revolution" shifted attention to what goes on in the black box of the mind. Thinking became a legitimate topic for scientific inquiry, and this combined with trends in learning theory to stimulate an understanding of how to activate the mind rather than just observe behavioral results of its (unknowable) processes. When applied to adults, educational principles could no longer assume an empty vessel into which an instructor inserted predetermined content. It did not take long for this assumption to be questioned for all learning at any age. For coaching, this trend provided a pillar to lift coaching from *teaching* to *experiencing*.

Over time, cognitive psychology has developed extensive overlap with neuroscience. Psychologists and brain researchers have asked similar questions about how memories are formed and the role of awareness and attention in the activation of memories. They have collaborated in discovering how people can carry on complex activities considering the limited capacity of working memory. In considering research on insight, or how to draw on out-of-awareness brain resources in order to resolve dilemmas, David Rock developed a Four Faces of Insight Model© (Rock, 2006) that we have included here as a useful guide for coaches.

With knowledge of the purpose and limits of cognitive processes, coaches can help clients make decisions and solve problems through being able to:

7. Communicate in short, specific sentences that maximize limited working memory.
8. Move among thinking levels so as to be able to simplify, chunk, and shift perspective with ease.
9. Facilitate their own and others' insights by:

- Creating and inviting a quiet mind.
- Focusing on connections rather than details.
- Allowing insights to emerge without interruption.
- Noticing and attending to insights when they emerge.
- Encouraging the flow to action.

How Can We Feel Better?

Psychotherapy is an *application* of medical and psychological theory with its own history that predates scientific psychology. For that reason, we deal with psychotherapy separately from psychology. Because it is a practice that uses psychosocial means to elicit change, psychotherapy has much to offer as bedrock for coaching. However, its roots in mechanistic assumptions resulted in an ongoing argument over what determines mental illness: heredity or environment? A systemic view says both are important, but human creativity and meaning making also play a role. Coaches may use many psychotherapy techniques as long as they avoid attempting to treat mental illness. Psychotherapy approaches described in chapter 10 reveal a trend from assuming that people's personalities and behaviors are *determined* by objective forces to seeing them as *constructed* by the active, unique, meaning-making capacity of human beings.

It is common for clients to come to coaches rather than psychotherapists because "I'm not sick — I just feel there's something more." To be fair, many psychotherapists see their practice as helping people live their lives more fully. But coaching has emerged as part of a desire to accentuate the positive. Nowhere is this practiced more consciously than in the new field of positive psychology, which studies what it means to be truly, authentically happy and fulfilled as a human being anyplace in the world. Along with research into resilience and emotional intelligence, this orientation provides a pillar that coaching has relied on in the shift from and emphasis on *illness* to a focus on *strengths*.

Neuroscience has provided a platform for utilizing emotions as summarizers of our state of mind—integrators of information from our bodies, minds, and relationships. Our survival has depended on the ability to summarize all these inputs so as to know whether to move toward what we perceive to be rewarding or to withdraw from what we perceive to be threatening. Yet emotions tell us not only about the reward or danger out there but also the processes our brain uses to gather and transmit that information. Sometimes our danger-alert process is too sensitive, and we find ourselves withdrawing when we should be, we later realize, moving forward. And vice versa.

Understanding how a threat response may be triggered by something other than an actual threat, or by a threat that demands a response minus the cognitive shutdown that threats elicit, helps coaches and their clients keep cool under pressure. Coaches who apply these principles are able to:

10. Shift attention to solutions rather than problems.
11. Recognize and explain the brain's reaction to threat; for example, difficulty in maintaining the "big picture" when experiencing stress.
12. Label and reappraise intense negative emotions and help others learn to do the same.
13. Recognize without taking personally the automatic danger response when one's own or another's status is threatened.

HOW CAN WE GET ALONG?

Management attempted to make itself more scientific by embracing Taylorism at the beginning of the 20th century. However, the fact that Taylorism dealt with organizations and teams and work groups militated against a totally individualistic approach. From the beginning, some management theorists stressed the human "soft" side of management concerns, despite the business school emphasis on numbers, thus providing useful bedrock for coaching. Organizations recognized this by relying on industrial/organizational psychology and social psychology for much of the theoretical principles on which their practices were based. The numbers orientation of meta-analysis has helped introduce a higher-level systemic view. Even 50 years ago, there were indications of a shift from *hierarchy* to a more systemic-related *participation*.

Beginning in the mid-20th century, some managers and consultants were so insistent on introducing a new perspective to organizational life that Art Kleiner (2007) called them "heretics." They were rejected by organizational powers in the same way that religious heretics were and continue to be. Now we know they were not heretics at all but visionary leaders. Their heresies are today the orthodoxy of organizational coaching, and these principles inform all coaches, whether they work directly with organizations or not; there are few clients for whom the workplace and the place of work in their lives are not likely to be fertile topics for coaching. One former heresy was that workers should have a voice in planning their work. Now management's job of *telling* people what to do is being replaced by leadership skills of *listening* to workers' own ideas, thus engaging their creativity and leadership capacity.

The integrative field of social cognitive and affective neuroscience provides a platform for recognizing that our brains are made for social participation and that we are a profoundly social species. David Rock founded a new field of NeuroLeadership to bring these insights into the business world. We actually are able to imagine how others think and to respond accordingly. Therefore, being informed that status, certainty, autonomy, relatedness, and fairness are associated with brain areas that produce strong reactions can help us know how to avoid those reactions and how to calm them when they occur, especially when they are the result of relationship ruptures or conflict.

Coaches who are aware of these approaches are able to help clients get along with others more effectively by utilizing the capacity to:

14. Engage in collaborative, contingent conversations that lead to attuned relationships and repair ruptured ones.
15. Examine "mistakes" or conflict so as to know better which intuition or internal voice to listen to and which to ignore in the future.
16. Reduce the danger response and increase the reward response by enhancing:
    - Status.
    - Certainty.
    - Autonomy.
    - Relatedness through trust.
    - Fairness.

These 16 competencies represent a beginning understanding of how we can reformat our own brains or, in Jeffrey Schwartz's terms, "self-direct our own neuroplasticity." Daniel Siegel would call it "using our [social] minds to create our brains."

As a child, Linda was supposed to be taking a nap but couldn't sleep. She had just eaten a cracker before being put to bed and noticed that a cracker crumb looked like a tooth. "I wonder," she asked herself, "if I wished hard enough, could I turn this cracker crumb into a real tooth?" Her interest was not just scientific theory testing. There was also the matter of the tooth fairy. She put the crumb under her pillow and wished and wished as hard as she could. But the crumb remained a crumb. She concluded at that point that even wishing with all her might would not make magic happen.

If the adult Linda could talk to that napping child, she would tell her she was right in one way but wrong in another. Although she could not just sit on her bed by herself and wish for a tooth to be created, human beings working together in the future would invent materials that could make teeth at least as good as the ones we grow ourselves, although a tooth fairy might not agree. And someday it would be possible to anchor a replacement tooth permanently in a person's mouth.

Although individual humans cannot create magic by wishing alone, we as a species can overcome seemingly insurmountable obstacles. We can join together to create a system marked by dynamic stability, increasing complexity, and a more humane species. We can use our minds and relationships to potentiate and evolve new brains.

Internet Links

4Therapy Network: www.4therapy.com/consumer (retrieved 4 April 2008).

Adler International Learning Inc.: www.adlerlearning.com (retrieved 10 January 2009).

American Psychiatric Association: www.healthyminds.org (retrieved 12 April 2009).

American Psychological Association Help Center: www.apahelpcenter. org (retrieved 12 April 2009).

Center for Narrative Coaching: http://narrativecoaching.com (retrieved 5 April 2008).

Dyer, Wayne: www.drwaynedyer.com (retrieved 5 January 2008).

Ekman, Paul: www.paulekman.com (retrieved 24 January 2008).

The Foundation of Coaching: www.coachingcommons.org (retrieved 10 January 2009).

Gallup Organization: www.gallup.com (retrieved 29 June 2008).

Harvard Medical School & McLean Hospital, Institute of Coaching: www.harvardcoaching.org (retrieved 1 June 2009).

Hay Group®: www.haygroup.com (retrieved 12 April 2009).

High Performing Systems Inc.: www.hpsys.com (retrieved 1 June 2009).

International Coach Federation: www.coachfederation.org (retrieved 31 December 2007).

International Consortium for Coaching in Organizations: www. coachingconsortium.org (retrieved 29 July 2008).

International Journal of Coaching in Organizations: www.ijco.info (retrieved 29 July 2008).

Internet Mental Health: www.mentalhealth.com (retrieved 4 April 2008).

The Journal of Positive Psychology: www.tandf.co.uk/journals/titles/17439760. asp_ (retrieved 29 June 2008).

Legacy Leadership®: www.coachworks.com (retrieved 1 June 2009).

Maharishi Vedic University: www.maharishi.org (accessed 5 January 2008).

MentorCoach™: www.mentorcoach.com. (retrieved 12 April 2009).

Multi-Health Systems Inc.: www.mhs.com (retrieved 1 June 2009).

NeuroLeadership Institute & Summit: www.neuroleadership.org (retrieved 29 July 2008).

Results Coaching Systems Inc.: www.resultscoaches.com (retrieved 30 March 2008).

Robbins, A. (2008). Home Page. www.tonyrobbins.com/Home/Home. aspx (accessed 5 January 2008).

Social Cognitive and Affective Neuroscience: http://scan.oxfordjournals.org (retrieved 8 March 2008).

Social Neuroscience: www.psypress.com/socialneuroscience (retrieved 8 March 2008).

Society for Psychotherapy Research: www.psychotherapyresearch.org (retrieved 1 June 2009).

The Shadow Coach™: www.theshadowcoach.com (retrieved 29 June 2008).

University of Pennsylvania Authentic Happiness: www.authentichappiness. sas.upenn.edu/Default.aspx (retrieved 29 June 2008).

University of Pennsylvania Positive Psychology Center: www.ppc.sas. upenn.edu/ppquestionnaires.htm (retrieved 29 June 2008).

University of Toronto. Ontario Institute for Studies in Education Department of Adult Education and Counselling Psychology: http:// aecp.oise.utoronto.ca/cert/leadership-coaching.html (retrieved 1 July 2008).

References

Adams, M. (2004). *Change your questions, change your life: 7 powerful tools for life and work.* San Francisco: Berrett-Koehler.

Adler, A., & Brett, C. (1998). *What life could mean to you.* Center City, MN: Hazelden.

Allen, D. (2001). *Getting things done: The art of stress-free productivity.* New York: Viking.

Allen, R. E. (Ed.). (1991). *Greek philosophy Thales to Aristotle* (3rd ed.). New York: Free Press.

American College of Sports Medicine. (2006). *ACSM's resources for the personal trainer.* Baltimore, MD: Lippincott Williams & Wilkins.

American Psychiatric Association. (2000). *Diagnostic and statistical manual of mental disorders* (4th ed., Text Revision). Washington, DC: Author.

American Psychological Association. (1999). Social psychology Once overlooked, now a staple. *APA Monitor Online, 30*(11). Retrieved September 16, 2007, from http://www.apa.org/monitor/dec99/ss8.html.

Anderla, G., Dunning, A., & Forge, S. (1997). *Chaotics: An agenda for business and society in the 21st century.* Westport, CT: Praeger.

Ansbacher, H., & Ansbacher, R. (Eds.). (1956). *The individual psychology of Alfred Adler.* New York: Basic Books.

APA Help Center. (2008). *The road to resilience.* Retrieved June 29, 2008, from http://www.apahelpcenter.org/featuredtopics/feature.php?id=6.

Argyris, C. (1982). *Reasoning, learning, and action: Individual and organizational.* San Francisco: Jossey-Bass.

461

Argyris, C. (1990). *Overcoming organizational defenses: Facilitating organizational learning.* Englewood Cliffs, NJ: Prentice Hall.

Argyris, C. (1993). *Knowledge for action: A guide for overcoming barriers to organizational change.* San Francisco: Jossey-Bass.

Argyris, C., & Schön, D. (1974). *Theory in practice: Increasing professional effectiveness.* San Francisco: Jossey-Bass.

Argyris, C., & Schön, D. (1978). *Organizational learning: A theory of action perspective.* Reading, MA: Addison-Wesley.

Asch, S. E. (1955). Opinions and social pressure. *Scientific American, 193,* 31–35.

Bandler, R., & Grinder, J. (1975, 1976). *The structure of magic I & II.* New York: Science and Behavior Books.

Bandura, A. (1977). *Social learning theory.* Englewood Cliffs, NJ: Prentice Hall.

Bandura, A. (1986). *Social foundations of thought and action: A social cognitive theory.* Englewood Cliffs, NJ: Prentice-Hall.

Barfield, T. (Ed.). (1997). *The dictionary of anthropology.* Oxford: Blackwell Publishing.

Baron, S., & Schmidt, R. A. (1991). Operational aspects of retail franchisees. *International Journal of Retail and Distribution Management 19*(2),13–19.

Bateson, G. (2002). *Mind and nature: A necessary unity.* Cresskill, NJ: Hampton Press.

Batson, D. (1991). *The altruism question: Toward a social-psychological answer.* Mahwah, NJ: Erlbaum Associates.

Baumeister, R. F., & Leary, M. R. (1995). The need to belong: Desire for interpersonal attachments as a fundamental human motivation. *Psychological Bulletin, 117,* 497–529.

Bechtel, W., Abrahamsen, A., & Graham, G. (Eds.). (1998). *The life of cognitive science: A companion to cognitive science.* Oxford: Basil Blackwell.

Beck, A. T. (1976). *Cognitive therapy and the emotional disorders.* New York: International Universities Press.

Beers, M. H. (2004). *The Merck manual of medical information* (2nd Home Ed.). New York: Pocket Books.

Begley, S. (2007). *Train your mind, change your brain: How a new science reveals our extraordinary potential to transform ourselves.* New York: Ballantine Books.

Bereiter, C., & Scardamalia, M. (1993). *Surpassing ourselves: An inquiry into the nature and implications of expertise.* Chicago, IL: Open Court.

Berg, I. K. (1994). *Family based services: A solution-focused approach.* New York: Norton.

Berger, P. L., & Luckmann, T. (1966). *The social construction of reality: A treatise on the sociology of knowledge.* Garden City, NY: Anchor Books.

Bergquist, W. (2003). *Creating the appreciative organization: Six strategies for releasing human capital.* Sacramento, CA: Pacific Soundings Press.

Bergquist, W. (2007a). Appreciative organizational coaching and the release of human capital. *International Journal of Coaching in Organizations, 2007*(3), 66–75.

Bergquist, W. (2007b). The application of appreciative perspectives to the coaching enterprise. *International Journal of Coaching in Organizations, 2007*(4), 44–54.

Bergquist, W., & Mura, A. (2005). *Themes and variations for postmodern leaders and their coaches.* Sacramento, CA: Pacific Soundings Press.

Biswas-Diener, R., & Dean, B. (2007). *Positive psychology coaching: Putting the science of happiness to work for your clients.* Hoboken, NJ: John Wiley & Sons.

Blosser, P. (1973). Principles of gestalt psychology and their application to teaching junior high school science. *Science Education, 57,* 43–53.

Boulding, K. (1985). *The world as a total system.* Beverly Hills, CA: Sage.

Bowden, E.M., Jung-Beeman, M., Fleck, J., & Kounios, J. (2005). New approaches to demystifying insight. *Trends in Cognitive Sciences, 9,* 322–328.

Bowlby J. (1951). *Maternal care and mental health.* Geneva: World Health Organization.

Bowlby, J. (1969). *Attachment, attachment and loss* (Vol. I). London: Hogarth Press.

Bowlby, J. (1973). *Separations: Anger and anxiety, attachment and loss* (Vol. II). London: Hogarth Press.

Bowlby, J. (1980). *Loss: Sadness & depression, attachment and loss* (Vol. III) (International psycho-analytical library no.109). London: Hogarth Press.

Boyatzis, R. E., & McKee, A. (2005a). Resonant leadership. *Personnel Psychology, 59*(2), 467–471.

Boyatzis, R. E., & McKee, A. (2005b). *Resonant leadership: Renewing yourself and connecting with others through mindfulness, hope, and compassion.* Boston: Harvard Business School Press.

Boyatzis, R. E., Smith, M. L., & Blaize, N. (2006). Developing sustainable leaders through coaching and compassion. *Academy of Management Learning and Education,* 5(1), 8–24.

Brafman, O., & Brafman, R. (2008). *Sway: The irresistible pull of irrational behavior.* New York: Doubleday.

Braham, B. (2006). *A heuristic inquiry into the impact of a vipassana meditation practice on executive coaching.* In I. Stein, F. Campone, & L. J. Page (Eds.), *Proceedings of the Third ICF Coaching Research Symposium.* Washington, DC: International Coach Federation.

Breger, L. (2000). *Freud: Darkness in the midst of vision.* New York: John Wiley & Sons.

Bridges, W. (2003). *Managing transitions: Making the most of change* (Rev. ed.). Cambridge, MA: DaCapo Press.

Bridges, W. (2004). *Transitions: Making sense of life's changes* (Rev. ed.). Cambridge, MA: DaCapo Press.

Briggs, J., & Peat, D. (1999). *Seven life lessons of chaos: Timeless wisdom from the science of change.* New York: HarperCollins.

Brock, V. (2008). *A perspective on the history of coaching.* Retrieved January 10, 2009, from http://www.coachingcommons.org/category/museum/.

Brothers, L. (1997). *Friday's footprint: How society shapes the human mind.* New York: Oxford University Press.

Brothers, L. (2001). *Mistaken identity: The mind-brain problem reconsidered.* Albany, NY: State University of New York Press.

Brown, R. (2003). *Social psychology: The second edition.* New York: Free Press.

Brownmiller, S. (1975). *Against our will: Men, women, and rape.* New York: Simon & Schuster.

Bruner, J. S., Goodenough, J., & Austin, G. (1956). *A study of thinking.* New York: John Wiley & Sons.

Buber, M. (1970). *I and thou.* (Walter Kaufman, Trans.). New York: Charles Scribner's Sons.

Buckingham, M. (2007). *Go put your strengths to work: 6 powerful steps to achieve outstanding performance.* New York: Free Press.

Buckingham, M., & Clifton, D. O. (2001). *Now, discover your strengths.* New York: Free Press.

Buckingham, M., & Coffman, C. (1999). *First, break all the rules: What the world's greatest managers do differently.* New York: Simon & Schuster.

Burnham, T., & Phelan, J. (2000). *Mean genes: From sex to money to food: Taming our primal instincts.* New York: Penguin.

Burton, A. K., Tillotson, K. M., Symonds, T. L., Berk, C., & Mattheuson, T. (1996). Occupational risk factors for the first-onset and subsequent course of low back trouble. *Spine, 21,* 2612–2620.

Bushe, G. R. (2007). Appreciative inquiry is not (just) about the positive. *OD Practitioner, 39*(4), 33–38.

Cameron, K. S., Dutton, J. E., & Quinn, R. E. (Eds.). (2003). *Positive organizational scholarship: Foundations of a new discipline.* San Francisco: Berrett-Koehler.

Cannon, W. B. (1927). The James-Lange theory of emotion: A critical examination and an alternative theory. *American Journal of Psychology, 39,* 10–124.

Career Partners International. (2008). *ROI of Executive Coaching.* Retrieved June 24, 2008, from http://www.cpiworld.ca/default.asp?tier_1=21&tier_2=27&content=51.

Carson, R. (2003). Taming your gremlin: A surprisingly simple method for getting out of your own way (2nd ed.). New York: HarperCollins.

Cherniss, C. (1999). *The business case for EI.* Consortiume for Research on Emotional Intelligence in Organizations. Retrieved June 29, 2008, from http://www.eiconsortium.org/reports/business_case_for_ei.html.

Chopra, D. (1989). *Quantum healing: Exploring the frontiers of mind/body medicine.* New York: Bantam Books.

Cialdini, R. J. (1984). *Influence: How and why people agree to things.* New York: Morrow.

Cialdini, R. J. (2007). *Influence: The psychology of persuasion.* New York: Harper Collins.

Clippinger, J. (Ed.). (1999). *The biology of business: Decoding the natural laws of enterprise.* San Francisco: Jossey-Bass.

Coghill, R. (2007). *Expectations vs. experience: Constructions of individual subjective reality.* Presentation at The First Global Neuroleadership Summit, Asolo, Italy, May 14–16. Retrieved January 24, 2008, from http://neuroleadershipsummit2007.blogspot.com/.

Coles, R. (1970). *Erik H. Erikson: The growth of his work*. Boston: Little, Brown.

Collins, J. (2001). *Good to great: Why some companies make the leap . . . and others don't*. New York: Harper Collins.

Constantine, P. (2007). *The essential writings of Machiavelli*. New York: Random House Library.

Cook-Greuter, S. (1999). *Post-autonomous ego-development: A study of its nature and measurement*. Dissertation, Harvard Graduate School of Education.

Cooperrider, D. L, & Whitney, D. (1999). *Appreciative inquiry*. San Francisco: Berrett-Koehler, 2005.

Cosmides, L., & Tooby, J. (1997). *Evolutionary psychology: A primer*. Center for Evolutionary Psychology. Retrieved December 31, 2007 from, http://www.psych.ucsb.edu/research/cep/primer.html.

Cozolino, L. (2002). *The neuroscience of psychotherapy: Building and rebuilding the human brain*. New York: W. W. Norton.

Creswell, J. D., Welch, W. T., Taylor, S. E., Sherman, D. K., Gruenewald, T. L., & Mann, T. (2005). Affirmation of personal values buffers neuroendocrine and psychological stress responses. *Psychological Science*, *16*, 841–920.

Cross, K. P. (1981). *Adults as learners*. San Francsico: Jossey-Bass.

Crow, S., & Eckert, E. D. (2000). Videotape and discussion follow-up of the Minnesota Semistarvation Study participants. Ninth International Conference on Eating Disorders, May 4–7, New York City.

Csikszentmihalyi, M. (1991). *Flow: The psychology of optimal experience*. New York: Harper Collins.

Csikszentmihalyi, M. (1996). *Creativity: Flow and the psychology of discovery and invention*. New York: HarperCollins.

Darwin, C. (1859). *On the origin of species by means of natural selection: Or the preservation of favoured races in the struggle for life*. London: John Murray.

Deci, E. L., & Ryan, R. M. (1985). *Intrinsic motivation and self-determination in human behavior*. New York: Plenum Press.

de Groot, A. D. (1965). *Thought and choice in chess*. The Hague: Mouton.

DeJong, P. & Berg, I. K. (2002). *Interviewing for solutions*. Pacific Grove, CA: Brooks/Cole.

Deng, M-D. (1992). *365 Tao: Daily meditations*. New York: Harpercollins.

Dennett, D. (1991). *Consciousness explained*. New York: Penguin.

de Shazer, S. (1985). *Keys to solution in grief therapy.* New York: Norton.

Deutschman, A. (2006). *Change or die: The three keys to change at work and in life.* New York: Regan/HarperCollins.

Diener, E. (1984). Subjective well-being. *Psychological Bulletin, 95*(3), 542–575.

Diener, E., & Diener, C. (1996). Most people are happy. *Psychological Science, 7,* 181–185.

Dilts, R. B. (1983). *Roots of Neuro-Linguistic Programming.* Cupertino, CA: Meta Publications.

Dollard, J., & Miller, N. (1950). *Personality and psychotherapy: An analysis in terms of learning, thinking and culture.* New York: McGraw-Hill.

Drake, D. B., Brennan, D., & Gortz, K. (Eds.). (2008). *The philosophy and practice of coaching: Insights and issues for a new era.* Hoboken, NJ: John Wiley & Sons.

Dreikurs, R., & Soltz, V. (1964). *Children the challenge.* New York: Hawthorn Books.

Duke University Medical Center. (2000). *Effect of exercise on reducing major depression appears to be long-lasting.* Retrieved January 5, 2007, from http://www.dukenews.duke.edu/Med/exercise.htm.

Edelman, G. (1987). *Neural darwinism: The theory of neuronal group selection.* New York: Basic Books.

Eisenberger, N. I., Lieberman, M. D., Kipling, D. & Williams, K. D. (2003). Does rejection hurt? An fMRI study of social exclusion. *Science, 302, (5643),* 290–292.

Ekman, P. (2003). *Emotions revealed: Recognizing faces and feelings to improve communication and emotional life.* New York: Times Books.

Ellenberger, H. F. (1970). *The discovery of the unconscious: The history and evolution of dynamic psychiatry.* New York: Basic Books.

Ellis, A. (1957). Rational psychotherapy and Individual Psychology. *Journal of Individual Psychology, 13,* 38–44.

Ellis, A. (1974). *Humanistic psychotherapy: The rational-emotive approach.* New York: McGraw-Hill.

Ellis, A. (2003). Early theories and practices of rational emotive behavior theory and how they have been augmented and revised during the last three decades. *Journal of Rational-Emotive and Cognitive-Behavior Therapy, 21,* 3/4.

Eriksson, P. S., Perfilieva, E., Bjork-Eriksson, T., Alborn, A. M., Nordborg, C., Peterson, D. A., et al. (1998). Neurogenesis in the adult human hippocampus. *Nature Medicine, 4* (November), 1313–1317.

Erwin, E. (1978). *Behavior therapy: Scientific, philosophical and moral foundations.* New York: Cambridge University Press.

Evans, D. R., Hearn, M. T., Uhlemann, M. R., & Ivey, A. E. (2004). *Essential interviewing: A programmed approach to effective communication.* Belmont, CA: Brooks/Cole-Thompson Learning.

Eysenck, H. J. (1952). The effects of psychotherapy: An evaluation. *Journal of Consulting Psychology, 16,* 319–324.

Eysenck, H. J. (1953). *Uses and abuses of psychology.* London: Penguin Harmondsworth

Eysenck, M. W., & Keane, M. T. (2005). *Cognitive psychology: A student's handbook* (5th ed.) Hove and New York: Psychology Press, Taylor & Francis Group.

Farb, N. A., Segal, Z. V., Mayberg, H., Bean, J., McKeon, D., Fatima, Z., et al. (2007). Attending to the present: Mindfulness meditation reveals distinct neural modes of self reference. *SCAN 2,* 313–322.

Feigenbaum, M. J. (1978). Quantitative universality for a class of non-linear transformations. *Journal of Statistical Physics, 19,* 25–52.

Festinger, L. (1957). *A theory of cognitive dissonance.* Stanford, CA: Stanford University Press.

Frankl, V. E. (1984). *Man's search for meaning.* New York: Washington Square.

Fredrickson, B. (2001). The role of positive emotions in positive psychology: The broaden-and-build theory of positive emotions. *American Psychologist Special Issue, 56,* 218–226.

Freeman, L. C. (2004). *The development of Social Network Analysis: A study in the sociology of science.* North Charleston, SC: BookSurge, LLC.

Freud, S. (1995). *The Freud reader.* New York: W. W. Norton.

Gagne, Robert (1965). *The conditions of learning.* New York: Holt, Rinehart and Winston.

Gagne R. M., & Briggs L. J. (1974). *Principles of instructional design.* New York: Holt, Rinehart & Winston.

Gallese, V., Fadiga, L., Fogassi, L. & Rizzolatti, G. (1996). Action recognition in the premotor cortex. *Brain, 119,* 593–609.

Gallwey, T. (1981). *The inner game of golf* (Rev. ed.). New York: Random House.

Gallwey, T. (1987). *The inner game of tennis* (Rev. ed.). New York: Random House.

Gallwey, T. (1997). *The inner game of skiing* (Rev. ed.). New York: Random House.

Gallwey, T. (2001). *The inner game of work: Focus, learning, pleasure and mobility in the workplace.* New York: Random House.

Gardner, H. (1983). *Frames of mind: The theory of multiple intelligence.* New York: Basic Books.

Gardner, H. (1985). *The mind's new science: A history of the cognitive revolution.* New York: Basic Books.

Gardner, H. (1993). *Frames of mind: The theory of multiple intelligences* (2nd ed.). (10th anniversary). London: Fontana Press.

Gatchel, R. J., Polantin, P. B., & Mayer, T. G. (1995). The dominant role of psychosocial risk factors in the development of chronic low back pain disability. *Spine, 20,* 2702–2709.

Ghiselin, M. T. (1973). Darwin and evolutionary psychology. *Science, 179*(4077), 964–968.

Gladwell, M. (2005). *Blink! The power of thinking without thinking.* New York: Little, Brown.

Gleick, J. (1987). *Chaos: Making a new science.* New York: Penguin.

Goffman, E. (1959). *The presentation of self in everyday life.* New York: Doubleday Anchor.

Goldberg, M. C. (1998). *The art of the question: A guide to short-term question-centered therapy.* New York: John Wiley & Sons.

Goldsmith, M. (2003). Changing leadership behavior. In H. Morgan, P. Harkins, & M. Goldsmith (Eds.), *Profiles in coaching: The 2004 handbook of best practices in leadership coaching.* Retrieved December, 31, 2007, from http://www.marshallgoldsmith.com/articles/article.asp?a_id=1&p_id=2.

Goleman, D. (1995). *Emotional intelligence: Why it can matter more than IQ.* New York: Bantam Books.

Goleman, D. (2006). *Social intelligence: The new science of human relationships.* New York: Bantam Books.

Goleman, D., Boyatzis, R., & McKee, A. (2002). *Primal leadership: Realizing the power of emotional intelligence.* Cambridge, MA: Harvard Business School Press.

Grant, A. (2003). Keeping up with the cheese! Research as a foundation for professional coaching of the future. In I.F. Stein & L.A. Belsten

(Eds.), *First ICF Coaching Research Symposium.* Mooresville, NC: Paw Print Press, pp. 1–19.

Green, C. D. (2007). Classics in the history of psychology. Retrieved August 27, 2007, from http://psychclassics.yorku.ca/Krstic/marulic.htm.

Greenberg, L. (2002). *Emotion focused therapy: Teaching clients to work through their feelings.* Washington, DC: American Psychological Association.

Greene, R. (1998). *The 48 laws of power.* New York: Viking Press.

Gross, J. J. (1998). The emerging field of emotion regulation: An integrative review. *Review of General Psychology, 2,* 271–299.

Gross, J. J., & John, O. P. (2003). Individual differences in two emotion regulation processes: Implications for affect, relationships, and well-being. *Journal of Personality and Social Psychology, 85,* 348–362.

Gross, J. J., Richards, J. M., & John, O. P. (2006). In D. K. Snyder, J. A. Simpson, & J. W. Hughes (Eds.). *Emotion regulation in families: Pathways to dysfunction and health.* Washington, DC: American Psychological Association.

Grow, G. O. (1991). Teaching learners to be self-directed. *Adult Education Quarterly, 41*(3), 25–149.

Guastello, S. (2000). Nonlinear dynamics in psychology. *Discrete Dynamics in Nature and Society, 00,* 1–20.

Guest, S. (2007). Appreciative inquiry and coaching—AI is not (just) about the positive: An interview with Gervase Bushe. *International Journal of Coaching in Organizations, 2007*(4), 22–28.

Haley, J. (1971). *Changing families: A family therapy reader.* New York: Grune & Stratton.

Hassed, C. (2008). *The essence of health: The seven pillars of wellbeing.* North Sydney, Australia: Ebury Press, Random House.

Haviland, W. (2002). *Cultural anthropology* (3rd ed.). Burlington, VT: University of Vermont.

Hawkins, J., & Blakeslee, S. (2004). *On intelligence.* New York: Henry Holt.

Heidegger, M. (1977). *Basic writings.* D. F. Kudl (Ed.) New York: Harper & Row.

Herrnstein, R., & Murray, C. (1994). *The bell curve: Intelligence and class structure in American life.* New York: Free Press.

Hoffman, E. (1994). *The drive for self: Alfred Adler and the founding of Individual Psychology.* Reading, MA: Addison-Wesley.

References

Holbeche, L. (2005). *The high-performance organization: Creating dynamic stability and sustainable success.* St. Louis, MO: Butterworth-Heinemann.

Holland, J. H. (1998). *Emergence: From chaos to order.* New York: Oxford University Press.

Houshmand, Z., Livingston, R. B., & Wallace, B. A. (Eds.). (1999). *Consciousness at the crossroads: Conversations with the Dalai Lama on brain science and Buddhism.* T. Jinpa (Trans.). Ithaca, NY: Snow Lion Publications.

Howard Community College. (2007). *What is wellness.* Retrieved December 27, 2009, from http://www.howardcc.edu/students/wellness_center/index.html.

Howell, W. C. , & Fleishman, E. A. (Eds.). (1982). *Information processing and decision making.* In E. A. Fleishman (Series Ed.), *Human performance and productivity, Vol. 2.* Mahwah, NJ: Lawrence Erlbaum Associates.

Hubble, M. A., Duncan, B. L., & Miller, S. D. (1999). *The heart & soul of change: What works in therapy.* Washington, DC: American Psychological Association.

Hudson, F. M. (1999). *The adult years: Mastering the art of self-renewal* (Rev. ed.). San Francisco: Jossey-Bass.

International Coach Federation. (2008). *Core competencies.* Retrieved July, 26, 2008, from http://www.coachfederation.org/ICF/For+Current+Members/Credentialing/Why+a+Credential/Competencies/.

Jay, M. (1999). *Coach 2 the bottom line: An executive guide to coaching performance, change, and transformation.* Victoria, BC: Trafford.

James, W. (1950). *The principles of psychology* (Vols. I & II). Mineola, NY: Courier Dover Publications. (Originally published 1890)

Johns, G., & Saks, A. M. (2005). *Organizational behavior: Understanding and managing life at work* (6th ed.). Toronto: Pearson Education Canada.

Johnson, S. (2006). The neuroscience of the mentor-learner relationship. In S. Johnson & K. Taylor (Eds.), *The Neuroscience of Adult Learning,* special issue of *New Directions for Adult and Continuing Education, 110* (Summer, 2006), 63–69.

Jonassen, D. H., & Grabowski, B. L. (1993). *Handbook of individual differences, learning, and instruction.* Hillsdale, NJ: Lawrence Erlbaum Associates.

Jung, C. G. (1923). *Psychological types,* Vol. 6 of *Collected works of Carl Jung.* Princeton, NJ: Princeton/Bollingen. (Originally published 1921 as *Psychologische typen.* Zurich: Rascher Verlag.)

Kabat-Zinn, J. (2005). *Coming to our senses: Healing ourselves and the world through mindfulness.* Carlsbad, CA: Piatkus Books.

Kaplan, R. M., & Saccuzzo, D. P. (2005). *Psychological testing: Principles, applications, and issues.* New York: Thomson Wadsworth.

Keller, C. (1986). *From a broken web: Separation, sexism, and self.* Boston: Beacon Press.

Kellert, S. (1993). *In the wake of chaos.* Chicago: University of Chicago Press.

Kempermann, G., Kuhn, H. G., & Gage, F. H. (1997). More hippocampal neurons in adult mice living in an enriched environment. *Nature, 386*(6624), 493–495.

Kerr, M. E., & Bowen, M. (1988). *Family evaluation: An approach based on Bowen theory.* New York: W. W. Norton.

Keys, A., Brozek, J., & Jemscje, A. (1950). *The biology of human starvation.* Minneapolis, MN: University of Minnesota Press.

Klein, N. (2007). *The shock doctrine: The rise of disaster capitalism.* New York: Metropolitan Books/Henry Holt.

Kleiner, A. (2008). *The age of heretics: A history of the radical thinkers who reinvented corporate management* (2nd ed.). (A Warren Bennis book.) Hoboken, NJ: Jossey-Bass.

Kluckhohn, C., & Murray, H. A. (1948). Personality formation: The determinants. In C. Kluckhohn & H. A. Murray (Eds.), *Personality: In nature, society and culture* (pp. 35–48). New York: Knopf.

Knight, R.N. (July 1986). Franchising from the franchisor and franchisee points of view. *Journal of Small Business Management,* 8–15.

Knowles, M. (1986). *Using learning contracts.* San Francisco: Jossey-Bass.

Knowles, M. S., Holton, E. F., & Swanson, R. A. (1998). *The adult learner: The definitive classic in adult education and human resource development* (6th ed.). Woburn, MA: Butterworth-Heinemann.

Knox, A. B. (1986). *Helping adults learn.* San Francisco: Jossey-Bass.

Kolb, B., & Whishaw, I. Q. (2003). *Fundamentals of human neuropsychology* (5th ed.). New York: Worth Publishers.

Kolb, D. A. (1984). *Experiential learning.* Englewood Cliffs, NJ.: Prentice Hall.

Kolb, D. A., & Fry, R. (1975). Toward an applied theory of experiential learning. In C. Cooper (Ed.), *Theories of group process.* London: John Wiley & Sons.

References

Kopp, R. R. (1995). *Metaphor therapy: Using client-generated metaphors in psychotherapy.* New York: Bruner/Mazel.

Kopp, R. R. (2007). An empty sadness: Exploring and transforming client-generated metaphors. In G. W. Burns (Ed.), *Healing with stories: Your casebook collection for using therapeutic metaphors* (pp. 30–43). Hoboken, NJ: John Wiley & Sons.

Kotter, J. P. (1996). *Leading change.* Boston, MA: Harvard Business School Press.

Kotter, J. P., & Cohen, D. S. (2002). *The heart of change: Real-life stories of how people change their organizations.* Boston, MA: Harvard Business School Press.

Kounios, J., Frymiare, J. L., Bowden, E. M., Fleck, J. I., Subramaniam, K., Parrish, T. B., & Jung-Beeman, M. (2006). The prepared mind: Neural activity prior to problem presentation predicts solution by sudden insight. *Psychological Science, 17,* 882–890.

Kroeber, T. (1961). *Ishi in two worlds: A biography of the last wild Indian in North America.* Berkley: University of California Press.

Kübler-Ross, E. (1969). *On death and dying.* New York: Routledge.

Kuhn, T. (1962). *The structure of scientific revolutions.* Chicago: University of Chicago Press.

Labonté, R. (1983). Keeping fit in a sick society: The ideology of health promotion. *Our Generation,* Summer, *16*(1).

Labov, W. (2006). *The social stratification of English in New York City.* (2nd ed.). New York: Cambridge University Press.

Laske, O. (2007). *Measuring hidden dimensions, Vol. 1: The art and science of fully engaging adults.* Medford, MA: Interdevelopmental Institute Press.

László, E. (1972). *The systems view of the world.* New York: George Braziller.

Lavenda, R. H., & Schultz, E. A. (2003). *Core concepts in cultural anthropology* (2nd ed.). New York: McGraw-Hill Higher Education.

Layard, R. (2003). *Happiness: Has social science a clue?* Lionel Robbins Memorial Lectures, London School of Economics. Retrieved June 29, 2008, from http://cep.lse.ac.uk/events/lectures/layard/RL030303.pdf.

Layard, R. (2005). *Happiness: Lessons from a new science.* New York: Penguin.

Lazarus, R. (1991). *Emotion and adaptation.* New York: Oxford University Press.

Leonard, T. (1998). *The portable coach: 28 surefire strategies for business and personal success.* New York: Scribner.

Lerner, H. G. (1989). *The dance of intimacy: A woman's guide to courageous acts of change in key relationships.* New York: Harper & Row.

Levitin, D. J. (2006). *This is your brain on music: The science of a human obsession.* New York: Penguin.

Lewin, K. (1947). Group decision and social change. In T. M. Newcomb & E. L. Hartley (Eds.), *Readings in social psychology* (pp. 340–344). New York: Henry Holt.

Lewin, K. (1975). *Field theory in social science: Selected theoretical papers.* Westport, CN: Greenwood Press.

Lewin, K. (1999). *The complete social scientist: A Kurt Lewin reader* (1st ed.). Martin Gold (Ed.). Washington, DC: American Psychological Association.

Lewin, K. (2008). Lewin quotes. Retrieved April 20, 2008, from http://psychology.about.com/od/psychologyquotes/a/lewinquotes.htm.

Lewin, R. (1992). *Complexity: Life at the edge of chaos.* New York: Macmillan.

Lieberman, M. D. (2007). Social cognitive neuroscience: A review of core processes. *Annual Review of Psychology, 58,* 259–289.

Lieberman, M. D., Eisenberger, N. I., Crockett, M. J., Tom, S. M., Pfeifer, J. H., & Way, B. M. (2007). Putting feelings into words: Affect labeling disrupts amygdala activity to affective stimuli. *Psychological Science, 18,* 421–428.

Libet, B., Gleason, C. A., Wright, E. W., & Pearl, D. K. (1983). Time of conscious intention to act in relation to onset of cerebral activity (readiness potential): The unconscious initiation of a freely voluntary act. *Brain, 106,* 623–642.

Lindeman, E. C. (1926). *The meaning of adult education.* New York: New Republic. (Republished in a new edition in 1989 by The Oklahoma Research Center for Continuing Professional and Higher Education.)

Lorenz, E. N. (1963). Deterministic aperiodic flow. *Journal of Atmospheric Science, 20,* 130–141.

Losee, Robert M. (1997). A discipline independent definition of information. *Journal of the American Society for Information Science, 48,* 254–269.

Luthans, F., Youssef, C. M., & Avolio, B. J. (2007). *Psychological capital: Developing the human competitive edge.* New York: Oxford University Press.

Lyubomirsky, S., King, L and Diener, E. (2006). Guidelines for national indicators of subjective well-being and ill-being. *Journal of Happiness Studies,* 7(4).

Maas, J. B. (2001). *Power sleep: The revolutionary program that prepares your mind for peak performance.* New York: Harper Collins.

Maddi, S. R., & Kobasa, S. (1984). *The hardy executive: Health under stress.* Homewood, IL: Dow Jones-Irwin.

Magner, Lois N. (1992). *A history of medicine.* New York: Marcel Dekker.

Mahoney, M. J. (1991). *Human change processes: The scientific foundations of psychotherapy.* New York: Basic Books.

Marshall L., Born J. (2007) The contribution of sleep to hippocampus-dependent memory consolidation. *Trends in Cognitive Science, 11,* 442–450.

Maslow, A. H. (1943). A theory of human motivation. *Psychological Review, 50,* 370–396. Retrieved June 26, 2008, from http://psychclassics.yorku.ca/Maslow/motivation.htm.

Maslow, A. H. (1968). *Toward a psychology of being.* New York: Van Nostrand.

Maslow, A. H. (1971). *The farther reaches of human nature.* New York: Viking Press.

Masson, J. M. (1984). *The assault on truth: Freud's suppression of the seduction theory.* New York: Farrar Straus & Giroux.

Mayer, J. D., Caruso, D. R., & Salovey, P. (2000). Emotional intelligence meets traditional standards for an intelligence, *Intelligence, 27,* 267–298.

Mayer, J. D., Salovey, P., & Caruso, D. R. (2001). *The Mayer-Salovey-Caruso Emotional Intelligence Test (MSCEIT).* Toronto: Multi-Health Systems, Inc.

Mayo Clinic. (2006). *The Mayo Clinic plan: 10 essential steps to a better body & healthier life.* New York: Time Inc.

Mayo, E. (1933). *The human problems of an industrial civilization.* New York: Macmillan.

McGregor, D. (1960). *The human side of enterprise.* New York: McGraw-Hill.

Mead, M. (2001). *Sex and temperament in three primitive societies.* New York: Perennial.

Medawar, P. B. (1972). *The hope of progress.* London: Methuen.

Meichenbaum, D. (1977). Cognitive-behavior modification: An integrative approach. Boston: Kluwer Boston.

Mercola, J. (1998). *33 Secrets to a good night's sleep*. Retrieved June 24, 2008, from http://www.mercola.com/article/sleep.htm.

Mikkelsen, A., Saksvik, P. O., Eriksen, H. R., Ursin, H. (1999). The impact of learning opportunities and decision authority on occupational health. *Work and Stress, 13*(1), 20–31.

Milgram, S. (1967). The small world problem. *Psychology Today, 2*, 60–67.

Milgram, S. (1974). *Obedience to authority: An experimental view*. New York: HarperCollins.

Miller, G. A. (1956). The magic number seven, plus or minus two: Some limits on our capacity for processing information. *Psychological Review, 63*, 81–93.

Miller, G. A. (2003). The cognitive revolution: A historical perspective. *Trends in Cognitive Science, 7*(3), 141–144.

Miller, J. B., & Stiver, I. P. (1998). *The healing connection: How women form relationships in therapy and in life*. Boston: Beacon Press.

Minsky, M. (1986). *The society of mind*. New York: Simon & Schuster.

Minuchin, S. (1974). *Families and family therapy*. Cambridge, MA: Harvard University Press.

Moreno, J. L. (Ed.). (1960). *The sociometry reader*. New York: Free Press.

Murphy, J. S., & Hudson, F. M. (1995). *The joy of old: A guide to successful elderhood*. San Francisco: Jossey-Bass.

Myers, I. B., McCaulley, M. H., Quenk, N. L., & Hammer, A. L. (1998). *MBTI Manual (A guide to the development and use of the Myers Briggs type indicator)* (3rd ed.). Palo Alto, CA: Consulting Psychologists Press.

Nathan, P. E., & Gorman, J. M. (Eds.). (1998). *A guide to treatments that work*. New York: Oxford University Press.

Negoianu, D., & Goldfarb, S. (2008). Just add water. *Journal of the American Society of Nephrology 19*. Retrieved January 2009, from www.jasn.org. (Published online ahead of print) .

Neisser, U. (1976). *Cognition and reality: principles and implications of cognitive psychology*. New York: W. H. Freeman.

Nisbett, R. E. (2003). *The geography of thought: How Asians and Westerners think differently . . . and why*. New York: Free Press.

Nisbett, R. E., & Ross, L. (1985). *Human inference: Strategies and shortcomings of social judgement*. New York: Prentice-Hall.

Norcross, J. C. (Ed.). (2002). *Psychotherapy relationships that work: Therapist contributions and responsiveness to patients.* New York: Oxford University Press.

Ochsner, K. N., Bunge, S.A., Gross, J., & Gabrieli, J. D. E. (2001). *Rethinking feelings: Explaining the neurocognitive mechanisms of emotion control.* Paper presented at the UCLA Conference on Social Cognitive Neuroscience, April 2001, Los Angeles, California.

Ochsner, K. N., & Lieberman, M. D. (2001). The emergence of social cognitive neuroscience. *American Psychologist, 56,* 717–734.

O'Connor, A. (2006). The claim: Skipping breakfast can affect your mood and energy levels during the day. *New York Times,* February 21. Retrieved January 5, 2008, from http://www.nytimes.com/2006/02/21/health/21real.html?_r=1&oref=slogin.

Olalla, J. (2004). *From knowledge to wisdom: Essays on the crisis in contemporary learning.* Boulder, CO: Newfield Network.

Olalla, J. (2008). Interview with Julio Olalla. W. H. Bergquist, interviewer. *International Journal of Coaching in Organizations, 2,* 6–31.

Olson, A. K., Eadie, B. D., Ernst, C., & Christie, B. R. (2006). Environmental enrichment and voluntary exercise massively increase neurogenesis in the adult hippocampus via dissociable pathways. (Special Issue on Neurogenesis.) *Hippocampus, 16*(3), 250–260.

Orem, S. L., Binkert, J., & Clancy, A. L. (2007). *Appreciative coaching: A positive process for change.* San Francisco: Jossey-Bass.

Ormrod, J. E. (1990). *Human learning: Principles, theories, and educational applications.* Columbus, OH: Merrill.

Orlinsky, D. E. (2007). *Collaborative research: How different are coaches and therapists?* Paper presented at 11th Annual International Coach Federation Conference, Long Beach, California, November 3.

Orlinsky, D. E., & Rønnestad, M. H. (2005). *How psychotherapists develop: A study of therapeutic work and professional growth.* Washington, DC: American Psychological Association.

Ormrod, J. E. (1990). *Human learning: Principles, theories, and educational applications.* Columbus, OH: Merrill.

OSS Assessment Staff. (1948). *Assessment of men: Selection of personnel for the office of strategic service.* New York: Rinehart.

Page, L. J. (1998). The crisis in mental health theory. *International Journal of Mental Health, 27*(1), 33–61.

Page, L. J. (2001). One of a kind. Introduction to D. Eckstein & R. Kern, *Psychological fingerprints: Lifestyle assessment and interventions*. Dubuque, IA: Kendall/Hunt.

Page, L. J. (2005). Research as "expertising": A reading guide for practicing coaches. In I. F. Stein, F. Campone, & L. J. Page (Eds.), *Proceedings of the Second ICF Coaching Research Symposium*. Washington, DC: International Coach Federation.

Page, L. J. (2006). Thinking outside our brains: Interpersonal Neurobiology and organizational change. *International Journal of Coaching in Organizations*, 2006 (2), 22–31.

Page, L. J. (2007). My grandmother's kitchen: A metaphor for organizations in the new paradigm. *International Journal of Coaching in Organizations*, 2007(4), 6–61.

Page-Hollander, L. (1973). *Sex role, speech, and status: An analysis of public telephone conversations*. Dissertation, Princeton University. Ann Arbor, MI: University Microfilms.

Pagels, H. R. (1998). *The dreams of reason: The computer and the rise of the sciences of complexity*. New York: Simon & Schuster.

Panksepp, J. (1998). *Affective neuroscience: The foundations of human and animal emotions* (Series in Affective Science). New York: Oxford University Press.

Parsons, T. (1968). *The structure of social action*. Glencoe, IL: Free Press.

Pashler, H. E. (1997). *The psychology of attention*. Cambridge, MA: MIT Press.

Peltier, B. (2001). *The psychology of executive coaching*. New York: Brunner-Routledge.

Penland, P. (1979). Self-initiated learning. *Adult Education Quarterly*, 29(3), 170–179.

Perry, B. D. (2006). Fear and learning: Trauma-related factors in the adult education process. In S. Johnson & K. Taylor (Eds.), *The Neuroscience of Adult Learning, special issue of New Directions for Adult and Continuing Education, 110* (Summer, 2006), 21–27.

Peters, T., & Waterman, R. (1982). *In search of excellence*. New York: Harper & Row.

Peterson, C. (2006). *A primer in positive psychology*. Oxford: Oxford University Press.

Peterson, C., Park, N., & Seligman, E. P. (2006). Greater strengths of character and recovery from illness. *Journal of Positive Psychology, 1*, 17–26.

Peterson, C., & Seligman, M. E. P. (2004). *Character strengths and virtues: A handbook and classification.* New York: Oxford University Press.

Piaget, J. (1928). *The child's conception of the world.* London: Routledge and Kegan Paul.

Pinker, S. (2002). *The blank slate: The modern denial of human nature.* New York: Penguin Putnam.

Plutchik, R. (2007). *The nature of emotions.* Retrieved January 24, 2008, from http://www.fractal.org/Bewustzijns-Besturings-Model/Nature-of-emotions.htm.

Porter, M. E. (1980). *Competitive strategy: Techniques for analyzing industries and competitors.* New York: Free Press.

Pralahad, C. K., & Hamel, G. (1990). The core competence of the corporation. *Harvard Business Review,* May–June.

Pratt, D. D. (1998). Ethical reasoning in teaching adults. In M. Galbraith (Ed.), *Adult learning methods* (pp. 113–125). Malabar, FL: Krieger.

Prigogine, I. (1996). *The end of uncertainty: Time, chaos, and the new laws of nature.* New York: Free Press.

Prilleltensky, I. (1994). *The morals and politics of psychology: Psychological discourse and the status quo.* Albany, NY: State University of New York Press.

Prochaska, J. O. (1979). *Systems of psychotherapy: A transtheoretical analysis.* Homewood, IL: Dorsey Press.

Prochaska, J. O., Norcross, J. C., & DiClemente, C. C. (1994). *Changing for good: A revolutionary six-stage program for overcoming bad habits and moving your life positively forward.* New York: William Morrow.

Quartz, S. R., & Sejnowski, T. J. (2002). *Liars, lovers, and heroes: What the new brain science reveals about how we become who we are.* New York: William Morrow.

Rader, M. & Gill, J. H. (1990). *The enduring questions: Main problems of philosophy* (4th ed.). Belmount, CA: Wadsworth.

Ratey, J. (2003). *The user's guide to the brain.* London: Abacus.

Rath, T. & Clifton, D. (2004). *How full is your bucket?* New York: Gallup Press.

Redfield, R. (1953). *The primitive world and its transformations.* Ithaca, NY: Cornell University Press.

Reinardy, J. R. (1992). Decisional control in moving to a nursing home: Postadmission adjustment and well-being. *Gerontologist, 32*(1), 96–103.

Reivich, K., and Shatte, A. (2002). *The resilience factor: 7 essential skills for overcoming life's inevitable obstacles.* New York: Broadway Books/ Random House.

Ridley, M. (1999). *Genome: The autobiography of a species in 23 chapters.* New York: HarperCollins.

Rimm, D., & Masters, J. (1974). *Behavior therapy.* New York: Academic Press.

Rizzolatti, G., & Craighero, L. (2004). The mirror neuron system. *Annual Review of Neuroscience 27*, 169–192.

Rizzolatti, G., Fadiga, L., Gallese, V., & Fogassi, L. (1996). Premotor cortex and the recognition of motor actions. *Cognitive Brain Research 3*, 131–141.

Rizzolatti, G., Sinigaglia, C., & Anderson, F. (Trans.). (2008). *Mirrors in the brain: How our minds share actions, emotions, and experience.* New York: Oxford University Press.

Rock, D. (2006). *Quiet leadership: Six steps to transforming performance at work.* New York: Collins.

Rock, D. (2008). SCARF: A brain-based model for collaborating with and influencing others. *NeuroLeadership Journal, 1*, 44–52.

Rock, D. (2009). *Your brain at work.* New York: Harper Business.

Rock, D., & Schwartz, J. M. (2006a). A brain-based approach to coaching. *International Journal of Coaching in Organizations, 2006*(2), 32–43.

Rock, D., & Schwartz, J. M. (2006b). The neuroscience of leadership. *Strategy+Business, 43*. Retrieved April 20, 2009, from http://www. strategy-business.com/media/file/sb43_06207.pdf.

Rogers, C. R. (1951). *Client-centered therapy: Its current practice, implications and theory.* London: Constable.

Rogers, C. R. (1969). *Freedom to learn: A view of what education might become.* Columbus, Ohio: Charles E. Merrill.

Rolls, E. T., & Deco, G. (2002). *Computational neuroscience of vision.* New York: Oxford University Press.

Rose, S. (2005). *The future of the brain: The promise and perils of tomorrow's neuroscience.* New York: Oxford University Press.

Rosenthal, R., & Jacobson, L. (1992). *Pygmalion in the classroom,* (Expanded ed.). New York: Irvington.

Rosenthal, S. M., & Page, L. J. (Eds.). (1998). Market madness and mental illness: The crisis in mental health care — 1 & 2. *Special Issues of International Journal of Mental Health, 27*(1&2).

480

Rossi, E. (1991). The wave nature of consciousness. *Psychological Perspectives*, *24*, 1–10.

Rotter, J. B. (1954). *Social learning and clinical psychology*. New York: Prentice-Hall.

Rowley, L. (2005). *The elusive American dream*. Retrieved June 29, 2008, from http://finance.yahoo.com/columnist/article/moneyhappy/979.

Rushall, B. (1996). Goal-Setting. *Coaching Science Abstracts*, *2*(2). http://www-rohan.sdsu.edu/dept/coachsci/csa/vol22/table.htm (retrieved 29 December 2007).

Sanders, S. H. (2000). Risk factors for chronic, disabling low-back pain: An update for 2000. *APS Bulletin 10*(2).

Sandstrom, J., & Smith, L. (2008). *Legacy leadership: The leader's guide to lasting greatness*. Dallas: CoachWorks Press.

Sartre, J-P. (1993). *Being and nothingness: An essay on phenomenological ontology*. Hazel E. Barnes (Trans.). New York: Washington Square Press. (Originally published 1943).

Satir, V. (1983). *Conjoint family therapy* (3rd ed.). Palo Alto, CA: Science & Behavior Books.

Satir, V. (1988). *New peoplemaking*. Palo Alto, CA: Science & Behavior Books.

Savery, J. R., & Duffy, T. M. (1995). Problem based learning: An instructional model and its constructivist framework. *Educational Technology*, *35*, 31–38.

Schoenfeld, B., Weinberg, R. S., & Gould, D. (2003). *Foundations of sport and exercise psychology*. Champaign, IL: Human Kinetics.

Schön, D. A. (1983). *The reflective practitioner: How professionals think in action*. New York: Basic Books.

Schön, D. A. (1987). *Educating the reflective practitioner*. San Francisco: Jossey-Bass.

Schriver, J. (1995). *Human behavior and the social environment: Shifting paradigms in essential knowledge for social work practice*. Boston: Allyn & Bacon.

Schuyler, D. (1971). *Cognitive therapy: A practical guide*. New York: Norton.

Schwartz, J. M., & Begley, S. (2002). *The mind & the brain: Neuroplasticity and the power of mental force*. New York: ReganBooks, HarperCollins.

Schwartz, J. M., Stapp, H. P., & Beauregard, M. (2004). Quantum physics in neuroscience and psychology: A neurophysical model of mind–brain interaction. *Philosophical Transactions of the Royal Society of London, Series B: Biological Sciences* doi:10.1098/rstb.2004.1598. Retrieved January 1, 2008, from http://www.jstor.org/journals/00804622.html.

Schwartzer, R., & Leppin, A. (1992). Possible impact of social ties and support on morbidity and mortality. In H. O. F. Veiel & U. Baumann (Eds.), *The meaning and measurement of social support* (pp. 65–84). New York: Hemisphere.

Segerstrom, S. C., & Miller, G. E. (2004). Psychological stress and the human immune system: A meta-analytic study of 30 years of inquiry. *Psychological Bulletin, 130* (4), 601–630.

Seligman, M. E. P. (1990). *Learned optimism: How to change your mind and your life.* New York: Free Press.

Seligman, M. E. P. (2002). *Authentic happiness: Using the new positive psychology to realize your potential for lasting fulfillment.* New York: Free Press.

Selye, H. (1956). *The stress of life.* New York: McGraw-Hill.

Selye, H. (1974). *Stress without distress.* Philadelphia: J. B. Lippincott.

Senge, P. (1990) *The fifth discipline: The art and practice of the learning organization.* New York: Currency Doubleday.

Sherif, M., Harvey, O. J., White, B. J., Hood, W. R., & Sherif, C. W. (1961). *Intergroup conflict and cooperation: The Robber's Cave experiment.* Norman, OK: University of Oklahoma Institute of Group Relations.

Siegel, D. J. (1999). *The developing mind: Toward a neurobiology of interpersonal experience.* New York: Guilford Press.

Siegel, D. J. (2001). Toward an interpersonal neurobiology of the developing mind: Attachment relationships, "mindsight," and neural integration. *Infant Mental Health Journal, 22*(12), 67–94.

Siegel, D. J. (2007a). *The mindful brain: Reflection and attunement in the cultivation of well-being.* New York: Norton.

Siegel, D. J. (2007b). Mindful therapy: The brain, the mind, relationships and the development of well-being. Workshop sponsored by General Practice Psychotherapy Association, Toronto, 22 October 2007.

Siegel, D. J., & Hartzell, M. (2003). *Parenting from the inside out: How a deeper self-understanding can help you raise children who thrive.* New York: Jeremy P. Tarcher/Putnam.

Sigerist, H. E. (1951). *A history of medicine: Primitive and archaic medicine, Vol I.* Yale Medical Library Publication No. 27. New York: Oxford University Press.

References

Sigerist, H. E. (1961). *A history of medicine: Early Greek, Hindu, and Persian medicine, Vol. II.* Yale Department of History of Medicine Publication No. 38. New York: Oxford University Press.

Silbiger, S. A. (1999). *The ten-day MBA: A step-by-step guide to mastering the skills taught in America's top business schools* (Rev. ed.). New York: William Morrow.

Silsbee, D. (2004). *The mindful coach: Seven roles for helping people grow.* Marshall, NC: Ivey River Press.

Simons, D. J., & Chabris, C. (1999). Gorillas in our midst: Sustained inattentional blindness for dynamic events. *Perception, 28,* 1059–1074.

Smith, B. (2007). Coaching emotional intelligence: The business case for human capital. *International Journal of Coaching in Organizations, 3,* 8–20.

Srivastva, S., Cooperrider, D., & Associates (Eds.). *Appreciative management and leadership: The power of positive thought and action in organizations.* San Francisco: Jossey-Bass.

Stapp, H. P. (2007). *Mindful universe: Quantum mechanics and the participating observer.* A. C. Elitzur, M. P. Silverman, J. Tuszynski, R. Vaas, & H. D. Zeh (Eds.), The Frontiers Collection. Berlin: Springer-Verlag.

Starns, O. (2004). *Ishi's brain: In search of America's last "wild" Indian.* New York: W. W. Norton.

Stein, I. F. (2008). *Enacting the role of coach: Discursive identities in professional coaching discourse* (Doctoral dissertation, Fielding Graduate University, 2008). *Dissertation Abstracts International, 69* (03).

Stewart, I. (1989). *Does God play dice?: The mathematics of chaos.* Oxford, UK: Basil Blackwell.

Stewart, M. (2006). *The management myth.* Retrieved April 13, 2008, from http://www.theatlantic.com/doc/prem/200606/stewart-business.

Stoltz, P. (1997). *Adversity quotient: Turning obstacles into opportunities.* New York: John Wiley & Sons.

Sun Tzu. (1983). *The art of war.* J. Clavell (Ed.). New York: Delacorte Press, Random House.

Surrey, J. L., Stiver, I. P., Miller, J. B., Kaplan, A. G., & Jordan, J. V. (1991). *Women's growth in connection: Writings from the Stone Center.* New York: Guilford Press.

Swanson, R. A., & Law, B. D. (1993). Whole-part-whole learning model. *Performance Improvement Quarterly, 6*(1), 43–53.

Tabibnia, G., Satpute, A. B., & Lieberman, M. D. (2008). The sunny side of fairness: Preference for fairness activates reward circuitry (and disregarding unfairness activates self-control). *Psychological Science, 19*, 339–347.

Tang, Y. (2007). Presentation at The First Global Neuroleadership Summit, Asolo, Italy, 14–16 May. http://neuroleadershipsummit2007. blogspot.com/ (retrieved 27 May 2008).

Tang, Y.-Y., Ma, Y., Wang, J., Fan, Y., Feng, S., Lu, Q., et al. (2007). Short-term meditation training improves attention and self-regulation. *Proceedings of the National Academy of Sciences of the United States of America, 104*, 17152–17156.

Tang, Y.-Y., & Posner, M. I. (2008). The neuroscience of mindfulness. *NeuroLeadership Journal, 1*, 33–37.

Taylor, F. W. (1964). *Scientific management, comprising Shop management: The principles of scientific management* and Testimony before the Special House Committee. New York: Harper & Row.

Taylor, K. (2006). Brain function and adult learning: Implications for practice. In S. Johnson & K. Taylor (Eds.), *The Neuroscience of Adult Learning,* special issue of New Directions for Adult and Continuing Education, *110* (Summer), 71–85.

Thomas, W. H. (1996). *Life worth living: How someone you love can still enjoy life in a nursing home: The Eden Alternative in action.* Acton, MA: VanderWyk & Burnham.

Tight, M. (1996). *Key concepts in adult education and training.* London: Rutledge.

Toffler, A. (1984). Foreword. In Prigogine, I., & Stengers, I., *Order out of chaos: Man's new dialogue with nature* (pp. iii–xx). New York: Bantam Books.

Tough, A. (1971). *The adult's learning projects: A fresh approach to theory and practice in adult learning.* Retrieved April 11, 2008, from http://allentough.com/.

Tough, A. (1982). *Intentional changes: A fresh approach to helping people change.* Retrieved April 11, 2008, from http://allentough.com/.

Towne, H. R. (1886). Engineer as economist. *Transactions of the American Society of Mechanical Engineers 7*, 425ff.

United Press International. (2001). *Exercise "better than drugs for depression."* Retrieved April 3, 2008, from http://www.healthy.net/asp/templates/ news.asp?Id=1937.

References

Vaihinger, H. (1911, 1925). The philosophy of "As If"; A system of the theoretical, practical and religious fictions of mankind. (Published in 1911 as *Wie die Philosophie des Als Ob entstand*). Leipzig: Felix Meiner Verlag.

van der Kolk, B., McFarlane, A. C., & Weisaeth, L. (Eds.). (1996). *Traumatic stress: The effects of overwhelming experience on the mind, body and society*. New York: Guilford Press.

van Praag, H., Shubert, T., Zhao, C., & Gage, F. H. (2005). Exercise enhances learning and hippocampal neurogenesis in aged mice. *Journal of Neuroscience, 25*(38), 8680–8685.

Vedantam, S. (2006). Drugs cure depression in half of patients: Doctors have mixed reactions to study findings. *Washington Post*, March 23, 2006. Retrieved January 5, 2008, from http://www.washingtonpost.com/wp-dyn/content/article/2006/03/22/AR2006032202450.html.

Virchow, R. (1962). *Disease, life, and man: Selected essays*. L. J. Rather (Trans.). New York: Collier Books.

von Bertalanffy, K. L. (1968). *General system theory: Foundations, development, applications*. New York: George Braziller.

Vroom, V. (1995). *Work and motivation* (Rev. ed.). San Francisco: Jossey-Bass Classics. (Originally published in 1964)

Vygotsky, L. S. (1978). *Mind and society: The development of higher psychological processes*. Cambridge, MA: Harvard University Press.

Wagner, U., Gais, S., Haider, H., Verleger, R., & Born, J. (2004). Sleep inspires insight. *Nature. 427*(6972):352–355.

Weick, K. E. and Sutcliffe, K. (2001). *Managing the unexpected: Assuring high performance in an age of complexity*. San Francisco: Jossey-Bass.

Weinberg, G. (1975). *An introduction to general systems thinking*. New York: Corset Wiley.

Wellner, A. S. & Adox, D. (2000). Happy days: What can America learn from the positive psychology movement? *Psychology Today*, May/June 2000. Retrieved April 5, 2008, from http://psychologytoday.com/articles/pto-20000501–000015.htm.

Wheatley, M. (1992). *Leadership and the new science: Learning about organization from an orderly universe*. San Francisco: Berrett-Koehler Publishers.

White, F. (1998). *The overview effect: Space exploration and human evolution*. Reston, VA: American Institute of Space Aeronautics and Astronautics.

White, M, A. (2007). *Maps of narrative practice*. New York: W.W. Norton.

White, M., & Epston, D. (1990). *Narrative means to therapeutic ends.* New York: W.W. Norton.

Whitmore, J. (1996). *Coaching for performance* (2nd ed.). London: Nicholas Brealey Publishing.

Whitworth, L., Kimsey-House, H., & Sandahl, P. (1998). *Co-active coaching: New skills for coaching people toward success in work and life.* Palo Alto, CA: Davies-Black Publishing.

Wiener, N. (1948). *Cybernetics: Or the control and communication in the animal and the machine.* Cambridge, MA: MIT Press.

Wiener, N. (1950). *The human use of human beings.* Cambridge, MA: Da Capo Press.

Williams, G. P. (1997). *Chaos theory tamed.* Washington, DC: Joseph Henry Press.

Williams, P., & Davis, D. C. (2002). *Therapist as life coach: Transforming your practice.* New York: Norton.

Wlodkowski, R. J. (1985). *Enhancing adult motivation to learn.* San Francisco: Jossey-Bass.

Wright, T. A. (2003). Positive organizational behavior: An idea whose time has truly come. *Journal of Organizational Behavior, 24,* 437–442.

Yerkes, R. M., & Dodson, J. D. (1908). The relation of strength of stimulus to rapidity of habit-formation. *Journal of Comparative Neurology and Psychology, 18,* 459–482.

Zimbardo, P. G. (2007). *The Lucifer effect: Understanding how good people turn evil.* New York: Random House.

Zull, J. E. (2006). Key aspects of how the brain learns. In S. Johnson & K. Taylor (Eds.), *The Neuroscience of Adult Learning, special issue of New Directions for Adult and Continuing Education, 110* (Summer), 3–9.

Index

Index

Infants:
  brain development of, 103
  conversations with, 424
  mental maps of, 105
Influence, in social psychology, 385–386
Information:
  life as flow of, 21–22, 25
  processing of, 305
  unresolved loops of, 265
Information Processing and Decision Making (W.C. Howell), 163
Inhibiting, by working memory, 250
Inner game, 281
The Inner Game of Golf (Timothy Gallwey), 145
The Inner Game of Skiing (Timothy Gallwey), 145
The Inner Game of Tennis (Timothy Gallwey), 145
Inner Game of Work (Timothy Gallwey), 145
Inquiry, appreciative, 83, 281, 414–416
Inquiry mode of instruction, 238
Insight, 221, 264, 268–271
Insight inventory, 406
Insight theory, 293–294
Instinctual hunger, 214
Instruction, modes of, 238
Insults, 434–435
Integrated body-mind training (IBMT), 91–92
Integration, 97, 348
Integrity versus despair stage (development), 208
Intellectual wellness, 138–139
Intelligence:
  emotional, 340–343
  and prediction, 260
  psychometrics for, 200–201
Intelligence quotient, 200
Intention, mirror neuron activity and, 100–101
Intentional Change Model, 84
Intentionality, 281
Interdevelopmental (IDM) Institute, 208
Internal control, 389
Internal locus of control, 231
Internal models, of self-organizing systems, 79

International Coach Federation, 10, 316, 425
International Consortium for Coaching in Organizations, 14
International Psychoanalytical Association, 282
Internet Mental Health (Web site), 319
Internet resources, 319, 459–460
Interpersonal neurobiology, 109, 427
Interpretations:
  and emotions, 355–356
  of metaphors, 312–313
Interviews:
  entry, 317–318
  nondirective, 375
Intimacy versus isolation stage (development), 208
Intuition, 223, 433–434
I/O (industrial/organizational) psychology, 381–383
iPod, 79
Irrational beliefs, 297–301
Ishi, of the Yahi tribe, xiii–xiv, xvi, 1, 2, 6, 27, 44, 275, 449
Ishi in Two Worlds (Theodora Kroeber), xiv
Isolation, 126, 157, 428
I-Thou relationships, 39
Ivey, Allen, 292

J

James, William, 183, 192–194, 210, 348, 364
Jay, Mike, 10
Jefferson, Thomas, 332
Jen, 64
Jnana, 61
Johnson, Sandra, 365, 425
Jonassen, D. H., 229
Judger state, 346
Jung, Carl, 201, 282–283

K

Kahneman, Daniel, 332
Kaplan, R. M., 341
Karma, 61, 62
Keane, M. T., 222, 249, 260

497

Index